The Power of Sex

The Social Construction of Sex, Genders and Sexualities

Other Books by Anthony Synnott

The Body Social: Symbolism, Self and Society (Routledge, 1993)

Aroma: The Cultural History of Smell, with Constance Classen and David Howes (Routledge, 1994)

Shadows: Issues and Social Problems in Canada (Prentice-Hall, 1996)

Re-Thinking Men: Heroes, Villains and Victims (Ashgate, 2009)

The Power of Sex

The Social Construction of Sex, Genders and Sexualities

by

Anthony Synnott, PhD

Gordian Knot Books

An Imprint of Richard Altschuler & Associates, Inc.

Los Angeles

 For information, or special orders contact the publisher, Gordian Knot Books/Richard Altschuler & Associates, Inc., at 10390 Wilshire Boulevard, Suite 414, Los Angeles, CA 90024, (424) 279-9118, or Richard.Altschuler@gmail.com.

Library of Congress Control Number: 2016939468
CIP data for this book are available from the Library of Congress

ISBN-13: 978-1-884092-21-3

Gordian Knot Books is an imprint of Richard Altschuler & Associates, Inc.

Cover Layout and Design: Inspire Creative Works

Printed in the United States of America

Distributed by Ingram

For

Rowan, Gabriel, Connor, Liam and Jasper

With all my love

Contents

Foreplay

Sex is everywhere, sells almost everything, can be used to obtain many things, is how we were conceived, and for many people—as an expression of loving—it *is* everything. It can be immensely enjoyable, energizing and health-giving—if it doesn't kill you.

But it is also immensely controversial. Whom we have sex with, when, where, why and how is all very difficult.

What's the problem? Sex is probably our favorite indoor and outdoor pastime—or was, or will be. It is normal and natural; we were all conceived this way, perhaps with love and passion, except for a few by artificial insemination or without consent. Why cannot consenting adults do whatever they want . . . wherever, whenever, however, and with whomsoever they want?

The quick answer is two words: cultural norms; or quicker still, one word: laws. But what these norms and laws are, how they vary from culture to culture, and how and why they change over time would require more than two words: in fact, a book—this book.

Indeed, sex is hugely problematic. It may be fun, good exercise and great for the heart, but almost everything to do with the genitals and sex is hotly debated: prostitution, pornography, nudity, homosexuality, masturbation, contraception, abortion, paraphilias, circumcision, divorce, clitoridectomies and genital cosmetic surgeries—to name only a few topics of controversy related to sex.

We may love sex and need it, but sex is not clean and clear like a quadratic equation: It carries a lot of baggage. This includes male and female supremacism, misogyny and misandry, homophobia and heterophobia. Men and women may define sex differently (with major variations within each population), employ double standards and often complain bitterly about each other's attitudes and sexual behaviors. Then there is the debate about male and female sexual dysfunctions, and the role that pharmaceutical companies may play in medicalizing normality. On top of that there is a tendency to impose male/female binaries on what is a sexual continuum.

Then there is the whole issue of different cultural practices, values and beliefs. The *Kama Sutra* and the *Bible* are eons apart, despite the romantic *Song of Songs*. Chinese eroticism that involves loving the lotus is far removed from the erotic stone carvings of the Hindu temples of Khajuraho, which in turn are quite different from the Christian cathedrals; and the homosexual rituals of some of the highlands of Papua-New Guinea are different, again, from how the English typically or stereotypically do sex—with humor (how else?)—which, in turn, contrasts with the alleged pragmatism of the French and seemingly polarized Americans, who are somewhat divided between Puritanism and addiction. The Japanese famously celebrated sex with the Shunga art form, but they celebrated it in contrast to the European Christian tradition. So globally just about everything associated with sex is a muddle.

Finally, the ethics of sex—what is right or wrong, good or bad—is personally subjective, culturally relative and historically contingent. And not everyone cares about ethics. Exploring sex, sexes and sexualities is fascinating, but reader discretion is advised. Still, as Freud said: "*Nil humanum alienum a me puto.*" ("I do not consider anything human alien to me.")

This is neither a "how-to-do-it" manual nor a guide to 100 or 365 positions with illustrations and diagrams of body parts. It is meant to be a loving, light and enlightening—and lingering (the same etymology as lingerie)—look at sex, cultural norms, historical developments, personal stories (not mine), the rise of sexology, and the politics of sex—painted not only in 50 shades of grey but in all the colors of the rainbow.

Also, this is not a therapy manual. It is not intended to replace the work of professional sexologists and sex therapists, such as *Sex for Dummies* by Ruth Westheimer, *Sex Life* by Pamela Stephenson-Connolly and *Sex Drive* by Bella Ellwood-Clayton. It is a multi-disciplinary exploration of sex: a synthesis of memoirs, history, anthropology, sociology and psychology, and discussions about changing ideas and attitudes and how people enjoy themselves—or not. Lord Chesterfield famously wrote of sex: "The pleasure is momentary, the position ridiculous, and the expense damnable." Plus one probably has no clothes on. This is known as the bad attitude to sex!

Sophia Loren equally famously remarked that the most erotic part of the body is the brain; but equally, so far as sex is concerned, the brain is also the most problematic; i.e., as regards personal and cultural norms and values.

Sex may be almost everywhere, especially since Freud so kindly told us about sex symbols—think the Eiffel Tower, the Empire State Building and grain silos. He also mentioned vaginal symbols, without naming them as such, including putting on shoes, packing boxes or groceries, looking for change in your purse and exploring caves—and then the whole world begins to symbolize sex. It really is just about everywhere, not just on billboards or in bed; so much so that the United States has been described by some Americans as a "raunch" culture, "pornified" and "hypersexual."

But even though sex is nearly everywhere, selling everything, it is still a very taboo topic. We do not discuss our sex lives with everyone, as we do the weather or the news; perhaps we don't even discuss it with anyone, including our partners. So maybe this book will help to open up the discussion.

Sex is the electricity and chemistry that keep relationships alive and vibrant and the glue that keeps them together; but historically, cross-culturally and socially, confusion is all.

Sex and sexualities used to be relatively simple. People were male or female and homosexual or heterosexual. Now it is more complicated. People may still be male or female but they may also be intersex, transitioning, transgender, transsexual, she-males, or, in many cultures, a third sex, or two spirits: ambisexual. The same is true for sexual orientation: People may be heterosexual or homosexual, but also possibly bisexual, asexual, egosexual, polysexual and, now, pansexual, with paraphilias abounding. So sex is all a maze and a minefield and a muddle. The old 2x2 model—m/f, gay/straight—has disappeared. Exploration requires care.

And the sexual realities keep changing. In 2015, in the United States alone, the Supreme Court legalized gay marriage; Bill Cosby ("America's Dad") was accused of multiple rapes; Bruce Jenner, an iconic male, very publicly transitioned to Caitlyn Jenner; Miley Cyrus announced that she was pansexual and introduced a relatively new word into the sexual lexicon, with the implication that there are now more than three sexualities; Ashley Madison—the online dating service marketed to people who are married—was hacked; and flibansarin, also known as Addyi, was approved by the FDA as a treatment for hypoactive sexual desire disorder in women. What next?

Section 1—Sex

Chapter 1
Sex

In the beginning was sex. We were all conceived one way or another by sex, in bed or on the kitchen table or in a Petri dish or by IVF or in a passing meadow. We survived our mother's pregnancy and our birth, both hazardous times, and even infancy, and now we can enjoy ourselves. We deserve it.

Sex is one of our greatest pleasures. It is often intimately associated with love and the creation of new life. Sex is at the heart of our most personal relations, and also intimately linked with more mundane government policies and even the survival of the species. Sex is the primordial act of creation. In this act, humans are as gods. Sex has populated the world to the number of over seven billion people. This is a powerful force—biologically, personally and socially.

Sex is also one of our greatest pains, resulting in unwanted pregnancies, sexually transmitted infections (STIs), HIV/AIDS, ruined careers, betrayals, divorces, homicides, suicides—hate as well as love and death as well as life.

Sex has been enjoyed and suffered since the dawn of humanity, obviously, yet it still remains fascinating, mysterious and elusive. Sex is discussed endlessly in bedrooms and cafes, written about eternally from the *Kama Sutra* to Reddit, sung about in opera arias and Blues, Country and Western, jazz, and pop songs, and watched on Skype and Pornhub. It seems to be forever new.

Sex is studied professionally by sexologists, psychologists, sociologists, and cross-culturally by anthropologists; legislated by lawyers; prosecuted by the criminal justice system; sold by sex workers and paid for by their clients; moralized by the religious authorities; recommended by the medical profession; dissected by biologists; debated by ethicists; advertised and filmed nearly everywhere; deconstructed by post-modernists; and even investigated by the U.S. Congress back in 1998, with the incident between Bill Clinton and Monica Lewinsky. Still, it is practiced by almost everyone (though occasionally repressed or sublimated)

Pleasurable, painful, and fascinating, sex is also immensely controversial, which is remarkable, really, considering that it is so normal a drive, that we were all conceived by sex, and that the birds and the bees do it without any major problems (or so it seems). Yet we argue about who is allowed to do what, with what, to whom, and when and where and why, and what it all means, if anything. And despite all the arguments, sex codes vary widely.

The penalty for getting sex "wrong" by any particular local standard may range from harassment charges to prison to death, depending on the society and historical period. Particularly controversial are such issues as adultery, prostitution, nudity, pornography, homosexuality, pedophilia, polygamy, masturbation, sodomy, contraception, abortion, premarital and extramarital sex, divorce, circumcision and clitoridectomy. Indeed almost everything to do with sex and the genitals is controversial.

So sex is everywhere and all the time, to judge by the world population growth rate, but it is also everywhere controversial, hence the morality police and the legislations and investigations. Sex may be a personal, pleasurable and intimate affair, but it is also, as Michel Foucault has pointed out, the nexus of society: the intersection of public and private, personal desire and government policy to raise or lower national birth rates in order to increase economic growth or to reflect changing societal values and norms. Sex may be personal but it is also highly political.

Hugh Hefner, the founder of *Playboy*, stated: "I believe that sex is the primary motivating force in human history" (Petersen, 1999: ix). Readers may agree or not, or it may be true for some people but not for others. Some might make the claim for money or power or simply survival; but it is not a bad debating topic.

Yet despite the power, ubiquity and controversies about sex, there is surprisingly little agreement about what sex is.

What Is Sex?

The question of what constitutes sex was raised with particular poignancy and vividness after the relationship between Monica Lewinsky and Bill Clinton was publicized in 1998. Bill Clinton declared on television: "I did not have sexual relations with that woman." Some believed him. Some did not. But it all depends on how he or we define "sexual relations."

A *Time*/CNN survey polled Americans on this issue and found a surprising range of opinion on what sex is. The question was: "If Clinton and Lewinsky did the following, should it be considered sexual relations?"

Table 1.1: What are Sexual Relations?

	Sexual Relations	Not Sexual Relations
Kissed each other in a romantic way	40 percent	53 percent
Touched each other in areas such as the breasts or buttocks, directly or through clothing	59 percent	35 percent
Touched each other in the genital area either directly or through clothing	69 percent	25 percent
Engaged in oral sex	87 percent	7 percent

Time, 10 August 1998: 22. "Not sures" and "Refused to answer" not included.

Clearly there was massive disagreement about what sex is and what sexual relations are. This is a little hard to explain. A national poll of Canadians conducted by *Maclean's* found similar disagreement. Referring to the "activities of U.S. President Bill Clinton," the question was: "Do you personally consider having oral sex with someone to whom you are not married to be adultery?" 71 percent said Yes; 22 percent said No; and 7 percent did not know or refused to answer (*Maclean's*, 28 December 1998).

Eighty-seven percent of Americans thought oral sex with someone to whom you are not married constitutes sexual relations, but 7 percent did not, and only 71 percent of Canadians thought it is adultery. Are Canadians more sexually tolerant than Americans? It would appear so. Does their sexual behavior differ? We will discuss that later. The fact, however, that 40 percent of Americans considered romantic kissing to be "sexual relations" is curious. Do they consider their romantic kissing partners in their total count of those with whom they have had sex? Surely not, it would most definitely seem.

The huge difference in the responses indicates the extent of the disagreement about what sex is and what sexual relations are. It also clarified the vast cultural gap between American and French values. Francois Mitterand, a former President of France, enjoyed his wife and his mistress, with whom he had a daughter and appeared in public together on occasion. This was not considered to be either a scandal or a secret, and it was ignored by the press and the general public as a purely personal matter. The contrast with the American reaction to Clinton is extreme. The actress

Catherine Deneuve seemed to summarize French perplexity when she said: "America is a strange country. Most pornographic films are made here, and yet you have the President of the United States on trial for having an affair. Incredible!" (*Time*, 17 August 1998)

Incredible perhaps, but even more incredible was the congressional effort to define "sexual relations." They were defined as "When the person knowingly engages or causes contact with the genitalia, anus, groin, breast, inner thigh, or buttocks of any person with an intent to arouse or gratify the sexual desire of any person" (*Time*, 24 August 1998). Selective bodily contact, not penetration, therefore defines "sexual relations" in this case. Not even fellatio counts here, which would have let Clinton off the hook, since there is no mention of mouths! It's amazing—just made for "Saturday Night Live." Groping is now sexual relations, but fondling the hair or face is OK, and the outer thigh is fine, too, but not the inner one, as if there is a dividing line. And foot fetishists are also in the clear.

Sigmund Freud, in one of his finer moments, opined: "Seriously, it is not easy to discover what is covered by the concept 'sexual'" (1982:344). True enough.

Post-modern Sex

Sex is not what it was. So much has changed in a lifetime. The language has changed, the attitudes, the practice, and the technology.

The language: So many new words have entered the sexual lexicon since the 1960s: the pill, Viagra, Addyi, cock-rings, butt-plugs, bullets, swinging, barebacking, cottaging, transgendered, transsexual, transitioning, she-males, intersexual, pansexual, egosexual, safe sex, cybersex, vanilla sex, stalking, sexual harassment, cock-blockers, player-haters, bikinis, thongs, vibrators, Petri dishes, jelly bracelets, arm candy, toy boys, trophy wives, cougars, commando, booty calls, outercourse, rainbow parties, hook-ups, bug-chasers, blended families, parental alienation syndrome, surrogacy, sperm and ovum banks, sex predetermination, abortion-on-demand, pro-life and pro-choice, designer babies, spare parts babies, embryo-evaluation, women's rights, gay rights, men's rights, starter marriages, gay marriages, genital piercing, vasectomies, penile enlargement, labiotomies, vaginoplasties, date rape, spousal rape, battered wife syndrome, paternity fraud, paternity suits, deadbeat dads, monstrous mums, groupies, freebies, roofies, heterosexism, homophobia, heterophobia, misogyny, misandry, queer theory, on-line sex (even with a webcam), Kegel exercises, Ashley Madison and, recently, anal bleaching (don't!)—plus an alphabet of acronyms: AI(D), ARVs, BDSM,

BGLTI, DNA testing, ED, HIV/AIDS, HPV, IUDs, IVF, MSM, NRTs, RU-486, STDs, STIs and the elusive G-spot.

The changed vocabulary—and there is much more—indicates the changed realities of sex today. Not that all the above are totally new to humanity (though many of these words are not in my computer dictionary), but now they are institutionalized on "Main Street" and are part of the vocabulary of the media.

Breaking this list down into its component parts we can see a number of processes at work: the mechanization, commodification, commercialization, chemicalization and politicization of sex, and the changed cost-benefit analysis of sex.

Every decade has seen major shifts in the evolution of sex and gender. The 1950s saw the first successful sex change operation, the publication of *Playboy* and considerable new research on sexualities. The 1960s witnessed the marketing of the pill, which divorced sex from pregnancy and transferred fertility control from men to women, resulting in plummeting fertility rates and increased education, job participation and income levels for women; then there was the women's movement and the gay movement; and with Elvis, the Beatles, and the Rolling Stones, there emerged the "sexual revolution." In the 1970s, the new reproductive technologies (NRTs) emerged, which divorced pregnancy from sex, and in the U.S. Roe v. Wade gave women the right to abortion. HIV/AIDS exploded in the 1980s, which dramatically altered the cost-benefit equation of sex. The 1990s saw the massive increase in Internet pornography. The dawn of the new century saw the expansion of gay rights; and in the second decade, many are concerned about the rights of lesbian, gay, bisexual, transgender, intersex, queer and questioning (LGBTIQQ) individuals, working to continue decreasing the incidence of HIV/AIDS globally, achieving low fertility rates in parts of Asia and western Europe, the effects of Internet porn on viewers and, in the U.S. the protection of the rights of gays to marry, and the attempted defunding of Planned Parenthood and effectively rolling back Roe v. Wade, and so much more.

The Pill: After receiving FDA approval in 1960, the birth control pill gave women control over their fertility and freed them from their biology, which immediately resulted in a long series of consequences: a plummeting birth rate that resulted in increased enrollments of women in education and the labor force, which, in turn, caused women to have increased incomes and resulted in a shift in the economic and political balance of power in both the family and the state. All these changes chimed with the so-called sexual revolution (perhaps earlier inaugurated by the publication of *Playboy* in 1953) and, probably not coincidentally, an increased divorce rate, following changing divorce legislation. Again, all this facilitated the rise of the women's movement after the 1968 protest against the Miss America Beauty Pageant, which, in turn, echoed the Civil Rights movement. And this, in turn, facilitated the rise of the gay rights movement after the violent protests against police harassment at the Stonewall Inn in New York in 1969. This soon expedited the men's movements from the seventies, notably the National Organization of Men against Sexism (NOMAS) and the National Coalition for Men (NCFM). The former is largely about men's wrongs, the latter about men's rights. Not much consensus there. This little pill has had a major impact on gender relations over many decades and all around the world.

The latest developments include more pills for male erectile dysfunction and, in 2015, Addyi for female hypoactive disorder, a condition that some suggest may not exist as defined (Ellwood-Clayton, 2012).

Commodification: Sex has always been a commodity, bought and sold in the market-place and the brothel, legal in some countries, illegal and punishable by death in others. Today sex slavery and sex trafficking have created a horrendous modern problem, followed in the annual reports of the U.N. Office on Drugs and Crime and other organizations.

But prostitution is not the only type of commodification. We now have sperm and ovum *banks*—the word is significant—with catalogues of potential donors and price lists that are very similar to the farming catalogues that market bull sperm. The only difference is price, and the farming catalogues include color photographs of the bulls. One anonymous would-be parent advertised: "Wanted: One well-bred, smart, sporty Stanford egg. Price $100,000 (Avery, 2000). This was then a record for "selective breeding."

The pill divorced sex from pregnancy. The new reproductive technologies divorced reproduction from sex. Louise Brown was the first person conceived in a Petri dish in 1978; she died in 2012. So one can have sex without children and children without sex. The process of vitrification, the freezing of sperm and ova, means that people can have children later, and still without sex; but perhaps both semen and ova will be healthier because younger—or not, because frozen.

Rosie Read, an 18-year-old English university student, offered her virginity on eBay. She said that she would rather have sex with a stranger than have three years of poverty. Of course. Why give it away for free when you can sell it on eBay? She received more than 400 offers in three days, and accepted the offer of 8,400 pounds from a 44-year-old engineer; but as a lesbian, she says she did not enjoy it at all. Nor did he, presumably. Oh, well. Still, the money will have been some consolation.

Chemicalization: The pill began this process, chemicalizing contraception, and it has continued with the chemicalization of both male sexuality, with Viagra, Cialis and Levitra, and of female sexuality, with the 2015 FDA approval of Addyi, as mentioned earlier. All this may well have reduced anxieties about unwanted pregnancies and increased sexual pleasure, but the physiological costs down the road of the absorption of so many chemicals into the body are not yet known.

Mechanization: Museums of sex have now been established in many cities, displaying dildos from around the world, sculptures, phalluses, postcards, photographs, and pictures—all testifying to our human interest in sexuality and in maximizing pleasure. Any sex shop is also a museum, in its own way, with costumes, books and magazines, chocolates and lubricants, "adult" or erotic movies.

One of many major differences in post-modernity is the battery-operated machine, the sex toy: sexual pleasure for as long as the battery lasts. This must be why they advertise the energizer *bunny*, since the bunny is the most famous sex symbol of all, as reflected in, for example, the Playboy Bunny" the phrase "fucked like rabbits," and the Easter Bunny as the symbol of resurrection. Yet all the teaching in schools about the mechanics of sex could be complemented by lessons on the mechanization of sex and, more importantly, the emotions rather than the motions.

Politicization: The politics of sex have been transformed with so many traditional relations between the sexes now criminalized, for better and also for worse. Batteries of legislation designed to protect women from the nasty behaviors of nasty men have been passed. These include laws about stalking, sexual harassment, violence against women, rape-shield laws, marital rape, domestic violence (previously considered a private matter), the battered-wife syndrome, preventive homicide (of the husband), and deadbeat dads (failure to pay court-ordered payments). A wide range of behaviors has been criminalized. Some have argued that these behaviors were already actionable under existing legislation, and that the new politics merely infantilize women, demonize men and create double standards. Others disagree, of course, hence the legislation which is intended to maximize justice and equity.

An excellent example (but trivial) of politics involved with sex is the complaint of one woman who disliked the missionary position. She explained that "It's political in every way" (Hite, 1987: 547), expressing what she may have seen as patriarchy. So true, but the reverse position, with the woman on top, is equally political. So the number of positions is steadily reduced for the politically and symbolically sensitive people out there. Are there any apolitical positions? The imagination boggles again.

Criminalization: The criminalization of some activities has also been accompanied by the de-criminalization of others in many countries, such as abortion, prostitution and homosexuality, discussed below.

Economics: The economics of sex is everywhere also. It is not just that sex is used to sell many things, but everything sexual is for sale, and every body part is sexualized. Specialty stores sell sexy lingerie, sex games, and magazines with such evocative titles as *Pussy*, *Hard On,* and *Tits*. They cater not only to heterosexual and homosexual tastes, but also to interests in BDSM, anal sex and all sorts of fetishisms; and they are all readily available for anyone to see on the Internet. Video stores rent "adult" movies: the name changes from "dirty movies" to "blue movies" to "porn movies" to "adult movies" to "erotica" indicate the total change in attitudes since the sexual revolution in the 1960s. Pornography and erotica are discussed in more detail later.

The economics of sex includes not only prostitution and pornography but also movies, sex stores, books and magazines, university courses, much of the retail, advertising and cosmetic industries, legislation . . . the list is endless. Even a date requires expenditures on food and drink, cosmetics and clothing, and cars and gas. Sex is a mainstay of the economy, largely unrecognized but of incalculable value.

Sex was once almost exclusively heterosexual and romantic in the classic Hollywood movies starring Humphrey Bogart and Lauren Bacall, Spencer Tracy and Katharine Hepburn, Rock Hudson and Doris Day, and everything with Marilyn Monroe. As in fairytales, the couple lived and loved happily ever after, and the sex was kissing. Now sex may be heterosexual, homosexual, egosexual, bisexual, pansexual, polysexual, solo, virtual or phone. Whatever.

So sex is not what it was: the contraceptive pill and the little blue pill, the accelerated commodification, NRTs, AIDS, machines and batteries, chemicals, legislation, criminalization and de-criminalization, the politics, economics and media, the Internet, and more permissive attitudes—all have affected our sex lives for better and for worse. In post-modernity sexuality is now sexualities.

The Sex Nexus: Michel Foucault

The French historian Michel Foucault had a rather different angle on sex and sexualities. He refused to enter the sex wars with arguments about types of sex, their various meanings, gendered or otherwise, and the statistics on frequency rates, the average number of partners, satisfaction rates, fidelity/infidelity rates—and all the quantitative or qualitative data of sexologists and sociologists. Nor did he follow the Krafft-Ebing route of sexual pathology. And he largely ignored Freud's contributions to the stages of psycho-sexual development, symbolism, complexes, dreams, jokes, polymorphous perversity, infantile sexuality, sexual orientations and so on.

In his three-volume *History of Sexuality*, Foucault's contribution has been both considerable and singular. This was not a history along the usual chronological lines (Henriques, 1961; Bullough, 1976, 1979; Tannahill, 1982; Petersen, 1999); rather, he emphasized the centrality of sex in both personal and social life. The former was well known, the latter less so. He suggests that, during the Victorian era, sex and sexuality had become the subject of "a multiplicity of discourses . . . in demography, biology, medicine, psychiatry, psychology, ethics, pedagogy and political criticism" (1980:33). Ecclesiastic authorities still pontificated and legislators still legislated; but they were not the only voices. The age of the expert had dawned.

Foucault placed sex and sexuality at the heart of social life. Psychologists locate the self at the center of their discipline, political scientists place power at the center, anthropologists culture, sociologists society, economists money, historians time, geographers place and astronomers space. But Foucault insisted on sex—and he has a point.

> [Sex] was at the pivot of the two axes along which developed the entire political technology of life. On the one hand it was tied to the disciplines of the body: the harnessing, intensification, and distribution of forces, the adjustment and economy of energies. On the other hand, it was applied to the regulation of populations. . . . Sex was a means of access both to the life of the body and the life of the species . . . [so] it was tracked down in behavior, pursued in dreams; it was suspected of underlying the least follies, it was traced back into the earliest years of childhood.

> . . . But one also sees it becoming the theme of political interventions, economic interventions (through incitement to or curbs on procreation), and ideological campaigns for raising standards of morality and responsibility: it was put forward as the index of a society's strength, revealing of both its political energy and its biological vigor. (1980:145-6)

In this view, sex is not simply a personal matter; it is also political, economic and demographic—an affair of state. The two axes of private life and public life intersect with sex. Sex is the nexus of society.

This analysis of sex ties in with Foucault's analyses of the institutions of the clinic, the asylum and the prison—or the sick, the mad and the bad—in his earlier works. Here he had emphasized the essentially disciplinary nature of society and its institutions in the production of 'docile' bodies, i.e., as social control.

> The historical moment of the disciplines was the moment when the art of the human body was born. . . . What was then being formed was a policy of coercions that act upon the body, a calculated manipulation of its elements, its gestures, its behavior. The human body was entering a machinery of power that explores it, breaks it down and rearranges it. A 'political anatomy', which was also a 'mechanics of power', was being born . . . Thus discipline produces subjected and practiced bodies, 'docile' bodies. (1979:137-8)

All the institutions of society are power systems—machinery, in his graphic imagery—which work through the body to control the self. Note: he emphasized the body, not the mind, which had been prioritized since the ancient Greeks and Paul, through the Renaissance to Descartes, Rousseau and Freud. The "anatomo-politics of the human body" (1980:139) is the key and is everywhere.

> The workshop, the school, the army were subject to a whole micro-penalty of time (lateness, absences, interruptions of tasks), of activity (inattention, lack of zeal), of behavior (impoliteness, disobedience), of speech (idle chatter, indolence), of the body ('incorrect' attitudes, irregular gestures, lack of cleanliness), of sexuality (impurity, indecency). . . . It was a question of making the slightest departures from correct behavior subject to punishment. (1979:178)

The family, the school, the military, the factory, the prison and the clinic all enforce rules of bodily behavior—even, or especially, about sexuality and sexual behavior. Punishment creates docility. The sexual body is under constant surveillance. "The gaze is alert everywhere" (1979:195).

Foucault's second major contribution to sexology was attending to the regimentation of sexuality in our society. Pierre Trudeau once remarked that "The state has no business in the bedrooms of the nation." He was wrong. All the legislation on sexuality, homosexuality, abortion rights, prostitution, and especially AIDS policies indicates how wrong he was. The state is everywhere, like Big Brother in George Orwell's *1984*—and it is not going away. Foucault noted that the "anatomo-politics" of the individual body is paralleled by the "bio-politics of the population" (i.e., the "species body"), which regulates fertility rates, birth control, health and population growth rates (1980:139). This is the state's business in the body politic and sex. And just as state policies vary, so also do they change.

Concrete examples include the one-child policy initiated by Chairman Mao in China in 1979, which is still in place generally, though there are many exemptions, such as for rural families, ethnic minorities, and parents with handicapped children. The policy was modified in 2013 to permit couples, if one spouse is an only child, to have two children. The policy has had four major consequences over nearly the last 40 years: First, there has been a high rate of economic growth, which was the intent of the policy. Second, there have been some unintended consequences, such as a grossly skewed gender imbalance of about 120 boys to 100 girls, which exists because Asian peoples tend to want boys (to save on dowries, sometimes, but also because girls usually become members of the husbands' families); this situation may create problems down the road as many men will have no one to marry. Third, there has been a low fertility rate, which fell from 6.2 in 1965 to 1.7 in 2011, far below the replacement rate of 2.1; this decline created the so-called demographic dividend, i.e., the bulge of working age adults, which facilitated the economic boom. This situation has resulted in the fourth major consequence of the low birth rate: an increasingly high dependency ratio, which ironically may slow the economic growth rate. The fertility rate in Japan, South Korea and Taiwan has fallen to 1.4 or lower (Beech, 2013; *Economist*, 11 July 2013; 22 August 2015). The phrase "demographic crisis" used to refer to the population boom, but now it refers to the population bust in many countries in the world, with the notable exceptions of India and countries in Africa.

Japan illustrates the political and economic importance of sex—well, strictly speaking, the importance of fertility rates, but you cannot have fertility rates without it. The birthrate there has fallen to 1.4 per female, the lowest in the world after South Korea. The nation is beginning to shrink demographically, as documented by the 2005 census, which showed that the number of deaths exceeded the number of births for the first time. So the population is shrinking and graying. Not good. The median age of the population is 44 years, which is among the highest in the world and increasing; and the population of working age (15-64) individuals is decreasing. The population is expected to fall by 38 million (from 127 million in 2010) in the next 40 years, when it is predicted that 40 percent of the Japanese will be over 65. Some European countries are in similar boats, notably France and Italy. There are solutions. These include encouraging women to stay in the labor force, encouraging retirees to reenter the labor force, increasing immigration, and raising productivity (*Economist*, 20 November 2010; 22 August 2015). Also more sex. That is my contribution.

Other examples of attempts to alter population size and characteristics include the sterilization program of Indira Gandhi in India, the Nazi eugenics program, the AIDS policies—or lack of same, in Mbeki's South Africa—and, more routinely, the "child allowances" of the Welfare State. Every nation has its cultural norms and rules that regulate virtually everything about sexuality and sexual intercourse. Prostitution may be punishable by death by stoning in some Islamic nations (although this is rare in practice), but it has been legalized in the Netherlands since the early 1980s and the "Window Ladies" are available for an average of about 50 Euros, according to the official 2012 tourist brochure. Homosexuality was illegal in the United Kingdom until it was decriminalized in 1967, but it was decriminalized much earlier in Sweden, in 1944, and much later in the U.S., in 2003; and it is still illegal in many parts of the world—an indication of different cultural norms. In the United States, bans on interracial marriage were not struck down by the Supreme Court until 1967 and abortion was illegal until Roe v. Wade in 1973. In Ireland, it is still illegal, in 2015. The U.S. Congress investigated Clinton's "sexual relations" which, while nominally about whether he had lied to Congress, was surely more about what he had done or not done.

Attitudes

Our attitudes to sex and to sexualities vary widely, depending on a host of factors such as age, sex, religion, religiosity, political orientation (e.g., liberal or conservative), culture and, especially, personality. This was illustrated with particular clarity in the Clinton-Lewinsky affair, and is still evident in the range of attitudes to such issues as homosexuality, prostitution, pornography, extra-marital sex and so on. It is probably as well to know a partner's attitudes to sex before everyone gets too involved with everyone else, for if partners disagree, there will be problems. However, attitudes can, and do, change.

Many researchers have studied our attitudes to sex, and love, and our behavior too (see Chapter 4), and tried to box us all into their neat compartments, with their own labels. This is a useful enough exercise, though unfortunately they all tend to build different compartments, so it is a bit confusing. But so is life, and so is sex.

Helen Fisher, professor of anthropology at Rutgers, has tried to explain why we are attracted to particular people, in her latest wonderful book *Why Him? Why Her? How to Find and Keep Lasting Love* (2010). It includes our attitudes to sex. She starts with the neuro-transmitters, the chemicals that influence the biology of our personality; and personality is, she says, 50 percent genetic, 50 percent social: an even split of nature/nurture, biology/psychology. She developed a personality test (included in her book) based on her knowledge of four neurotransmitters, which are found in varying amounts and ratios in everyone: dopamine, serotonin, testosterone and estrogen. These, in turn, generate four different personalities, which she labeled, respectively, Explorers, Builders, Directors and Negotiators. The top two determine our personality. She is an Explorer/Negotiator. Explorers are attracted to Explorers, her research shows, and Builders to Builders, on the "birds of a feather" theory of love; but Negotiators and Directors are attracted to each other, on the "opposites attract" theory. The success of any developing relationship will depend upon many other variables, of course, including education, status, religion, and luck (that's hard to measure); but personality, whether similar or complementary, is certainly a powerful factor.

So is sex. In a chapter on "The Chemistry of Dating," Fisher says that Explorers are looking for Play Mates, Builders for Help Mates, Directors for Mind Mates and Negotiators for Soul Mates—with the rider that one's second dominant personality trait will qualify the search. Thus, "dating is entertainment to the Explorer, social participation to the Builder, and an investment of time and energy to the Director; it is the search for a deep and authentic personal connection to the Negotiator." Furthermore, Explorers need adventure, Builders want loyalty, Directors need sex, and Negotiators need romance: for them, sex and love are intertwined (2010:137-8).

She insists that we all need sex: "If you want to keep your sex life active, have more sex." It's all chemical. "Keep the chemistry for lust, romantic love and attachment in the brain waves daily"—and not just in the bedroom (2010:230-1).

She has noted that our sexual needs and desires are variable in many dimensions due to these personality differences, which embrace so much—how we doodle, our vocabularies, even how we decorate cakes, if we do. So our personalities influence who we will love and our attitudes to sex; and, presumably, vice versa: our attitudes to sex influence both our sex lives and our love lives, which may or may not be distinct.

Fisher does note that some people are more sexual than others, have stronger libidos, more sex partners, and so on. At the top of the list of relatively asexual people is Jim Gibbons, Governor of Nevada, who announced that he had not been intimate with any woman, including his wife, since 1995: "I'm living proof that you can survive without sex for that long." But his deposition was in response to a sexual-harassment lawsuit (*Time*, 8 March 2010:16). Yet not everyone would envy him for his allegedly sexless state or his apparent asexuality.

Asexuals are thought to constitute about 1 percent of the population in the U.S. The Asexual Visibility and Education Network (AVEN), founded in 2001, defined asexual as follows: "An asexual is a person who does not experience sexual attraction." This is not to be confused with celibacy, which is a choice, not an orientation. The AVEN website offers opportunities for asexuals to discuss their situations, their relief that they are not alone, and sometimes their anti-sexuality. Anthony Bogaert has been interviewing asexuals for a decade, and his book *Understanding Asexuality* introduces what he calls the fourth sex (really a sexual orientation, not a new sex) and upsets some of our conventional ideas. He points out that this is not a pathology, and that asexuality is normal for many people at some times in their lives, usually pre-pubescence and old age, but also during crisis times of illness, after break-ups and high stress, among others. Indeed, he flips the discussion by arguing that love and sexual desire are a type of madness. He cites the examples of sports celebrities, politicians and celebrities whose recklessness and stupidity damage their lives and reputations.

In his jargon: ". . . people's cognitive functioning is impaired significantly when preoccupied with sex . . ." (2012:98). Or, more plainly, they were thinking with the wrong head. Young men skateboard dangerously to impress young women; young women diet dangerously or go to tanning salons to impress. He could have gone on about the madness of sex: excessive expenditures, immoral and/or illegal behaviors (including stalking, sexual harassment and coercion), the frequency of becoming overwrought, the agony of jealousy leading to violence, etc. Tick off enough items here and that would warrant the inclusion of sexual desire in the DSM-5 as a disorder. In this view, the asexuals may be the lucky ones and the sane ones.

Nothing illustrates this madness better than addiction. A cover story of *Newsweek* explored what it described as "The Sexual Addiction Epidemic," featuring "Valerie" who explained: "I lost two marriages and a job. I ended up homeless. I was totally out of control." Specifically, "She had serially cheated on both her husbands . . . logging anonymous sex in fast-food restaurant bathrooms, affairs with many men, and one-night stands too numerous to mention. . . ." (Lee, 2011:50) The list went on: phone sex chat lines, on-line pornography, compulsive masturbation, exhibitionism, sex for money . . . Eventually she attempted suicide and woke up in hospital. This was the turning point, rock-bottom, and then she went for treatment.

Various experts explained that sex addiction has exploded into an epidemic due primarily to the rise of Internet pornography. The Society for the Advancement of Sexual Health estimates that 3-5 percent of the population in the U.S. might be sex addicts, or about nine million people. The number of therapists treating this condition has risen from under 100 a decade ago to over 1,500. (It's a growth industry.) The demographics have shifted: Still 90 percent male, they say, but expanding beyond the middle-aged to include the older and younger sets, as well as more women, like "Valerie." Women are more often described as "love addicts," tending to fall into dependent relationships with unrealistic expectations (Lee, 2011). So are we back to the old binary once more, i.e., that men want sex, women want love? Or is this more stereotyping and double standards? Simultaneously this topic was spotlighted in the movie "Shame" (2011), directed by Steve McQueen and starring Michael Fassbender.

The Diagnostic and Statistical Manual of Mental Disorders, Vol. 5 (DSM-5) by the American Psychiatric Association (APA)—sometimes known as the "Bible of Psychiatry"—has recently been revised, and sex addiction is now redefined as Hypersexual Disorder. The complete definition is available at http://www.dsm5.org together with a long list of other sexual dysfunctions (APA, 2013:423-50).

There are many sexual personality types, from Fisher's four types to the extremes of asexuals and addicts, hedonists and ascetics; but there are also sensory types. In *Living Sensationally* (2008), Winnie Dunn, professor in the Department of Occupational Therapy Education at the University of Kansas, suggests that there are four major sensory types of people, with high or low thresholds of sensory stimulation and active or passive self-regulation. So we have a 2x2 table: the Seekers (who have high thresholds of tolerance and actively seek sensory stimulation of one or more of the senses); the Sensors (who are hypersensitive to all or some of the senses, and so have a low threshold of tolerance and are passive); the Bystanders (who are rather oblivious, don't notice their bruises, don't think about color co-ordination, don't mind bright lights or loud noises but don't seek them out); and their polar opposites, the Avoiders (who actively avoid noise, lights, crowds and over-stimulation).

Dunn has a survey questionnaire so that readers can discover their sensory type and perhaps clarify some of their sensory problems with their partners. She includes chapters on food, dress, work and leisure, and relationships, and suggests that while sensory opposites may attract for a while, they will certainly grate in time. All these types have their joys and pleasures, but different sensory types will have certain difficulties in relationships and with sex.

How Dunn's four sensory types might be synthesized with Fisher's four personality types is a matter for future research, though the Explorers and the Seekers seem like they would make a good match, for a while. In any event, both these authors offer very useful insights into our sexual and sensory types. Both authors assert that the basic binaries between the highly-sexed and the asexual, the sensual and the ascetic, are overridden by more nuanced considerations of personality type and sensory type.

The Chicago University study *Sex in America* interviewed a random selection of almost 3,500 Americans about every aspect of their sex lives, attitudes and practices. The researchers gave nine key statements requesting Likert-type scale responses: "always, almost always, sometimes, or never wrong" (Michael et al., 1994: 231). The statements asked if premarital, extramarital and same-gender sex and pornography are always wrong (four separate questions). And a series of Agree/Disagree questions: "I would not have sex with someone unless I was in love with them," "My religious beliefs have guided my sexual behavior," "A woman should be able to obtain a legal abortion if she was raped" or "If she wants it for any reason." The authors divided the responses into Traditional, Relational and Recreational, with each subdivided for a total of eight "normative orientations" (Michael et al., 1994:234). Twenty-four boxes is too complex for us here; suffice it to note, however, that the responses sometimes varied from 100 percent to 0 percent. These issues are extremely divisive, and the major fault lines, predictably, are gender, age, religiosity and marital status. We seem to have strong opinions on what is right and wrong about sex, and we are prone to considerable disagreement. Sex is a battlefield.

In sum, in terms of attitudes to sex and the laws of attraction, Fisher stresses the chemicals that determine personality types, Dunn looks to the sensory types. Both agree on four main types, but the relation between them is not yet clear. The Chicago sociologists find three main types differentiated by attitudes (i.e., not by chemicals or by sensory types), and determined or influenced by a battery of variables, especially religiosity but also age, gender and marital status. There are also, however, the asexuals and the hypersexuals, the romantics and the instrumentalists, the hedonists and the ascetics. It is all a muddle.

Meanings

What does sex mean? Everything or nothing? Or something in between? Where is it on a continuum from 1-10? Does it consume your life and thoughts? Or can you take it or leave it?

It is axiomatic that sex means different things to different people. For some it may be virtually meaningless: "It didn't mean a thing!" they explain. It was, perhaps, "just" a one-night stand; there is no emotional involvement, no affection. I do not love him or her; actually I don't even like him or her. Sex does not constitute a relationship. It is just sex: fun, maybe money. For others sex means almost everything. It is a giving of oneself to another; it is physical, emotional, even sacred, the ultimate—a union, a communion and a communication: love.

The former types—once labeled promiscuous, then permissive and now self-labeled "free spirits"—may be found presumably among sex workers, escorts, and the more hedonistic and sexual. They would include the Recreational types in the Chicago sex survey and, also, the more pragmatic and instrumental, who will use sex to achieve their goals and to get what they want. It is an asset: part of their erotic capital, in Hakim's phrase, to be invested wisely and profitably.

The meanings of sex are multiple, therefore, and certainly not polarized between "disorder" and "order," addiction and non-addiction, pleasure and pain. We can probably distinguish four dominant and partly different meanings.

For some people sex may be recreational: fun, needed every Saturday night and requiring no emotional involvement. It is purely physical, a nice feeling, as after a good meal or a stiff drink. This is Recreational sex. For others, sex may be a means of livelihood, full-time or part-time, when the ships or a convention or the Olympic Games come to town. It's a job. This is sex as purely financial, following the laws of supply and demand. This would include prostitution or, in the new terminology: sex work; and it is dangerous work: sex for profit. It would also include those with a more instrumental than romantic attitude to sex, using their erotic capital to their best advantage, as mentioned earlier. For still others sex may be Relational: wanting to be together, to have a romantic relationship, perhaps being in love. Later sex may be more about having children: procreation. The two Rs and the two Ps are recreation, prostitution, relation, and procreation; and all four might follow each other in sequence, one after the other. Clearly sex does not mean the same thing for everybody, and what sex means changes over time. Also, there are two other minority behaviors: rape, which is coercive and criminal sex; and incest, which may be consensual and recreational (see below) or rape. So this gives five types of sex.

Having drawn these lines we can promptly trip over them, since in practice these types often blend and blur. Couples trying to have children are probably having fun too: procreation and recreation as well as relational sex. And sex workers have relationships, children and often have fun too, depending on their status. Furthermore, recreational sex is a broad term that subsumes a multitude of motivations: mercy sex, revenge sex, friendship sex, trophy sex, or the horny, anonymous sex of the one-night stand, in which pregnancy may, nonetheless, follow.

Despite the overlaps, however, it is useful to keep the basic distinctions in mind, and not get them confused. The novelist Terry McMillan has the mother of four children lamenting precisely this confusion: "All four of 'em married the wrong person for the wrong reasons. They married people who only lit up their bodies and hearts and forgot about their minds and souls. To this day I still don't think they know that orgasms and love ain't hardly the same thing" (2001:12). Seemingly they confused sex and love, recreational and relational sex—a not uncommon mistake.

The bestselling Brazilian author, Paulo Coelho, whose books have sold more than 65 million copies in 60 languages, has other ideas. In an interview, he affirms that "sex is a physical manifestation of God . . . a blessing." And: "I think that sexuality is first and foremost the way that God chooses for us to be here on earth, to enjoy this energy of love in the physical plane." He excludes rape and pedophilia (1998:185-6). This is sex as loving and spiritual and transcendent—far beyond relational. Elsewhere he speaks of sex (not even love) as "the language of the soul" (2005:139). Yet he is acutely aware of how problematic sex may be in so many ways and, after interviewing sex workers in the Netherlands, reported that it only lasts, on average, 11 minutes (2005:11). That's about one cigarette. But did these sex workers say that it was "a physical manifestation of God" or "the language of the soul"? I doubt it. I reckon they would have said it was 50 Euros.

Meanings may vary, therefore, from nothing (favorite assertion: "It didn't mean anything!") to prostitution, recreation, relational, procreation; in a word (excluding rape and incest), from nothing to cash, fun, love, children, crime and God.

No doubt meanings change over time as we age, from "Can't get enough of it" to "Can't get any of it!" to "Don't want it anymore." Plato told the story of the aging Sophocles: "How about your service of Aphrodite, Sophocles—is your natural force still unabated?' To which he replied: "Hush, man, most gladly have I escaped this thing you talk of, as if I had run away from a raving and savage beast of a master" (*Republic* 329, 1984:578). So he was delighted at his loss of desire, which shows that the issue is not new. Plato thought that this was "a good answer," but maybe it was just sour grapes.

Augustine was not so sure. His conflict between his love of sex and his love of God required him to prioritize, he thought, and to renounce sex in pursuit of the kingdom of heaven; hence his famous prayer: "Give me chastity and continence, but not yet" (BookVIII:7; 1975:169).

So sex means different things to different people, and the meanings may change over time. So much depends on what we desire: Do we prefer good sex or a good night's sleep? Or chocolate? Much depends on whether we are ascetics or hedonists, sex-negative or sex-positive.

Hedonism and Asceticism

An obituary of Felix Dennis described him as "a hedonist and media magnate." Hedonist? He said that he had spent $100 million on drugs, drink and high living in just one decade, [and the rest he just wasted] and he had

14 mistresses on his payroll. He was also an ironic and whimsical poet (*Economist*, 5 July 2014):

They tell me I'm riddled with cancer
So I'm planning to croak with elan
If you'll pass the cigars and decanter
I'll be dying as hard as I can.

He did, too, of throat cancer, at the rather young age of 67. Hedonism is an ancient Greek philosophy, asserted by Aristippus, a friend of Socrates, who founded the Cyrenaic school, and insisted that "bodily pleasures are far better than mental pleasures." He practiced what he preached and lived a luxurious life (*Laertius*, *Vol. 1*, 1972:219). This contrasted with the Epicurean school, founded by Epicurus (341-270 BCE), who also valued pleasure: "We call pleasure the alpha and omega of a blessed life. Pleasure is our first and kindred good." But they considered mental pleasure superior to physical pleasure (*Laertius Vol. 2*, 1972: 655).

Hedonism of one sort or another seems to have been the prevailing philosophy of the Greek and Roman cultures, with vomitoria for diners and bread and circuses for the plebs, brothels in Pompeii and elsewhere, and sexual activities graphically decorating public and private places. Yet asceticism also persisted, in both the military training of Sparta and the spiritual practices of Orphism, whose practitioners abstained from meat, wine and sexual intercourse. (Etymologically, the word ascetic is from the Greek *askesis*, which referred to military training.) Orphism, and the belief that the body is the tomb of the soul *(soma = sema)* influenced such leading lights as Pythagoras, Socrates and Plato, and then neo-Platonism and Christianity.

In traditional Christianity, the ascetic life was valued by St. Paul, particularly to achieve salvation. "I harden my body with blows and bring it under complete control, to keep myself from being disqualified after having called others to the contest (1 Cor. 9:25). The body is both "the temple of the Holy Spirit" (1 Cor. 6:19) but also the enemy: hence the need for control. As he explained to the Galatians: "What I say is this: Let the Spirit direct your lives, and you will not satisfy the demands of human nature. For what our human nature wants is opposed to what the Spirit wants, and what the Spirit wants is opposed to what our human nature wants. The two are enemies" (Gal. 5:16-7; cf. Rom 7:14-24). Paul was highly dualistic but the dualism was internal: a war within the self between the body (and human nature) and the Spirit.

Later the emphasis shifted from this hostility to the imitation of Christ, who prayed, fasted in the wilderness, resisted the temptations of the devil, and was crucified. Thomas a Kempis (1380-1471), whose book *The Imitation of Christ* has been described as "probably the best known and the best loved book in Christendom," stressed the value of suffering: "Jesus has many who love his Kingdom in heaven, but few who bear His Cross. He has many who desire comfort, but few who desire suffering. He finds many who desire His feast, but few His fasting. All desire to rejoice with Him, but few are willing to suffer for His sake . . ." (1980: 83). Suffering, in this view, has transcendental and spiritual value, and is redemptive.

Priests and nuns take vows of poverty and chastity, and sometimes in the contemplative orders vows of silence, as they lead, ideally, ascetic lives in pursuit of holiness. The late Pope Paul II regularly flagellated himself, like many other saints, including St. Francis of Assisi, St. Catherine of Sienna and St. Ignatius, as part of the imitation of Christ and what was known as the mortification of the flesh. Bonaventure's life of St. Francis is an extraordinary testament to the amount of pain and suffering a person can voluntarily impose upon himself without killing himself; it is also a tribute to what a modern theologian says is an outdated spirituality (Bonaventure, 1978; Nelson, 1978).

Ascetics are found in many faiths. The Five Pillars of Islam require the declaration of faith, prayers five times a day, fasting during Ramadan, pilgrimage to Mecca (the Hajj), and the giving of alms. Asceticism is notable in the Shia ritual of self-flagellation on the day of Ashura, mourning the death of the grandson of the Prophet Muhammad, Imam Hussein, at the battle of Karbala in 680.

In India, the adherents of Jainism, who number over four million, are particularly ascetic, taking vows of non-violence (against animals and insects as well as humans), truthfulness, non-stealing, celibacy and, effectively, poverty. Also, I was informed near a Jain temple in India that they cannot take transport: They must walk.

Sexual asceticism was institutionalized by the Puritans in England, Scotland and New England in the seventeenth and eighteenth centuries. These descendants of Swiss Calvinism and Scottish Presbyterianism were committed to "purity," in contrast to what they perceived as the excesses of the Catholic Church. They were epitomized not only by Calvin and John Knox but also by Oliver Cromwell, who defeated the Royalists and Cavaliers in the English Civil War, secured the execution of Charles I in 1649, and took great delight in killing Catholics, especially priests and monks, in Ireland. The battles and beheadings by the Puritans on one side of the Atlantic were matched by the Witchcraft Trials in Salem on the other, and the executions of 20 men and women for alleged witchcraft in 1692 (Bremer, 2009).

Puritanism was not all about sex, as the term is usually applied today, but mostly about doctrine and democratizing religion; but sexual behavior was imbricated in the spiritual lifestyle. As Max Weber put it: "The sexual asceticism of Puritanism differs only in degree, not in fundamental principle, from that of monasticism . . . [S]exual intercourse is permitted, even within marriage, only as the means willed by God for the increase of His glory according to the commandment, 'Be fruitful and multiply'" (1968:158).

So no theater in Cromwell's England, no dancing in Calvin's Geneva, no alcohol, no music (Weber, 1968:118-22)—and absolutely no twerking. Ironically, Puritanism is now best exemplified by the Vatican and the teachings of the Church, which the Puritans once so vigorously condemned, as well as by the so-called "religious right" in the United States. This is not only a personal matter, in terms of what we as individuals think is right or wrong: it is also political, as governments either fund or refuse to fund abortions and abortion clinics in developing nations, proclaim or do not proclaim abstinence policies, legalize or prosecute prostitution, condemn or subsidize the use of contraceptives, valorize or demonize homosexuality, etc.

Hedonism is not all about sex either, but in so far as it is, it is associated with Lothario, Casanova and, more recently, Wilt Chamberlain, Warren Beatty, Erroll Flynn, Catherine Millet, Chelsea Handler, Felix Dennis, Georges Simenon, sex workers, and so on. Nymphomania used to be a term reserved for women but could probably be more accurately applied to men. Now we label extreme sexual hedonism "sex addiction," and famous people are always trooping off to clinics to be treated. Now it is renamed again in the *DSM-5* as "Hypersexual Disorder," which does not sound quite so glamorous.

The slogans of hedonism are many and various: "*Carpe diem*," said the Romans, a phrase echoed later by the English poet Herrick: "Gather ye rosebuds while ye may;" and also by the rock stars: "Sex, drugs and Rock 'n' Roll," and the older slogan, "Eat, drink and be merry, for tomorrow you die;" and also the reminder that "You only live once."

In the Euro-American culture, citizens have often had a vexed, perplexed and ambivalent attitude to pleasure and the body and to sex as well as gender, caught as they have been between hedonism and asceticism, and, therefore, different ethics. On the one hand people are obsessed with sex. This is evident in the rise of Internet porn, the gossip magazines and magazines like *Cosmopolitan* and *Playboy*, cosmetic surgery, including genital surgeries for both sexes, sexologies and sexographies, beauty, the fashion and advertising industries and, of course, this book and others that focus on sex.

On the other hand, there is a lot of free-floating guilt attached to sexual matters. So much sex is immensely controversial: prostitution, abortion, contraception, masturbation, homosexuality, women going topless—or top-free in the new lexicon—or breastfeeding in public, adultery (a death-penalty offence in some places, like homosexuality), and of course, sex itself: with whom or with what, safe or not. And all this guilt and controversy are tied up with a range of attitudes, from misogyny to misandry and homophobia to heterophobia, together with conflicting demands for equal rights, identical duties, or special privileges.

Guilt is not the same as asceticism; but in so far as individuals are required to restrain themselves, then sexual asceticism is required. Doctors are not allowed to have sex with their patients, lawyers with their clients, presidents with their interns and professors with their students—even if all concerned are single, consenting and adult. Such behavior is widely considered dishonorable and unprofessional and, therefore, grounds for a wide range of sanctions, from official reprimands to disbarment to firing to impeachment—rather than tolerant smiles. No such strictures seem to apply to gardeners, plumbers, electricians, carpenters, and other so-called "blue-collar" workers; they are just lucky and smiling.

Sexual asceticism (abstinence, celibacy, restraint) is widespread in both spiritual and secular domains. It sometimes seems that everything sexual is either sinful or illegal or both, even though it's not fattening, good exercise, and so good for you. The range from sex-positive to sex-negative, from obsession to prohibition, indicates the deep and wide ambivalence, indeed, conflict. This can be illustrated with several recent examples: prostitution, abortion, contraception and misogyny.

Prostitution

In the Red Light district in Amsterdam, the Window Ladies, as they are called, show themselves to be available in cubicles. The sex work is regulated and licensed by the city, and advertised in the tourist brochures, with the rate 50 Euros on average, when I was there in 2012 armed with recommendations and telephone numbers for the more expensive men's clubs.

Yet in the quiet tourist town of Kennebunck, Maine, a 29-year-old Zumba instructor was charged with engaging in prostitution. This activity earned her $150,000 over 18 months. Not bad. The police have made public the names and addresses of some of the clients, with more to follow (*Gazette*, 19 October 2012). The irony here, of course, is that if she had done it for free, she would not have been charged, nor would names have been released. So the real offence is charging money.

More recently in Brazil, where prostitution is legal, the sex workers were reportedly very upset that Brazil lost in the 2014 World Cup, because their incomes were severely reduced. "It's not even worth it coming to work," sighed one woman whose weekly income had fallen from the equivalent of $600-700 to $300. Trafficking is not an issue in Brazil, where the waiting lists for high-end brothels, known as *termas,* are two years (Nolen, 2014).

In Canada the Supreme Court declared, "It is not a crime to sell sex for money." This was the decision in the 2013 Bedford case, where the court struck down the prostitution legislation as being unduly restrictive of the rights of sex workers. The Conservative government is now, in 2015, considering new legislation, Bill C-36, which will criminalize customers and pimps rather than sex workers, in order to protect the women. This has provoked the usual controversy. Sex workers have argued that they want sex work decriminalized for buyers and sellers, and have asserted that they are not victims, nor trafficked. The Liberal opposition is quiet since this is so widely regarded as a moral issue, but they tend to argue for free trade, modeled on the Netherlands, New Zealand and Brazil. You can buy and sell guns, so why not sex? Furthermore, it infantilizes women, telling them what they can and cannot do. And if you can sell sex but clients cannot buy it, what is the point? The government is responding to the Robert Pickton case. He was a pig farmer convicted of murdering six women in British Columbia and suspected of killing another 20 women, but he confessed to a cellmate that he had killed 49 women; all this over a period of about 20 years. He is thought to have fed their bodies to the pigs. The government is also following the "Nordic model" of Sweden and elsewhere, in an effort to prevent trafficking and eventually eliminate prostitution, while providing support services for those women affected. Some doubt the effectiveness of the model, worrying that prostitution will go underground and the profession will become even more dangerous for women.

There are basically three models of prostitution. One, the so-called Nordic model, asserts that prostitution is simply another example of patriarchy, which exploits women and facilitates the trafficking of women, with the proposed policy that customers should be penalized and the sex workers, who are defined as victims, should be given counseling. A second model, which is fairly common and traditional, is the "moral model," that prostitution (adherents do not use the term sex work, which sounds too close to social work) is wrong, and the prostitutes should be penalized. The third model is the belief in the free market and sex between consenting adults, as in Germany, the Netherlands, Brazil, Nevada and elsewhere. Prostitution, the "oldest profession in the world," is not going away, but it might go underground, which is more dangerous for everyone. Still, the rise of trafficking has indicated that there are limits to freedom, and the rise of male prostitution or sex work has indicated that there are limits to the feminist "male privilege" model. So whether prostitution or sex work should be decriminalized, criminalized or institutionalized is hotly debated.

Meanwhile, the Internet has "liberated" the whole business. The *Economist* discussed "The Sex Business" in a lead article with a rare disclaimer that "some may find the topic distasteful." The article lists various websites both for advertising by prostitutes and comments by clients, notes the price differentials between various cities, and "average hourly mark-ups" for services rendered, comments on the fall in prices since the 2007-8 recession and, in Europe, with the influx of women into the European Union from eastern Europe, notes the decline in street walkers (about 10-20 percent in the U.S. by one estimate), and the rise in escort services, massage parlors, and such websites as Ashley Madison and Tinder. Male prostitutes account for about one-fifth of the commercial labor force. The author concludes that, overall, members of the oldest profession will profit from the Internet, like so many others (9 August 2014).

Abortion

The Guttmacher Institute provides all the facts and figures on abortion on its website. To summarize some of the salient data: About 44 million abortions were performed worldwide in 2008 (the latest data available). The abortion rate for women aged 15-44 was 29 per 100,000 in 2008. World-wide nearly half of all abortions were unsafe and often illegal, resulting in 47,000 deaths and 13 percent of all maternal deaths, plus another 8.5 million complications from such abortions requiring medical care, which one-third do not receive. Conditions vary widely from Africa and Latin America, where almost all abortions are illegal and unsafe (except for South Africa, which legalized abortion in 1997, and Mexico City) to Europe and North America. Still, in Europe, about 30 percent of pregnancies end in abortion. In the U.S. about one-half of pregnancies are unintended and one-third end in abortions, with 1.1 million abortions performed in 2011.

The facts and figures are significant, but so are the politics and values. Roe v. Wade in 1973 legalized abortion in the U.S., but the issue is still controversial, with voters divided between pro-choice and pro-life, and several abortion providers in the U.S. have been murdered. *Time* magazine headlined the abortion issue in a cover story "40 years ago, abortion rights activists won an epic victory with Roe v. Wade. THEY'VE BEEN LOSING EVER SINCE." Roe v. Wade established women's rights to abortion, a procedure which had hitherto been illegal, but the details of regulation were left to the individual states, some of which have passed legislation effectively limiting women's rights to abortions. As of 2013, four states now have only one abortion clinic. In 2011, 24 state legislatures passed 92 provisions restricting abortions. About 30 states do not cover the costs of abortions, except in cases of rape, incest or threats to the health of the potential mother (Pickert, 2013). So women's rights are in conflict with states' rights, and, by and large, Republican values conflict with women's rights values

A complicating factor is that a generational shift seems to have occurred within the women's movement, which is still largely led (or dominated, as some would say) by the second wave feminists who won the victory in 1973. The younger feminists apparently refer less to "choice" and more to "reproductive justice"—a more inclusive term that includes such issues in the culture wars or, some say, the war against women, as contraception, child care, gay rights, health insurance and economic opportunity. As one activist (Pickert, 2013:45) explained: "The pro-choice movement would focus on 'Let's open more clinics.' The anti-choice movement would say, 'Let's stop women going into them.' [W]e would say, 'Let's ask why there is such a high rate of unintended pregnancies in our communities." About 50 million legal abortions were performed in the 40 years after Roe v. Wade—which is about the same number as were killed in World War II between 1939 and 45. The rate has declined by about a third, from 30 per 100,000 in 1981 to about 20 per 100,000 in 2008, due to several factors: a decrease in the number of doctors willing to perform them (down from 2,908 in 1982 to 1,720 in 2011; it is dangerous); a decrease in the number of clinics due to state regulations (primarily by Republican legislators ostensibly to protect women's health by raising clinic standards and requirements); and better birth control information and use, probably partly due to Planned Parenthood (Pickert, 2013).

Susan Faludi wrote an interesting essay in *Harper's* on this ideological generation gap. She asserts that "The contemporary women's movement seems fated to fight a war on two fronts: alongside the battle of the sexes rages the battle of the ages." This latter battle is between second- and third-wave feminists, not very politely described as between the prudes and the sluts. She situates herself between the two groups as the youngest of the old and the oldest of the young, and refers to the "war" in terms of matricide and sororicide—which is surely overkill, way too homicidal for arguing over leadership, policies and votes. The debates are not just about abortion but also pornography (see Chapter 11), in arguments between, for example, Gail Dines—who is very worried about its proliferation, increasing violence and degradation, and effects on both practitioners and viewers— and Caitlin Moran—who wants better porn. It is also about prostitution and sex work: some want the prostitutes arrested, others want the clients arrested, still others advocate for the rights of sex workers, and then there are those who want everyone to leave everyone alone.

The 2012 U.S. election campaign reignited the gender wars and the culture wars, largely with the statement by Todd Akin, who said: "If it's a legitimate rape, the female body has ways to try to shut that whole thing down." As opposed to what? An illegitimate rape? Really! Then Paul Ryan said, "The method of conception doesn't change the definition of life"—but of course it does change the meaning of both life and life-chances. Both men are Republicans, against abortion, and anxiously looking for ways to roll back Roe v. Wade.

Meanwhile, in Northern Ireland the first abortion clinic was opened in 2012: a sign of the changing times. And in France the National Assembly has voted both to fully reimburse the costs of all abortions and to pay for all contraceptives for minors aged 15 to 18.

More than 1,000 women die every year in Latin America, and one million are hospitalized due to complications from "backstreet" abortions (*Economist*, 8 June 2013:40). It is difficult to justify this sort of slaughter, even if you are the Pope, whose church condemns abortion.

Contraception

Contraception is seen by some as not only a moral issue but also, therefore, a political and legal issue. The wealthy Green family, rooted in the Evangelical Christian faith, decided to challenge President Obama's Affordable Care Act on the grounds that it requires companies to cover the costs of contraceptive methods. The family considers this to be immoral, against God's law, and an infringement of their civil rights and freedom of religion (Van Biema, 2014). The issue is controversial, of course, and one commentator remarked that the Green's "battle for their freedom of religion violates that of their employees." Another stated: "In my opinion, an honorable person has tolerance for other people's beliefs" (*Time*, 23 July 2014:2). U.S. presidential candidate Rick Santorum stated in 2012: "One of the things I will talk about . . . is I think the dangers of contraception in this country . . . [contraception] is not okay. It's a license to do things in the sexual realm that is counter to how things are supposed to be."

Misogyny

Misogyny still plagues relations between the sexes and, therefore, sexual relations. Consider the following:

• Pakistan: The shooting of 15-year-old Malala Yousafzai in Pakistan, in October 2012, by the Taliban, for advocating more education for women, has horrified the whole world and focused renewed attention on the rights of women and global misogyny. Then in May 2014, the 25-year-old Farzana Parveen was stoned to death by her own family for marrying the man she loved.

• India: This was followed by the gang rape, torture and murder of the unnamed student in India, in December 2012. The culprits were caught and sentenced to death, though one committed suicide in prison.

Since then far more attention has been paid to the plight of women in Pakistan and India and around the world, and penalties have been increased. When I visited India in 2012, the parents of a 14 year old girl were convicted of the misnamed honor killing of her and the murder of a servant. The parents were both professionals (dentists) and were sentenced to life.

In remarks that received international coverage, Babulal Gaur, an Indian state minister in President Modi's BJ Party, described rape as "sometimes it's right, sometimes it's wrong." And agreeing with a critic of the death penalty, he added: "Boys commit mistakes. Will they be hanged for it?" Apparently a rape is committed in India every 21 minutes (Gottipati, 2014).

• Egypt: At the celebrations in Tahrir Square for the election of Abdel Fattah el-Sissi in June 2014, a video posted on YouTube shows dozens of men assaulting a woman, with other assaults reported at the same time. The president had the (unprecedented) grace to visit one of the women in hospital and apologize.

• Nigeria: The Islamist Boko Haram abducted hundreds of girls from villages in the north. Some escaped but others were apparently married to the militants or enslaved. The men and the boys were usually killed.

• Canada: Robert Pickton was convicted in 2007 of the murders of six women, charged in the deaths of 20 more women, and he admitted to killing 49 women. This was followed by the 2014 Royal Canadian Mounted Police (RCMP) report on 1,181 murdered and missing aboriginal women from 1980-2012. Of these 1,017 were murdered and 164 are missing. Indigenous women constitute 4.3 percent of the Canadian population but 11.3 percent of the missing and 16 percent of all female homicides

• Turkey: The President of Turkey, Recep Erdogan, rejected equal rights for women, saying: "You cannot put men and women on an equal footing. It is against nature. They were created differently" (*Gazette*, 25 November, 2014).

• U.S.: "RAPE. The crisis in higher education" was the cover story of *Time* (26 May 2014), stating that "for young women, America's campuses are dangerous places," and that "19 percent of U.S. undergraduate women are victims of sexual assault while in college."

This conflation of rape and sexual assault is part of a problem: There is a difference between rape and an unwanted kiss or butt pat or threat, but the author states that "more than half" of these assaults were rape. How much more? Reliable statistics are hard to come by but, still, more than 10 percent of female undergraduates raped must be a huge number, barely examined. Alcohol was involved in three-quarters of the cases. One study found that only 6 percent of male students reported behavior that fitted definitions of rape, but more than half were repeat offenders committing, on average, six rapes each. Another report states that 90 percent of rapes were committed by 3 percent of offenders. How do they get away with it? Many victims do not report the crime; about one-third of the (potential) victims were not sure if a crime had been committed, revolving around the issue of consent. Others were worried about either a second rape by the authorities or their reputations. And not all university and police authorities have been adequate in their responses to allegations of rape. The penalty for rape, in one case, was 10 years; for a woman it may be years of trauma and fear. In May 2014 the Obama Administration listed 55 schools under investigation for Title IX violations with respect to sexual assault, and Congressional legislation may be pending (Grey, 2014).

Rape is not simply a campus problem. The allegations by so many women against Bill Cosby, and in England, the allegations against celebrities, including Bill Savile and Rolph Harris, plus the cover-ups that have precluded investigations have appalled and disappointed many people. The good news is that the rape-rate, at least in the U.S., is falling steadily. The FBI records on its website show that 79,770 rapes were reported in 2013, for a rate of 25.2 per 100,000 females. (The rate for males is not reported, despite the frequency of prison rapes.) This amounts to a rape every six minutes, but this is 6.3 percent lower than in 2012 and 16.1 percent lower than in 2004. However, many, perhaps most, rapes are not reported.

Do we in North America and Western Europe live in a "rape culture?" Is the phrase useful? Accurate? Like "car culture" or, in the U.S. especially, "gun culture"? Opinions are hotly contested. If one believes, extrapolating from U.S. university data, that 90 percent of the rapes are committed by 3 percent of the men, from FBI data that the frequency of rapes has fallen by 50 percent in the last 50 years, and from criminal data that the sentence for rape may be 10 years, then the answer is probably no, especially if one compares this with India. It is not a cultural norm, but it happens. If one recognizes, however, that allegations of rape are often not reported, not believed, and, if reported and recorded, are often not adequately investigated, that research on the topic is small-scale and barely funded, and that, therefore, the issue is camouflaged and should be researched better and legislated, then the answer might be yes.

War involves the killing of men and often the rape of women. The *Economist* has estimated the horrifying totals of rapes from the Soviet army in Germany (100,000 to two million), the Indian army in the Bangladesh war of 1971 (200,000), the Bosnian war of 1992-5 (20,000), the Sierra Leone civil war of 1991-2002 (over 50,000), and the Rwandan genocide of 1994 (500,000), with the war in the Congo continuing. What is new is the use of rape as a deliberate tactical weapon of war in the Bosnian war, when women were separated into "rape camps" for systematic, organized rape. This policy was replicated in Darfur (Sudan) and Rwanda (*Economist*, 15

January 2011); and it is perpetuated by Boko Haram in Nigeria and ISIS in Iraq, Syria, and elsewhere today.

Misogyny is still a global problem with a long and bloody history. Universal human rights are not recognized everywhere and, even if recognized, are not always practiced (Morgan, 1970; Miles, 1991; Gilmore, 2001; Holland, 2006; Synnott, 2009)

Dualism

The roots of all this ambivalence to sex, body and gender are deep and three-fold, at least in the "West," for want of a better word, including ancient Greek philosophy, the Judeo-Christian tradition and Cartesian the mechanism. The common denominator in these three traditions is dualism: male/female (Pythagoras, Aristotle), mind/body (Plato, Paul) and soul/body (Christianity, Descartes). All three are intermingled and linked to other binaries; and they have also been ranked in a moral hierarchy for millennia, leaving a problematic legacy which is only now being challenged, and even reversed: from patriarchy and male supremacism to (if not matriarchy) female moral supremacism, and from misogyny to misandry—but still dualism.

To explore all these historical, philosophical themes in dualism in detail would take us too far afield, and besides it is fairly well-known territory, with many people, including me, having tried to tackle some of these issues (Hertz, 1960; Needham, 1973, 1979; Ranke-Heinemann, 1990). Suffice it to suggest that mind/body and the related soul/body dualism may have originated in Orphism, as Antony Flew suggests (1984:259), but it was certainly embraced and perpetuated by Plato. Furthermore both Parmenides and Pythagoras developed 10 sets of "Opposites," which, they argued, explained change; and the latter included male/female in his Table of Opposites—a theme developed by Aristotle into male supremacism, knotting, among other things, male/female, mind/body and soul/body dualism together (Synnott, 1993).

All this was totally congruent with mythology, including Hesiod's story of Pandora that, in turn, chimed with the story of Adam and Eve in Genesis. Ultimately all three sources, Hesiod's mythology of Pandora, the Genesis theory of Eve, and Aristotelian philosophy of gender coalesced into a male supremacist unity. All this was and is totally antithetical to harmonious gender and sexual relations. Again, both Jesus Christ and St. Paul were highly dualistic in terms of good and evil, heaven and hell, God and Satan, the right and left hands, mind and body, sheep and goats, light and darkness, life and death; and, in Paul (but not in Christ), male and female. And all this permeated European thought for centuries; the sting was that the theoretical triple dualism evolved into this triple hierarchy of values: male over female, mind over body, and soul over body.

The above just sketches the very broad outlines of the historical origins of dualism, developed further in modernity by René Descartes, widely acknowledged as the founder of modern philosophy. His effort to develop a rational philosophy based on mathematical first principles was in some ways a disaster. Descartes distrusted the senses and the body as a source of reliable knowledge. Here he followed Plato in much of his philosophy, but he was less extreme. Descartes just distrusted the body, but Plato thought it was evil and a prison of the soul, and he repeated his ideas frequently in *Phaedo* (65-6, 81), *Phaedrus* (250c), *Cratylus* (400c) and in the *Republic* (437). This view was echoed by Saint Paul, as mentioned earlier, and other church fathers. So it has a long and deep tradition.

Descartes reinforced these traditions. He trusted his brain: "*Cogito, ergo sum*" ("I think, therefore I am"). He continued: "This 'I', that is to say, the mind, by which I am what I am, is entirely distinct from the body" (1968:53-4). And as to this body, Descartes wrote: "I considered myself, firstly, as having a face, hands, arms, and the whole *machine* made up of flesh and bones, such as it appears in a *corpse* and which I designated by the name of body" (1968:104; emphasis added). A machine? A corpse? Whatever happened to sensuality? How different Western philosophy would have been if Descartes had stubbed his toe—hard—on his way to his desk and founded his philosophy on the undeniable reality of physical pain and bad language. Or if he had fallen madly in love with some glorious woman, a love which was madly reciprocated with hot sex. (Two of the many big "ifs" in history.) But he didn't, and physical binarism, with body-negativism and sex-negativism, has plagued us ever since. He didn't think that his own thinking might be as untrustworthy as his senses, due to forgetfulness, miscalculations, false assumptions, bad judgment, biases, prejudices etc. So body-negativism and its attendant sex-negativism were institutionalized in Western culture, religion and philosophy (Synnott, 1993).

These may be some of the philosophical origins of Western dualism, but the anthropologists Robert Hertz (1960) and Rodney Needham (1973) suggest that dualism originated in our understanding of the human body (male/female, right/left, two arms, legs, eyes etc.). Needham even suggests that "The universal incidence of dual symbolic classification . . . suggests the possibility that to classify by binary opposition is a natural proclivity of the human mind" (1979:57). After all, the human brain has two hemispheres (commonly known as "left brain" and "right brain") just like the human bottom—a wonderful sympathy and symmetry between brain and butt, top and bottom.

The British feminist Ann Oakley has extrapolated these binaries while engaged, oddly, in a discussion of the supposed merits of qualitative versus quantitative methods in sociology. Supposedly, the former is female and the latter is male, i.e., warm, personal caring versus cold, hard numbers. She appeals for a rejection of this binary, basically male/female as opposite, but offers a long list of parallels: "hard/soft; masculine/feminine; public/private; rational/intuitive; intellect/feeling; scientific/artistic; social/natural, control/understanding; experiment/observation; objective/subjective; autonomy/dependence; voice/silence" (1998:709). The binaries no longer apply to gender, or at least not as much as they did. They are more likely now to misrepresent gender than to represent it, with such vast shifts in the balance of power, family structures, occupational and educational distribution, and wealth.

The origins of our Western dualism may lie primarily in Greek philosophy, Christian theology, Cartesian philosophy or in the physical body—or just in the common-sense construction of the in-your-face realities of personal and political relations: male/female, me/you, us/them, war/peace; or of time: day/night, now/then; or of space: north/south, east/west, here/there, left/right, up/down, forward/backward; or of status: adult/child, slave/free . . . and many more. Yes? No? Or a third option: Maybe.

"Three" admits of more nuanced possibilities and options than two, and negates or qualifies the simple binary, as Dundes (1980) has demonstrated. So we have the Holy Trinity, the Three Wise Men, Plato's three types of people, the Triple Crown in horse-racing, the trifecta in betting, the three cardinal virtues (Faith, Hope and Charity), the three kingdoms of nature (Animal, Vegetable and Mineral), the three cardinal colors (red, yellow and blue), the three traditional Fates (who control Birth, Life and Death), and the three Graces, painted by Rubens, who bestowed beauty and charm.

In language we can interject intermediate terms: small/medium/large, before/during/after, right/left/straight, us/them/neutral, hot/cold/warm, and so on. In fairy tales, three is almost magical: the three bears and the porridge, the three little piggies, Cinderella and her two sisters, and, as we shall soon see, three sexes. Then we have the beginning, the middle and, at last, the end.

*

It must make a huge difference in attitudes to sex and to life if the gods are, like Zeus, obsessed with sex and definitely sex positive. Zeus seduced and married numerous goddesses, nymphs and mortals and had many children. He was a philanderer of epic proportions, with a full, rich sex life, and not always moral. By modern standards Zeus was a womanizer and a serial rapist. The Greek gods and goddesses were certainly anthropomorphic, and Zeus as top god enjoyed his sexual pleasures without restraint or conscience.

In this the mythical Zeus stands in stark contrast to the crucified Christ. The imitation of Zeus is far from the imitation of Christ, which is generally understood as prayer, fasting, work, and asceticism of various types, including, for the clergy, vows of poverty and chastity and, for those in the contemplative orders, vows of silence. The Desert Fathers took asceticism to extremes, becoming hermits in the desert and, like many monks and ascetics today of various faiths, relying on charity or alms for their survival.

The *Qur'an* has a beautiful sura: "Women are your fields: go, then, into your fields whence you please" (sura 2:223). This may seem a bit patriarchal to Westerners, especially, but one has to remember the time in which it was written. I imagine that Islamic feminists have updated the interpretation of this sura for equality's sake. Furthermore, a later sura (2:228) asserts: "Women shall with justice have rights similar to those exercised against them," which is widely interpreted to mean equal rights, though this is not always granted, notably by the Taliban. But then the sura continues: "although men have a higher status than women." The *Qur'an* remains open to different interpretations. Paradise, too, will be a sexy place. Virgins await the young men, and young men await the women (sura 52:24). In any event, this suggestion to enjoy ploughing your fields indicates a vastly more positive attitude to sex, women and pleasure than either Plato or Paul. And the idea that Paradise is sexual must also be more attractive to many than the Thomistic idea of the Beatific Vision, however beautiful and wonderful the sight.

Similarly, the *Kama Sutra*, composed in the fourth century in India, indicates the joy of sex for both men and women. It describes and names numerous positions and is now likely to be fully illustrated. It is still a classic present for Valentine's Day. The past still teaches the present with older values.

Again, the image of a fat and smiling seated Buddha conjures up a vastly different spirituality than the crucified Christ, even though Vatican II emphasized the glory and joy of the resurrection.

In many parts of the world, the phallus has been worshipped as a fertility god (Monick, 1987; Vanggard, 1972); and in some parts of the world today it still is, along with the vagina (Blackledge, 2003; Wolf, 2012). But sex and gender often remain problematic.

Perhaps attitudes to sex would be more positive if we were more fully aware of the health benefits of sex. Sexologists now insist on the wide range of mental and physical health benefits of sex—well, they would, wouldn't they? But the list is impressive. Sex increases blood circulation, produces oxytocin, which lowers blood pressure and increases happiness feelings, produces endorphins and immunoglobin A, which boosts the immune system, helps ward off colds and viruses, and raises testosterone levels, which strengthen bones; it also burns calories (how many depends on you), is excellent cardio, which strengthens the heart and other muscles, and relieves stress (Ellwood-Clayton, 2012:21-3). So if you don't feel like it, do it anyway—*especially* if you don't feel like it. If sex were a pill, it would be extremely expensive (of course, sex sometimes is too), but with multiple benefits; and we would take it every day.

Chapter 2
Gender

"*Vive la difference!*" say the French about gender, and well they might. The differences are obvious and amazing, and account for the world population explosion from about one billion in around 1800 to 1.65 billion in 1900 to 6 billion in 2000 and over 7 billion today (www.prb.org). That's a fair amount of sex over the years.

Yet there are paradoxes with gender. The DNA of males and females is 99 percent identical and their chromosomes are identical except for only one chromosome out of 46 on 23 pairs: the sex chromosome. Women have the XX and men the XY. So chromosomally we are 98 percent identical. But socially we define ourselves as opposite sexes. We are biologically virtually identical, yet we define ourselves as socially opposite. Some even say that there is a battle between the sexes and that they are at war. This is all very strange.

Others negate this difference and insist on the unity of the species, Homo sapiens, and assert the United Nations Universal Declaration of Human Rights that "All human beings are born free and equal in dignity and rights." This does not preclude the probability that different populations will have to argue and fight for their rights. Nonetheless, the two main theories of gender—difference theory (or two-world theory) and similarity theory (or one-world theory)—tend to be seen as contradictory rather than complementary.

Equal rights is pretty much a given in the so-called Western world, but differential rights are asserted elsewhere, and differential values also, as we have seen. Still, it's the difference that creates the electricity, the magnetism, the spark and the sparkle—and the trouble. And it is how we assess and apply the differences within our common humanity and how we negotiate and navigate the multiple rights and duties and cultures that create the gender politics.

That one chromosomal difference between males and females packs a mighty punch, not only in different physiologies that result in different lifestyles stemming from pregnancy and childbirth potentials and actualities, but also in different hormone levels, which likely affect cognitive and behavioral development. Women have, on average, five times more estrogen than men, 10 times more progesterone and 15 times less testosterone. Furthermore there are differences in brain structure and function, which are coming under the usual controversial scrutiny (Brizendine, 2010). How all these variations affect us is still not entirely clear for four main reasons: first, because it is so difficult to separate biological variance from social conditioning; second, because these differences are averages, and the range within each sex is probably considerable; third, because the effects of class, social race and culture are confounding factors, and likely override the significance of gender in social relations; and fourth, because the hormonal balances and brain functions change over time.

Nonetheless, XX and XY are still powerful forces, especially of love. Mostly men and women are attracted to each other as "opposite" sexes, though some individuals, of course, are sexually attracted to others of the same sex. The interesting thing is the degree to which we socialize ourselves in opposite directions; this is, perhaps, less than we used to over the millennia until the pill . . . but still.

It all starts with "Is it a boy or a girl?" And then the expectations and training begin, often with the colors pink and blue. Then come the toys. Toys-R-Us and Wal-Mart are basically gender segregated into blue and pink sections, to make it easier for us to buy "gender-appropriate" toys: guns, cars, trucks, planes, water-pistols, and Leggo for boys, and Barbie dolls, food things, house things, and dresses for girls—though both are frequently given the same things, such as painting and crayon sets (but they probably often draw different things) and books (but different types of books), and maybe video games. Overall, toys are still very binary and socialize cleanly and clearly into "opposite" sexes. No wonder men and women so often have difficulty with each other.

Despite the U.N. Universal Declaration of Human Rights, we clearly are neither universally all free nor equal in dignity and rights. The statement is not a description of reality but rather a utopian prescription. Again, equality in human rights does not mean identity: Men and women are not the same, and might just possibly be entitled to different rights, duties, and responsibilities, and to differential protection under the law. This is debated. Also, equality in rights does not necessarily mean identity in values, goals and interests. These three factors can and do create problems both between and within the two sexes.

Love relations between people are cross-cut by conflict relations, which, in turn, impact our sex lives. XX and XY are not just about the sexy bits, and chromosomes, hormones and brain functions. They are about what being a man or a woman means, and what being masculine and feminine is.

"He was not man enough for me," a friend explained when I asked her why she was getting divorced. This brings us to the second paradox of gender. Male or female is biology and masculine or feminine is social, and the paradox is that there may be a disconnect between the two. Not all men are masculine or equally masculine. This particular man had problems with alcohol, police and work—all related of course; he was "not man enough," needed to "man up." Similarly, just as some men are more masculine than others, so some women are more feminine than others. There is a continuum of masculinity, from the proverbial wimps, losers, dorks, geeks, nerds and sissies (i.e., somewhat feminine) to the hunks and jocks and alpha males. What we might call the Masculinity Quotient ranges from the alpha males to the omega males, with the majority probably somewhere in the middle. Similarly we can develop a Femininity Quotient from the "butch" (i.e., somewhat masculine) to the ultra-feminine actresses who shine and smile on our screens. This constitutes an *intra*-gender continuum.

The third paradox of gender, following from the second, is that some men may be relatively feminine, even female-identified, and some women may be relatively masculine, even male-identified. In the extremes, this may be a form of gender dysmorphia and lead to sex-change operations. Thus, some men may be more feminine than some women and some women may be more masculine than some men. This requires a few definitions of masculinity and femininity. My own research indicates the considerable overlap between what my students identify as typically or stereotypically male or female qualities and their own personal ones. Men often identify as warm and women as tough.

The gender binary is not so binary after all. It is an *inter*-gender continuum: The genders overlap, and are not mutually exclusive in terms of temperaments and self-definitions. These three paradoxes can also help us to better understand the inter-gender problems of relating, as well as the intra-gender problems, such as they are. Gender is now a problem. It is not something we have, like a golf ball, but something we do and also something we undo (as Judith Butler has noted) in our own different ways.

Post-modern Gender

Gender, like sex, is not what it was. There used to be two genders, neatly, cleanly and clearly distinguished, and immutable. Now gender is more complicated. Consider the following:

• Thomas Beatie was born a woman, then had sex reassignment surgery in Hawaii, had her breasts surgically removed, took hormone therapy, lived as a man for years, but kept his female sex organs. He married Nancy, who impregnated him/her—a pretty neat post-modern trick—with donor sperm and a syringe; and in 2009, she had his second child. He also receives hate mail and he and his wife run a store called "What is Normal?" He is, therefore, the father *and* mother of his children: social father and biological mother. The daddy is mommy and the mommy is daddy.

• The South African runner, Caster Semenya, who became the 800-metre world champion in 2009, is said to be not totally female, though she was raised as a female with, apparently, the appropriate genitalia. The International Olympic Committee, which had introduced gender verification tests after evidence that Soviet athletes were not always what they said they were, dropped them in 1999. Gender verification proved to be too delicate a personal issue and also too complicated to assess. Not all the criteria of gender necessarily match, e.g., hormones, primary and secondary physical characteristics, psychological orientation, etc. Semenya seems to be both male and female, biologically: perhaps a female dominant hermaphrodite—"intersexed" in the new terminology. Neither genitals nor chromosomes nor hormones can apparently adequately define sex. Gender testing is not an exact science.

• The unhappily named "Octomom," Nadya Suleman, had eight children by in-vitro fertilization (IVF) in 1999, to join the other six she already had, for a grand total of 14. This is another aspect of post-modern gender: the pushing of the biological fertility boundaries by the new reproductive technologies. There is yet another: She cannot support herself at present and has no husband to support her, so she and her children are supported by the state, i.e. the taxpayers, whether they like it or not. One-hundred years ago, however, the mother would not have been supported by the state, and most or all of her children would have surely died.

• Norrie May-Welby became the first person in the world to be genderless—gender-free or neuter, in the new lexicon—after Australia gave "hir" a certificate stating "sex not specified." Norrie famously declared that designation, stating that "The concepts of man or woman do not fit me." Norrie was born male but fed up with discrimination because of his androgyny, so he began the gender transition process by taking the prescribed hormones and having the appropriate surgery, then he decided to stop taking the hormones and being who "zie" (the new word for he/she) was. The New South Wales government eventually issued the certificate, as offered to men and women in transition, to facilitate international travel, but also recognized that zie does not fit into the conventional physical, psychological and hormonal boxes of male/female. The government later withdrew the certificate, and Norrie has appealed. Zie has her own blog on Facebook entitled "The Happy Eunuch." A combination, I guess, of Hollander's "The Happy Hooker" and Germaine Greer's "The Female Eunuch," which discusses her sex life and the problems with gender binaries.

• A 66-year-old man went to see his doctor in Hong Kong, concerned about an abdominal swelling. The doctor found a cyst on his ovaries and informed him that he was a woman. The man apparently had two rare genetic conditions: Turner syndrome, which affects females and causes chromosome problems, and congenital adrenal hyperplasia, which increases male hormones and resulted in a micro-penis and a beard (Kesterton 2013).

Post-modern sex began with the pill but, as with sex, so with gender. The rapid decline in fertility rates, the rise in divorce rates, and the increased role of the state in the family (e.g., with child allowances, welfare, legislation governing alimony and child support, etc.) meant that more women could and did enter the labor force, could and did continue their higher education, and not only began to compete with men but also to surpass them in both educational qualifications and income levels.

The husband is no longer the "head" of the family, the sole provider, the patriarch. In many families the old gender-roles are reversed. Gender is not what it was.

But, actually, gender never was what we always thought it was! That has been one of the most fascinating insights of post-modernity. We always thought that there were two genders. We were either male or female, fixed at birth, and either heterosexual or homosexual: a 2x2 table into which we all fit.

Not anymore. Now we know that we can be *both* sexes at once, the genders are *not* fixed, there are, or may be, more than two genders, and, furthermore, that sexual orientations can change quite unexpectedly and surprisingly. We can change sex: Gender reassignment surgery will do that. Many people have changed their sex. Technically, or at least in social science, gender is the social and cultural expression of the sexual being, which is biology. So we should really be talking about sex reassignment surgery. In any event, anatomy is no longer destiny, as it mostly was held to be in Freud's time.

Clearly, Mother Nature sometimes, somehow screws up, giving the wrong gender identity to the physical body: Psyche and soma do not match. *How* this happens is not as clear as that it *does* happen. But then in the process of gender (or sex) reassignment surgery, some might stop halfway; and if they can, some of course will do so. So we have the new she-men: both male *and* female at the same time. Some men may live as women, as depicted in such films as "The Crying Game" and "M. Butterfly;" and then there are others who, like Thomas Beatie, live as a married man, with his/her children and with female genitalia. Virginia Woolf described in *Orlando* (1928) the gradual evolution of a man into a woman over the centuries. That was remarkably prescient, for now it is possible over a few years. In post-modernity, life is full of surprises and options.

The *DSM-5* has a few pages on what it calls Gender Dysphoria, including the clinical description: "Individuals with gender dysphoria have a marked incongruence between the gender they have been assigned to (usually at birth, referred to as *natal gender*) and their experienced/expressed gender" (APA, 2013:453). This has involved a newish vocabulary of gender assignment and gender reassignment, gender identity, dysphoria, transgender (referring to identity) and transsexual (referring to sex-change or gender reassignment, usually involving hormone therapy and surgery (APA, 2013:451-9).

So much for "male or female, fixed at birth": Now you can not only change your sex but you can also be both at once. In fact, the idea that we are, or can be, both genders at once, is not entirely new. Charles Darwin was the first to broach this topic. He was controversial not only because he said that we were all descended from the ancestors of apes, sort of like cousins of the great apes. What he actually said was even more astonishing. In a letter to a friend he wrote: "Our ancestor was an animal who breathed water, had a swim bladder, a great swimming tail, an imperfect skull and undoubtedly was a hermaphrodite! Here is a pleasant genealogy for mankind" (1887: Vol. 2:266). Darwin's theory of evolution not only blurred the lines between the species but also between the genders: We are not only descended from the ancestors of apes but, before that, from a hermaphrodite fish—so an original gender *biological* unity.

Following Darwin, Freud emphasized the *psychological* unity of humanity. In 1910 he wrote: "It is popularly believed that a human being is either a man or a woman. Science, however, knows of cases in which the sexual characters are obscured" (Vol. 7.1977:52). Then he added: "In human beings pure masculinity is not to be found either in a psychological or a biological sense. Every individual on the contrary displays a mixture of the character-traits belonging to his own and to the opposite sex" (Vol. 7, 1977:142). Isn't it interesting that even when he is saying that we are *not* opposite, he still refers to us as "opposite" sexes? It is hard to think outside our traditional categories or boxes.

Twenty years later, Freud reiterated his earlier points, with a stronger emphasis: "Man is an animal organism with (like others) an unmistakably bisexual disposition. The individual corresponds to a fusion of two symmetrical halves . . . We are accustomed to say that every human being displays both male and female impulses, needs and attributes (Vol. 12, 1977:295).

The word "bisexual" in this context really means "bigender." Freud is not referring to those who are sexually attracted to both men and women, but to the psychic composition of men and women as comprised of male *and* female "impulses, needs and attributes"—which begs the question as to what they are and how they differ.

The other point is that the notion of human beings as "a fusion of two symmetrical halves" is reminiscent of Plato's theory of love. In the *Symposium*, Plato offered a myth about the origins of love, stating that originally humans were all globular and of three sexes descended from the sun, the moon or the earth. They decided to attack heaven, but Zeus was not amused and cut them all in half. It is an odd story, and I suspect his audience rolled their eyes. But the conclusion is interesting, as the bisected individuals try to find their other half in order to be whole again. This bisection "left each half with a desperate yearning for the other, and they ran together and flung their arms around each other's necks, and asked for nothing better than to be rolled into one . . . each of us is seeking for the half that will tally with himself" (190-1; 1963:543-4). This is the couple as one: globular. One is not complete without the other, and some still refer to their partners as their "other half."

Carl Jung, a former disciple of Freud's, developed the idea of psychological bigenderism, which affirmed both "halves" their opposition—Logos to Eros and Sol (Sun) to Luna (Moon)—but also their unity: "In the unconscious of every man," he said, "there is *hidden* a feminine personality, and in that of every woman a masculine personality" (1983:221; emphasis added). Maturity, he insisted, consists in integrating the hidden into the conscious.

If post-modern sex began in 1960 with the pill, post-modern gender might be said to have started with Darwin's assertion of the descent of Homo sapiens from a hermaphrodite fish. What a fall! What a capsize of the old hierarchy! This blurring of biological gender was followed by Freud's, and later Jung's, assertions of psychological bigenderism, and, later still, by the realization that, biologically, humans are conceived as female. All this is further complicated by gender-neutrality. Sweden is now introducing the term "hen" to replace the gender identifiers of "han" (male) and "hon" (female). While support for this new usage has come from LGBT groups, it has also come from teachers in nurseries and kindergartens, and from others concerned that children should be free to grow up without gender biases (Noack 2015). The social reconstruction of gender continues apace.

Transgender

Darwin argued, from evolution, that humans are all biologically descended from bigendered fish. The later discovery that humans are 98 percent chromosomally identical confirmed his insight. Jung later insisted that humans are also psychologically bigendered. But neither went so far as to challenge the conventional gender order of male/female, blue/pink, Mars/Venus, guys/dolls and Adam and Eve.

Today we are more accustomed to gender as a continuum, recognizing masculine women and feminine men, and to sexual orientation as varied: heterosexual, bisexual, homosexual, pansexual and asexual, with a few paraphilias thrown in for good measure as well as to complicate any ideas that gender and sexuality might be simple. The first successful sex change operation was performed on George Jorgensen, who became Christine, in 1951. He was not the first to have such an operation, however. One of the earliest attempts was in Germany, in 1930, on the then-famous artist Einar Wegener. He became Lili Elbe but died the following year from sex-change surgical complications (Morris, 1974:45-6). The story of Wegener/Elbe was depicted in a 2015 feature film starring Eddie Redmayne as the transgendered artist.

Gender reassignment surgery is now not uncommon, and many have written about their experiences: Jan Morris (1974) and Kate Bornstein (1995) are among the most well-known of these authors. Morris explains: "I was born with the wrong body, being feminine by gender but male by sex, and I could achieve completeness only when the one was adjusted to the other" (1974:26). In this view, gender is *psyche*, not body. How we *feel* is your gender—which throws a large spanner into the traditional works.

Indeed, this generates the idea that we *do* gender rather than that we *are* gender. Our gender is what we choose it to be. This is an idea more popular in the relevant circles than with U.S. Customs. You can try this at home but not at the border.

Judith Butler is the apostle of this social construction of gender: how we identify and how we perform gender. But perhaps she starts from Simone de Beauvoir's insights. In *The Second Sex* de Beauvoir brilliantly echoed Marx on class, but refers to different classes: "Humanity is divided into two classes of individuals whose clothes, faces, bodies, smiles, gaits, interests and occupations are manifestly different" (1953:xx-xxi). Butler said much the same thing, although less clearly; but she makes the points that individuals *decide* about this, and may not identify with the ascribed sex of birth. Anyone can perform either sex, for gender is only performance: ". . .acts, gestures, enactments generally constituted as performances are *performative* in the sense that the essence or identity that they otherwise purport to express are *fabrications* manufactured and sustained by corporeal signs and other discursive means" (1990:136).

Given that all the world's a stage, one may perform with smiles and gaits however one wants. But Butler has been criticized for confusing the part with the whole and ignoring biology and the body. Pregnancy, childbirth, lactation and menopause are not the same as clothes or smiles; and Martha Nussbaum is furious that Butler has ignored the real problems of real women in the real world, and argues that her "hip quietism" "collaborates with *evil*" (1999; emphasis added).

Transexuality has been a rather private matter affecting a relatively small number of individuals until recently, despite the memoirs by Morris, Bornstein and others. But it began to gain more publicity with the winner of the Eurovision Song Contest in 1998, a transexual Israeli woman, Dana International. An ultra-Orthodox rabbi and also deputy health minister declared: "Dana is an abomination. Even in Sodom there was nothing like it." But Dana responded: "No-one has a monopoly on the Lord and the Lord has proven where He stands" (Kalman, 1998).

Then Chastity Bono, the daughter in the popular "Sonny and Cher Comedy Hour," began the seven-year transitioning process to becoming a man—Chaz. In a frank interview, Chaz explained: "There's a gender in your brain and a gender in your body. For 99 percent of people, these things are in alignment. For transgender people, they are mismatched. That's all it is.

It's not complicated, it's not a neurosis. It's a mix-up. It's a birth defect, like a cleft palate." With the transition he said: "I expected to feel better and happier, but I really underestimated the impact my transition would have. I didn't realize that life could be this easy, that life could be this comfortable. It was unimaginable." He added that he talks less, wants more sex than his longterm partner, and likes gadgets more; and he suggests that there is more to biology than we realize (Wilson 2011).

The issue gained more traction in popular awareness with Jenna Talackova, a transgendered beauty queen, Miss Universe Canada. She was expelled from the Miss Universe Beauty Pageant in 2012 by Donald Trump, who owns it, on the grounds that she was not born female. He reversed his decision a few days later after furious criticism.

Awareness expanded further with the starring role of the transgendered Laverne Cox in the popular Netflix series "Orange is the New Black" and her role as a speaker for the transgender rights movement. Her profile was heightened when she was featured on the cover of *Time* (9 June 2014), with the lead article exploring what *Time* called "America's next civil rights frontier."

Then Bruce Jenner, a Gold Medal winner for the decathlon in the 1976 Olympics, married three times with 10 children and step-children, began transitioning, with even more publicity. She is now Caitlyn Jenner and explained in an interview with *Vanity Fair*: "I'm not doing this to be interesting. I'm doing this to live" (Bissinger, 2015:52).

Just as gender does not determine sexual orientation, so the trans community has insisted that physical genitalia do not determine gender as psychic identity. As Bissinger phrases it: "You can be born a woman with male genitalia, just as you can be born a man with female genitalia" (2015:52).

Trans individuals constitute between 0.3 percent and 0.5 percent of the population of the U.S. (*Time*, 13 June 2015:31)—which is up to 1.5 million individuals—though there may be many more who are feeling disconnects between their biology and their psychology. Apparently about 65 percent of Americans report that they have a friend or relative who is homosexual, but only 9 percent say that they have one who is trans; still, that 9 percent of the population is quite a lot of people: about 29 million. Steinmetz, from whom this data is drawn, writes that "nearly 80 percent of young trans people have experienced harassment at school; 90 percent of workers say they've dealt with it on the job . . . [and] 41 percent have attempted suicide compared with only 1.6 percent of the general population" (2014:44, 46). (Comparing the young with the general population seems like oranges and apples; I suspect that age may be an intervening variable here.) According to *Time*, eight transgender minority women were killed by June 2015 alone (13 June 2015:31). Several organizations now support the transgendered population, including the National Center for Transgender Equality, the Transgender Law Association and the World Professional Association for Transgendered Health. While it is easier than it was to change official documents, many insurance plans prohibit hormone treatments and surgeries for transitioning individuals, though some states prohibit this prohibition (Steinmetz, 2014). So the battles persist.

Some battles are in process. The Vancouver School Board in British Columbia has passed a three-point new policy to protect the rights of the transgendered. In the future they will not be known as him/her, he or she or his or hers but as "xe, xen and xyr." Second, they will be able to use their own or other toilets and join whichever sports teams they prefer. Third, the parents will not be kept informed of any gender identity issues that the students may be facing. A board member explained: "We're standing up for kids and making our schools safer and more inclusive." Two members were forced to resign. The large Chinese and Korean communities have protested particularly forcefully, asserting that the authorities are intruding over parental rights, that parents have a right to know and that this is a medical issue not a psychological one. The journalist Margaret Wente, who reported on this suggests the following:

> What we have here is a profound culture clash between world views, traditional and post-modern. One stresses family obligations, duty, conformity and responsibility to others. The other stresses self-expression, individual rights and radical autonomy. One believes that people are essentially male or female. The other believes that that belief is the root of many of our problem. No school policy yet devised is inclusive enough to include both of them. (2014:A13)

Another battle is being fought between radical feminists ("Radfems") and transgenderists, since the former do not accept the latter as women and consider them to be men. This seems to be a minority position within feminism, but Robin Morgan articulated it clearly:

> I will not call a male "she"; thirty-two years of suffering in this androcentric society, and of surviving, have earned me the title

> "woman"; one walk down the street by a male transvestite, five minutes of his being hassled (which he may enjoy), and then he dares, *dares* to think he understands our pain? No, in our mothers' names and in our own, we must not call him sister. (Goldberg, 2014:24)

Eloquent though she is, Morgan has survived very well; and while defining the essence of woman as "suffering" and "pain," which these transitioners are prepared to assume, she unfortunately ignores the suffering of men. Pity. And the suffering of the transgendered. The irony is that trans women suffer more discrimination than other women. They cannot serve in the U.S. army, they can be fired in most states, they experience high levels of violence, and 41 percent of survey respondents had attempted suicide. The National Center for Transgender equality and the National Gay and Lesbian Task Force, which monitor developments, estimate that one in 30,000 men and one in 100,000 women seek gender reassignment surgery, but still more identify with the other sex.

Opponents of the Radfems, which some call TERFs (trans exclusionary radical feminists), consider them transphobic and hate groups. Radfems, in turn, prefer their events, lectures, camps and so on to be restricted to "womyn-born-womyn" and believe that female-to-male transitioners merely want to raise their status in the androcentric (as they see it) world, while male-to-female transitioners are described as "autogynophiliacs": an erotic compulsion or paraphilia rather than an identity. It does get more complicated. An abortion support group declares: "We recognize that people who identify as men can become pregnant and seek abortions" (Goldberg, 2014: 28).

Juliet Jacques, who transitioned from male to female, and writes about her experience, suggests that trans people have highlighted the debates about what it means to be male or female, masculine or feminine—much as homosexuals have done; for they are not so much opposite sexes or a continuum, as others argue, but more a four- dimensional kaleidoscope. She says that "the most difficult question was, simply, 'Why?' I don't know what caused my gender dysphoria—nature, nature or some combination: it just *is* . . ." (2014).

Some battles have been won. When I applied for a visa for India two years ago, in 2013, I had to check one box with the following options: male, female, transgender. But India has a long tradition of recognizing transsexuals, who are known there as *Hijras* (Nanda, 1999). And the English language has already changed with the *DSM-5*.

Morris switched from one gender to the other, and argues that there are only two sexes, which overlap but are not the same. Kate Bornstein, however, disagrees: "I identify as neither male nor female . . . but as a third" (1995:3-4, 98). She said that as a transsexual she faced "urinary segregation" at IBM, since both the men and the women refused to let her use their washrooms.

In sum, the more trans people become celebrities (International, Talackova, Cox), the more celebrities become transgendered (Bono, Jenner), and the more authorities (e.g. India, Australia) recognize realities beyond the "two" sexes, the more quickly and easily will the general public come to terms with the new realities of gender.

Intersex

Anne Fausto-Sterling (1993), a developmental geneticist, says there are five sexes or more, depending on many factors, but including the "intersexed." Our norm of two, she says, is "in defiance of nature." She suggests that we recognize "true" hermaphrodites, as well as male or female dominant "pseudo" hermaphrodites, as three distinct sexes. In the past, such gender-genital ambiguity was regarded as a medical emergency requiring "corrective" surgery, to ensure that the infant would fit normally into our binary system. Today, however, thanks largely to the efforts of Cheryl Chase and the Intersex Society of North America, which she founded, a new consensus has emerged: (a) Optimally children should be assigned a gender as soon as possible after birth; (b) The baby's genes, hormones, genitals, internal organs, electrolytes, gonads and urine should all be examined; (c) Doctors should counsel parents not to immediately demand corrective surgery, but to wait.

The burden of research suggests that surgery generally has negative consequences, and that it is the parents, not the children, who have the problems with "disorders of sexual development." One young woman discovered she was intersex when her professor listed some of the symptoms: "No periods, can't have children, ambiguous genitals." She cried for a week but concludes: "Now I think intersex is pretty weird but kind of sweet" (Weil, 2006:4-5).

One of these disorders is androgen-insensitivity syndrome, whereby a fetus with male (XY) chromosomes cannot adequately metabolize androgen. Another is congenital adrenal hyperplasia, which masculinizes girls' genitals at birth. Then there are boys with a micro-penis and girls with clitoromegaly, an enlarged clitoris. To operate or not, that is the question? (Weil, 2006). Intersex tends to refer to biology; trans refers to psychology and the much-disputed brain. While some refer to a male or female brain (generally male brains are better connected within each hemisphere and back to front, and female brains are better connected across the hemispheres and side to side), others prefer to stress the similarities and the overlaps between the brains, which they say are not especially different, and are formed, perhaps, as much by the environment as by biology.

So gender is not what it was in the 1950s. In 1950 the norm was male/female, heterosexual/homosexual. Only four quadrants. Boring. Now the norm is a continuum of males to females, as well as masculine to feminine, not necessarily coinciding with gender; and which also includes transgendered, intersexed, she-males, and transitioning—a far more complex, varied number of "genders," which also conveys the viewpoint and message that we are all bigendered. And some in these categories are also bisexual even polysexual and asexual, not to mention the huge number of sexual paraphilias out there. Now it is a fuller, richer, much more muddled, weird and sexier world, which suggests a "four-dimensional kaleidoscope."

Sexologies

Sexology as the scientific study of sex was initiated by Richard von Krafft-Ebing (1840-1902), professor of psychiatry at the University of Vienna. His *Psychopathia Sexualis* (1886) became the foundation of modern sexual pathology, investigating such matters as sadism, masochism, fetishism, bestiality, nymphomania, incest, necrophilia, corpse-mutilation, rape, sex murders, pedophilia . . . a long list.

Such practices might horrify or disgust most people, which is why some are criminalized. But two aspects of his work are particularly interesting: first, he used case studies, and second, although he condoned punishment for illegal sexual activities, he was a compassionate man, referring to these "unfortunate people" whose letters to him "reveal sufferings of the soul in comparison to which all the other afflictions dealt out by Fate appear as trifles" (1946:iii). Unfortunately this work was neither about sex as joy or fun nor about sex as healthy—it was about sex as sick, however compassionate.

His book was very popular. It went through 12 editions from 1886 to 1946 and deeply influenced Freud. Yet the book was about pathology and set sexology off in the wrong direction. It was all about what's wrong with sex. There was nothing about what Alex Comfort famously described as *The Joy of Sex* (1972). Still, he was a pioneer, and both Freud and Havelock Ellis acknowledged their debts to him.

Since Freud is discussed elsewhere, here we will be brief. Certainly his impact upon sexology has been enormous. He asked the central questions that had never been asked before, listened, analyzed, generated theories, and advanced our understanding to new levels. He insisted on the centrality of the sexual drive in human life, and his insights into the human condition remain useful. Many of his terms, ideas, and areas of analytical concern remain in current use—probably more than any other thinker of his time: id and libido; ego and super-ego; the stages of psycho-sexual development; free association; his discussions of dreams, jokes and (Freudian) slips; processes like repression, sublimation, displacement, identification, fetishism, regression, fixation, conversion, transference, substitution, resistance, and projection; symbolism; the importance of the unconscious; infantile sexuality ("polymorphous perversity"); the Oedipus and Electra complexes; Eros and Thanatos; death wishes and reality principles . . . and more. Freud brought sexuality into the academic—even popular—domain.

Although he has been widely criticized by some for his theory of penis envy, his alleged misunderstanding of female orgasms, and for his famous question, "What does a woman want?" (Jones, 1954:468), his name—despite a viewpoint that critics say suggests misogyny—was on both the American and the British lists of the Top 100 Most Important People of the Twentieth Century—a tribute to his genius!

Havelock Ellis published his seven-volume *Studies in the Psychology of Sex* (1898-1928), and then a more accessible one-volume *Psychology of Sex*. In his Introduction, he gracefully recommended Freud's *Introductory Lectures on Psychoanalysis*. This is not what most academics do: They usually try to shoot down the competition. Ellis includes chapters on sexual deviation, in which he cites Krafft-Ebing, but also chapters on love and marriage; so here sex is switched from pathology to being more about love and marriage, and horse and carriage. A major paradigm shift. He insisted that "no sharp boundary line exists between normal and abnormal. All normal persons are a little abnormal in one direction or another . . ." (1934:vi). What a relief. The abnormal is normal.

He pointed out that homosexuality is normal (1934:214-5). He noted that women do have sexual desire, but that the social requirements of "modesty" inhibit the expression of their desires, and thus camouflage and even distort the reality (1934:335-7). And masturbation too is normal rather than, as Freud argued, a perversion. He cited the anthropologists Bronislaw Malinowski and Margaret Mead for their discussions of youthful sexuality and sex play and the wide range of cultural "normality." Citing Mead, he said: "Nearly every little girl masturbated from the age of six or seven, more or less in secret, the boys also, but more usually in groups, and casual homosexual practices are common" (1934:103).

He argued that the universality of sexual desire, the normalcy of masturbation, the need to sexually experiment to maximize pleasure, and homosexual sex are normal; and while Ellis no doubt helped to transform contemporary sexual relations, his work also reflected the post-World War I relaxation of Victorian sexual morality, the flapper era, the Moulin Rouge, the emergence of sun-tanning and nudism, jazz, Valentino and Hollywood.

In the 1940s and 1950s, the landmark Kinsey reports (1948, 1953) on the sexual behavior of American men and women presented tables of statistical data on what people actually did, but little qualitative data on what it meant—how important or delightful it all was. Alfred Kinsey at Indiana University was an entomologist by training, specializing in wasps, and he applied the same scientific methods to Americans as he did to the wasps: dispassionate, quantitative and nonjudgmental. Love was not mentioned. He argued that more was known about the sexual life of wasps than humans. Among his findings about men: 8 percent had sex with animals, 10 percent were gay, 50 percent had been unfaithful to their spouses, and 90 percent masturbated. While these findings were later qualified, they set the benchmarks for future researchers. He also found that 25 percent of wives had cheated on their husbands and 60 percent masturbated to orgasm. In this, he negated the old virgin-whore dichotomy and showed that women had a libido too, unlike Hollywood's Doris Day and Audrey Hepburn, which is why Marilyn Monroe was so important as a successor to Mae West. These were descriptions of sex as it was, not as Americans thought it should be or believed it to be.

William Masters and Virginia Johnson at St. Louis University followed up with *The Human Sexual Response* (1966), which took an entirely physiological approach to sex analyzed in the laboratory and measured. Starting their research with prostitutes and continuing with volunteers, they emphasized the importance of the clitoris in female satisfaction (hitherto apparently under-researched) and multiple orgasms, and later pioneered sex therapies for non-orgasmic women and the use of surrogates. The book was a bestseller and highly controversial; and, perhaps, as Petersen implies, the beginning of the end of phallocentrism. Soon afterwards the battery-operated vibrator was marketed (Petersen, 1999).

Meanwhile, the scientific sexologists had been bypassed by events. First, the pill was developed, tested and then marketed with FDA approval in 1960. The consequences, direct and indirect, were enormous. This facilitated the hippy movement and the sexual revolution, replete with the slogans "Make Love, Not War!" "Sex, Drugs and Rock 'n' Roll," and "Free Love." The specific gender highlights of these two decades include the 1953 publication of *Playboy* magazine, founded by Hugh Hefner, featuring Marilyn Monroe as the first centerfold. This was followed by *Penthouse* magazine (1969) and *Hustler* magazine (1974)—all appealing to male sexuality. In a similar sexually liberated vein, Helen Gurley Brown wrote her bestselling book *Sex and the Single Girl* (1962), which advocated sex before marriage. She later became the editor of *Cosmopolitan* magazine, which became the forum of women's sexual "liberation." Meanwhile, in France Simone de Beauvoir published *The Second Sex* (1949, published in English in 1953), which was followed in the United States by Betty Friedan's *The Feminine Mystique* (1963) to huge acclaim. The National Organization of Women (NOW) was founded in 1965 by Betty Friedan and others. Then, in 1968, the second wave of the women's movement was inaugurated by the mass protest against the Miss America Beauty Pageant in Atlantic City.

But it was not just books and magazines. Sex was in music: The crooner Frank Sinatra of the 1940s was replaced by the gyrations of Elvis in the 1950s and Beatlemania in the 1960s. And musicals: "Hair" and "Oh! Calcutta!" And film: Brigitte Bardot, Jane Fonda, and the Bond movies, leading up (or down) to Internet porn. And the tell-all memoirs, of which more later. Now, some say, we live in a hypersexual, pornified, raunch culture (Dines, 2010; Levy, 2005: Paul, 2005.)

More recently, sexologists have turned to the personal stories and advice from practicing therapists and clinical psychologists, including Bella Ellwood Clayton and Pamela Stephenson-Connelly, to name two of many, with very different orientations from the pathologies of Krafft-Ebing, the theories of Freud, the statistics of Kinsey and the physiology of Masters and Johnson. Sexology has come a long way over time.

Sexologists, the pill, legislation, the popular print media, television, Hollywood, the sexual revolution, the women's movement, the new reproductive technology and gay rights have all affected sexual behavior in numerous ways. Indeed, post-modern sex, at its extremes, is light-years away from the fifties norms and the ideals of the nuclear family, the dog called Spot and the white picket fence.

The English writer Penelope Fitzgerald once wrote: "It sometimes strikes me that men and women aren't quite right for each other." Well, on a good day . . . But it's not all about men and women; sometimes sex and love are about men and men and women and women. And here, too, the changes in values and attitudes and policies have been very rapid. Now they can become each other.

"Gay Is Good"

"Gay is good" was the slogan of gay rights activist Frank Kameny, who died in 2011. Kameny fought in World War II but was fired from his Civil Service job in the 1950s for being gay. He then became an activist for gay and lesbian rights, and is known as the "Father of the Gay Rights Movement." In 1968 he coined the slogan for which he is famous, after watching students on TV shouting Stokely Carmichael's slogan "Black is Beautiful," and thinking that gays needed a slogan too. He received an apology from Barack Obama before he died. It seems fitting to use his rallying cry as the title of this section, which explores the changing attitudes, values and policies about gays—the changing "social constructions," as the sociologists say. Indeed, the transformation in Western social constructions of homosexuality has been remarkable: from social problem to pride, from wrong to rights, from the closet to parades, from sin and crime and sexual deviant to normal and a personal matter, from bad to—in Kameny's word—good.

The history and sociology of homosexuality have been discussed by many (e.g., Bullough, 1979; Nardi, 2000; Aldrich, 2012). We will focus primarily on Euro-America, beginning with the sentencing of Oscar Wilde to two years in prison in 1895 for "gross indecency between males." In retrospect, it is more likely that it was for flaunting his liaison with the son of the powerful Lord Douglas. Others with the same sexual orientation were not so charged. This was homosexual sex as *crime*.

Homosexuality was also defined or constructed as a *sin*, following interpretations of the words of the Lord to Moses in Leviticus: "Thou shalt not lie with mankind as with womankind: it is abomination" (18:22); and "If a man also lie with mankind as he lieth with a woman, both of them have committed an abomination; they shall surely be put to death; their blood shall be upon them" (20:13).

Some believe that these are the orders of God, valid forever. Others think that these are interesting ideas about the culture of the Israelites in about 800 BCE, have no relevance today, and should not be taken literally; but if they were to be taken literally, then homosexuality would be a criminal offence—homicide—which is also a sin and against another commandment. Plus, one might wonder why God was so interested in the sleeping habits of the Israelites: Two chapters are concerned almost exclusively with what or whom they should not sleep—who also must be put to death.

In discussing the literal interpretations of the Bible, James M. Kaufman penned an open letter to Dr. Laura Schlesinger, a popular conservative-radio talk-show host in the U.S., who opposed homosexuality, noting the many biblical allowances and prescriptions that are prohibited and illegal today. (Actually he denied that he wrote it, but it is brilliant.) These include permission to own slaves (Lev 25:44) and to sell daughters into slavery (Exodus 21:7), requirements to kill any neighbors who work on the Sabbath (Exodus 35:2), and prohibitions against hair-trimming, touching the skin of a dead pig, planting two different crops in the same field, wearing two different kinds of thread, and eating shellfish . . . very many prohibitions. While some of these permissions and requirements may be criminal offences today, the prohibitions are largely ignored by both Christians and Jews. Clearly, in invoking Leviticus, the religious right is cherry-picking its causes. Why are they not protesting against barbers, football players, cotton and polyester blends, shellfish in restaurants and fish-markets? And why are they not killing their Sabbath-working neighbors, owning slaves, and selling their daughters? The point is obvious.

By the end of the nineteenth century, homosexuality was widely regarded as both crime and sin. Attitudes began to shift with the pioneering work in pathology by Krafft-Ebing, in psychoanalysis by Freud and, especially, in sexology with Havelock Ellis, who acknowledged his great debt to Freud. He was particularly dogmatic: "Homosexuality has always and everywhere existed. It is normal." It is also important for three main reasons: "(1) its wide diffusion and the large place it has played in various epochs of culture; (2) its frequency in civilization today, and (3) the large number of distinguished persons who have manifested this aberration"—aberration in the statistical or biological sense rather than the moral. He added that homosexuality "may be called "natural," from its frequency among animals, especially the primates (1934:215-9), and therefore it should be decriminalized, as he said it was in France and elsewhere in Europe.

As the premier sexologist writing in English, Ellis was extremely important in the re-evaluation of homosexuality; but the Depression and World War II put his agenda on the back-burner. Then, in 1948, two events were further turning points in this process. The United Nations announced the Universal Declaration of Human Rights, which stated, in part, "All human beings are created equal in dignity and rights." This was a massive reversal in the thinking about humanity from Plato and Aristotle, which had been predicated on the belief that we are all *unequal*. This belief was institutionalized not only by gender (sexism) and race (racism) but also by ethnicity, religion (the Crusades, Inquisition, anti-Semitism and the Holocaust) and basic biology—as it is so often today.

The second event was the publication of *Sexual Behavior in the Human Male* by Kinsey, Pomeroy and Martin, as earlier mentioned. The authors found, to the astonishment (and sometimes horror) of many people, that 37 percent of the total male population had had some homosexual experience to orgasm, and so had most teenagers, leading the researchers to conclude that homosexuality and heterosexuality lie along a continuum—they are not mutually exclusive. In their words: "The world is not to be divided into sheep and goats. Not all things are black nor all things white. It is a fundamental of taxonomy that nature rarely deals with discrete categories" (1948:639). Given that "both Jewish and Christian [faiths] have considered this aspect of human sexuality to be abnormal and immoral" (1948:610), the researchers had to tread carefully in reporting that homosexual sex was both normal and frequent and avoid commentary about morality. Their calculations and statistics are now rather amusing, as they were compiled before the pill, the sexual revolution and the women's movement. The researchers note, for example, that "6.3 percent of the total number of orgasms is derived from homosexual contacts" compared to 69.4 percent from heterosexual and 24 percent from masturbation or nocturnal emissions, and only "0.3 per cent of the outlet . . . from relations with animals of other species" (1948:610). I love the phrasing: "outlet" and "animals of other species," because it is so formal and archaic sounding today.

They concluded that "The homosexual has been a significant part of human sexual activity since the dawn of human history, primarily because it is an expression of capacities that are basic in the human animal"(1948: 666). So the attack on traditional attitudes escalated, and the blurring of old certainties and binaries continued: Darwin blurred the human/animal binary, Freud and Jung blurred the male/female binary, and now Ellis and Kinsey blurred the heterosexual/homosexual binary. But it all takes time.

In 1954, Alan Turing committed suicide. Turing was a brilliant mathematician, a war hero, handsome and gay. As a Professor of Mathematics at Cambridge University, he led the team at Bletchley Park (now open as a Museum) that broke the German Enigma code. His team is credited with shortening World War II by two years and, thereby, saving millions of lives. After the war, he became a professor at Manchester University, but homosexuality was illegal and he was arrested and charged with gross indecency. He was offered the choice of prison or "treatment," that is, chemical castration. He chose the latter and never recovered. The man was a genius lost to us. A spokesman for Google said, "Without his ideas we would not only have no Google, we would also have no Internet, no mobile phones, no laptops, no email, no Facebook, no YouTube—and the world would have a GDP substantially less than it is today." And the computer revolution would have happened 20 years earlier and in the UK, not Silicon Valley. "All the principles of computation go back to Alan Turing," the spokesman added, with his work going back to a paper he first published in 1936 at the age of 24, and then another revolutionary paper in 1950 that is generally credited with launching the field of Artificial Intelligence. He was to computers, they say, what Newton and Einstein were to physics; and his work ranks with Stephenson's Rocket, the Wright Brothers Flier, nuclear power stations and spacecraft as changing our worlds. Finally, in 2009, after a petition to Downing Street, the Prime Minister publicly apologized for Turing's treatment at the hands of the British Justice system (Hanlon, 2011). Then a stamp was issued featuring and honoring Turing. He had already been listed by *Time* magazine as one of the 100 most influential people of the twentieth century. In 2013, Turing was granted a Royal Pardon, and in 2014 a film about him "The Imitation Game" was released.

In 1948, the human rights revolution, epitomized by the 1948 U.N. Universal Declaration of Human Rights, facilitated the rise of the Civil Rights Movement in the United States, which, in turn, facilitated the rise of the Women's Movement, which, in turn, inspired the rise of the Gay Rights Movement, and then the men's movements and the Transgender Rights Movement. The process has been cumulative, and the ripple effects are still spreading slowly around the world.

Meanwhile, following the *Wolfenden Report* (1957) in the U.K., homosexuality was decriminalized in the U.K. in 1967 and in Canada the following year. The issue has been far more controversial in the United States, where Kameny coined the phrase "Gay is good" in 1968; but everything came to a head with the Stonewall protest in 1969.

Stonewall was another turning point in the emerging Gay Rights Movement in the United States. It was a gay bar in New York, which the police periodically raided. But on one famous occasion the raid was resisted successfully by the patrons, the police withdrew, gay rights were asserted and vindicated and the stereotype of gays as effete or feminine was effectively destroyed. It took a while for these ideas to be enacted in law and culture, but this was the beginning. The Lambda Legal Defense and Education Fund was founded in 1971 to advance and defend gay rights.

A fourth turning point was the decision by the American Psychiatric Association to remove the definition of homosexuality as a "sexual deviation" from the *DSM-3* in 1974. Homosexuality began to be reconsidered as within the "normal range" of sexual expression—as Ellis had argued 40 years earlier and Kinsey did 26 years earlier. How long does it take?

So, for many people, homosexuality was redefined from sin and crime and sick to normal, natural and, as Kameny put it, good—and all this in 75 years! This constituted a massive change among legal, ecclesiastical and medical authorities, as well as the general public, and the process is still continuing. But the process has not been without rollbacks.

HIV/AIDS was first reported by the Center for Disease Control (CDC) in Atlanta, Georgia, in 1981, after the deaths of a number of gay men in San Francisco. At first the casualty rate was low and the disease was dismissed as the "gay plague;" but the casualty rate increased, as the disease spread to intravenous drug users and then to the straight population; finally, the medical experts realized that the disease was global and that the death rate was a huge problem, economic, political and demographic. The medical model of the disease was countered by the moral model, since it was defined by some Christian fundamentalists as God's curse on homosexuals. This epidemic created a huge backlash against gays but also united the gay community, which had been sequentially empowered by the sexologists Ellis and Kinsey, the activist Kameny, and then the militarism of Stonewall, the legalism of Lambda Legal, the APA decision, and the legal initiatives in the U.K. and Canada.

The epidemic also injected risk back into sexuality—not the risk of unwanted pregnancies but the risk of death. The human cost has been high: About 35 million have died, but the latest UNAIDS Global Report, for

2014, is more optimistic than earlier reports. The Report estimates that about 35 million people are now living with HIV, which is more than in previous years, since the antiretroviral therapy is reaching more people. There were about 2.1 million new infections of HIV in 2013, but that is a 38 percent decline from about 3.4 million in 2001. And the number of AIDS deaths was 1.5 million in 2013, down from 2.3 million in 2005, a decline of 35 percent. So this is substantial progress. The 2013 Report includes a 10-point program of action for the following years (UNAIDS, 2013, 2014). Globally, the expenditure on treatment and prevention costs about $19 billion per annum (*Economist*, 26 July 2014:65).

The virus has killed over 650,000 Americans, but the numbers have dropped from 50,000 deaths per annum to 15,000; yet there are still about 50,000 new infections every year, amounting to about 1.1 million people with HIV, including 76 percent male, 44 percent black, and 33 percent white. Transmission of HIV is 53 percent male to male sex, 27 percent male to female sex and 15 percent by contaminated needles (Park, 2014).

AIDS is now redefined as a chronic illness rather than a death sentence, and the battle against it is slowly being won. The tide is turning but now Ebola and SARS are on the horizon. Presenters at the International AIDS Conference in Melbourne in 2014 noted the four different prevention methods of HIV transmission: education, condoms, drugs (especially the antiretrovirals, or ARVs) and circumcision. They noted that the ARVs reduce the risk of transmission ("treatment as prevention") and that a new drug, Trovada, seems to reduce infection rates by 90 percent; so it is recommended as "pre-exposure prophylaxis" for those at high risk. Finally, decriminalizing prostitution would reduce infection rates by about one third. The latter offers a medical model of prostitution in contrast to the moral model (it's a sin, or at least bad for communities); the feminist model (they are victims, and some are) applied in Sweden and elsewhere; and the liberal model of free trade applied in the Netherlands and Germany. As can be seen, models and muddles proliferate again.

Apparently apes and monkeys have had SIV, the Simian Immunodeficiency Virus, for thousands of years—at least 32,000 to be more precise. This is the precursor to our HIV and humans must have been exposed to it very often. So how did a mild monkey disease turn into this pandemic? The monkeys themselves seem to have adapted to SIV and developed some sort of immunity to it. And the ancestor virus to SIV may have existed for millions of years. There are, in fact, two HI viruses: HIV-1, the most common, and HIV-2, which is milder and rarely found outside West Africa, having originated with sooty mangabeys. The earliest confirmed HIV case was discovered in blood from a man in Kinshasha in 1959. So what made the virus global? The two main theories are the mass-production and use (and reuse) of syringes in the 1950s to combat yaws, syphilis, malaria, smallpox, polio and so on (though some point out that syringes had been in use earlier). The other theory, which is complementary rather than contradictory, points to increased population migration and the rapid expansion of African cities in the twentieth century—an expansion due, in part, to declining mortality rates, which was partly due, in turn, to the syringes, and which resulted in red-light districts, sex workers and, as today, the spread of HIV (McNeil, 2010).

Two consequences of the emergence of HIV/AIDS in the U.S. were the Supreme Court decision in Lowers v. Hardwick in 1986 to uphold a lower court decision that sodomy was a crime. This was a huge step back for human rights and also for the authority of the psychiatric profession. Then, in 1998, Matthew Shepherd was brutally tortured and murdered in Wyoming because he was gay, which revolted the country and received worldwide publicity. This was followed by the murders of Aaron Webster in Canada in 2001, David Morley in London in 2004 and Brian Williamson and Steve Harvey in Jamaica in 2005 and 2006, respectively. In California, a Baptist minister preached that homosexuality is "a monstrous sin against God." (It always amazes how many people are convinced they know what God thinks, and even more amazing that they so rarely agree.) His supporters announced "No tears for Queers," "AIDS is God's curse," and "Repent or Perish" (*Time*, 16 December 2002). The climate began to change as the general public began to realize that the murderers, not the gays, were the sick people, and that homophobia, not homosexuality, is the problem.

Perhaps this murder was the tipping point and the turning of the tide. Or perhaps it was the Ellen DeGeneres' lesbian kiss on prime time TV in 1997. In any event, the U.S. Supreme Court in Lawrence v. Texas (2003) overturned its earlier 1986 ruling and decriminalized homosexual activities in the remaining 14 states where it was still a crime—36 years after the U.K., a time gap similar to their abolitions of slavery. By 2003 in the U.S., "Will and Grace" had become the most popular TV sitcom, and this was followed by "Queer as Folk" and "Queer Eye for the Straight Guy," which all normalized what had so recently been criminalized. Another indication of changing attitudes was the box office successes of "Brokeback Mountain" and "Capote" in 2005. *Newsweek* (20 March 2000; 7 July 2003 and *Time*

(10 October 2005) foregrounded gay issues in cover stories: From closet to front page in no time flat.

Another turning point was the $11.2 billion award in damages by a jury to a man who was fired by the billionaire hotelier Leona Helmsley after she learned that he was gay (*Time*, 17 February 2003:11). The tide continued to turn when, in 2009, Iceland elected its first openly gay head of state as Prime Minister, Johanna Siguroardottir. Another glass ceiling broken.

In 2010, the U.S. Congress voted to repeal the Clinton-era policy of "Don't Ask, Don't Tell," which had resulted in 14,000 men and women leaving the U.S. military (Hulse, 2010). And in 2012, Tammy Baldwin became the first openly gay candidate to be elected to the U.S. Senate. At the same time, voters in four more states voted to legalize same-sex marriage, for a total of nine, plus the capital. These vicious culture wars are more of a problem than the numbers would seem to warrant, but they also suggest that only 2.7 percent of men and 1.3 percent of women had had same-sex sex in the previous year (Michael et al., 1994:174-6). This does not mean that they were all gay or lesbian, nor that all gays and lesbians had had sex the previous year: some might have retired from the game, others might have had a famine year, and others might just have lied; but it does suggest that these wars about rights and equity are a widespread tribute to a sense of justice and fair play for a small minority.

Bullying remains a major problem for many gays and lesbians in high school and university, and causes suicides every year. Bullying may be verbal or physical but the new cyber-bullying is particularly difficult to deal with since it is anonymous. Some schools have initiated "diversity clubs" for those who feel persecuted (not just gays). The YouTube video "It gets Better" has helped many, as the comments indicate. The suicide of Tyler Clementi in 2010, a Rutgers University student, and a number of others after that, prompted President Obama to call a White House Conference on bullying (*New Yorker*, 6 February 2010). And several initiatives have been established by different authorities to help LGBTIQQ teens, especially, to cope with homophobia (Pascoe, 2007).

In his inaugural address to Congress in 2012, President Barack Obama sent a trailblazer message on gay rights: "We, the people, declare today that the most evident of truths—that all of us are created equal—is the star that guides us still, just as it guided our forebears through Seneca Falls and Selma and Stonewall." Here he echoes the Declaration of Independence but also squarely equates the Gay Rights Movement with the Women's Rights Movement and the Civil Rights Movement. He added: "Our journey is not complete until our gay brothers and sisters are treated like anyone else under the law—for if we are truly created equal, then surely the love we commit to one another must be equal as well" (*New York Times,* 22 January 2012). Gay rights are human rights.

Meanwhile in Russia, President Putin tried, unsuccessfully, to ban gay athletes from competing in the 2012 Olympic Games.

Another turning point was when Pope Francis remarked: "If a homosexual person is of good will and is in search of God, I am no-one to judge." This may not change the theology of Aquinas, but it does change the attitudes and practice. The Pope, a former nightclub bouncer, was voted "Person of the Year" by *Time* in 2013 (23 December 2013).

Despite the progress in human rights in some parts of the world, problems remain. Homosexuality is illegal in 76 countries, mostly in Africa and the Middle East, and six of them have the death penalty. In Uganda in 2009, a government "backbencher" introduced the "Anti-Homosexuality Bill," which proposed the death penalty for HIV-positive gay men and prison for those not reporting gays. A newspaper published names and addresses. Vigilantism followed. Some American evangelicals, who still regard homosexuality as a sin that should be criminalized, preach against the "homosexual agenda." A film "Call Me Kuchu" (gay or transgendered) documents the discrimination and the murder of gay activist David Kato (Sharlet, 2010; *Economist*, 10 November 2012). The gay son of a colleague cannot return to his native Iran for fear of his life. In Nigeria in 2014, President Jonathan Goodyear signed legislation banning gay marriage and other activities, including gays organizing meetings. Being gay is still dangerous.

Yet all this panic in so many countries about sin, crime, right and wrong, good and evil and knowing the mind of God should really be seen in historical and cross-cultural perspective. Europeans and Americans have tended to divide humans historically into either male or female and heterosexual or homosexual in sexual orientation: a neat, clean and clear division, 2x2, of watertight compartments. Recently they have questioned the gender binary—with transgendered, transexuals, and intersexed, plus the Darwinian idea of a biological continuum and the Freudian and Jungian ideas of a psychological continuum. This was followed by Bornstein's notion of three sexes and Fausto-Sterling's of five sexes. Similarly, the sexual orientation binary of homosexual or heterosexual has also been crossed by asexuals, egosexuals, pansexuals and bisexuals. The old traditional binaries are now largely destroyed, at least in some circles; yet in others the moral panic of homophobia still persists, and in still others homoeroticism is normalized.

Homoeroticism was approved most famously in ancient Athens. In the *Symposium* (217-9), Alcibiades blandly mentions his failure to seduce Socrates; and also in the *Symposium* (211b) Plato discusses how the understanding of absolute beauty begins with a beautiful boy. An ancient text stated firmly: "Marriage is a remedy devised by the necessity of procreation, but male love alone must rule the heart of a philosopher" (in Mottier, 2010:10). And the homosexual practices in parts of New Guinea were discussed earlier.

Indeed, as the anthropologist Rafael Ramirez notes about his native Puerto Rico, homosexuality may be more or less acceptable. Sexuality there is far more subtle, nuanced, gentle and complicated than it is in the U.S. or Nigeria, among many other countries. Puerto Ricans recognize a continuum of sexual behavior rather than the usual Western binary of gay or straight. Ramirez refers to a typology of men: the straight, who know nothing of *el ambiente*—the gay world; the *ententido*—the man who may or may not have had homosexual relations but considers himself heterosexual; the *ponca*—a self-defined heterosexual whose claims are not accepted by gays; the *bugarron*—who also claims to be heterosexual despite *ambiente* activities because he is the penetrator and plays a male "game"; and the *loca*—who claims to be and is recognized as gay. There are also, however, the *locas de closet, locas vestidas* (drag queens) and the *locas partidas* (effeminate men). This is a very different reality, vocabulary and sensitivity from the binary Western constructions of sexual behavior and orientation. Ramirez does add that, while there is stigma attached, the climate is changing and gay pride is now being asserted (Ramirez, 1999).

Interestingly, lesbianism has not provoked the same debate and fury as male homosexuality. Perhaps this has been because of fear of AIDS, which hit the male community harder than the female; the lack of a challenge to traditional ideas of masculinity; or the greater range of emotional expression and intimacy expected or permitted of women. Certainly lesbians have been discriminated against, but murders have seemingly been rare or non-existent.

The first point here is that the American binary, gay or straight, is rejected for a more sophisticated categorization of sexual orientation. The second is that there is no necessary relation between sexual orientation and identity. The term homosexual was probably first coined in 1868 by a Hungarian journalist and later popularized by Krafft-Ebing, reaching the

English language in translation in 1892, where it was maintained by Ellis. The earliest known use of the word heterosexual in the English language was also in 1892, but it referred to recreational sex as opposed to procreative sex. The significance of this naming process is that it reifies the behavior into an identity. What you *do* constitutes who you *are*. This was new. People had always engaged in same-sex sex but they were not defined by these actions. Now they were. Labels and identities were pinned on them by others. As Foucault put it: "The sodomite had been a temporary aberration; the homosexual is now a species" (in Mottier, 2010: 44). But what sort of species? That depended—a sinner for the fundamentalists, a criminal for the courts and a sexual deviant in psychiatry. Such has been some of the prevailing wisdom, now capsized.

Still, the term homosexual is now being challenged and displaced. It is not necessarily a self-definition but a label imposed by others, and often a negative label. MSM—men who have sex with men—is an abbreviation that emerged in the mid-1980s to describe men who have sex with other men but do not identify as gay: "It's not who you are, it's what you do." Mottier notes the complexity of the terminologies, citing this example: "he might be homosexual, but he's not gay" (2010:127). This affirmation articulates sexual orientation but does not define identity, and the self is labeled by oneself not by the other. The evolution of the terminology demonstrates the evolution of thinking: homosexual from the mid-1800s in Europe; gay and lesbian 50 years later; then MSM and WSW (or, in England, WLW, i.e., women who love women; note the difference: men have sex with men but women love women! And men don't love men?) Also, there is the designation MSM/TG (transgender). In addition, there have been the shifts from "gay" to "gay and lesbian" to "gay, lesbian and bisexual," to LGBT, and now tp LGBTIQQ (Boellstorff, 2011:297). Even the originally pejorative terms like "fag," "dyke" and "queer" have now been appropriated as self-assertive; so the group Queer Nation has the slogan ""We're queer, we're here" (Mottier, 2010:127).

Jane Ussher has explained that it is necessary to distinguish between material and discursive elements in understanding about being lesbian or gay; she rejects the essentialist idea of earlier sexologists that doing equals being, and insists that "being (or doing) 'lesbian' or 'gay' isn't just about same-sex sex" (1997:132). An act does not become a type of person or an identity. It all depends on the context, phenomenology and meaning—the discursive element (or the social construction) as in ancient Athens or Puerto Rico. She discusses the changing historical context of homosexuality. In the U.K. the death penalty for sodomy between men was in effect from 1553 until the act was repealed in 1861, when the penalty was reduced to between 10 years and life. Though the laws were less concerned with women, occasional legislation in France, Italy and Spain did condemn women who had sex with other women to burning at the stake (1997:133). One member of parliament (MP) stated in 1921 that sex between women "saps the institutions of society," "stops childbirth," "produces neurasthenia and insanity" and "causes our race to decline" (1997:135). Another MP commented on the verdict in a child custody case in 1994: "We don't put children in the hands of the insane. Why should we put them in the hands of the perverted?" (1997:138).

The early sexologists blamed the body for lesbianism—a certain masculinization—notably Krafft-Ebing and Ellis. The later psychiatrists blamed the mind: neurosis, as in the *DSM IV*. Then Foucault and others blamed societal labeling, as we have seen, and further stigmatization; and still, for men, biology is credited or blamed as genetics or birth order or birth number or any number of other hypotheses. Some researchers suggest that neither genetic nor personal nor social factors determine a sexual orientation, but, perhaps, a complex interacting, synergistic collection; others suggest that the cause does not matter: Deal with it. The facts that some people are bisexual and some change their orientation in midlife are confounding realities for any simple theory of orientation. Ussher's own interviews explore the multiple meanings of being lesbian. Some were more essentialist, some more constructionist, just to blur the distinctions. This is an example of a woman who is more reductionist: "I started fancying women when I was in like the first year of infant school . . ." And another woman: "I'd say I was born one." Another woman only seems to have realized it when her aunt named it and asked: "So do you think you're a dyke, then?" And the realization was not always appreciated: "It's a complete hassle, being, coming out and being gay, I mean I didn't, I didn't like it . . . sometimes I still think God, you know, it would be so much easier to be straight . . . but you're sitting there and you have all these feelings and stuff." Ussher thus comments: "Material and discursive factors act together to define what it is to be lesbian" (1997:148-150).

Ussher goes on to explore what being lesbian means in practice: fashion, style, community, sex, politics, and women's rights, plus issues involving violence, parental rejection, isolation, depression, sex and pleasure. Her main point is that exploring "the relationship between the material and discursive" is essential to understanding lesbians or gays (1997:155).

Americans seem more vexed by questions of gay rights and gay marriage than, say, the British or Canadians, but less vexed than, say, the Saudis, Gambians and Ugandans (*Economist*, 11 October 2014). In June 2013, the U.S. Supreme Court struck down the Defense of Marriage Act (DOMA) but the decision was close: 5 to 4. Justice Kennedy wrote: "DOMA writes inequality into the entire United States Code." The *New York Times* declared this a "Victory for Equal Rights." (27 June 2013). The Supreme Court decision was precipitated by Edith Windsor, who was engaged in 1967 and married in Canada in 2007, after which she was handed a bill for over $350,000 for a refund from her spouse's estate. Under DOMA, her marriage to Thea Spyer was not legal. So she fought and won and was named by *Time* as one of the "Persons of the Year" (Gray, 2013). Recently, Tim Cook, Apple CEO, declared publicly: "I consider being gay among the greatest gifts God has given me" (*Time*, 17 November 2014). In May 2015, the Irish voted by referendum to legalize gay marriage. Then in June 2015, the U.S. Supreme Court legalized gay marriage, 11 years after the state of Massachusetts and 14 years after the Netherlands. By June 2015, same-sex marriages were legal in 18 countries.

Today, homosexuality is not the social problem—homophobia is; and some say heterosexism, transphobia and even emerging heterophobia. But misogyny and misandry still persist. Sex, sexes and sexualities remain remarkably controversial globally.

*

One striking aspect of all these gender activists—from Beatie and May-Welby to the sexologists, from Krafft-Ebing, Freud and Ellis to Kinsey, Masters, and Ellwood-Clayton—is how different they all are: They might be discussing different species. How they conceptualized sex and sexualities is certainly fascinating, as is the reality they purport to discuss; but even in this short chapter, one could get worried about the wide range of expert opinion on the topic, and about the conflicts of rights: women's, gays, men's and trans, as well as parental and grand-parental. The other striking aspect about all these theories and practices of sex and sexualities, whether from Oscar Wilde's conviction or from the marketing of the pill, is the rapidity of all these changes: from Queen Victoria's alleged advice on sex to "lie down and think of England" to twerking.

We all live in our own sex worlds. We were conceived in sex and live our sex lives and love lives as best we can, with ups and downs and, of course, ins and outs, and occasional famines. And our sex worlds permeate everything and imbue the rest of the world with the halo of eroticism. It is not just about the microcosm of "the couple" and sex, but about the glances, the smiles, the imagination, the poetry, the mind-reading, the surprises, our feelings and desires on the bus, at a meeting, in the mall, selecting apples at the supermarket—chemistry and electricity.

Still, we are all different. At the polar extremes are those who live for their "liaisons": sexual adventures with no emotional commitment. Newness is all—new partners, new experiences and new sex; they value their independence, no clinging; they value their privacy, no questions. They are instrumental, not affective, in their relations (not relationships). Intimacy is suffocating: "Give me space!" They value distance. Formerly they were called promiscuous (negative), whether men or women, then permissive, and now free spirits (very positive). Others, at the other extreme, are searching for love, a soul-mate, union and communion. They try to compromise, ride the waves and negotiate problems. They are not restless. Sex and love go hand in hand and the bond is somehow sacred—it is not just an itch to be scratched.

The majority of people are probably somewhere between the extreme romantics and the extreme recreationals. Then mix in the multiple sexualities: hetero/homo/bi/pluri/ego/virtual/hyper and asexualities; now note the range of intensities; stir in the many paraphilias; add the personal baggage, wounds and sensitivities. Then blend in, gently, the many possible "oppositions" and intersectionalities of class, culture, race, faith, language, politics and personality; and then let it all simmer for a while. Quietly add children, money and job worries, divorces and blended families and in-laws and outlaws—and voila! Enough action to keep sexologists, therapists and relationship gurus—and everyone else—quite busy.

Chapter 3
Desire

Lust at first sight. Desire may arise suddenly, as soon as we meet someone, and hot desire is often triggered by beauty. Attraction can be instantaneous. The chemistry is right. Lust mutates into love. But, equally, desire often gently declines and subsides as we become more intimate with each other over time. The novelty wears off. The challenge has been met. The curiosity wanes. The affair dies a natural death. Lust mutates into disinterest. Sad but true. The compensation is that this does not always happen. Perhaps the happy couple is away from each other often, so desire is rekindled anew. "Absence makes the heart grow fonder," some say. Others are more pessimistic: "Out of sight, out of mind."

The stereotypes are well-known. Men want sex and women want intimacy. Men are more angry and upset about physical infidelity and women by emotional infidelity. Men will scatter their seed wherever they can or, more bluntly, screw anything that moves if possible; but women are far more careful. Women go for quality, men go for quantity. Women usually say no; men usually say yes. Men want to find a place; women need to find a reason. The more partners people have, the lower her reputation drops, and the higher his flies.

These stereotypical binaries and polarities and differential expectations of men's and women's sexual desires and behavior may be well-known but they may also be inaccurate. They may also be self-fulfilling prophecies. And they are certainly vast generalizations, which require interrogation.

Warren Farrell is concise and blunt: Men want a sex object and women want a success object, but he advocates that we need to "go beyond woman [sic] as sex objects and men as success objects to both sexes as objects of love" (1993:371). This we might describe as the trade theory of desire. Desire may not be quite that polarized: Both parties sometimes just want sex, and sometimes men want a success object, no doubt, and women want a sex object, a cute "toy boy." People trade what they have for what they want—which will depend on what they have and have to offer: perhaps beauty, sexiness and youth for wealth and security for themselves and their children; and hopefully everyone is happy. April–September marriages are sometimes like that. The marriage of Anna Nicole Smith and billionaire J. Howard Marshall, 63 years her senior, might have been a case in point. The sex/success trade-off is not the whole story, of course, as there are so many other variables in play; but that is one theory and it has its utility for some.

Recent research suggests that attraction is much more complicated than such a trade: We tend to trust people who look like us and our family of birth, but we are not necessarily so sexually attracted to them: "trust-worthy but not lust-worthy," as one researcher puts it (De Bruine, 2002, 2004, 2005). This would make evolutionary sense: Sexual relationships with siblings and/or progeny are, in evolutionary terms, dysfunctional; hence, perhaps, the virtually universal incest taboo.

Attraction is not just a matter of looks, sex objects and success objects, of course. Personality, intelligence, humor, style—almost anything and everything—may attract and incite desire. Still, Elizabeth Browning advises:

> "Do not say 'I love her for her smile—her look—her way
> Of speaking gently,—for a trick of thought
> That falls in well with mine, and certes brought
> A sense of pleasant ease on such a day'"

For all things change. Just "love me for love's sake." Some things may not change much, like leopards' spots; and smells may be one of those things. Research seems to increasingly indicate the importance of aromas, subliminally, on the self and in attraction. Beauty is well-understood, smell not so much, and the story is long and complicated. It began with the observation that lizards and snakes seem to smell with their tongues, flicking them in and out rapidly. This led to the discovery of Jacobson's organ (named for its discover, Ludvig Jacobson, in 1811)—a different odor receptor from the nose found in many animals, and all amphibians, but not most birds. Further research over the years discovered that the organ connects to the hypothalamus rather than to the more recently-evolved thalamus—the reptilian brain rather than the mammalian brain. More recent research indicates the importance of this organ in regulating sexual activity in small mammals, such as mice, guinea pigs and voles. If researchers remove the organ, the pheromones (chemicals) emitted by others of their species cannot be detected, and sexual activity declines or ceases. (I wish they would leave them all alone). Most humans have the organ in the nasal septum, but it is often damaged; and, anyway, this personal scent is often overpowered by general cleanliness and camouflaged by deodorants, shampoos, etc., so, perhaps, our aroma is not as powerful as it is with mice (Watson, 1999).

The original research on mammals and reptiles had moved on to humans. In the early 1970s, an undergraduate student, Martha McClintock, noticed that many women in her dormitory maintained the same monthly rhythm. She suspected pheromones, and she and others continued research along those lines. No one had thought that humans would be so physically affected by their chemical emanations. Turns out we are, and more. New discoveries about the major histocompatibility complex (MHC) may help to explain the chemistry of desire and love. Apparently mice, men and women are sexually attracted to those whose autoimmune system is most different from their own, and, therefore, complementary; so any children from such unions would have a wider range of MHC genes and superior immunity to disease. But apart from the children, the personal benefits are said to be better orgasms, greater happiness and living happily after—except that the most biologically suitable MHC candidate may not be the most socially suitable individual. Research indicates that women, smelling the T-shirts of men, preferred those with MHC most different from their own, unless they were taking oral contraceptives—which raises difficult questions about biology and desire (Wedekind et al., 1995; Glaser, 2002).

The attraction is probably subconscious, but interested individuals can take swabs from inside the cheeks of potential mates and, for a fee, ScientificMatch in Boston will match them with those of optimum biological compatibility. Beauty (or at least biological suitability) is now in the nose of the beholder.

Attraction and desire may seem simple: "I want you! NOW!!" but the science is complicated. The most recent research suggests that women have a dual sexuality. When women are ovulating they tend to feel sexier and desire more masculine men—aggressive and competitive; when they are not ovulating, they tend to prefer more feminine men—men more like themselves, gentler, who they think will make good husbands and fathers. But the pill prevents ovulation. So the researchers worry that women on the pill will be choosing mates whom they otherwise (i.e. off the pill) would not choose: i.e., nurturing types who resemble themselves. When and if, however, they go off the pill, desire will wane and the relationship may fall apart. Also, the more feminine men have similar MHC genes, so biologically they are less suitable mates than the more masculine men, especially for the children. In sum, the researchers worry that the pill may lead women to make poor choices in mate selection, and they want further research to clarify the "maladaptive side-effects of Pill use on mate choice, attractiveness, relationship satisfaction, divorce probability and offspring health"

(Bielski, 2009). What is a girl to do? Well, clearly, with two sexualities, in order to be completely sexually fulfilled (which should be a right), she needs two men, one for when she is ovulating and one for when she is not. Oh, the joys of science!

Plus, *what* we desire can be very problematic. Paraphilias are discussed in Chapter 13, and while some can be relatively harmless, they can also be, or develop into, the criminal and lethal.

Similarly, *how much* we desire is important. Intense desire can be problematic, causing totally inappropriate behavior, impulse sex, STIs, unwanted pregnancies and, yes, getting laid but also getting laid off, or both. But lack of desire is also increasingly being recognized as problematic.

Between 7 percent and 15 percent of women aged about 20-60 are distressed over their lack of desire—more than are worried about other issues, like painful intercourse or difficulty orgasming, though all the data on these issues are suspect due to lack of research funds. One woman declared: "I'm actually O.K. with never having sex again." But she's not O.K., which is why she is attending the clinic. Another woman is more forthright: "I want to feel horny. I want to want."

Dr. Lori Brotto is a leading expert on women's hypoactive sexual desire disorder (HSDD) and was in charge of redefining this condition for the *DSM-5*. At present, the redefinition is brief and applies to both sexes: "persistently or recurrently deficient (or absent) sexual fantasies and desire for sexual activity." But some critics think that this is too simple and too male a definition. Women's desire may be more complicated. Dr. Brotto works on sensory awareness and body awareness, but also on reversing the conventional model of desire. The traditional model is that desire precedes arousal. Dr. Brotto believes that the first step in reducing HSDD is not desire but a "willingness to be responsive." The new model, therefore, especially for women, is that willingness precedes desire (Bergner, 2009b). One should not wait for desire to arise, in this theory of desire, but it will arise once you are willing and get started. Action creates the passion, not vice versa.

The Australian sexologist Bella Ellwood-Clayton, author of the excellent *Sex Drive* (2012), is quite concerned about female desire, and wrote the entire book about it. One issue is asymmetry of desire, or "desire discrepancy." Mismatched sex drives are difficult to negotiate and may have serious consequences for the relationship. She notes that "Rom-Coms and women's literature seem to be all about *finding* love, not tending to it" (2012:34). She adds that "once in a secure relationship, a woman's sex drive begins to plummet." And she cites a German study that found "four years into a relationship, less than half of 30-year-old women desired regular sex. After 20 years the rate dropped to 20 percent. Men's libido, on the other hand, remained pretty constant. Oh how predictable!" (2012:35).

She is particularly vexed by this entire discussion of HSDD, apparently the most common form of the broader Female Sexual Dysfunction (FSD). She and others are concerned about the "corporatization of sex" by the pharmaceutical companies, which in turn "drives commercialization, which feeds consumerism," and then the medicalization of normality (2012: 159). Their definition of FSD (for the corporations fund most of the research) is, she argues, for profit, not benefit. She agrees with Dr. Brotto that the whole concept of HSDD should be re-evaluated by objective researchers and with comparative and cross-cultural data. HSDD is rarely physiological in origin, but usually relational, and often not subjectively defined as a problem, let alone a medical disorder. Basically the argument is that the pharmaceutical companies and their paid sex researchers are creating a nonexistent disease based on "faulty" statistics (e.g., that 43 percent of Western women have FSD). We do not even know what normal is; but whatever it is, it is probably neither normal somewhere else nor for everyone.

That said, there may be problems. A recent *Time* report, using national data, avers that 69 percent of porn actresses say they greatly enjoy sex compared to only 33 percent of nonperforming women. This may be explained by other data—that only 29 percent of women reach orgasm during sex compared to 75 percent of men (*Time*, 8 September 2014:83). If correct, these are two huge gaps in sexualities. Then again, desire itself can be problematic. The lack of desire is sometimes portrayed in semi-humorous terms. One survey asked: "Which would you prefer: a good night's sleep or a good night of sex?" 63 percent of the women preferred sleep compared to only 44 percent of the men. This was a random sample of residents of Toronto, but the figures were high, I thought, indicating a wider problem of HSDD than one might expect, and, also, a wide gap between men and women that is indicative of both mismatched sexualities and high male HSDD rates (Southworth, 1999). Or, perhaps, the women were really much more tired—the double load, maybe. This may be normal, not pathological.

Lust

What is the difference between desire and lust? My compact edition of the *Oxford Dictionary* defines desire as "Unsatisfied appetite, longing, wish, craving," and lust as "Have strong or excessive desire." So the difference here is simply a matter of degree: Lust is just a stronger desire. But wait, lust has a second meaning derived from the Bible and theology, says the dictionary: "sensuous appetite regarded as sinful, animalistic desire for sexual indulgence, lascivious passion." So here's the rub: sexual, sinful, animal, i.e., subhuman—the meanings are all synonymous and all negative. And this is confirmed by the allocation of lust as the third of the "seven deadly sins."

All this echoes a couple of the 10 Commandments: "Thou shalt not commit adultery" and "Thou shalt not covet thy neighbor's wife." That's a bit much, since one cannot help coveting, can one? So we are condemned even by our ideas and imagination, it seems. But clearly sex is dangerous territory. "Genesis" has proven difficult to interpret. The Lord said: "Be fruitful and multiply" (Gen. 1:28), which we might interpret as "Have sex and have children"—a fair enough divine commandment. But down here on earth there is massive controversy about whom we can have sex with, when and where and how and why; and, equally, there is debate about how many children we should have, or should not have, given the world population growth rate and China's still-prevalent one-child policy. God stirred up a hornet's nest with that one.

St. Paul was very much against lust: "To be carnally minded is death" (Rom 8:25), "Make not provision for the flesh, to fulfill the lust thereof" (Rom 13:14); then, in his letter to the Galatians, Paul gets quite carried away:

> The flesh lusteth against the Spirit, and the Spirit against the flesh so that ye cannot do the things ye would . . . Now the works of the flesh are manifest, which are: immorality, uncleanness, licentiousness, idolatry, witchcrafts, enmities, contentions, jealousies, anger, quarrels, factions, parties, envies, murders, drunkenness, carousings, and suchlike." (Gal. 5:17, 19-21)

This is very clearly sex-negative and body-negative, and a component part of the "Western" cultural heritage, which still persists, as does dualism. Others wrote and spoke in the same vein for centuries (Badinter,1989; Ranke-Heinemann, 1990). Hence, the insistence of moralists on asceticism, mentioned earlier. Such sex and body negativism are only recently being challenged.

This next-world focus of traditional Christianity has been capsized in post-modernity and post-Christianity. Simon Blackburn has composed a slim, witty and erudite volume, *Lust* (2004). He points out that lust has had bad press compared to love and friendship, and cites Shakespeare's sonnet

129 on lust, with the last couplet: "All this the world well knows; yet none knows well/To shun the heaven that leads men to this hell."

Blackburn notes that "We would none of us be here without it." Lust, that is; and he intends "to lift it from the category of sin to that of virtue" (2004:3). That is the postmodern capsize. Schopenhauer, like God and Paul, was very much against lust, which, he said,

> exerts an adverse influence on the most important affairs, interrupts the most serious business at any hour, sometimes confuses even the greatest minds, does not hesitate with its trumpery to disrupt the negotiations of statesmen and the research of scholars, has the knack of slipping its love-letters and ringlets even into ministerial portfolios and philosophical manuscripts. (Blackburn, 2004:3)

And, I might add, sociology textbooks (not mine). To which Blackburn's response is surely, "Yes, Arthur, but well worth it!" Here Schopenhauer exemplifies what we discussed earlier: the asceticism and sex-negativity of so much Christian teaching, together with Plato's idea that the body hinders the mind and Descartes' theory that the body is only a machine, a corpse. No pleasure here.

Blackburn's book is a tour-de-force: He is at home with everyone from Plato and Lucretius to Paul, Augustine, Aquinas, Shakespeare, Kant, and Freud, as well as in tune with evolutionary psychology and the contemporary United States. And it is amazing how all these lovers of wisdom are so interested in lust. His favorite is Thomas Hobbes, whom he quotes:

> The appetite which men call LUST . . . is a sensual pleasure, but not only that; there is in it also a delight of the mind: for it consisteth of two appetites together, to please and to be pleased; and the delight men take in delighting, is not sensual, but a pleasure or joy of the mind, consisting in the imagination of the power they have so much to please. (2004:87-8)

The symbiotic pleasure in pleasing and being pleased is reciprocal, and Blackburn describes this "pure mutuality" as a Hobbesian unity. And surely this is virtue not vice. But equally, though Hobbes is defining LUST, it seems to me that he is defining LOVE. In *Leviathan*, Hobbes clarifies the distinction: "Natural lust. *Love* of persons for pleasing the sense only. . . . The passion of love. . . . *Love* of one singularly, with desire to be singularly beloved" (Pt. 1: 6; emphasis in original).

Here, love is potentially "pure mutuality" while lust is "merely" sensory gratification of the self, not the other, and we return to the bad press lust receives and the tradition that it is a sin. The comparison between the two was expressed most lyrically by the English writer, Jeanette Winterson: "What you think is the heart may well be another organ."

St. Augustine

Augustine, like Paul but not Blackburn, was a fierce opponent of lust. This is Augustine (354-490), Bishop of Hippo in North Africa. We meet him at a turning-point in his life, age 32, with a girlfriend, a son, and a mother, Monica, praying for his conversion to Christianity. He is on the brink. And in his *Confessions*, he tells the story of: ". . . how you released me from the fetters of lust which held me so tightly shackled and from my slavery to the things of this world" (Bk. VIII: 6).

So, lust was the problem. While he was mulling over these things, a Christian friend came to visit and told him of two friends of his who had suddenly converted from the service of the state to the service of God, after reading about the life of St. Antony (my patron saint), the Abbot of the Desert Fathers. Augustine was deeply moved:

> You were showing me before my own eyes so that I could see how sordid I was, so deformed and squalid, how tainted with ulcers and sores. . . . As a youth I had been woefully at fault, particularly in early adolescence. I had prayed to you for chastity and said 'Give me chastity and continence, but not yet.' (Bk. VIII: 7)

The famous prayer was answered, but not without more trauma:

> My inner self was a house divided against itself . . . I was beside myself with madness that would bring me sanity. I was dying a death that would bring me life. I knew the evil that was in me, but the good that was soon to be born in me I did not know. (Bk. VIII: 8)

He had a crisis, went into the garden, pulled his hair, hammered his head, and hugged his knees during "this agony of indecision." Then he had a vision: "While I stood trembling at the barrier, on the other side I could see the chaste beauty of Continence in all her serene unsullied joy, as she modestly beckoned me to cross over and to hesitate no more" (Bk. VIII: 11. Still in the garden, weeping, suddenly Augustine heard a voice singing: "Take it and read, take it and read." So he did. He picked up Paul's epistles and read the first passage: "Not in reveling and drunkenness, not in lust and wantonness, not in quarrels and rivalries. Rather, arm yourselves with the Lord Jesus Christ; spend no more thought on nature and nature's appetites." (Bk. VIII: 12) [Rom 13:13-4]

So he did and rejoiced: "At last my mind was free from the gnawing anxieties of ambition and gain, from wallowing in filth and scratching the itching sore of lust" (Bk IX).

But Augustine went further, and in his *City of God* formulated the doctrine of original sin: that the original sin of the first parents stained the entire human race; this explained the problem of evil, in his view. "The sin which they committed was so great that it impaired all human nature—in this sense, that the nature has been transmitted to posterity with a propensity to sin and a necessity to die" (Bk XIV:1).

To be fair, he politely rejected the Pauline hostility to the body, explaining that humans have free will, and that many sins are mental rather than physical; so the problem is the will not the flesh, mind not body: "It is an error to suppose that all the evils of the soul proceed from the body." He added later that "Man's will, then, is all-important" (Bk XIV: 3, 6). But lust was one of the sins of the flesh.

The long tradition of lust as vice is rooted in both Greco-Roman and Judeo-Christian mythologies. The lusts of Paris and Helen for each other caused the 10-year Trojan War and the death of Paris. The lust of Zeus for Leda resulted in his rape of her, as a swan. The lust of Samson for Delilah and Holofernes for Judith resulted in the deaths of both men. The lust, or desire, if you prefer, of King David for Bathsheba resulted in the killing of her husband, Uriah; but, the Bible says, "The Lord was not pleased with what David had done," and punished him (2 Sam. 11:27).

More recently, lust is associated with many sex scandals (e.g., Bill Clinton, Tiger Woods, John Edwards, Eliot Spitzer, Iris Robinson, Dominique Strauss-Kahn, and General Petraeus, among many others); and lust is also associated with divorces, homicides, suicides, careers destroyed, and damaged adults and children, in the wake of men and women following their bliss in an individualistic entitlement culture.

So we have portraits of lust as vice and as virtue, depending, perhaps, on the definition and, perhaps, on the consequences—what we do with our lusts—under the surveillance of both the Lord and the State. And lust is mostly male, in mythology and in the media, though not necessarily in reality.

Blackburn concludes: "Nature makes fools of us. We are puppets of our hormones and genetic programs. But nature repays us with pleasure" (2004:125). And such pleasure. We are born by pleasure through lust as virtue, and we may be hurt through lust as vice. To live is to lust, and to live is to desire, and often to desire sex. Which brings us to Darwin's theory of sex.

Sex, Evolution and Darwin

Charles Darwin published *The Descent of Man, and Selection in Relation to Sex* in 1871. He had already discussed the evolution of species through natural selection, the struggle for survival and the survival of the fittest in *The Origin of Species* (1858), but the evolution of humans and sexual selection were new themes, and even more controversial.

Sexual selection, he wrote, "depends on the advantage which certain individuals have over other individuals of the same sex and species, in exclusive relation to reproduction" (Pt. 2, Ch. 8). The theory of evolution by natural selection referred to species, while sexual selection referred to individuals, though it does have evolutionary implications. This selection process is of two types: weaponry in the "law of battle," applying particularly to mammals, and "charm" applying particularly to birds. Darwin loved birds and devoted four chapters to them, but only two to humans. The law of battle applies almost universally to males, who seek out females but must first defeat other males, then charm the female of their choice. "It is certain that with almost all animals there is a struggle between males for possession of the female" (Pt. 2, Ch. 8). Not the most "PC" phrasing, perhaps, and this was before *Cosmopolitan* magazine indicated otherwise; but consider the male weaponry both for attack (against other males) and defense (against predators). This includes tusks, horns, antlers, teeth, hooves, claws, stings and smells (think skunk); and, with birds, beaks and spurs. The arsenal is formidable. Darwin also wrote about everything else from worms and reptiles to beetles and fish; but his point is well taken.

On charm, he described the male courtships with songs, aerial dances, drumming, the peacock-type feather display, iridescence, crests, necklaces, epaulettes, the bright colors (reds, yellows, blues, greens) of plumage, the bower-birds nesting behaviors, with examples piled on examples. We too can see the city pigeons strutting around the females, cooing gently and fluffing up their iridescent neck plumage. Eventually the female chooses: "though they may not always select the strongest or best armed, they will select those which are vigorous and well-armed, and in other respects the most attractive" (Pt. 2, Ch. 8).

There is what he calls a "double selection" of females by males and of males by females; but he admits that sexual selection is "an extremely complex affair, depending, as it does, on ardor in love, courage, and the rivalry of the males, and the powers of perception, taste, and will of the female" (Pt. 2, Ch. 8). Such couples are likely to breed earlier, to have bigger litters with more pups, kittens, fledglings, kits, chicks or babies and (since they are born earlier of more vigorous parents) higher survival rates. The others are left to fight over or to charm the rest, and breed later with lower survival rates. Hence, the sexual selection and, thought Darwin, the gradual beautification of all these species.

As for humans, Darwin discussed the law of battle among men for women in "barbarous nations," for which there was not much evidence, so he had to refer to gorillas. Perhaps a contemporary sociologist would add barroom brawls and the occasional homicide in love triangles, not to mention Helen and the Trojan War. Yet Darwin is good on beauty and beautification, by both men and women, to charm and attract the opposite sex; and for men to appear terrible in battle against other men. He emphasized the relativity of beauty, stating that "Hardly any part of the body, which can be unnaturally modified, has escaped" (Pt. 2, Ch. 19). He commented also on the pain and suffering endured for beauty's sake and the benefits beauty brings. But, again, his main point is the evolutionary consequences through inheritance of this favoring of strong men and beautiful women, in this complicated calculus of what we now call erotic capital, an important component of the broader social capital (Hakim, 2010).

In the end, therefore, the strongest and wealthiest men were likely to have more children "than would the weaker, poorer and lower members of the same tribes" (Pt. 2, Ch. 20). Second, he thought that "women have become more beautiful, as most persons will admit, than men" since men are valued for their ability "to defend and support them," not primarily for their beauty (Pt. 2, Ch. 20). Finally all those characteristics by which human populations vary—the shape of the nose, the cheekbones, the presence or absence of hair and its texture, the color of the skin, the shape of the head, the height etc.—all these things are partly adaptation to the environment. Darwin argued that: "of all the causes which have led to the differences in external appearance between the races of man . . . sexual selection has been by far the most efficient" (Pt. 2, Ch. 20). So we are descended from "a hairy quadruped furnished with a tail and pointed ears" (Pt. 2, Ch. 21) and, before that, from some sort of fish. How embarrassing.

But sexual selection is not just about bodies and beauty. It also affects minds in birds and beasts:

> Courage, pugnacity, perseverance, strength and size of body, weapons of all kinds, musical organs . . . bright colours, stripes and marks, and ornamental appendages, have all been indirectly gained by the one sex or the other, through the influence of love or jealousy, through the appreciation of the beautiful in sound, colour or form, and through the exertion of a choice . . . (Pt. 2, Ch. 21)

Darwin could not quite say it. We can. That choice, that sexual selection, is based on "the appreciation of the beautiful." Beauty is certainly defined variously among humans, as Darwin had noted, but power, strength and protective and supportive abilities count among humans too. This is part and parcel of erotic capital.

There is a corollary. If beauty has an evolutionary function, as Darwin so plausibly argues, then surely we all have a duty to the future of the human species to be as beautiful as possible, by any means necessary. Now there is a fresh marketing idea for the cosmetic surgery industry: "It's not vanity, darling, it's my duty to humanity."

But the same argument would apply to "courage, pugnacity, strength and size of body . . . " so it gets out of hand, especially as the evolutionary point of beauty is to maximize fertility.

Sex, Fun and Jared Diamond

Darwin explained the evolution of species, including humans; and Jared Diamond, the Pulitzer Prize-winning author of *Guns, Germs and Steel*, takes Darwin a step further, by explaining the evolution of human sexuality in his prior book, *Why is Sex Fun?: The Evolution of Human Sexuality*. I had expected it to be very short—"because it feels so good"—with a possible chorus, as in the song, "so it must be right." This would have the additional advantage of short-circuiting so much of ethics and law, and simplifying moral debate. But no. It may still be fun, but Diamond argues that, compared to the 4,300 other mammalian species and the 30 million or so other animal species, human sexuality is, and I quote, "weird." Indeed, he describes humans as "The Animals with the Weirdest Sex Life." Speak for yourself, mate, I say to myself.

Darwin pointed out how similar human sexual selection is to other species. Diamond points out how different it is, in seven ways. Let him count the ways (1997: ix-x; 4-6):

- Long-term sexual partnering. Most humans engage in a contractual marriage, though there are different types.
- Co-parenting. This is a sexual union but also involves joint rearing of their children; especially unique is the role of the father.
- The privatization of sex.
- Concealed ovulation, in contrast to most mammals.
- Sex is mostly for fun rather than procreation or "instinctive."
- Female menopause.
- The size of the penis

Not much weird about this, we might say, because we are so used to it and, therefore, he says, speciesist. His questions are: Why are we the only species like this? Why are we unique? What evolutionary purposes are served? And he attempts to demonstrate the evolutionary functions of all these diverse sexual strategies.

Some of this work is too technical to summarize, but two points are particularly important. He calls us "weird" because we are unique. But so are many of the species he discusses. Take the praying mantis—please—or the black widow spider. I have seen the former in Maine and the latter in Mexico; both are stunningly beautiful and both kill their mates. There is a lesson here, folks: The mantis male "is routinely eaten by his mate just after or even while he is copulating with her." This, says Diamond, "clearly involves the male's consent," because he approaches her and does not try to escape till she bites his head off, by which time it is too late. But Jared, please, maybe he was hoping for a kiss. Did you think of that? Jared argues that this sexual cannibalism helps the survival of the species by giving her the protein she needs, etc. (1997:11). At the risk of being speciesist, however, if I were the being-cannibalized guy, I might take issue: "Bugger the species, Jared, what about ME? This is not equity feminism. This is murder."

The other issue is the penis. He seems to be upset that it is so large. Who is he kidding? He must be the only North American who thinks that. Is he projecting? (Excuse the pun.) Still, I'm sure that there is cosmetic surgery for it, as there is for breast-reduction and fat-reduction. But I have never heard of it. *Au contraire*. The usual discussion is about penile enhancement. Lovely word—compared to breast augmentation. Augmentation just means bigger, whereas enhancement means bigger and *better*.

He says that the erect penis in gorillas is about 1¼ inches and in chimpanzees is about 1½ inches, but in humans it is about five inches (others say more, on average). You want a project? Measure the erect penis on a gorilla.

He asks: "Are those extra couple of inches of the human penis a functionally unnecessary luxury?" (1997:143). Is he kidding? We discussed this earlier. In one word, NO!

Still, it is curious that these great apes, so much larger and stronger than we are, but also not so smart (they didn't invent paraphilias), have so much smaller penises. Why? Read Diamond on Fisher's runaway postulate and Zahari's handicap model, and the high opportunity cost of large penises on available biosynthetic energy—and weep or laugh, as the case may be. His answer is that they are functionally unnecessary, and that they come at a high cost. I suspect that most men would disagree and assert that they are functionally useful and convey many benefits. But Diamond is talking physiologically and I am talking socially.

The Pill

The greatest change in the evolution of human sexuality was, perhaps, not the opposable thumb or walking on two legs or the expansion of the brain—which distinguish us from other primates—but chemical: the invention of the pill that received FDA approval in 1960. For the first time, women were able to control their own reproduction and, in the developed world, the birth-rate plummeted. Some women did not want so many children and some wanted none at all. But the pill famously facilitated the sexual revolution, with its dogma of "free love" or, more often, free sex. Also, especially for women, more sex, fewer children, more education, better jobs, higher income, more power, and greater equality. A peaceful revolution.

The pill divorced intercourse from procreation, i. e., it allowed for sex without pregnancy. From the pill in 1960 to the Petri dish in 1978, the building of sperm and ovum "banks," and catalogues of the donors—all these phenomena indicate that sex and conception are becoming increasingly depersonalized and commodified. The pill facilitated not only the sexual revolution and the declining fertility rate but also the increasing registration of women in tertiary education, an increasing proportion of women in the labor force.

As a result of these changes, the pill also facilitated a shift in both the economic balance of power in the family and the political balance of power in the state, which ultimately led to changes in the Divorce Acts (1968 in Canada and 1970 in the U.S.), increases in divorce rates, and new family structures: blended families, cohabiting individuals, households with single mothers and fathers, and a sharp increase in fatherless boys. These were sequential changes, but also interactive.

The women's movement, usually dated from 1968, and the protest against the Miss America Beauty Pageant in Atlantic City, both reflected and reinforced all these trends: demographic, familial, educational, economic and political. The status of women in the developed world has changed profoundly, and remarkably quickly and peacefully, for such seismic shocks over the last 50-plus years.

Perhaps the greatest impact of the pill has been on women's psyche. As one enthusiast explained: "It's magic, a trick of science that managed in one fell swoop to wipe away centuries of female oppression, overly exhausting baby-making, and just marrying the wrong guy way too early . . . These days, women's twenties are as free and fabulous as they can be" (Grigoriadis, 2010:46-7). But she does add the qualifier that, after 10 or 15 years on the pill, "one anxiety—Am I pregnant?—is replaced by another— Can I get pregnant?"

And it is not just that the quality of the eggs begin to decline after the mid-30s; so does the quality of the sperm of a same-age partner—a double difficulty. In vitro fertilization (IVF) works well, but the younger the better. About 64 percent of women aged 30 conceived successfully in one cycle of IVF, 47 percent at age 35, 28 percent at age 40, and only 2 percent at age 44-plus. One expert thinks that, in the future, young women and men will deposit their eggs and sperm in a bank for freezing and then go and get sterilized (Grigoriadis, 2010:123). A bit bleak, not too romantic: "Come on, darling, let's go down to the bank and make a withdrawal!" "OK, dear."

There is a third possible, but controversial, downside. In an essay entitled "Dr. Rock's Error," Malcolm Gladwell offers a must-read but complicated analysis of research on the pill and women's health. Dr. Rock was one of the three people credited with developing the pill and succeeding in getting FDA approval. As a devout Catholic, and because the pill replicates women's hormonal production—merely extending the so-called safe period—he considered it "natural." The pill includes only the natural hormones progesterone and estrogen. Pope Paul VI condemned it in 1968 with the encyclical "*Humanae Vitae*." Rock's error, wrote Gladwell

(2009:107), was that "He was consumed by the idea of the natural" to placate his church.

Flash forward to the1980s, when anthropologist Beverly Strassman went to live for two and a half years with the Dogon of Mali—a pre-industrial people who did not practice contraception—to study female fertility and what is "natural," in a biological not a theological sense. On average, a Dogon woman has menarche at age 16, gives birth eight or nine times, breastfeeds for about 20 months, and so has her period about 100 times in her lifetime. In contrast, the average American woman has an earlier menarche at 14, has few if any children, does not breast feed for long, if at all, and has between 350 and 400 periods. Strassman says that this shift through the demographic transition from high to low fertility is very significant, since "women's bodies are being subjected to changes and stresses that they were not necessarily designed by evolution to handle" (2009:111). The consequences of this "incessant ovulation," some suggest, are a number of physical adversities, including abdominal pain, fibroids, anemia and cancer, especially ovarian and endometrial cancer, since every ovulation requires cell division and the possibility of cell mutation.

Meanwhile, Malcolm Pike, an American medical statistician, visited Japan to try to determine why Japanese women had breast cancer rates six times lower than American women that somehow rise almost to American levels when they migrate to America. Two factors stood out. One was that the risk rate rose sharply during the reproductive years but slowed after menopause; the other was that women who had had their ovaries removed were at much lower risk. So the cancer had something to do with reproduction. But what? The researchers found that women born at the turn of the century had menarche at 16.5 years —much later than Americans. They calculated that this gap accounted for 40 percent of the difference in breast cancer rates. (They also thought that age at first pregnancy and number of children did not matter, which, given Strassman's work, seems counter-intuitive; but Japan has a low fertility rate.) Then, the average post-menopausal Japanese woman weighed 100 pounds, compared to the American average of 140 pounds—another 25 percent of the difference. Finally, diet: Women in rural Japan and China lived on an extremely low-fat diet, and so produced only 75 percent of the amount of estrogen that American women did. They thought that these three factors explained most of the difference in breast cancer rates.

So it does seem as though the pill has more widespread consequences for women's health than was expected. One point that Gladwell overlooked is the genetic basis for some cancers, notably breast cancer. Angelina Jolie brought this to public attention with her double mastectomy as preventive surgery, since, with the rare BRCA1 and 2 genetic mutations, she was at high risk of both breast and ovarian cancers. Ovarian cancer is also considered a risk factor for Jewish women of Eastern European origin.

For all the billions of dollars invested in cancer research and cure, breast cancer still kills about 40,000 American women every year (about the same number since 2000), and a good deal of panic prevails around the "C word." Yet the chance of dying from breast cancer is about 1 in 4,566, and it is responsible for only 3 percent of the total number of about 1.3 million women's deaths every year, while heart disease causes 22 percent of the deaths, other cancers 15 percent, and Alzheimer's 5 percent (O'Connor, 2015). For all the successful medical research on cure, perhaps we should look more at social science research on prevention. There has been much less attention paid to the social issues surrounding cancer raised by Strassman and Pike, including weight, low-fat diet, number of pregnancies, duration of breast feeding, and frequency of menstruation. This research could be done quickly and easily with surveys and interviews in hospitals and clinics during annual checkups. Still, the World Health Organization (WHO) did issue an advisory on carcinogenics in October 2015, including a wide range of products from processed meats to air, but that does not deal specifically with the social science of breast cancer or other cancers.

Humans are still evolving, as Darwin showed, and our sex lives are still evolving, as Diamond and the pill indicated, each in their different ways. And more pills are hitting the market. What next? The male contraceptive pill? Or a female "desire" pill? Yes, just arrived: Addyi. Or new and improved dildonics?

Jealousy

One of the consequences of this tangled trinity of desire and lust and sex and love is often jealousy. Books on jealousy abound, like jealousy itself. But this is not a review of all the literature, just some pointers on the existential anxieties, a glance at some of the contradictory and complementary theories, and some counter-intuitive findings of some researchers. Where to begin? Perhaps lightly, with Judith Viorst, the American humorist and poet, describing a familiar situation in "Confessions of a Jealous Wife":

> Over on the other side of the room there is a 19-year-old girl with long hair parted down the middle, a clingy dress about an inch

> shorter than her hair and the clear-eyed, fresh-faced look of someone who is not awakened by babies at six in the morning. She is hanging on to my husband's every word as if he were Warren Beatty, only smarter, and he is hanging on to her every word as if she were Simone de Beauvoir, only better-looking, and I am beginning to feel like Othello. (1977:17)

So, here it begins, and she shares her ideas and experiences: "I think the everyday kind of jealousy has less to do with a fear of overt sexual betrayal than it does with a fear of intimacy that excludes us" (1977: 21). She describes her "get-him-jealous" game, throwing things, including a custard pie, but eventually concludes: "on those days when I happen to be feeling mature and secure I'm also going to admit that a man who wasn't attractive to other women, a man who wasn't alive enough to enjoy other women, a man who was incapable of making me jealous, would never be the kind of man I love" (1977: 24).

Fine. But what about those days when someone is not feeling "mature and secure," and there is a realistic—or unrealistic—fear of "sexual betrayal?" It can get worse. The villainous Iago rightly warns Othello: "O! Beware my lord, of jealousy: It is the green-ey'd monster which doth mock the meat it feeds on" (Othello, Act 3, Scene 3).

Why green, I wonder?

Jealousy is a two-edged sword that cuts both the lover and the beloved; and in the case of Desdemona and Othello, it killed them both. This jealousy, which Freud called "delusional," is now sometimes known as the "Othello Syndrome." The other iconic story of jealousy is Euripides' play, *Medea.* Medea is in love with Jason, of Golden Fleece fame, and they have two children. But Jason has to marry another, for political reasons. Medea seems to take it well and presents the queen with a poisoned wedding dress. The queen dies, Medea kills her two children and flees.

Jealousy is also biblical, beginning with Cain and Abel. Proverbs (27:4) states that "Anger is cruel and fury overwhelming, but who can stand before jealousy?" Even God is jealous, and admits it, and threatens punishment. The second commandment states:

> Thou shalt not make to thyself any graven image, nor the likeness of anything that is in the heavens above, or in the earth beneath, or in the waters under the earth. Thou shalt not bow down to them nor worship them: for I the Lord thy God am a jealous

God, and visit the sins of the fathers upon the children unto the third and fourth generations. (Exodus 20:4-5)

God meant what He said and said it often. He destroyed Sodom and Gomorrah and sent the flood from which He rescued only Noah and his wife and the animals. Jealousy may be a "green-ey'd monster" but it is also an attribute of the all-powerful divinity. It is hardly worth provoking a jealous god. That invites retribution. Same goes for jealous humans. Hardly worth the risks, really.

So jealousy is rooted in Greek literature and Judeo-Christian faith, and it is also deeply personal, as Judith Viorst confessed, and also Roland Barthes: "As a jealous man, I suffer four times over: because I am jealous, because I blame myself for being so, because I fear that my jealousy will wound the other, because I allow myself to be subjected to banality" (in Baumgart, 1991: vi).

Similarly Valerie Trierweiler, the former mistress of the French Prime Minister Francois Hollande, confessed: "I will readily admit to it: I am jealous. I have been jealous with every man I have loved. I do not know how not to be when I am in love." She added: I could not stand seeing other women put their heads on [Francois's] shoulder and hold him by the waist . . . I have even sent a few of them packing. Would these women have liked me to cosy up to their husbands?" (Johnson, 2015:25-6). Probably not, but apparently her behavior irritated the French electorate, as she recognized, and, perhaps, the prime minister also.

All that said, there is more, of course. Anthropologists argue that jealousy is not a universal phenomenon but, rather, culturally relative, possibly arising in cultures that practice monogamy and in which men, especially, regard women as "theirs," i.e., as property. Margaret Mead (and others) writing about the South Seas, remarks on the easy sexuality of the locals, though her work has been criticized. And Diamond Jenness, writing about the Arctic, mentioned the utility of spouse exchange (See Chapter 4).

Freud

According to Freud, "Jealousy is one of those affective states, like grief, that may be described as normal. If anyone appears to be without it, the inference is justified that it has undergone severe repression . . . The three layers or grades of jealousy may be described as (1) *competitive* or normal, (2) *projected*, and (3) *delusional* jealousy" (1981, Vol. 10:197).

We are probably all familiar with normal jealousy, unfortunately. Freud suggests that "essentially it is compounded of grief, the pain caused by the thought of losing the loved object" (loved "person" would be better, in my opinion), mingled with feelings of hostility to the rival and perhaps self-criticism. Projective jealousy is imputing to the other the same sort of faithless behavior that one has done oneself, or would like to do. While mild flirtations at a party might be regarded as harmless by some people, for the jealous person they are not. And delusional jealousy is simply paranoia: The beloved is not being faithless with a third party; it is all in the jealous person's mind and mixed up, says Freud, with homosexuality (1981, Vol. 10:197-9).

But scholarship on jealousy has come a long way since Freud, and there is now far more research on jealousy from many different perspectives. It is a complicated emotion. Trust is necessary in relationships, but blind trust is as delusional as paranoid jealousy, and a form of self-deception or wish-fulfillment. A balance is necessary between trust and mistrust or suspicion—a healthy skepticism, perhaps, or alertness.

Ayala Pines

Ayala Pines is a clinical psychologist who has practiced with individuals, couples, and group workshops in California and Israel, including with convicted murderers. Her book *Romantic Jealousy* discusses in somewhat depressing detail her conclusions. She adopts five theoretical approaches to jealousy, depending on the circumstances, all of which are both useful and different. She is aware, of course, of the dire consequences of jealousy: "Murder, aggression, hatred, lowered self-esteem, depression, suicide and suicide-attempts, domestic violence, destruction of romantic relationships, marital problems, and divorce" (1998:11).

She defines jealousy as "a complex reaction to a perceived threat to a valued relationship or to its quality," and suggests that "Jealousy . . . lies somewhere in the gray area between sanity and madness." But she also describes it as the "shadow of love" (1998:5, 13, 17). Pines is cautiously optimistic that jealousy may be "growth-enhancing' (1998: xii)—if it doesn't kill you. She surveyed over 700 people asking: "Are you a jealous person?" and found that 54 percent said yes and 46 said no, so a fairly even split. She said that their experiences had been somewhat similar, but that their different self-perceptions had important consequences for coping. An appendix includes a questionnaire for self-evaluation and the calculation of a sort of Jealousy Quotient.

The five approaches are the psychodynamic approach, which focuses on the individual, asking why someone is very jealous or not. Explanations are sought in the early family experiences but are multi-factorial, including, among other things, witnessing parental infidelity, the experience of losses, mental illness, and having a small penis—factors that are often unconscious (1998:45-65).

The systems approach goes beyond the individual and family background to consider the couple relationship. Unlike the psychodynamic approach, the emphasis is on the present, not the past, the conscious, not the unconscious, and not why the individual is jealous but, rather, what the problem is—which is not always obvious. An affair may be seen as a form of communication or of escape, and Pines offers case studies to illustrate both types. Any affair will likely generate intense jealousy, but the point is that there is reciprocity. Jealousy is useful to both parties in some ways, and both are responsible for causing the problem or being complicit, even if only one is identified as the jealous party. For instance, some enjoy the jealousy, seeing it as a sign of love; others create it, to affirm their value. A vicious circle of "pursuer—distance" may develop, and one of many techniques to resolve this pattern may be role reversals. As one theorist put it, the couple see themselves trapped in a plot, but they are, in fact, the authors of the plot. Critics point out that this approach ignores early childhood experiences and the unconscious, but Pines (1998) argues that both early family experiences and couples interaction have to be addressed.

The sociobiological approach emphasizes the gender factor in jealousy, suggesting an evolutionary function and a genetic basis for differential jealousies. Thus, it is said that males react with anger and females with depression, due to different meanings attached to sex. Pines summarized the research: "Women generally connect sex with affection, closeness, intimacy. Men generally connect sex with achievement, adventure, control, or pure physical release" (1998: 95). This is based on research summarized in 1992, now over 20 years old, and much has changed. But that is the theory. Pines notes that jealousy is normal, a reassuring point to couples in jealousy mode, but also that what attracted the couple to each other is often, ironically, the cause of the jealousy. As to who is more jealous, men or women, the data indicate that they are about equal in terms of intensity, frequency and triggers, but not in their responses. Why not? Because women know who their children are, but men are faced with dealing with "paternity uncertainty"—a very different situation that implies the possibility of spending a lifetime raising someone else's kids, and thus being a fool. So it is not surprising that men might react more violently, since more is at stake. It is said that after an affair, men are more likely to deny the significance of the relationship (no time to deal with it) or to leave, while women are more likely to try to improve the relationship. Women are apparently more likely to try to induce jealousy, according to one researcher (Viorst, previously discussed), for five reasons: to gain a reward, to test the strength of the relationship, for revenge, to boost self-esteem or to punish the partner. This is done in numerous ways, but you may not have known that they were deliberate. Related to this discussion, one survey of 554 societies found that only 135 practice monogamy; most societies practice polygamy and only four practice polyandry. In some cultures, the penalties for female adultery are (or have been) much higher than for male adultery, possibly because the social costs are higher. In sum, the sociobiological approach argues that the differential costs and benefits of jealousy are determined by evolution and genetics over millennia. In this controversial view, jealousy is important for genetic survival (1998:91-112).

Finally, the social-psychological approach emphasizes how culture and different cultures frame jealousy and the appropriate responses to jealousy. This is the domain of anthropology, and Pines reviews the many diverse ways peoples cope and deal with jealousy (1998: 113-32).

The anthropologist Ruth Benedict reported on the Zuni of the American south, among whom she lived, who coped with infidelity with equanimity and without anger or violence. "If she is unfaithful, it is normally a first step in changing husbands . . ."—a simple and easy process. If he is unfaithful, she will ignore it until the family gets irritated; then, as the wife explained: ". . . 'I didn't wash his clothes. Then he knew that I knew that everybody knew, and he stopped going with that girl.' It was effective, but not a word was passed" (1968:77). Yet, among the nearby Apache, the man was entitled to cut off part of her adulterous nose. What she was entitled to do was not stated (1968). Similarly, the Dobuans of Melanesia get very upset. Benedict lost her anthropological cool in describing them: "They are lawless and treacherous. Every man's hand is against every other man" (1968: 94). Strangely, to "Western" cultures, "faithfulness is not expected between husband and wife . . .," but when infidelity happens, "If it is the husband, he breaks his wife's cooking pots. If it is the wife, she maltreats her husband's dog." He may attempt suicide, and usually fails, but then the relatives step in and the unhappy relationship continues. Yet, in Dobu, "Men and women alike rate sex satisfaction high and make achievement of it a matter of great concern. . . . The stock sex teaching with which women enter marriage is that the way to keep their husbands is to keep them as exhausted as possible" (1968: 99-100, 121). These and so many other different cultural attitudes to sex and reactions to adultery rather negate the theme of universal bio-determined genetic responses to sexual infidelity.

Pines (1998) also explores situations where jealousy is either controlled, reduced or absent. This includes a commune of 15 women and 17 men and two children in California known as Keristans, who practice what they call polyfidelity, that is, lifelong fidelity to each other while rotating sexual partners on a regular basis. She also interviewed swingers, noting the distinction between what one author described as "person-centered sex" compared to "body-centered sex" and "residential and psychological monogamy," a distinction that also applies to those who practice open marriages. Some of this is funny. A man describes an open marriage scene: "You wake up in the morning naked under the blankets after spending the night making love. Suddenly her husband comes into the bedroom, says good morning to you, and then starts an argument with her about who was supposed to take out the garbage last night (1998:135).

Surreal, yes. Clearly it is impossible to go into more detail in this nuanced and sophisticated set of analyses; but this outline may be just sufficient to give a taste of the complexity of this common and normal, as well as pathological, experience. To love is to be jealous, at times, for most people in the West, who so emphasize marriage, monogamy and soul-mates. Pines ends on a positive note, that extreme jealousy can be controlled with psychiatric techniques to help jealous individuals and their mates.

Nancy Friday

Nancy Friday offers a different and personal perspective. She wrote a 500-plus-page blockbuster of a book on the topic, titled *Jealousy: Why We All Feel It, How to Overcome It* (1987)—very candid, chock-full of stories, interviews and ideas. She had already written best-sellers about women's fantasies, men in love and mother-daughter relationships, so she is something of an expert in matters of the heart. She says right away that: "I was jealousy personified" and "I had never known love without jealousy" (1987:1, 6).

She explores dependence, attachment and detachment, love and hate, power, the Oedipus complex (Freud), preconscious memory and the mother/breast (Klein), narcissism, sibling rivalry, self-esteem and envy. Jealousy is complicated.

An anthropologist affirms: "I see jealousy as a positive force. If a relationship is good, it is worth fighting for . . . If jealousy had not served an important purpose, it would have evolved out of the species. I think men are *absolutely* more jealous than women. They have to know who their children are." An analyst disagrees and echoes Freud: "Jealousy has its roots in unhealthy patterns of development. It is tied up with ownership. As such it is always pathological." And a social psychologist disagrees with both of them: "Jealousy flows from threats to self-esteem or threats to the equality of my relationship. Being in a low-power position is one of several ways that either or both of these threats become magnified" (Friday, 1987:31-4). Some think that there is a genetic predisposition to jealousy; others that it derives originally from the earliest relations with, first, the mother then, sequentially, the father and siblings, and that it affects subsequent adult relations. This is Friday's view, as she discusses her absent father and her mother's preference for her sister.

So there we have it, the expert lack of consensus. That jealousy is good and useful or, perhaps, bad and pathological; it is normal, anyway, maybe genetic in origin or, perhaps, originates in parental or sibling rivalry; or maybe it is a function of low self-esteem or powerlessness. I'm sure that clarifies jealousy.

According to Friday (1987:130), "Every love relationship is a balance of power," but that is precarious, for "She loves his power. She hates his power." It is not so much economic or political power, though these may be factors, but, rather, the power he has over her emotions, feelings and happiness: psychological power. And women live more in their emotions and identify, more with their relationships than men do, she says. Power *over* is resented, for it inhibits the power *to be*. As she puts it (1987:481): "We are bound to hate the ones we love. Who could have hurt us more?" A bit bleak.

She emphasizes throughout the importance of *two* parents—to double the love and to spread the infant's rage, and because fathers and mothers love differently. And she discusses how she learned to cope with her jealousy, partly by understanding it much better, thanks to her interviews, but also, I suspect, by sexing up her life and de-sacralizing, de-romanticizing and instrumentalizing sex. Jealousy is not necessarily always about sex. It is not necessarily always about love. It may be about upbringing. Still, the old excuse "it didn't mean a thing" may be true for the subject but it may not be true for his or her lover. It may be devastating.

Friday thanked her husband, Bill, in the Acknowledgments page, then proceeded in Chapter One to detail a torrid affair with Jack, which seems to have unleashed the sex maniac within, or the Bad Girl, as she describes herself. She talks about them walking around the deserted office building on weekends, naked, and how he licked his sperm off her face; then, later, how she picked up a French soldier on the beach; then, later still, a threesome with two men, a foursome with three men, and a voyage with Mr. Parker, before she came home and married Bill.

One might suspect that Bill could have been the teeniest bit jealous of all this, don't you think? But in all the 500-plus pages on jealousy, and despite all the interviews, Bill's views on jealousy are not recorded. Perhaps he was/is not the jealous type.

David Buss

The evolutionary psychologist David Buss argues that jealousy has an evolutionary purpose: It strengthens the love between the couple. He suggests that it is "a kind of old-fashioned mate insurance, an evolutionary glue that holds modern couples together." He adds that "The total absence of jealousy . . . portends emotional bankruptcy" (2000a: 54, 57). In brief, no jealousy, no love. It's a good thing, despite all the negative press that jealousy receives—unless it kills you, of course.

He also reports on the research on jealousy. In one study of dating university students, 33 percent reported that "jealousy posed a significant problem in their current relationship." This is the negative, problematic side of emotion. But, in another study, 31 percent of the women surveyed said that they had deliberately provoked their partner's jealousy, and they explained the many strategies they had used to do so. Only 17 percent of the men had done this. Another study explored why partners would deliberately provoke jealousy: 38 percent of the women surveyed said that it was to try to increase a man's commitment and 40 percent to test the strength of the bond between them. It must have tested some of them to the breaking-point (2000b:210-5). (Oh! *That's* how strong it was! Now I know. Wow! Not quite strong enough! Oh, well!). And they may wish to boost their self-esteem by basking in the sunshine of someone else's admiration and desire.

What is counter-intuitive in all this is that a longitudinal study over seven years found that the most jealous partners in the original survey were also the most likely to get married and to be together seven years later (2000a). The conclusion seemed to be that the depth of love *and* jealousy were tangled up together—pleasure and pain both. But this was just one study with a small sample, so this conclusion should be tentative. Furthermore, they may be still together, but the quality of the relationships is not known. Together isn't everything. Is it?

In his book *The Dangerous Passion: Why Jealousy Is as Necessary as Love and Sex*, Buss explains that men and women feel differently about infidelity. Women agonize more about their partners' emotional infidelity, worried about the loss of commitment and support, while men worry about that too, no doubt, but more about physical infidelity, because of paternity uncertainty. Indeed, the estimates are that 9-10 percent of children are mistaken about who their biological father is (2000b:162, 171). This has become a publicized and politicized issue now, with attention being focused on the rights of the children versus the rights of the deceived dad not to support someone else's child or children, and efforts by states to avoid paying welfare (Driedger, 1997; Henry, 2006; Rawe, 2007; Padawer, 2009). It's a mess and heartbreaking.

Buss states that jealousy is "not a sign of immaturity" but a necessary defense mechanism against very real threats to relationships from other people. Women's infidelity is often what he calls "mate insurance," a backup plan. As one woman said: "Men are like soup—you always need one on the back burner" (2000b:20). Another woman opined: "Men are like tires; some get better mileage than others, but eventually they all wear out (2000b:166). The meaning of sex varies considerably between the sexes, too, with women generally valuing emotional commitment more than men. Buss then discusses "signal detection": signals of infidelity, "mate value," "desirability differences," "symbiotic pathology," "derogatory tactics," emotional manipulation, mate-switching and, for women, trading up and the costs and benefits of affairs. Buss also discusses "Error Management Theory," according to which a cost-benefit analysis implies the evolutionary utility of jealousy, since it is more costly to be complacent than to be jealous. No question but that jealousy may be pathological and lethal, but that is only one side of the story; the other side is what Buss calls emotional wisdom.

So here we have considered some of the views of a psychiatrist, a clinical psychologist, a journalist and an evolutionary psychologist. There does not seem to be much consensus, but their views are interesting and clarify the dimensions, meanings, functions and practice of jealousy, as well as both the gender difference, which Buss stresses, and the gender similarities. Buss's book is fascinating, practical, evidence-based and well-researched, but rather sad.

In any event, jealousy is clearly a complicated emotion: normal, but often problematic, sometimes deliberately provoked, potentially dangerous both emotionally and physically, even lethally, but paradoxically imbricated with love. I did meet one man who, so I heard later, had returned from work early, found his wife in bed with another man, and killed them both. Jealousy can be lethal, in fact, as in *Othello* and *Medea*. Indeed, jealousy is thought to be a leading cause of intimate/spousal homicides in the United States and Canada.

*

So sex is weird. Desire is good, lust is bad, or maybe good, but it's hard to tell the difference. Desire is good, love is fine, but it seems that the greater the desire and the love, the greater the jealousy, and that hurts— maybe enough to kill. And the "sexperts" totally disagree about jealousy: Maybe it's good for the species but bad for the soul, which seems like a contradiction. And maybe it's manufactured, deliberately, to test the loved one. Who knows? And desire may lead to jealousy, which may lead to divorce, battering, and homicide or to loving sex, marriage and children.

Desire, like jealousy, is more controversial than one might expect. The solution seems, as Judith Viorst advised, to be "mature and secure." But she contradicts Buss; and, anyway, there is not a pill for that. Perhaps age. Or death.

Chapter 4
Cultures

People are amazingly varied in their sexual values, attitudes, preferences and practices. To some extent this relates to gender, age and religiosity, and to some extent to national cultures; but, certainly, sex is also very personal in terms of attitudes and practice. Pollsters and researchers ask such personal questions: How many people have you slept with? How many were of the same sex? The opposite sex? How long is your average sexual intercourse? How old were you when you first had sex? If you are, or were, married or in a committed relationship, were you ever unfaithful? How often? Such impertinence! And, in the so-called culture wars, they might want to know your opinion on a wide range of topics, including homosexuality, prostitution, pornography, abortion, pre-marital sex and more, much like the University of Chicago sex study mentioned earlier. So here we might consider some of the personal, gender and national cultures, with paraphilias to be considered later.

Personal Cultures

Our sex lives vary enormously, from celibacy and asexuality to hedonism and BDSM. We are fascinated by the variety. Warren Beatty has supposedly slept with 12,775 women, according to his official biographer, including such high profile women as Jane Fonda, Julie Christie, Joan Collins, Madonna, Isabelle Adjani, Diane Keaton and, of course, his wife, Annette Benning. Beatty denies the numbers, which his biographer calculated from his statement that he could not get to sleep without sex. So three-and-a-half decades as a single man gives about that number—and no sleepless nights. His biographer ignored the possibility that he might have had sex with himself or with some women more than once. In any event, for Beatty sex seems to mean sleeping pills. Not the most romantic definition.

But, then, Gene Simmons, the lead singer of KISS, asserts that he had slept with 4,897 women, but who's counting? (*Economist*, 14 February 2015:76); and Wilt Chamberlain claims that he had slept with over 20,000 women. That is a lot of sleeping—and counting. Sex means numbers.

Robert Mapplethorpe claimed to have slept with over 1,000 men. The Nobel Prize-winning economist, John Maynard Keynes, led a gay life in his youth and, as an economist, he was, no doubt, unusually fond of numbers. In any event, he recorded his sexual statistics for posterity: 61 encounters in nine months during 1908-9 and 65 the following year, with details: ". . . the actor of Whitechapel, 16-year-old under Etna, lift boy of Vauxhall, Jewboy, Grand Duke Cyril of the Paris baths" (*Economist*, 9 May 2015: 80). This is all very anal.

Jenna Jameson, perhaps the most famous porn star ever, says that she has slept with "Somewhere between sixty and eighty people—men and women, on screen and off" (2004:516). So, about 70, give or take a dozen or so.

So sex means money, sleeping pills, numbers, anal collections, and, perhaps. fun and relaxation—and sometimes love. Many people are writing about their sex lives: their "sexographies." Things that were once private are now publicized. And what once might have been shameful now rakes in the sex dollars. Everyone is confessing or bragging about their sex lives, especially if—okay, when—they have been totally scandalous. But readers, being nonjudgmental in all this and avoiding such moral judgments as "totally scandalous," explain that "they" extend the boundaries of what is normally considered normal. And the public buys up the books enthusiastically. People are fascinated by the sex lives of other people.

While some just list the celebrities they have "slept with," in our charming euphemism, others are pushing other boundaries. In *My Horizontal Life: A Collection of One-night Stands*, Chelsea Handler describes her seemingly hilarious adventures with many men, vodka, ecstasy, pick-ups and break-ups. She has since written two more books that leaped to the top of the *New York Times* best-seller lists and, all told, she has sold more than a million copies. She has her own late-night show and tours madly. Her tell-all tales of sex, her ex, masturbation and beyond seem to amuse her audiences. And so we (or they) live our (or their) lives vicariously.

We live in a trophy culture. Wilt Chamberlain, Warren Beatty, Catherine Millet, Jenna Jameson, Tiger Woods—athletes, actors and actresses, and others—where opportunity knocks, have their recreations and seem to collect each other. Former baseball star Jose Canseco explains:

> Sex is a big part of the game. The main reason is that it's just so easy to find. Wherever baseball players go, women want them. The women let the players know they want them and they make themselves available . . . We're men; we have egos and libidos, and that's a tough set of forces to combat. (2005:91)

He described the women as, variously, "imports," "road beef," "slump-busters" and other players' wives (Canseco, 2005:95-7). In the U.K., however, the groupies *target* specific soccer players for the cash they can earn, by selling their stories to scandal-mongering papers like the now-defunct *The News of the World* and the *Sun* (Druckerman, 2007:84-5). These personal stories and memoirs may be cathartic for the survivors or simply money-makers, but they cover a wide range of topics from incest to BDSM.

Incest: In her best-selling memoir, *The Kiss,* Kathryn Harrison described her long, incestuous relationship with her father, a pastor. It all began with a chaste kiss goodbye at the airport, then, she wrote: "My father pushes his tongue deep into my mouth: wet, insistent, exploring, then withdrawn." She reflects:

> In years to come, I'll think of the kiss as a kind of transforming sting, like that of a scorpion: a narcotic that spreads from my mouth to my brain. The kiss is the point at which I begin slowly, inexorably to fall asleep, to surrender volition, to become paralyzed. It's the drug my father administers in order that he might consume me. That I might want to be consumed. (1997: 68, 70)

The affaire ended when her mother died. The family dynamics between her mother, her grandmother, her father and her were remarkably tangled in this memoir, which also disentangles them.

Mackenzie Phillips, the daughter of the late John Phillips, founder of The Mamas and the Papas, recently wrote in her memoir, and retold it on Oprah, that her father raped her when she was 19, on the night before her wedding (they were both high on drugs at the time), but that later the sex was consensual, for 10 years. Her stepmother says this is not true and that she has a history of mental illness and drug abuse. Her two half-sisters think it might be true. She says that she wants to expose an issue that receives little attention. (http://www.people.com/people/article/0.20308234.00.-html).

Anonymous Sex: In her *New York Times* bestseller, the French art critic Catherine Millet expounds on the joys of anonymous sex at orgies: "There could be up to about 150 people (they did not all come to fuck, some had come to watch) and I would take on the cocks of around a quarter or a fifth of them in all the available ways: in my hands, my mouth, my cunt and my ass" (2003:10).

She is proud to admit that she is the first to take off her clothes at parties to get fucked. "I was only really relaxed after I had removed my dress or my trousers." She recounts her favorite episodes and the men.

"During that hour, I was taken by about thirty men, several of them held me up against a wall, and then they lay me on the hood [of a car]." That's one man every two minutes, which seems fairly brisk work. She described her fantasies in detail, and a party when she decided on anal sex only, and different types of penises and styles of sex: "I was always completely available: at all times and in all places, without hesitation or regret, by every one of my bodily orifices, and with a totally clear conscience" (2003:12, 24, 36). Her husband is fine with all this: *C'est normale, n'est-ce pas*?

Pornography: Jenna Jameson's book *How to Make Love like a Porn Star* (which she was) has sold well and has a happy ending. Her mother died when she was three; her father, a cop, could not relate; she left home at 16; began making up to $4,000 a night as a stripper in Vegas when she was 17-18; became a model; got addicted to drugs; then became the top porn star in the United States. Somehow, however, she survived and lived to marry, have a son, reunite with her father and her brother, and to conclude: "All the wrong choices I had made served only to ferry me to the right place" (2004:571). Then she wrote a best-seller.

Prostitution: People seem to be fascinated by prostitution. Xaviera Hollander's *The Happy Hooker* (1975) was a best-seller, which she parlayed into being a "Sex Advisor" with *Playboy*. Evelyn Lau's *The Runaway* (1989) established her reputation as a writer, but she was definitely *not* a happy hooker. "I hate men . . . ALL MEN ARE THE SAME . . . God I hate men. I hate life" (1989:282-3). Natalie (Natalia) McLennan (2008) has described her rise and fall as New York's #1 escort, commanding $2,000 an hour, with a minimum of two hours, but becoming addicted to cocaine and heroin, until her arrest for tax evasion and imprisonment. Then came redemption. And another Canadian (they are sexier than you thought), Chester Brown (2011), has chronicled his sexual experiences with more than two dozen prostitutes, and his rejection of the idea of romantic love. However, he has now settled down to a monogamous relationship with one of them, whom he still pays. He argues for the decriminalization of prostitution, as do others, while the Canadian government is moving increasingly towards the criminalization of "johns" rather than "jills." Belle de Jour's *The Intimate Adventures of a London Call Girl* (2007) jumped to the top of the British best-seller lists. She described, in amazing and sometimes amusing detail, what she did, the security system provided by her madam, and informed everyone that her price was 200 pounds an hour. Her identity was finally revealed—by then she had a PhD and was a professor at a university. She is now something of a celebrity in literary circles.

The Vagina: "The Vagina Monologues," brought to theaters in many countries, created a discussion about vaginas, normally not a typical topic. Once it was out there, Susanna Kaysen told us about hers. She explained that something "went wrong" with her vagina. "Some days my vagina felt as if somebody had put a cheese grater in it and scraped. Some days it felt as if someone had poured ammonia inside it. Some days it felt as if a little dentist was drilling a little hole in it (2001:3).

She saw her gynecologist, who suggested antifungal cream and estrogen cream, and said "The more you use the vagina, the better its health" (2001:7). But sex hurt so the gynecologist sent her to an herbalist, then an internist, then a vulvologist. They tried everything from teabags to Novocain to baking soda to dilators/dildoes, and the vulvologist recommended surgery. Her adventure with her vagina continued for over a year and cost her her boyfriend. Eventually, she states, "I've become a vagina" (2001:110).

And then her vagina just died, with no pain but no sensation either. As she puts it: "When eros goes away, life gets dull. It's as if I'm colorblind. The world is gray" (2001:131). This went on for almost two years. Her last words on the topic: "My vagina keeps trying to get my attention. It has something important to say to me. I'm listening. I'm still listening" (2001:159).

BDSM: All this sexual information is almost overwhelming, and all the intimate confessions, or bragging, about numbers, names, and attitudes, stories of incest, anonymous sex, prostitution, pornography, the vagina—and just when you thought "that's it, what could be next?" along came the—not one, but three—novels in the *Fifty Shades* series of BDSM: Erotic romance for mature audiences, by E. L. James, which soared to the top of the best-seller lists from Australia to Canada to the U.S. Dismissed as "mommy porn," they unleashed a flood of more novels of the same genre. Then Sophie Morgan published her autobiographical *Diary of a Submissive* (2012). Here she describes her transformation from a normal, loved, English middle-class girl to a successful journalist who found intense pleasure in intense pain, both physical—by spanking, biting, hitting etc.—and psychological—by humiliation. She is happy with this and loves her tormentor. She could not explain this; no Dr. Freud here. She just described her life. "It may sound odd that such cruelty and humiliation inspired the thought, but . . . I knew I loved this twisted, clever tender man who got upset at people being cruel to animals but took joy in doing horrible things to me (2012:266).

Then, after one excruciating episode, James disappeared, dumped her, then reappeared and explained that he didn't like to hurt her anymore. He was sorry. She replied that he hurt her more by disappearing than ever he had before. He said he was sorry. Again. Often. She explained:

> When you hurt me I like it. I crave it. . . . Being so completely off-balance, being demeaned, being hurt, diminished, does it for me . . . Yes, you hurt me. But you do it with my permission . . . Yes you're sadistic. And maybe you need to get your head around that . . . And I'm happy being me—needing to be hurt . . . (2012:287)

So there are many sex stories out there and many very different values, attitudes, behaviors and problems. Dorothy Parker, in her poem "Pictures In The Smoke," is quite amusing on this: "Oh, gallant was the first love, and glittering and fine; The second love was water, in a clear white cup; The third was his, and fourth was mine; And after that, I always get them all mixed up."

Gender Culture

Gender culture raises other issues, some of which have been mentioned earlier. Sex researchers tend to favor either qualitative data (as above, the personal touch) or quantitative, the numbers—as with the *Kinsey Report* and the "*Time*/CNN Survey" clarifying the disagreements about what constitutes sex (Table 1.1).

The most comprehensive survey on sex (totally quantitative) in America was conducted out of the University of Chicago (mentioned earlier), with a random sample of nearly 3,500 Americans aged 18 to 59. The results show both some gender differences and similarities in gender culture and offer some surprises (Michael et al., 1994). In point form:

• Most of what we think about sex in America is, flatly, "wrong" (1994:14).

• The majority of men and women had only one sexual partner in the previous year or none at all (79 percent for men, 90 percent for women)—a high majority for both sexes (1994:35; cf. 176). Despite the images on TV and the tabloids, the American sex world is not a hotbed of promiscuity and free-range sex.

• Fidelity: Monogamy is the norm in marriage. Ninety-four percent of married couples had only one partner in the previous year; and more than

80 percent of the wives and about 75 percent of the husbands reported that they had been faithful to their spouses in their entire marriage (1994:101, 105, 214). So, the infidelity rates of 20-25 percent are not that much different.

• Numbers: In general, men report more sexual partners than women: 33 percent say that they have had more than 10 partners since age 18, compared to 9 percent of women; and while 34 percent of women have had one or no partners, only 23 percent of men fall into that category. That said, 29 percent of the women have had more partners than 44 percent of the men (the age breakdown is not presented), so the overlap is considerable, and the traditional stereotypes are not entirely persuasive. Equally, the disjunction between the numbers is not persuasive either. The numbers should add up, but do not; they are all, therefore, unreliable (1994:102). This question of numbers and, therefore, the apparent difference between male and female sexualities comes up all the time. The trouble is that the data are faulty and, therefore, distort our understanding of sexualities.

• Frequency: Americans can be divided into three groups: a third who have sex twice or more a week, a third just a few times a month, and a third a few times a year or never. And both the youngest singles and the oldest had the least partnered sex. Perhaps, surprisingly, there is little relation between the number of partners and amount of sex (1994:114-9).

Thinking: one of the biggest differences between the sexes concerned answers to the question "How often do you think about sex?" The majority of men (54 percent) responded "Every day" or "Several times a day," compared to only 19 percent of women; while 14 percent of women responded "Less than once a month" or "Never," compared to only 4 percent of men (1994:156). So, if you ask a man, "What are you thinking about?" you can guess.

Satisfaction: All this emphasis on numbers and statistics might seem to obscure our relation with sexual satisfaction, joy and pleasure. About 88 percent of married people reported great physical pleasure from their sex lives, and 85 percent received great emotional pleasure, too. These are much more encouraging results than from the Hite surveys. Counter-intuitively, the singles reported the least satisfaction (1994:123-6).

So, based on this survey are male and female sexualities the same or different? To this excellent question we can, for once, offer a definitive answer: yes and no, perhaps. Our sexualities seem to be similar in terms of the similar number of partners (one or none for most) and high fidelity rates. They seem to be dissimilar in terms of the much higher number of partners claimed by men, but we know that these figures are unreliable; they are also dissimilar in terms of thinking about sex: Men think about it far more often.

Yet, even when spouses agree about numerical frequency, they may evaluate it differently. This is very clear from the scene in Woody Allen's movie "Annie Hall" where the therapist asks Annie and her boyfriend, Alvy Singer, "Do you have sex often?" Alvy replies, "Hardly ever. Maybe three times a week," while Annie replies, "Constantly. I'd say three times a week."

The most striking feature of the survey is not so much the similarity/dissimilarity issue, the Mars/Venus dichotomy, the battle *between* the sexes in bed (as above), but the huge differences *within* each sex.

In quantitative terms, the researchers distinguished three populations: those with high, medium and low interest in sex, indicated in both sexes, by the number of sexual partners, the frequency of sex, the frequency of masturbation and the frequency of thinking about sex. The picture of the predatory male and the modest maiden is largely false. In number, for example, 15 percent of men report 21-plus sexual partners since age 18 and so do 3 percent of women (1994:109). This is a big difference, even if we allow for what we must call "male inflation," but a huge difference from those who have had under five partners. The stereotypes, which we discussed earlier, have a grain of truth but are also wildly inaccurate.

The wide range in behaviors reflects an equally wide range in attitudes and values. Again, there are three main groups: the Traditionals, largely ruled by religious beliefs, who tend to believe that teenage, pre-marital and extra-marital sex are all wrong, as are homosexuality and abortion; the Relationals, almost half the sample, who tend to be older and married, are more permissive, believing that sex need not be reserved only for marriage but should be loving, and that extra-marital sex is always wrong; and the Recreationals, more than a quarter of the sample, who disassociate sex and love, tend to be young and single and to have more partners and be in a high-risk category for STIs. The three categories indicate clusters of behavior and attitudes and are not water-tight compartments; furthermore, there are subsets within each category, e.g. prochoice or prolife, as well as in their attitudes to teenage sex, etc., mentioned above. This type of cross-category value conflict is, perhaps, the major component in the so-called "battle of the sexes" (1994:232-4); but this indicates that the battle of the sexes is misnamed, at least with respect to sex. It is not *between* the sexes but it is an ideological, political conflict of values *within* each sex. The so-called "culture war" and "gender war" intersect or cross-cut each other.

Indeed, even the idea of a "battle of the sexes" is a myth, at least as regards sex, with over 80 percent of the respondents of both sexes saying that they are emotionally *and* physically satisfied with their sex lives, whatever they may be.

A 2013 national sex survey of over 1,000 Canadian adults (18-49 years of age, so not very representative) found some surprising results—given the reputation of Canadians as being somewhat reserved and polite. Specifically, 225 have done it with two or more partners and another 295 would do it if they could; 85 have had sex in a canoe. The average number of partners in the sample was 12, though the number was higher with age, while nearly twice as many men as women have had 20 or more lovers and 17 percent have been strictly monogamous (Harris, 2013).

In sum, the definitions, experiences, attitudes and imaginations vary both within and between the sexes, as do double standards for both sexes. This is not so much a matter of lying as of perceptions, which vary all by themselves. Recent research indicates that both men and women apply double standards to their own behavior and their partner's. As reported in the journal *Men's Health* (April 2009:34), what men and women call sex depends on who is doing it—them or their partners.

Table 4.1: That Counts as Sex (in percent)

	M	F
I kissed another person deeply	12	5
My partner kissed another person deeply	24	13
I had oral contact with someone's breasts/nipples	14	5
My partner had oral contact with someone's breasts/nipples	33	20
I fondled someone's genitals	19	13
My partner fondled someone's genitals	46	28
I had oral contact with someone's genitals	41	36
My partner had oral contact with someone's genitals	65	62

Clearly men and women count differently, and women are easier on themselves and on men than men are; and both men and women apply double standards. Thus, "kissing deeply" does "count as sex" for a few women (5 percent) but for over twice as many men (12 percent); but far more think it "counts as sex" if their partner does it; likewise for the three other erotic behaviors. For oral sex, only 36 percent of women say it counts compared to 41 percent of men, but when it comes to their partners—hah! That's a different story. Women say that it does so count (62 percent) and men about the same (65 percent). No wonder men and women report such different numbers of partners. Men are much more likely than women to *raise* their sex score. Women do not count much of their sexual behavior as sex; they are so modest. But the same behavior by their partners does count: They are more judgmental. Both men and women usually do not count their oral sex as sex, but their respective partner's usually does count as sex. One wonders if penetration counts, or only if it is the partner's. Obviously this different counting could lead to some misunderstandings; but it does largely explain the aforementioned problem with numbers: Men and women define sex differently. Women say, "It doesn't count—unless you do it!" Men say, "Does so!—especially if you do it!" Oh, well. Evidently, men and women have very different definitional and, therefore, mathematical abilities: men inflate and women deflate their scores, and both have double standards. The table above illustrates very well both the numbers problem and the double standards.

Global Culture

The personal and gender sex cultures nestle within the very different national and ethnic cultures, though not always very comfortably. Cultures clash as violently as individuals. What is tolerable in some cultures is considered illegal and immoral in others. The list is familiar: homosexuality, fidelity, pornography, adultery, prostitution, even dating. Some of these conflicts are discussed here, but globalization and anthropology have raised some others.

A Swiss woman, Corinne Hofmann, visited Kenya on holiday somewhat recently and fell desperately, totally, in love with a Masai warrior. Her friends, both African and European, warned her against the relationship, but she ignored their advice. She tried to kiss him. He was horrified; and their first time in bed was, for her, a disaster. A female Masai friend explained the Masai facts of life: "Masai don't kiss. The mouth is for eating, and kissing—she makes a face—is contemptible. A man never touches a woman below the stomach, and a woman is not supposed to touch a man's penis. A man's hair and face are also taboo" (2007:21). Her friend also informed her about eating: "Lketinga can't eat this meat. No Masai warrior eats anything that a woman has touched, or even looked at. They are not allowed to eat in the presence of women: they can only drink tea" (2007: 24). The rules and norms about sex and marriage are infinitely various.

Anthropologists have worked very hard to describe the sex customs and values of other peoples, and to describe what might seem to be strange, though many of ours are strange enough (Lyons and Lyons, 2006). The incest taboo is variable. Homosexuality may or may not be illegal but not uncommon and denied. And a third sex is sometimes recognized: the *hijras* in India, the *fa'afafine* in Samoa, the *mahu* in Tahiti and Hawaii and the *fakaleitas* in Tonga (Lyons, 2006; Kottak, 2013). As we shall see, some practices anthropologists might find sensible (e.g., Jenness), others superior to our own, for one reason or another (e.g., Mead), and still others reprehensible or incomprehensible—but always fascinating, and in the tropics, especially so. The exotic is erotic.

Bronislaw Malinowski was, I think, the first anthropologist to systematically investigate the sexual practices of the other, in the Trobriand Islands. His *Sex and Repression in Savage Society* (1927) became a best-seller, perhaps, partly because of its garish title, but he did describe some customs very alien from those in England at the time. In his most well-known work, *Argonauts of the Western Pacific*, originally published in 1922—primarily about the *Kula* system of intertribal exchange economy and the major role of magic—he also discussed the sex lives of the islanders. "Chastity is an unknown virtue among these natives . . . As they grow up, they live in promiscuous free love, [and] . . . unmarried girls are openly supposed to do what they like." They have lineups for selection by boys, and when visitors arrive, girls are "expected to satisfy their sexual wants." Then again, during the gardening season, any strange man runs the risk that women will "seize him, tear off his pubic leaf, and ill-treat him orgiastically in the most ignominious manner" (1961:53-4). (Note his Western cultural assumption that chastity is a virtue.) He does admit that the women of Dobu are "an exception" (1961:42).

Malinowski followed in the tradition of the French navigator de Bougainville, who visited Tahiti in 1768, and was politely surprised by the overt sexuality of the locals, who canoed out to his ship: "[The men] pressed us to choose a woman, and to come on shore with her, and their gestures . . . denoted in what manner we should form an acquaintance with her." A naturalist on board believed that the Tahitians lived in a state of nature, a hypothetical state suggested by Rousseau: "The only god they know is the god of Love" (Wallace, 2003:18).

This eroticization of the South Seas was reinforced by Captain Cook's third and last voyages with HMS Bounty and HMS Resolution to Hawaii in 1778-9. His surgeon's mate was scandalized: "There are no people in the world who indulge themselves more in their sexual appetites. In fact, they carry it to a most scandalous and shameful degree." One of his fellow seamen was less worried: "We live now in the greatest Luxury, and as to the Choice & number of fine women there is hardly one among us that may not vie with the Grand Turk himself" (Wallace, 2003: 41, 46).

Paul Gauguin reinforced this trope of the sexy dusky maidens in the South Pacific by migrating to Tahiti for simplicity, health and, surely, sex. He has been attacked as a sexist, racist and imperialist (Wallace, 2003:110-3); but he was also an artist and, I think, he found there a superior lifestyle, not an inferior one.

Margaret Mead was also fascinated by sex and wrote a number of books in which sex figured prominently and politically. She was a prolific writer, including *Coming of Age in Samoa* (1928), *Growing up in New Guinea* (1930), *Sex and Temperament in Three Primitive Societies* (1933) and, finally, *Male and Female* (1949). Sexuality was, in her understanding, generally recognized and approved: Men and women were healthy and happy in their sexuality, and it began in childhood.

The general preoccupation with sex, the attitude that minor sex activities, suggestive dancing, stimulating salacious conversation, salacious songs and definitely-motivated tussling are all acceptable and attractive diversions, is mainly responsible for the native attitude towards homosexual practices. They are simply *play*, neither frowned upon nor given much consideration (1928/1968:115; emphasis in original).

In her lovely portraits of sunny and sexy lives devoid of guilt in the South Pacific, Mead echoed Malinowski, but without his apparent disgust. She also critiqued the U.S., challenged the prevailing biological determinism of gender, and her work was immensely popular. (It may not have been accurate and was severely criticized by Derek Freeman, an Australian anthropologist who followed Mead in the field.) Sex even sells anthropology.

Critical of the sexual norms of then-contemporary U.S., Mead insisted that "The more society . . . muffles the human body in clothes, surrounds elimination with prudery, shrouds copulation in shame and mystery, camouflages pregnancy, banishes men and children from childbirth, and hides breast-feeding," the worse for everybody (1949:146). The explicit comparison with the South Pacific was clear, the critique was heard, and practices have been modified and attitudes changed somewhat, partly because of her, but also because of Dr. Spock, the pill and the sexual revolution.

The Canadian anthropologist Diamond Jenness was a member of a scientific research team across the high Arctic from 1914-6. Traveling with an Eskimo (now renamed Inuit) guide to another village, he noticed a woman following them, so he asked: "Who is this woman, and why is she following us? It's only Snow-Knife's wife, he answered. She is coming with us to visit her two sisters. Don't trouble about her. She will stay with me throughout our journey, and in the meantime my wife will live with Snow-Knife" (1972: 53). Jenness explained that he had heard of this custom, but not understood it until he realized that it was a very sensible safety measure. Any strange visitor was liable to be killed, but men and women with wives and husbands in different villages—and they might have many—were considered to be members of the family, and so they were safe and (he did not say it) maybe loved. (While this was called wife-swapping, it was also husband-swapping).

A digression: He added that all a bride needed was "a meat knife, a sewing kit, a lamp, and a cooking pot." The groom provided "the home, skins, tools, and weapons" (1972: 56). How things have changed—and not entirely for the better. Five years later (in about 1921), he reported that the Eskimos of the Mackenzie River delta had been decimated by disease: The population fell from 2,000 to "a scant 200." He asked: "Were we the harbingers of a brighter dawn, or only messengers of ill-omen, portending disaster?" (1972:247). Disaster, actually. A couple of years after that, in a later edition of his work, he reported that many of his friends had died, first of an influenza epidemic, then of tuberculosis (1972:248).

So, globalization may be positive or negative: positive in the view of Mead, who thought that the sexual cultures of the Samoans and others were superior (i.e., less puritanical and more humane) to those of her native America, but negative in the view of Jenness, who was devastated by the lethal impact of his civilization on that of his friends.

A more startling account of gender and sex emerged from the research of the English anthropologist Evans-Pritchard among the Azande of the Sudan. One of his informants explained:

> In those days [late 19th century], if a man had relations with the wife of another the husband killed him or he cut off his hands and his genitals. So for that reason a man used to marry a boy to have orgasm between his thighs, which quieted his desire for a woman . . . Also there were some men who, although they had [female] wives, still married boys . . . They did for their husbands everything a wife does for her husband. (1974:36-7)

When the boys became men and warriors they might also marry a boy, and later they would marry a woman. So Azande male roles were very flexible: from bride to a warrior, to husband to a boy, to husband to a wife (Kottak, 2014: 179).

The American anthropologist Gilbert Herdt found a similar process among the Sambia of New Guinea—a tribe whose name he invented to convey anonymity. Where Malinowski had focused on the women, Herdt considered male sexuality and reported on what he called the "ritualized homosexuality" in Melanesia. The institutional pattern of same-sex transmission of semen to *create masculinity* in these cultures was most powerful and widespread . . . [Among the Sambia] the achievements of biological maturity and then fatherhood were believed to be solely the product of ritually constituted insemination (Herdt and Leavitt, 1998: 20; emphasis added). Men's sexuality had three stages: Boys provide sexual services to young men and receive semen from them to strengthen them so they can become warriors; then the boys become warriors and give their semen to boys; finally, warriors give their semen to women, both orally and vaginally, to produce milk (believed to be semen-related) and, also, to produce children. At first glance, this seems similar to the practice among the Azande, but there is all the difference between a warrior apprenticeship, marriage and sexual satisfaction and creating masculinity. So they switch from homosexual to heterosexual in a few years. Salazar (2006), commenting on Herdt's work, suggests that we should be careful about imposing Western sexual ideas on the Sambia, and that it seemed to him that maybe this was sex-as-nutrition, not as satisfaction—feeding the boy to manhood. But Herdt addressed this and suggested that "Homoerotic play takes precedence as the fellated's motive; the boy's growth is a latent social function of the bachelor's behavior (and is, I think, largely a rationalization on the men's part)"(2006:13-5).There is some logic to this, since semen is quintessentially male, but not a logic that will persuade contemporary prosecutors of pedophilia. This research has not, I believe, been replicated;

and since the original research was done in the sixties, these rituals may have changed; but if it was more about pleasure for the warrior than the nutrition and growth of the boy, then it was a clever ploy and an interesting facet of belief and faith.

Again, this may seem like the ancient Greece of Socrates in the *Symposium*, but not really, for then the logic was of mentoring, knowledge-transfer and like-mindedness from the older mentor to the beautiful young man.

What Evans-Pritchard and Herdt demonstrated was not only the extreme variability of the social construction of sexuality, but also of homosexuality and the relativity of virtue—a huge issue.

Add Hofmann, Malinowski, Mead, Evans-Pritchard, Jenness and Herdt together and it is clear that sexual practices, norms and morality are culturally relative. And that is just a small sample of the wide range of human sexual behaviors. Anthropology textbooks list even more practices (Kottak, 2014); and some will be discussed later (Chapter 11). Beliefs about what is right and wrong vary widely and are hotly debated.

The second point that emerges here is that while anthropologists and others may be interested in the sexual customs and values in other cultures, it seems clear that gender equality is closely linked to sexual equality, though admittedly both are hard to define. Much attention now is focused less on the sexual norms of others and more on human trafficking, mostly of women for sexual purposes, but also often *by* women (UNODOC, 2009; Cole, 2006).

Again, female genital mutilation is now widely regarded as a crime against women. UNICEF recently estimated that about 125 million women and girls have undergone this operation (*Time*, 5 August 2013:9). There was no mention of male genital mutilation.

Similarly, "gendercide" is catastrophic. The Indian economist Amartya Sen calculated in 1990 that 100 million baby girls were missing: killed, aborted or neglected to death, mostly in Northern India and China. The number is much more now, with boy/girl sex ratios at 120:100 in China, rather than a normal ratio of 105:100. The *Economist* reported recently that gendercide is now emerging in the Caucasus (21 September 2013).

A relatively recent major study of sexual behavior and attitudes is the 2007-8 Durex Sexual Wellbeing Global Survey (SWGS) (www.durex.com), which surveyed 26,000 people in 26 countries. Its first conclusion was that only 44 percent of participants are "fully satisfied" with their sex lives, although 66 percent said that sex is "fun, enjoyable and a vital part of life." Men are less satisfied than women, which bears out other research. Yet it does seem that nationality and sexual orientation are more significant variables than gender in the different vectors of sex. Although not all the data are presented for all vectors, in terms of sexual satisfaction, 78 percent of Nigerians report that they are satisfied, while only 10 percent of Japanese and 34 percent of the French say the same. This is a much wider range than anything reported about satisfaction in North America and surely requires more research. Frequency of sex is not always closely related to satisfaction: 87 percent of the Greeks and 82 percent of the Brazilians surveyed reported that they had sex every week, compared to only 34 percent of the Japanese. The British, Canadian and Americans were all in the 50-60 percent range. And neither satisfaction nor frequency necessarily correlated with the number of sex partners: Here, Austria wins, with men having had an average of 29 partners and women 17, compared to China with the least number. But the national league tables are cross-cut by the sexual orientation league tables. Among men, homosexuals reported, on average, 108 partners, bisexuals reported 21 male and 14 female partners and male heterosexuals came dead last with 13 partners. Among women, bisexuals report 13 male and 3 female partners, lesbians 11 and heterosexuals last, again, with only seven.

The SWGS is important, however, as indicating that *cultural* attitudes to sex may be even more variable than gender attitudes, varying by nation and by sexual orientation, in terms of being relatively sex-positive or negative, liberal or conservative. Indeed, this whole dichotomous or stereotypical conceptualization of men and women as sexually "opposite"—profligate vs. conservative, promiscuous vs. modest, good vs. bad, Mars vs. Venus, etc.—may be mostly a myth.

All things change, however, as Heraclitus noted so long ago. The National Opinion Research Center (NORC) at the University of Chicago surveyed married men and women about their fidelity in 1991 and, again, in 2002. Asked if they had ever had sex outside their marriage, 15 percent of the women said "yes" in 2002, up from 10 percent since 1991, while 22 percent of the men said "yes," the same as in 1991. So, female "adultery rates" (a new term, I think) are now approaching those of men, if we can assume that they both understood "sex" in the same way. We thus have an increasing disjunction between practice and attitudes, with infidelity rising while attitudes against it are hardening; but there is also an increasing convergence of husbands' and wives' infidelities: mostly faithful, but almost "equitable" in infidelity.

The whole matter of infidelity was pursued in some depth by former Wall Street journalist Pamela Druckerman in *Lust in Translation* (2007). She compiled a sort of league table of annual adultery rates for "married and cohabiting people who had more than one sexual partner in the last year" (in percentages), compiled from national probability samples of various recent dates for 39 countries. A selection from highest to lowest is presented in Table 4.2 below (Druckerman, 2007:61-3).

Table 4.2: League Table of Adultery Rates

	M	W
Togo	37.0	0.5
Cameroon	36.5	4.4
Brazil	12.0	0.8
Norway	10.8	6.6
China	10.5	n/a
Great Britain	9.3	5.1
U.S.A.	3.9	3.1
France	3.8	2.0
Italy	3.5	0.9
Switzerland	3.0	1.1
Australia	2.5	1.8
Bangladesh	1.6	n/a

Several points are worth noting: First, there is the vast range for men from Togo to Bangladesh—a 230 percent difference—and for women, from the high in Norway to the low in Togo. Second is the implausibility of these statistics, which should add up to equality but clearly cannot; this suggests that men and women define sex differently (a point we have discussed earlier). If you ask men and women how many people they danced with at a party, the numbers would be equal, assuming that they danced with each other. It is a matter of simple arithmetic. Nonetheless, the vast range of difference ought to make it impossible to generalize about men's and women's sexual appetites and performance, since the variations are clearly culturally determined. It is notable that Norwegian and British women "outperform" in adultery. Third, the stereotypes of Italian and French men as hypersexual are demolished by the data, as are the stereotypes of British men *and* women as not interested in sex (and, instead, preferring their pets). Fourth, Norway and Great Britain have the most willing women—but they are geographically far removed from the most willing men, in Togo and Cameroon—which, for the parties involved, would seem to be unfortunate.

Clearly, too, there are several different sex cultures out there. The Chicago survey emphasized three gender cultures within the United States. The Durex survey demonstrated the global cultures. Druckerman, however, has also emphasized socio-economic factors: the wealthier the country, in general, the lower the adultery rate (U.S., Italy, France, Australia, but not Great Britain). Religion and religiosity, however, are intervening variables. Bangladesh, with a low adultery rate, is one of the poorest countries in the world and largely Muslim. Although data from the Arab world and the Muslim world are almost nonexistent, religion is likely to be a major factor also (as in the United States). Togo is also very poor but has a high male adultery rate and a low female adultery rate; the discrepancy seems odd.

Druckerman also noted that while the French and the Americans have very similar rates of marital infidelity, attitudes to it are very dissimilar. About 16 percent of Americans have been unfaithful during their marriage, according to the Chicago survey: they do it, feel guilty mostly, and their spouses are devastated. The French do it, love it, and their spouses are irritated by it, but seem to accept it as part of married life. Former French presidents Francois Mitterand and Jacques Chirac were notorious womanizers. Chirac's wife knew this and opined that "Life is not a tranquil river . . . in this type of situation one puts forth a façade and one suffers the blows." Frenchmen like Chirac seem to see affairs "as one of life's pleasures, like *crème brulée*" (2007:142-3). The same is true for Catherine Millet (2003) in telling of her sex life. But most French men are not like Chirac and most French women are not like Millet. Nonetheless, according to the stereotypes, the French are pragmatic and the Americans are moralistic and puritanical.

In a review in the *Economist*, the author played on the old stereotypes: "Americans do it guiltily, Russians casually, Africans lethally and the French habitually" (31 March 2007). But the French sexual culture took a hit with the arrest in New York of Dominique Strauss-Kahn, the head of the IMF and a leading candidate to be president, on a charge of the sexual assault of Nafissator Diallo. Charges were later dismissed, but more scandals circled around him on his return to France, and protests against what was increasingly seen as a sexist and patriarchal sexual culture have escalated.

This reprised the critique of the sexual culture in the U.S. after the Anita Hill hearings in 1991 and the Clinton-Lewinsky affair in 1998.

Clearly, sexual cultures are various and, also, changing in many parts of the world, highlighted by these incidents. Similarly, in North America, the hook-up culture, drive-through marriages, the rise of common-law relationships, the drop in the fertility rate, the rise of Internet porn—all these trends signal other major changes in our sexual culture, for better or for worse.

The last word on numbers goes to one Tara Alexander, who wanted to get into the *Guinness Book of Records*. She selected the category of the greatest number of sex partners in one evening and had intercourse with 83 men (or, in the charming linguistics of the day, "brought eighty-three men to orgasm") and 24 orgasms; and she was filmed for cable TV (Petersen, 1999:350).

*

This fascination with sex is not new. The bible includes the "Song of Songs" (about 800 BCE), which purports to be a duet between King Solomon and, perhaps, the Queen of Sheba, and is, in its way, erotic. Out of India came *The Kama Sutra* in about the third or fourth century. In Rome, Ovid wrote *Ars Amoris (The Art of Love)* around 1CE, which is still amusing, cynical and wise. This was echoed in the twelfth century treatise *The Art of Courtly Love* (Capellanus, 1959) which has 31 rules for lovers, some of which still apply (though my students tend to disagree on which ones, which is interesting). These ideas about sex and love were followed by both Chaucer and Rabelais, who had some raunchy and funny stories in their work. One turning point was a steamy series of stories in *Memoirs of a Woman of Pleasure*, usually known as *Fanny Hill* (Cleland, 1748), which purported to be the memoirs and adventures of a "woman of pleasure"—so much sweeter a term than prostitute. The genre escalated with the violent fantasies of De Sade (1740-1814), notably *Justine*. Unfortunately, he tended to practice some of the cruelties that he imagined, so he spent 31 years of his life in prison. Some authorities say he was mad while others disagree. De Sade and Count Masoch will be discussed in more detail in a subsequent chapter.

Later came *The Life and Loves of Frank Harris*, banned in France, in four volumes published from 1922-27. They purport to be factual, but the stories cannot be verified and may be more wish-fulfillment than true. In fiction, James Joyce's *Ulysses* was first published in 1922 and promptly banned—and equally promptly pirated. The *Story of O* by Pauline Reage

(1954) was an erotic novel of bondage and submission echoing de Sade. D. H. Lawrence's *Lady Chatterley's Lover*, originally published in 1928, was finally reprinted by Penguin in the U.K. in 1960, and was promptly banned. The publishers were charged with the publication of obscenity (notably for the use of the words "fuck" and "cunt"), but the jury found for the defendants and gave a verdict of "not guilty."

Following the published treatises, the erotic stories and the fantasies appeared as films, and in the works of sexologists, and all began to merge and meld. The field is now wide open. *Playboy* (1953) was followed by *Penthouse* and the hard-core *Hustler*. Gay Talese's journalistic exploration and memoir of sex in America, *Thy Neighbor's Wife* (1983), was a shocker at the time but tame by today's standards. And now the tell-all memoirs by stars, sex workers (Hollander, Lau, de Jour and McLennan), free spirits, baseball players—some of which we have mentioned—all compete with each other for best-seller status.

In any event, the old stereotypes that men want sex and women don't, or not so much, are knocked down and out by some of these sexographies. Clearly, personal cultures are highly variable in terms of practice and meaning, and are deeply imbricated with gender cultures and global cultures. The disagreements about what sex is (Table 1.1), and what it means—from nothing to God; and the double standards (Table 4.1); and the unreliable statistics (Table 4.2); and the huge range of experiences and normalities reviewed by anthropologists and disclosed in memoirs of pornographers, prostitutes, and addicts, including treatises on vaginas or BDSM or incest—all this makes the sociology of sex absolutely fascinating.

Section 2—The Erogenous Zones

Introduction

Erogenous zones sound so sexy, almost naughty: "Access limited. Identification required. Private Property." The body, like the world, is divided into public and private parts, and semi-public ones, too.

Certainly all the parts of the body are potentially erogenous zones, from the hair on the head and the back of the neck to the eyes and lips and toes; but, with limited space, we will only linger on some of our most private parts: breasts, vaginas, penises, buttocks and, while we are there, the anus, not forgetting our skin, which keeps us all together as well as it can.

These erogenous zones are not only sexy sites, pleasure palaces; they are also sites of love and loving. And one of the most lyrical poems or songs of sexy loving and loving sex is "The Song of Songs" attributed to King Solomon in about 800 BCE; but it is a duet between two lovers, perhaps the King and the Queen of Sheba. It is erotic, praising so many parts of their bodies, so long ago; not much changes, except the similes. Here the woman loves her man:

> My beloved is white and ruddy, the chiefest among ten thousand. His head is as the most fine gold, his locks are bushy, and black as a raven. His eyes are as the eyes of doves by the rivers of waters, washed with waters and fitly set. His cheeks are as a bed of spices, as sweet flowers: his lips like lilies, dropping sweet-smelling myrrh. His hands are as gold rings set with beryl: his belly is as bright ivory overlaid with sapphires. His legs are as pillars of marble, set upon sockets of fine gold: his countenance is as Lebanon, excellent as the cedars. His mouth is most sweet: yea, he is altogether lovely. (5:10-16)

So every part and organ of the body is, or may be, an erogenous and erotic zone. Curiously, the Latin term for the sexiest bits, the genitals, is *pudenda*—things to be ashamed of. This term does indicate the historical roots of the widespread ambivalence to the genitals in the post-Roman and post-Christian culture. These attitudes have changed very rapidly, however, since the marketing of the pill and the sexual revolution in the sixties, although misogyny and misandry are still problematic in many parts of the world, and sex-negative and body-negative attitudes are not uncommon, as we shall see. Yet today, many believe that North Americans, particularly, are sex- and body-obsessed, to the degree that some say is problematic. On the positive side, the genitals are now more likely to be known as *Amanda*—things to be loved.

Everywhere in the world people decorate and even mutilate their bodies to beautify themselves, for beauty is erotic. Who and what are considered beautiful or handsome is almost infinitely variable: culturally relative, personally subjective and historically contingent. "Beauty is in the eye of the beholder," we say, which is true, but it is also in the culture of the beholder. Darwin was one of the first to develop this insight, with a long discussion on beautification techniques from around the world. Beauty, he argued, is an aphrodisiac and influences the "marriages" of mankind. "In civilized life man is largely, but by no means exclusively, influenced in the choice of his wife by external appearances." Likewise, he suggests, for "savages" (1981, part 2, chapter 19), but offers no observations about women.

The lotus was much beloved in China of old. The Golden Lotus was a foot and three inches long, with many broken bones (Ping, 2000; Levy, 1966). The Padaung, or Karen people of Myanmar, esteem the elongated neck, encircled by brass rings (Keshishian, 1979). In North America, the graceful swan neck of Audrey Hepburn was much admired, but Norah Ephron hated her neck—perhaps forgetting for the moment that one really cannot manage very well without it. She had a long list of types of neck; she was an aficionado of necks, as the Chinese were of the lotus: They include chicken, turkey, gobbler and elephant necks, with wattles or creases, and scrawny necks—fat, loose, crepey, banded, wrinkled, stringy, saggy, flabby and mottled necks. She was quite eloquent on the topic of necks. "The neck is a dead give-away. Our faces are lies and our necks are the truth" (2006:5).

Not much appreciation here, unless you love the painful truth. But contrast that with Wang Ping's comment on the lotus, that the feet became the face and emblematic of a woman's "gender, sex, beauty and class" (2000:226)—regardless of neck.

Anthropologists and photographers have excelled in illustrating the modes and meanings of body decoration and body modification. Certainly not all are intended to maximize personal allure or sex appeal. Some are to conform to cultural norms or religious beliefs, some to illustrate status or changes in status, some to be the same, others to be different or just for fun. Nonetheless, all that body painting, cicatrization, tattooing, branding, and piercing of just about anything that can be pierced; the cosmetic surgeries to augment breasts or penises; the muscularization and bulking-up of men and the slimming and dieting of women. Much of it does enhance masculinity or femininity over various times and places. The Maori Moko—deep incisions in the face in symmetrical patterns that are then inked-in with charcoal—contributed to the ferocious look of the warriors. The amputation of women's fingers in parts of New Guinea witnessed her loves when family members died: The loss of fingers symbolized her losses. Head deformation in various cultures identifies "us" and distinguishes "us" from "them"—as does circumcision, which may also mark entry into manhood, just as in some Australian aboriginal tribes the sub-incision marked the rite of passage from warrior to elder (Brain, 1979; Ebin, 1979; Virel, 1980).

Not that all this bodywork, often involving so much pain, was always about Eros directly, but, rather, indirectly, often defining what it means to be a man or a woman. Aesthetics and erotics are deeply connected.

In any event, the entire body is, or may be, an erogenous zone, since it is so sensitive, though insofar as beauty affects erotics, this too will be contingent. But here, for reasons of brevity and priority, we will just discuss five zones: the private zones of the vagina and the penis, and the semi-private/semi-public areas of breasts, buttocks and skin.

Chapter 5
Vagina

"The Vagina Monologues" (Ensler, 1998) popularized the vagina. Soon everyone was talking about their vaginas on stage and off, to whoever was interested—which, it turned out, was lots of people.

But the title is curious. Surely the vagina is often in dialogue with the penis, especially, but also with tongues and fingers and vibrators and who knows what else? "The Vagina Dialogues" (plural) would have been a more appropriate and sexier title. But, still, if a vagina is wandering around her apartment talking to herself, I suppose the monologue will suffice. Yet, surely, vaginas want someone or something to talk to, and there must be plenty of prospective partners out there.

Despite the changing attitudes over the last 50 or so years, attitudes to the genitals are still at the center of a host of controversies about who can do what and with what and to whom—involving nudity, abortion, masturbation, contraception, prostitution, pre-marital sex, extra-marital sex, marital sex, pornography (in film, art, literature), the new reproductive technologies (think Octomom), clitoridectomies, circumcision, penectomies and labioplasties. Such issues all tend to be discussed separately, as if they were all in watertight compartments; but they do have a common denominator: the genitals.

The clitoris is the only organ in the human body whose sole function is pleasure. No doubt "she" also has much to say, though her monologue is not out yet. Still, while the physiological functions of both organs are quite amazing, perhaps equally amazing are the monologues and dialogues *about* them.

The history, anthropology and sexology of these two friends and neighbors include Freudian psychoanalysis, Kinsey's statistics, the physiology in Masters and Johnson, the feminism of Greer and others, and the survey data from *Psychology Today* and the Hite reports—as well as what the vaginas said in their monologues. But we will not be discussing female circumcision and clitoridectomies; that has been done by many others.

Most of us were conceived in vaginas and birthed through vaginas, with only a few conceived in Petri dishes and birthed by caesarians. Billions of people owe their lives to vaginas. It is clearly a remarkable organ. (How much of an understatement is that?) It is also extremely controversial and, over the centuries, especially in the West, it has been widely misunderstood.

The misunderstanding begins with the word vagina (Latin: sheath)—as if the vagina is simply the sheath for the male sword or dagger, the penis. The precious weaponry is male, and the scabbard only a protective, and passive, device. Ignorance and, perhaps, misogyny is invested in the name, which is so far from the truth.

The vagina was also understood as simply a passageway. Crudely put: semen in, babies out. Certainly other items might go in (fingers, vibrators etc.) and other items flow out (blood, placenta, etc.); but the primary biological function of the vagina was thought to be the passive receptacle for semen (Latin: seed). The male spread his seed—the old expression "sowed his wild oats" articulates this idea well—and the female provided the fertile soil, so to speak, in which the seed germinated over the nine-month gestation period. From Aristotle and Pythagoras to the eighteenth century, the male was the active principle, the superior, the sun, the right side, reason, the head, while the female was the passive principle, the inferior, the moon (perhaps also suggesting "lunatic," from lunar), the left side, emotions, and the heart. Binaries again—as opposite sexes—but also hierarchies, higher and lower (Needham, 1979; Synnott, 1993).

Today, the wonder of the vagina is better understood and more appreciated. Catherine Blackledge, who has written a book on the topic, is lyrical. She initially confesses her ambiguous feelings and her "limited viewpoint" about her own vagina: "It was about sex, about pleasure, about bleeding, about pissing. It could also, unfortunately, be about pain. And, in the future, perhaps, it would be about childbirth." But then she wondered about her emotions: Was her occasional blushing when saying the word reflective of shame or embarrassment? This would be reflective of normative Western attitudes to sex generally and to the vagina in particular; plus, she saw it as a sign of her inferior status, "not being treated as well as a vagina-less person . . . downgraded because of my cunt" (2003:1-2). An obvious point: so many of the words used to describe sex and the genitals are insulting, curses and negatively loaded: cunt, dickhead, prick, fucker, fuck, etc. Our vocabulary testifies to our attitudes to sex and the body.

And the concept of the "vagina-less person" is a remarkable redefinition of the male, not only because he is *lacking* what "we" have but, also, because it capsizes the traditional Aristotelian theory of male superiority as well as the Freudian theory of penis envy.

Blackledge praises "the sheer beauty and diversity in design" of all the female genitalia that she examines, from chimpanzees to fruit-flies, including rabbits, birds and bees.

She praises the power of vaginas, which "store sperm, eject sperm, they destroy sperm and they carefully and precisely select the most genetically compatible sperm for them with their amazing genitalia." The old idea of one tiny sperm swimming bravely upstream to penetrate the ovum like an arrow is a myth. She points out that human ejaculates can contain hundreds of millions of sperm, yet only one, usually, might get "lucky." So the reproductive tract is a "chemical and physical death-trap for sperm" (2003:109). This is not my favorite image.

The courtship antics of the male amazed her by their complexity, as they did Darwin earlier, when the various species try to hook up their sexual geographies, or not. And she was appalled by the failures of science to understand the vagina, and by the religious value system of the West, "with its attitude of the vagina as the gateway to hell, the source of all trouble and strife in the world, and the potential downfall of men." Fair enough. I discussed this matter of gender attitudes in an earlier book (1993), and here Blackledge is referring to the Christian theologian Tertullian (c. 160-230), the myth of Eve in "Genesis," and the story of Pandora's Box in Hesiod, among others.

In contrast, she valorizes the belief systems in India and China, which "taught that female genitalia were the symbolic origin of the world, the source of all new life and the route via which longevity and eternal life could be attained." Here the vagina is an icon to be worshipped: the "divine vagina." And these ideas are expressed in their art. Furthermore, they seem to have been understood in the Paleolithic age in Europe, as demonstrated by some cave art and such well-known figurines as the Venus of Willendorf (about 22,000 BCE). Her anthropological and historical research seem to demonstrate fairly conclusively that "the vagina is icon, sacred, inviolable and worshipped. The site and source from which all human life springs. The font of all new life. The origin of the world" (2003:39).

So the vagina is variously sheath, passage-way, insult, gateway to hell, death-trap, pleasure-palace, beautiful, intelligent, powerful, icon, divine: worshipped and the origin of the world.

The Vaginal Revolution

Blackledge (2003) refers to the "vaginal revolution" in our understanding and appreciation of the vagina. This, perhaps, began with Gustave Courbet's painting "The Origin of the World" (1866), infamous then but famous now, which views a woman's body from her thighs to her breasts and focuses on her pubic area, including pubic hair. But since the picture could not be publicly and permanently exhibited for almost 100 years—the pubis is private—it was, perhaps, not the beginning but, rather, the beginning of the beginning. Still, the picture demonstrated a huge leap from Tertullian's theory that women are the "gateway to hell" to Courbet's "Origin of the World."

This artistic tradition flowered with Georgia O'Keeffe's portraits of flowers, which are often said to be thinly veiled vaginas, though she always denied this. The times were not ripe. Then Judy Chicago's "The Dinner Party" (1974-9), honoring the achievements of women, included even more explicit representations of the genitals. By then the times had changed.

One of the so-called "Kinsey reports," *Sexual Behavior in the Human Female*, published in 1953, shot onto the best-seller lists and arguably revolutionized American thinking about female sexuality. Kinsey and his team interviewed almost 6,000 women, and their findings shocked Americans. Among them was the discovery that almost half of the women had lost their virginity before marriage and that 13 percent had had sex with six or more partners (compared to 85 percent of the men and almost 50 percent of the men, respectively, for these same activities). Even more shocking than the data on premarital sex was the data on female adultery: of the entire sample, 20 percent of the married women had committed adultery by the age of 35, but, among younger women, the numbers rose to 40 percent; the average for men was 50 percent. Particularly controversial was his finding that women who had had premarital sex were more likely to be more orgasmic than those who had not.

Women were far more sexual and sexually active than had been thought. And Kinsey was later credited—or blamed—for the sexual revolution of the sixties. Certainly his sampling methodology was criticized, and his own pro-sex interest was thought to bias his analysis; but Kinsey was a scientist with a doctorate from Harvard, and the cat was out of the bag. This was women's sexuality as it was, not as some people thought it should be.

Today's readers might not be so surprised, shocked or startled by Kinsey's findings about women; but expert thinking (male experts, that is) about women's sexuality 60 years before Kinsey was pretty unanimous that women either had no interest in sex or very little interest; they were, perhaps, more interested in love. Krafft-Ebing had affirmed decisively in 1896: "Woman, however, when physically and mentally normal and properly educated, has but little sensual desire." He echoed an English doctor in 1882: "Women have less sexual feeling than men . . . as a rule women have nothing of what is understood as sexual passion." And an American physician spoke in similar terms: "Only in very rare circumstances do women experience one tithe the sexual feeling which is familiar to most men. Many of them are entirely frigid" (Blackledge, 2003:262). On the contrary, Kinsey argued, the desire was there but repressed by societal norms and conventions. He helped to relieve the pressure.

Then, in 1953, that same year, to make things worse for puritans and conservatives, Hugh Hefner published the first issue of *Playboy*, featuring Marilyn Monroe—the archetypal sex symbol of the day—as the centerfold. By the end of the decade, *Playboy* was selling a million copies a month (Petersen, 1999:231).

The sex drives of both women and men were being energized. Yet neither Kinsey nor Ellis nor Krafft-Ebing had discussed the clitoris or the vagina. Freud did so, but he was not very nice. In his 1905 treatise "Three Essays in the Theory of Sexuality" and his later 1931 essay "Female Sexuality," Freud explained his views. He described the clitoris as "a mutilated organ," i.e., not a penis—hence women had what he called "penis envy." And although in childhood the girl may enjoy infantile masturbation, in adulthood she "has the task of giving up what was her leading genital zone—the clitoris—in favor of a new one—the vagina." Or, one might suspect today, she is lucky and keeps both zones. In adulthood (Freud waxes poetic) the clitoris still has a function: "The task, namely, of transmitting the excitation to the adjacent female sexual parts, just as—to use a simile—pine shavings can be kindled in order to set a log of harder wood on fire" (1977, Vol. 7: 195, 371, 143). In sum, for Freud, the clitoris is mutilated, must be given up in maturity for the vagina and is akin to pine shavings.

All that changed with the publication in 1966 of *Human Sexual Response* by William Masters and Virginia Johnson. This was the physiology of sex, pure, unadulterated and divorced from love. They devoted an entire chapter to the clitoris, arguing for its centrality for orgasm, denying Freud's two types theory, and insisting that "clitoral and vaginal orgasms are not separate biological entities" (1966:67).

Their research was experimental: They filmed women masturbating and having sex with an artificial penis—transparent, lit up and with a camera—and filmed the orgasms. The book was a best-seller, transformed understandings of women's sexuality and was widely condemned by some. Yet oral sex was mentioned only once (it was illegal in almost every state at the time), and love not at all.

Meanwhile, the FDA had approved the first female contraceptive, Enovid, in 1960. By the end of the decade, a million American women were on the pill; and by the end of the next decade, 10 million (Petersen, 1999:261).

With the pill and the clitoris, the gateways to heaven, not Tertullian's hell, were wide open. These were the precursors to the "Sexual Revolution," the plummeting fertility rate, the increased female participation rate in the economy and in higher education, the women's movement, and a massive shift in the balance of gender-power.

Neighbors

The vagina and the clitoris are neighbors, and they say that good fences make good neighbors. But there are no fences in that part of the world, so there is rivalry. Freud favored the vagina, Kinsey ignored both, and Masters and Johnson celebrated the clitoris. But, as always, things get complicated.

Germaine Greer argued in the classic *The Female Eunuch* that "The banishment of the fantasy of the vaginal orgasm is ultimately a good thing, but the substitution of the clitoral spasm for genuine gratification may turn out to be a disaster for sexuality." Why? Because "Real gratification is not enshrined in a tiny cluster of nerves but in the sexual enjoyment of the whole person." Then, "Sex becomes masturbation in the vagina." Furthermore this is "the substitution of genitality for sexuality" (1971:42-4). But still, and Greer can be quite blunt: "A clitoral orgasm with a full cunt is better than a clitoral orgasm with an empty one, as far as I can tell at least" (1971:307).

The speed of change in sexual attitudes and practice is remarkable: Greer's sex-positive enthusiasm is so far removed from Krafft-Ebing of only 75 years earlier. The vagina and the clitoris seem quite different entities when constructed so variously from Freudian couches, Kinsey's statistics, the physiology of Masters and Johnson and the feminism of Greer. But what do women actually say for themselves?

In the mid-seventies, Shere Hite surveyed women across the United States with the question: "Do you think your vagina and genital area are ugly or beautiful?" She was the first to ask women what they thought about these parts of their anatomy—a horrific gap in social science research. The responses are intriguing and vary considerably, as this small selection indicates (1987:364-7):

"They're interesting, delicate, and fascinating in design."
"Beautiful—fantastic—wonderful."
"They're ugly, like an unhealed wound."
"They just 'are'. I wish I were a man."
"They look ugly but feel beautiful."
"Plain, but with charisma."

Hite (1987:619; adapted) also quantified the responses to her question from her sample of 932 women.

Table 5.1: Do You Think Your Vagina and Genital Area Are Ugly or Beautiful

	N	Percent
Beautiful Fascinating	347	37
Ugly	144	15
Average, OK, Natural, Neutral	407	44
Varied, Mixed Feelings, Strange	34	4

According to her data, therefore, just over one-third of the women are happy with their genitals, while 15 percent are unhappy, and about half are somewhere in between, viewing them as average, neutral, mixed, varied, etc. This is, perhaps, not quite the enthusiastic response that one might have expected about the sexual center of the female universe.

Hite argues that a "concern with cleanliness and odour is part of the more general problem of accepting female genitalia"; and that "The fact that there is no 'iconography' of women's genitals, while penises are glorified, is a further reflection of the way sex mirrors the general cultural inequality between men and women." Furthermore, "Our culture is still a long way from understanding, not to mention celebrating, female sexuality" (1987:364,379).

Yet her questions about masturbation, clitoral stimulation and orgasm evoked extremely enthusiastic responses from the women surveyed: no "problem of accepting female genitalia" there, it would seem. They apparently had no problems "celebrating female sexuality" either. So there is some contradiction between the responses to her questions and her analysis of these responses.

A survey conducted in the U.S. a few years earlier found that men were *more* dissatisfied than women with their genitals: only three percent of women were dissatisfied with the size of their genitals compared to 15 percent of the men; and only seven percent of the women were dissatisfied with the appearance compared to nine percent of the men (Berscheid, Walster and Bohrnstedt, 1973). By the criterion of these data, there is a more general problem of men accepting their male genitalia and most women were satisfied: a clear contradiction of Hite.

The wide range of women's opinions about their genitals is mirrored in the wide range of their attitudes towards men's genitals (Hite,1987:371-5). It seems probable that a few women have problems with sex and genitals generally, but most do not.

Men's attitudes to the clitoris and to women's genitals generally are also varied. Over 7,000 men responded to Hite's questionnaire on male sexuality, in which she asked two questions of relevance: "How do you feel about the clitoris?" and "How do women's genitals look?" It is unfortunate that she asked much more narrowly focused questions in her surveys to women, since, ironically, as a result we know more about the range and depth (or shallowness) of men's attitudes to the clitoris and to women's genitals than we do about women's attitudes.

Answers and attitudes varied from individual to individual, from the accepting to the rejecting to the hostile to the jocose to the ignorant to the gross to the sensitive. No doubt it is as interesting for women as well as men to know the range of responses; but apparently most men said they had never actually seen a clitoris—the lights were off, their lovers never showed them, etc. Some did not know about it: "I could never find my wife's. She doesn't seem to have one." One man said: "I have no feelings about it. She shouldn't have one." Others were neutral: "It is just a part of her that I caress now and then, but nothing to rave over." "What do I think about it? Nothing really."

Some were extremely enthusiastic: "It amazes me. It's the centre of my wife's entire sexual being. Every square micron must be packed with nerve endings because of her reaction when I touch it or even get near it." "I like to suck her, lick it, kiss it, talk to it, and she thinks I do a super job in it all." "It is the primary erotic centre of her body, tender and sensitive, and has to be treated with great care and emotion." (1981:658-63)

Men's feelings about women's genitals were equally varied, and there are too many to cite fully. Again, some men had not been able to look carefully: "I find that most girls are very much embarrassed if you examine them too much in the genital area." Some emphatically disliked them: too awful to quote. Most, by my estimate since the numerical data are not given, love them:

"I love my wife's genitals. They look big, pink, wet, warm, ready for fun, ready to respond to me, mysterious, powerful, something to explore. Wow!"

"I think women's genitals are about as lovely as something on this earth can get. I love the way they taste and smell. There have been some genitals about which I held a near-religious feeling; this was because they were attached to women for whom I felt a deep love." (1981:693-7)

Shere Hite was the first to ask these sorts of questions of women, and men; and the first to bring these private parts into the public eye, so to speak. And in so doing, she has contributed to the celebration of female and male sexuality.

One conspicuous exception to the general trend of silence is Natalie Augier's *Woman*, which has a chapter on the clitoris that is enigmatically entitled "The Well-Tempered Clavier." The Pulitzer Prize-winning author briskly dismisses penis envy, and penises: "Who would want a shotgun when you can have a semiautomatic?" (1999:58). Well, it depends what you want to kill! But it's an odd question, since both organs are usually more about birth and love than death and hate; and, anyway, shotguns have magazines, too. But apart from that slapshot at the penis, Augier is ecstatic about the clitoris: it's "a goddess," "Our Lady of Perpetual Ecstasy," "a private joke, a divine secret, a Pandora's box packed not with sorrow but with laughter," the nerve center of 8,000 fibers, a magic button, "a taut little baton, leading the way, cajoling here, quickening there, andante, allegro, crescendo, refrain." Encore! And "a woman's trick birthday candle, the one that keeps popping back no matter how hard you blow" (1999:58-72). The clitoris is surely a flexible reality: goddess, joke, secret, box, nerve center, button, baton and trick candle . . . any additions to the litany? Oh, yeah: semiautomatic.

*

Vaginas, like the clitoris, are also finally beginning to receive the public attention that they deserve. Augier is as delighted with vaginas as she is with clitorises. She makes her usual derogatory remarks about the penis: "A hose is a hose is a hose." This might evoke giggles, perhaps. And a hole is a hole is a hole, since she initiates this sort of debate. But after this old-style misandric sexist ritual to demonstrate her feminist credentials, she improves: "But the vagina, now there's a Rorschach with legs." She describes the vaginal stretching during child delivery: "The vagina is a balloon, a turtleneck sweater, a model for the universe itself, which, after all, is expanding in all directions even as we sit here and weep." It is also "sometimes thought of as a toothed organ, by analogy with the mouth: a hungry, sucking, masticating, devouring orifice, capable of depleting a man's resources fatally if he gives in to its allure too often." Here we touch on the notion of the devouring wife and metaphorical castration. "Or the vagina is the moist, soothing, kissing mouth"—a far more positive metaphor. She continues: The vagina can be "hands pressed together in prayer," and since it opens and closes, "it gives rise to the imagery of flowering, of bursting open: lotuses, lilies, leaves, split pecans, split avocadoes, the wings of a damselfly" (1999: 47-8). Lyrical stuff—the poetic equivalent of Judy Chicago and Georgia O'Keeffe.

And then there is the theater. Vaginas are "in" now, playing center stage at theaters around the world, thanks to Eve Ensler's hugely popular vignettes in "The Vagina Monologues" (1998). She interviewed over 200 women about their vaginas and the results are funny, wise, poignant, sad, glorious . . . the whole spectrum of life. The basic themes are that women should be able to say the word vagina without "shame and embarrassment," recognize the beauty and centrality of the vagina in women's lives and in life, and that women should love their vaginas and themselves. Also, there is a downside: "I say 'vagina' because I have read the statistics, and bad things are happening to women's vaginas everywhere: 500,000 women are raped every year in the United States; 100 million have been genitally mutilated worldwide." In sum, "Here's the place to release the myths, shame and fear. Here's the place to practice saying the word, because, as we know, the word is what propels us and sets us free. 'VAGINA'" (1998: xxii-xxv).

So this is a consciousness-raising and liberation exercise. But "shame and embarrassment" are the characteristic emotions? Really? Not according to the survey data from Hite and Berschied, which we have just reviewed. And to imply that only "bad things are happening" is just unconscionable.

She begins lightly with a long list of women's pet names for their vaginas, including pussy, pooki, twat, powderbox, dignity, coochi-snorcher, mongo, Gladys Siegelman, Connie, Mimi and more. She asks amusing questions: "If your vagina got dressed, what would it wear?" Answers include emeralds, a pink boa, and see-through black underwear. "If your vagina could talk, what would it say, in two words?" Answers include slow down, more, more, and yeah, yeah. "What does a vagina smell like?" Earth, God, a brand-new morning . . .

Then there are monologues on menstruation, masturbating to orgasm with Betty Dodson, rape (statistics above), clitoridectomy (inflicted on 80-100 million young women and girls, and last practiced in the U.S. in 1948), a panegyric on reclaiming the word cunt, an amusing prose poem on lesbian moaning, and a lyrical poem on her daughter-in-law giving birth. This is the only poem to the vagina I have read.

Certainly there is more to the vagina than the uninitiated might imagine; indeed this entire piece on a taboo site is important as removing the veil. Nonetheless, her pro-vagina monologue is seriously flawed by her anti-male bias. Her assertion that half a million women are raped every year in the U.S. is not substantiated by any data, and is contradicted by the Bureau of Justice Statistics (BJS). All the rape statistics are difficult for many reasons—the nature of consent, different state laws, alcohol consumption (hence diffused responsibility and awareness), non-reporting, and so on. Not least is the BJS conflation of rape and sexual assault. The good news is that reported rapes and sexual assaults have declined from 898,239 in 1993 to 300,165 in 2013. The bad news is that Ensler's conflation of rape and sexual assault camouflages the smaller (but under-reported) number of rapes. Assaults are far more common, and they include harassment, words, pats on the butt, i.e., not wanted but not violent either (Bureau of Justice Statistics, 2014). In addition, the rape data exclude rapes of men which, when prison rapes are included (which they are often not) outnumber female rapes (See Wikipedia "Rape Statistics," which I accessed 11 October 2015). No doubt the real number of rapes is higher than the recorded number, since some are not reported; but half a million seems like fear-mongering, moral panic and misandry. It is victim feminism—neither positive nor realistic. Why half a million? Why not three or six or 30 million? Second, while there is plenty about rape, clitoridectomy, masturbation, menstruation, birth and lesbian sex, there is nothing in the "Monologues" directly about heterosexual sex (except rape) or about love, which is a bit of an omission and reflects her bias and prejudice.

In light of this, may I offer my own contribution to what is often a dialogue not a monologue: "What does the vagina say to the penis?" Answers: "Hi! Welcome back!" "Oh, no! Not you again." "Dr. Livingstone, I presume." "No glovee, no lovee." "Not tonight, dear, I have a headache" (but I'm very good for headaches.) "Go away!" "Darling, the ceiling needs painting." "Have you finished yet?" "Come again soon, y'hear?" "What are you smiling at?" "Kiss me, you fool."

A digression: Be careful whom you kiss and where. A Brazilian woman recently attempted to murder her husband by inserting poison into her vagina and asking him to kiss her there. She did not realize how porous her vagina was. He refused but, instead, took his beloved attempted murderer to the hospital and saved her life. The reporter commented: "And they said chivalry is dead!" (McDonough, 2013).

Designer Vaginas

The hottest new sex surgeries are female genital reconstructions. Aesthetic surgery has moved far beyond the well-explored terrain of nose-jobs, liposuctions and face lifts, to include the more intimate zones of the body: the remodelling and "sexual enhancement" of the labia and the vagina.

Labiaplasties may be performed for practical and for aesthetic reasons. Some complain that their labia are too large or uncomfortable when they walk or cycle, or too painful when they have sexual intercourse. One woman explained that "My labia were so long that they showed through my clothes!" For such women, labiaplasties can bring relief. One woman told an interviewer: "This operation has changed my sexuality, my marriage and my life. I'd do it again in a heartbeat" (Havranek, 1998:146, 148).

Other women are simply not happy with the way things look and want the lips "tidied up," made more symmetrical or regular—beautified. Although most readers polled by *Cosmopolitan* said that their lips were "just right," some expressed concern or even—a new post-Freudian phrase—"labia envy." "I've always felt my outer lips are too big, and it makes me self-conscious, though I've never had a lover complain." Another seemed envious: "When I watch porn videos with my boyfriend, I do get a little freaked out by how large many of the stars' labia and clitorises are. My inner lips and clitoris are practically invisible. But when I share my insecurities with my guy, he always reassures me that he loves my 'teenie flower'" (Havranek, 1998:148).

Cosmopolitan even polled some men in their twenties on the topic: "Does he think you're a labia loser?" Again, not a usual topic for a family discussion around the dinner table. Some of their responses: "I can't say I recall ever seeing a vagina that turned me off." "I would guess that few men know an inner labia from an outer labia from a chaise longue. So I don't think men are bothered by labia of different lengths." "Trust me, if a man is close enough to see the fine details of your labia, the last thing he's likely to do is complain. Men expect each woman's genitals to be different, and it would be pretty boring if they all started looking the same thanks to cosmetic surgery" (Havranek, 1998:150).

The aesthetics of the labia—their size, shape and normalcy—are now beginning to receive the same sort of critical attention that the face has been receiving for so long. In a competitive age, both sexes have surely enough problems developing a positive body image without adding normative aesthetic standards to a hitherto relatively uncriticized zone of the body. Nonetheless, it does seem that even women's pubic parts are now not only going public but are also under the knife.

Vaginal surgeries are advertised as "empowerment" and as "rejuvenation." Since the diameter of the vaginal canal expands with aging and childbirth, some women request an extra suture or two in the vaginal wall muscles to tighten the circumference of the vagina and to enhance, allegedly, their own and, perhaps, their partners' sexual pleasure. There are other ways to improve vaginal muscle function, notably the Kegel exercises; nonetheless, this procedure is an alternative. The procedure may also be performed to remedy a condition of uterine prolapse. This may result in incontinence or in difficulty achieving orgasm. In such conditions, vaginal surgery, tightening the pubococcygeal or PC muscles, may improve this condition (Havranek, 1998:148, 150). Still, labioplasty is an increasingly popular surgery: up 49 percent from 2013 to 2014, according to the American Society for Aesthetic Plastic Surgery.

These procedures are, of course, controversial for many reasons. A psychologist commented that: "[Women's] insecurities are fueled by the very advertisements that prescribe a homogenized, prepubescent genital appearance standard for all women." She argues that such advertisements are totally unethical. A gynecologist pointed out that such surgeries may exacerbate sexual problems rather than resolve them. Little is known about the satisfaction rates after surgery, and any surgery carries risks. Some suggest that any pain caused by protrusion is more likely psychological rather than physical in origin; and they add that men protrude even further without any apparent problems, and that few if any men request penis reduction surgery. As with penile surgery, one suspects that the problem is usually between the ears rather than between the legs.

The Clitoris

With virtuoso performances at Judy Chicago's "Dinner Party," in Georgia O'Keeffe's artwork, in the monologues on international stages, in sexologists' surveys, and on operating tables, the female genitals are now public. But it has not always been so.

The clitoris, in particular, has had a mysterious history. Historians debate it and contemporaries wonder! The historian Thomas Laqueur declared that the clitoris was "discovered" by Renaldo Columbus of Padua in 1559—not long after his namesake, but no relation, discovered America (1990:64).

Recently, another historian, Katharine Park, has argued that the clitoris was, in fact, discovered (or rediscovered) by Charles Estienne of Paris in 1545. He described it as "a little tongue" (*languette*) and as part of a woman's "shameful member" (*membre honteux*), but he believed that it was connected to the urinary function. Contemporaries, however, credited the discovery to Gabriele Falloppia—he of the tubes fame—in 1550, who stated emphatically: "Modern anatomists have entirely neglected it, and do not say a word about it . . . And if others have spoken of it, know that they have taken it from me or my students" (Park, 1997:176-7).

Columbus, also known as Colombo, may not have discovered the clitoris, but he was acknowledged as the first to recognize the prime role of the clitoris in female sexual satisfaction: "It is the principal seat of women's enjoyment in intercourse so that if you not only rub it with your penis, but even touch it with your little finger, the pleasure causes their seed to flow forth in all directions, swifter than the wind, even if they don't want it to" (Park, 1997:177).

It seems likely that he was able to integrate his knowledge from the bedroom with that from the dissecting room. Colombo's story has been told in the historical novel, *The Anatomist* by Frederico Andahazi (1998). Interesting that the rise of science and scientific debate, one of the glories of the Renaissance, coincided with the witch hunts and the burning of Giordano Bruno at the stake in 1600. Glorious but brutal.

The debate was hot. Andreas Vesalius, the leading anatomist of his day, emphatically rejected this geographical discovery: "I have never once seen in any woman a penis . . . or even the rudiments of a tiny phallus" (Park, 1997:177).

The debate about who discovered what, and when, and what its function was is no doubt fascinating; but also interesting is the mystery of where the clitoris had disappeared to. It had been known to the ancients, the historians believe; and, apparently, orgasms were understood. Laqueur and Park seem to think that the mystery is due to a number of factors. First, the Dark Ages contributed to the massive destruction of knowledge in Europe. Indeed, according to Thomas Cahill (1996), it was the Irish alone who saved Western civilization. Second, the profusion and confusion of namings for the various parts of the anatomy in Latin, Greek and Arabic made it extremely difficult to determine exactly what was being discussed. And third, it was not until the dissection of human bodies was permitted by church and state in the sixteenth century that it was possible for physicians to dissect human cadavers. Indeed, it was Vesalius himself who revolutionized the science of biology, introduced dissection into medical schools and authored and illustrated the first textbook on human anatomy, in 1543. Galen (ca 129-99 AD) had founded experimental physiology with his work on wounded gladiators and animals, often monkeys, and his successes had ensured his admission to the court of the Emperor and Stoic philosopher Marcus Aurelius; but the limits of his methodologies became clear to Vesalius — nearly 14 centuries later!

Laqueur has also suggested that the ancient physicians privileged the male body with iconic status and were less concerned with the female body; also, quite apart from the language problems mentioned earlier, the ancients may not have had quite the same fascination with naming as did the early modern anatomists (1990:34-5).

Galen, the most distinguished physician since Hippocrates, the father of medicine, systematized contemporary medical knowledge, and his authority remained unchallenged until the sixteenth century. As a practitioner of dissection, but only on animals, he developed what might be called the inside-out theory of the genitals. He suggested the following (imaginary) experiment: "Turn outward the woman's [genital organs], turn inward, so to speak, and fold double the man's and you will find the same in both in every respect" (Laqueur, 1990:25).

The two anatomies are opposite, fit together, and match: the penis and the vagina, the scrotum and the labia, the ovaries and the testicles. This theory, or description, seems plausible; it fitted the practice of sexual intercourse.

Unfortunately, Galen was apparently unaware of the clitoris; and the new anatomists of the sixteenth century "discovered" the clitoris—a penis equivalent, as it seemed. This not only upset the traditional anatomies of gender, but it also capsized the traditional Aristotelian theory of gender, which Laqueur has described as the "one sex" model. Ultimately, the discovery also raised concerns about female sexuality, lesbianism and hermaphrodites. The implications of Colombo's discovery (or Estienne's or Falloppia's) were, therefore, immense.

The prevailing theory of gender among the ancients was propounded by Aristotle, that the adult male is paradigmatic of humanity. In a now notorious passage (737) in his *Generation of Animals*, he explained that "the female is, as it were, a mutilated male" (1984:1144)—also translated as an "impotent" or "imperfect" male. This definition has political and social implications, as Aristotle explained: "The male is by nature superior and the female inferior; and the one rules and the other is ruled; this principle, of necessity, applies to all mankind" (*Politics*, 1254; 1984:1990). Women, as adults, were, in turn, superior to children and, as free citizens, were superior to slaves, in a clean and clear vertical hierarchy of genders, age and status.

This Aristotelian teaching was congruent with the Judeo-Christian teaching in the book of "Genesis," just as the Pandora myth in Hesiod was congruent with the Eve story in "Genesis." Both traditions were integrated in the letters of Paul and, later still, consolidated by Thomas Aquinas (1225-74) in his *Summa Theologiae*, as the official doctrine of Christianity, at least until the Reformation.

This Aristotelianism was all speculative philosophy, however. In fact, many women exercised immense power: political, military, economic, spiritual or social. Reality frequently negated the theory, as reality so often does. Powerful women—including, among many others, Boadicea, Messalina, Eleanor of Aquitaine, Isabella of Spain, Queen Elizabeth I of England, abbesses galore, empresses, queens—lived well, or ill, despite Aristotle. No male was idiot enough to insult Elizabeth I, saying that she was only "an impotent male." The Red Queen would simply have screamed "Off with his head!"

Again, the literary works of the Renaissance and the early modern era, including writers like Rabelais, Cervantes, Castiglione and Shakespeare, confirm that gender realities did not conform to the theory.

All this seems to take us far afield from the clitoris. Yet this context of Greek philosophy, Christian theology, medicine, literature and history indicates that the discovery of the clitoris was, one might say, as momentous as the discovery of the New World. The gendered world, like the European world, was never quite the same again.

The debates at the time were hot and furious. There was the question of whether it existed or not. Estienne, Colombo and Falloppia said it did; Vesalius said it did not, except perhaps in hermaphrodites. This debate was resolved eventually, as we know, by trial and error, scientific method and, no doubt, hands-on research. Then there was the question of what it did. Estienne believed that it was associated with urination, probably because of its proximity to the urethra; Colombo related it to sex (Park, 1997:177).

The case of Marie le Marcis in 1601 illustrates many of these issues in human terms. Condemned to death for sodomy with another woman, she claimed to be a man with a hidden penis. Two medical commissions denied her claim, but on the third commission, one Jacques Duval, a surgeon from Rouen, found her to be a predominantly male hermaphrodite. Marie was spared to become Marin and to grow a beard. A professor of anatomy at the University of Paris, Jean Riolan, disagreed, arguing that the alleged penis was a prolapsed uterus. The disagreement, however, was not only anatomical, it was also philosophical, political and social.

Duval followed the "new" Hippocratic-Galenic tradition of gender, which recognized hermaphrodites as a third, intermediate, sex; Riolan followed Aristotle's binary, exclusivist model: Everyone is one or the other. Duval was a provincial, writing in French, pitted against the elitist Riolan, writing in Latin. And whereas Aristotle believed that women were mutilated/impotent/imperfect males, depending on the translation, Duval did not. He praised the uterus as "a lovable temple, august, holy, venerable and wonderful" (a major contrast to the Aristotelian view of the uterus as the source of female "hysteria"); and against Aristotle, again, he insisted: "Woman is not a failed male or imperfect animal, as maintained by Aristotle, who did not realize that she was formed by God the Creator, who makes nothing that is not whole and perfect" (Park, 1997:179-82).

Despite all this thinking and writing about the vagina and the clitoris in so many disciplines, they still do not seem to be well understood. Naomi Wolf (2012) has emphasized the genital-brain connections, the neurology and biochemistry of orgasms and the role of opioids; Robert King (2013) comments on the differential emphasis in medical texts on the clitoris, as internal or external. The external is well-known, but the internal? He quotes a physiologist who told him that the clitoris is an "iceberg organ, 7/8ths of it is always hidden." It is "not a tiny vestigial penis," as was believed for so long, but it is "larger than an (unerect) penis and a complex organ with 18 interacting parts, which in turn link to the brain's somatosensory cortex, which is (as we saw earlier) is in many respects different from that of males." All of which is to suggest that the relations between the genitals, orgasm, desire and the brain may well be much more complicated than has hitherto been imagined.

A Digression: Hermaphroditus

The Greeks had recognized hermaphrodites, at least in mythology; but whether they were recognized in law and practice is not clear. According to the legend told by Ovid, Hermaphroditus was the beautiful son of Hermes (Latin: Mercury) a son of Zeus and Aphrodite, the goddess of love (Latin: Venus). In his travels, the young man came to "a pool, a limpid shining pool," where dwelt a water-sprite named Salmacis. She "chanced to see / the boy and seeing, saw her heart's desire." She propositioned him gracefully, and requested directly "make me your bride!" The poor lad was desperately embarrassed:

A rosy blush
Dyed the boy's cheeks; he knew not what love was;
But blushes well became him; like the bloom
Of rosy apples hanging in the sun,
Or painted ivory, or when the moon
Glows red beneath her pallor . . .

Rejected, Salmacis yielded the pool and left, or pretended to. Hermaphraditus

Strolled to and fro and in the rippling water
Dipped first his toes, then ankle deep, and soon,
Charmed by the soothing coolness of the pool,
Stripped his light garments from his slender limbs.
Then Salmacis gazed spellbound, and desire
Flamed for his naked beauty and her eyes
Blazed bright as when the sun's unclouded orb
Shines dazzling in a mirror.

To cut a short lyric even shorter, the boy swam into the pool, Salmacis swam after him, caught him, entwined herself around him "like a snake" or "ivy wrapping round tall forest trees," and clung on, praying "Ye Gods ordain/No day shall ever dawn to part us twain!"

The gods heard her prayer and "They two were two no more, nor man, nor woman—One body then that neither seemed and both."

Ovid's tale is still poignant and poetic (Book 4:285-388; 1988:83-5), about a sort of magical sex, as the two merge and blend into one; but it has a fresh resonance in a post-modern age of gender-bending, bisexuality, transexuality, intersexuality and gender-denial, not to mention water-spritely assertiveness . . . which excuses the digression.

Orgasms

"An orgasm a day keeps the doctor away." This was the assertion of a recent British health pamphlet for high school students (Martin, 2009). Not surprisingly, many parents objected, fearing epidemics of STIs and more unwanted pregnancies, as well as rejecting the seeming insistence on the physical and recreational rather than the emotional and relational aspects of sex. Whether the students objected too is not recorded but, perhaps, for once teenagers might have agreed with the health authorities, or at least were willing to give it a try.

Still, the pamphlet does indicate a sex-positive valence, even a humorous attitude, but, perhaps, also an instrumental attitude: just a hint of commodification. The subtext might be "Save the National Health money: keep coming!" It's hard to tell, but the pamphlet implied that sex is more about good health than healthy relationships and personal happiness.

Orgasms have become extremely complicated and controversial recently, especially for women. Do women have one type of orgasm or two? If two, how are they different? Which is better? Which do women prefer? Do all women have a G-spot? Have they all found it? And what about female ejaculation? And on the matter of single and multiple orgasms, are some women just luckier than others, or are there some techniques or attitudes that can be taught and learned? Do Kegels help? That's apparently an easy question: The "sexperts" all say yes. So there is hope.

The first problem is location, location, location. In his *Three Essays on The Theory of Sexuality* (1905), Freud distinguished between clitoral and vaginal orgasms, and suggested that a woman transfers her "erotogenic susceptibility to stimulation" from the clitoris to the vagina as her "new leading zone" as she matures (Vol. 7, 1977:143-4).

Masters and Johnson totally contradicted this, addressing the following question: "Are clitoral and vaginal orgasms truly separate anatomic entities? From a biologic point of view, the answer to this question is an unequivocal No." They added that three subjects had orgasms responding to breast stimulation, "as well as to coital, clitoral-body, or mons area manipulation" (1966:66,67). This was definitive and scientific, it seemed, based on interviews and observations of hundreds of women, including 382 who were filmed having sex with an artificial penis: The camera was inside the penis. As Peterson put it: "Forget penis envy. The clitoris . . . was the only organ in the human body whose sole function was pleasure. Women had one. Men didn't" (1999:280).

Orgasms and the genitals were politicized further. In 1968 the second wave of the women's movement protested the Miss America Beauty Pageant in Atlantic city; and soon afterwards, in *The Myth of the Vaginal Orgasm* (1970), Anne Koedt escalated the protest from the city to the bedroom. Following Masters and Johnson she argued that all orgasms are clitoral.

All this leads to some interesting questions about conventional sex and our role in it. Men have orgasms essentially by friction with the vagina, not the clitoral area, which is external and not able to cause friction the way penetration does. Women have thus been defined sexually in terms of what pleases men; our own biology has not been properly analyzed. Instead we are fed the myth of the liberated woman and her vaginal orgasm—an orgasm which does not in fact exist. (www.cwluherstory.org)

She added that "It seems clear to me that men in fact fear the clitoris as a threat to masculinity." And she concluded: "The recognition of clitoral orgasm as fact would threaten the heterosexual *institution* . . . It would thus open up the whole question of *human* sexual relationships beyond the confines of the present male-female role system."

Susan Lydon echoed this reevaluation of orgasms in her essay "The Politics of Orgasm," criticizing, again, Freud's theory while emphasizing the findings of Masters and Johnson, but drawing out the politics. "The mythology [Freudian] remains intact because a male-dominated American culture has a vested interest in its continuance." Again: "The definition of normal feminine sexuality as vaginal, in other words, was a part of keeping women down, of making them sexually, as well as economically, socially and politically subservient." And, in believing in the myth of the vaginal orgasm, "the sad thing for women is that they have participated in the destruction of their own eroticism" (1970:200-4).

The irony, or the paradox, regarding this three-cornered argument about the mythology and politics of orgasms, was that the pill was now being marketed widely, taking everyone's concerns about pregnancy off the table, and Alex Comfort was writing *The Joy of Sex* (1972), countering the anger about vaginal orgasms as oppressing women. Who knew the debates could get so hot? And in the 1980s the G-spot ignited the debates all over again. Perhaps there are three zones.

Viagra was approved by the FDA in 2000. It works for most men most of the time, and by 2013 sales in the U.S. alone were over one billion dollars, with Cialis not far behind (www.drugs.com, accessed 11 October 2015). This expenditure testifies to men's and, perhaps, women's interest in sex, orgasm, pleasure and love, as it was more than the GDP of many nations (including New Zealand, Nigeria and Pakistan); if invested in micro-credit aid, it would transform any number of economies and lives. As it stands, it only transforms sex lives. Male sexual dysfunction drugs now net $4 billion annually globally (*Time*, 22 June 2015).

One complication involves different sexualities. We all live in different sexual worlds, but men's sexuality is often described as like gas burners: When you turn them on, instant flame and heat. Women's sexuality is more like electric burners: They take a while to warm up. Kinsey was surprisingly unsympathetic about this, pointing out that about three-quarters of all men orgasm within two minutes after (delicately) "coital entrance," and many within 10 or 20 seconds; and that is about the same for many primates, notably chimpanzees. He blames adverse female conditioning for the discrepancy (1948: 580). So, he probably annoys women for blaming them and annoys men for comparing them to chimps. Other sexologists are more tactful.

Hence, a basic mismatch between Adam and Eve. You would think that God or evolution (or both) could have managed this biology a little better if they wanted us to get along. Sexual incompatibility is built into our sex worlds. Thanks a lot! But, looking on the bright side, so is sexual compatibility. Timing may be problematic but our various bodily bits and pieces do seem to fit quite snugly and happily into each other. So thanks a lot for that—yes, really!

Certainly the world is overflowing with information about sex and orgasms: how to get them, more of them, better ones, longer ones and so on. Television talk shows, sex therapists, sexologists, magazine articles, shelves of books in bookstores and libraries, and university courses all recommending positions, toys, techniques, communication, music, atmosphere—simple, and so good for you.

The television series "Sex and the City" raised sexual awareness to new levels, though it appealed mostly to women, I suspect. There is no equivalent for men. And Meg Ryan showed how to fake it in the film "When Harry met Sally." But for those having sex, there is the triumph of achieving simultaneous orgasms, and most recently the blended orgasm: clitoral and vaginal/G-spot orgasms at the same time. Techniques and positions are available in your local *Cosmo* or online for those peak sexual experiences.

Vaginal, clitoral, multiple, simultaneous, blended, mythical or political: Who knew orgasms could be so complicated? And then the sexperts announce the joys of spontaneous orgasm or psychic coitus—said to be more common among women than men—and delayed orgasm for both men and women. In this view, the goal of sex, especially for the man, is not to come but to not come; or, in multi-syllabic terminology, penetration without ejaculation. So, whereas the traditional ideal is that both partners come, however they like, and then relax, sleep or whatever, the new ideal is that the male delays his orgasm for as long as possible so that his partner can enjoy him as long as possible. So the man delays his ejaculation, perhaps till the next day or two, then the build-up of sexual tension is more intense and the orgasm more explosive. This is the difference between the A-bomb and the H-bomb or, in a less military metaphor, between peasant sex and royal sex.

The peasant male has only one partner to please. The King has a whole harem to please. He cannot just please the first concubine he sleeps with, since he also has to pleasure the next, and the next. Imagine that! So the King has to delay his orgasm as long as possible to please as many as possible until the end. Absent the harem, the same applies now to the peasants. The longer the female partner is ecstatic, the better.

July 31st is National Orgasm Day in the U.K. Who decided this? I don't know, but probably some corporate advertising executive with something to sell; still, it does seem that orgasms deserve a day to themselves. Anyway, to celebrate this day, *Scarlet* magazine and the makers of an interesting device have polled thousands of women, mostly in the U.K., about their sex lives, and specifically their orgasms. You can participate at http://www.orgasmsurvey.co.uk.

Their findings do not give much cause for celebration, unfortunately. On the other hand there are some grounds for optimism in what is called "pelvic floor toning." This does sound too much like choosing between linoleum, hardwood flooring or wall-to-wall carpeting, but it is actually about muscles. Some of the main findings are:

- 45 percent of the respondents say that they "never" or "rarely" achieve vaginal orgasms through penetrative sex, but 34 percent do so "often" or "always."
- 29 percent "never" achieve vaginal orgasm through self-stimulation, but 22 percent always do.
- 38 percent say that they "never" or "rarely" achieve clitoral orgasm through penetrative sex, but 37 percent do so "often" or "always."
- 79 percent achieve clitoral orgasm through self-stimulation "often" or "always" (61 percent); only 8 percent never do.

Four points are apparent from the above: the wide range of women's orgasmic capacity and style; the distinction between vaginal and clitoral orgasm (despite the assertions of Masters and Johnson); the higher success rate of clitoral self-stimulation; and the relatively lower success rate of penetration in generating orgasms.

The researchers note that sex gets better with age, but if you can't wait, the secret seems to lie with the PC (pubococcygeal) vaginal muscle and its muscle tone. Women who said that their pelvic floor was good or very good or who exercise regularly were twice as likely to achieve vaginal orgasm as those who rated their pelvic floor as poor or very poor. And most of them never or rarely achieved vaginal orgasms. The secret (or a secret) is to exercise the PC muscles.

Apparently aging, childbirth, lack of exercise and menopause not only weaken the muscle, and therefore reduce contact between the penis and the vagina, but also the neural pathways to the brain weaken and need to be rebuilt or woken up. The American sexologist, Pamela Stephenson-Connolly, has reiterated the old chestnut "use it or lose it," but with the additional horror of the phrase "vaginal atrophy" (2011).

The Kegel exercises were explicitly intended to improve PC muscle tone; and the Pelvic Toner, available in White, Pearl or Sparkly Red, is also intended to help. According to their website, 80 percent of users reported an improved sex life within four weeks (www.iwabo.co.uk). The acronym in the Internet address is "I want a better orgasm."

No doubt doing the exercises and using the Pelvic Toner will help women to orgasm, but I wish it were not called a toner. The most common complaint at my office is "I've run out of toner." Now my imagination will be running wild, from my friends' computers to their pelvic floors and their PC muscles. But I digress.

There is, I think, a hint of "blaming the victim" in this report, like it's all, or mostly, their fault for their weak PC muscles. But this is only one of many factors in the occasional (or regular) inability to achieve orgasm. Other factors include the use of anti-depressants, alcohol (and alcoholism), stress, and hormone imbalance (hence the sometimes recommended HRT). And these factors apply to men, who are vulnerable to erectile dysfunction (ED), as well as to women. We can "blame" these factors too. Plus, the *Hite Report* (1987) on women's sexuality recorded many women complaining about their partner's sexual ineptness or selfishness—inadequacy, anyway; and her report on male sexuality has many men complaining of women's lack of interest in sex. So there are plenty of explanations for women and men not orgasming.

But still, working those PC muscles, and perhaps trying the Pelvic Toner, should help, if you need help. Ellwood-Clayton has criticized the entire Feminine Dysfunction theory, but suggests tantric yoga, mindfulness and other techniques to help improve women's sexual lives (2012: 250-72).

Then again, we might wonder about the importance of being in love, of fantasies and some of the paraphilias in having orgasms. Clearly the physical is all tangled up with the psychological, the emotional and, also, the cultural.

*

Since the clitoris was (re) discovered medically in 1545 or 1550 or 1559, depending on the authority, it has moved from literary obscurity to center-stage with "The Vagina Monologues" and the publicity generated by Masters and Johnson, feminists, Shere Hite, Natalie Augier, Susanna Kaysen and others. The old debates have sparked new understandings of female sexuality, gender equality, homosexuality (both female and male), hermaphroditism and a questioning of the entire Greco-Christian tradition.

Arguably this was the beginning of modernity, developing chronologically from Columbus' "discovery" of America (1492); Machiavelli's *The Prince* (1517), which eulogized power over virtue; Luther's theses on spiritual autonomy (1519); Copernicus' assertion of a heliocentric universe (1543); Harvey's discovery of the circulation of blood (1628); Descartes' *Treatise* (1637) on rationality; the execution of King Charles I (1649); and Newton's law of gravity (1687).

Which of these has had the greater impact on human life and love and civilization? Was it the discovery of America, the love of power not virtue, the assertion of spiritual autonomy, the heliocentric universe, the circulation of blood, rationalism, constitutionalism, the law of gravity—or the anatomical "discovery" and understanding of the clitoris between 1545 and 1559, with all its sexual, social and political implications and consequences?

Chapter 6
Penis

An arm is only an arm but the penis has many names: a dick or a prick, a cock or a cod, a dong or a prong or a schlong, a peter or a pecker; the list goes on and is almost poetic, musical: a tool, a hammer, a shooter, a sausage or a wiener, a John Thomas or J. T., a middle leg, a third eye . . . the slang terms are legion. And many men have their own pet names for their penis, as if it were a separate individual with a will of its own—which it sometimes, arguably, is. Clarence Thomas' pet name for his penis, Long Dong Silver, has now passed into American mythology.

The penis is at the center of male sexuality and a fine accessory to much female sexuality as well. Some might cavil at that and say that the brain is the sexiest part of the body, which is true in the sense that it is brainwork, desire and lust that get the penis working, but the brain only thinks, while the penis . . . OK, you get the picture.

A constellation of "stars" surround this "sun," including sperm and urine, of course, but also, among many other things, potency and impotence, erections and (ED), STIs, circumcision, castration, phallus worship, Freud and phallic symbolism, D. H. Lawrence, Viagra, masturbation (see below), performance anxiety, fathering and the creation of life—as well as pleasure, fun, absolute delight and sometimes pain.

Why does the penis have so many names? And sometimes (like the vagina) its own individual name? Presumably because of its enormous biological, personal and social significance. The list is long (please excuse some repetition):

- A source of pleasure, probably the principal source for most men for most of their lives.
- The organ of creation of new life: a godlike attribute.
- The organ of urination, for the disposal of waste products. So the sacred and profane, the life-creation and the waste disposal systems, are united in the same organ: a triumph of engineering.
- A status symbol in any public shower or private bedroom.
- A religious symbol, as the practice of circumcision unites both Jews and Muslims.
- Potentially an organ of disease and death through STIs and HIV/AIDS.

• It is the defining characteristic of the male sex and masculine identity; hence the importance of size, appearance and performance. Notoriously it is man's best friend, with his dog, which is why they both have names.

The average length of the erect penis is about 6 inches, from the Kinsey study of 3,500 American men. A later study of men from 27 countries suggested 6.4 inches, but there seems to be no data on the vexed questions of nationality and color (Morris, 2009:194). Men tend to be somewhat insecure in the highly competitive game of comparison shopping, and are vulnerable to what is suggested in the cartoon portraying a woman peering at a man's equipment on their first bedroom encounter and exclaiming, "Oh, cute! A starter kit!"

To keep everything in proportion, the penis of the boar is 1.5 feet long, the stallion 2.5 feet, the bull 3 feet, the elephant 5 feet and the blue whale 8 feet (Walker, 1979:299-300). (Who did all this measuring and how? Was someone strolling by an elephant with an erection and just happened to have a tape measure?) The blue whale weighs about 150 tons and is about 110 feet long. So the million dollar question is: which is better endowed, the male human or the male blue whale? By my rough calculations for length, the ratio for the whale is 8: 110 = 1:13.8, and for the average 5'10" male is 6.25:70 = 1:11.2. Inch for inch, relatively, humans win. We are probably the best endowed males in the animal kingdom. Grounds for celebration, until you see a stallion and remember that it is all relative.

Penises appear in three different shapes: blunt, bottle-shaped (a shaft thicker than the head) and prow-shaped (curving upwards) (Morris, 2008:195). One caveat: we will not be discussing the two things that penises would be most terrified of, if they could be, namely circumcision and castration. This has been discussed by others (Gollaher, 2000; Taylor, 2000; Colapinto, 2000).

Attitudes

Men don't talk about the penis much. They think about it a lot, but they don't talk about it. Strange. No doubt it's too personal. Taboo. They don't even write about it. Many of the books on masculinity don't even mention it—including mine, actually (Synnott, 2009); I had to excise the chapter on sex, so added some more for this book. Yet this is the distinguishing factor of the male of the species. Very strange.

So, what to say about this marvelous instrument of nature, which dangles between men's legs with bells on? The best works on the penis I found were David Friedman's *A Mind of its Own* (2001), which is a cultural history, and Susan Bordo's *The Male Body* (1957), which is largely about the penis and male sexuality in the contemporary United States, and includes discussions on Viagra, Lolita, Clinton/Lewinsky, size and so on. Desmond Morris is excellent also in *The Naked Man* (2008), but shorter.

There is not much research on male attitudes to the penis. In one survey, 15 percent of the men were dissatisfied with the size of their penis and 9 percent with the appearance; but homosexuals were much more likely than heterosexuals to have a low (below average) evaluation of their penises (45 percent compared to 25 percent), and they were also much more likely to have a low body-image score (33 percent compared to 25 percent) (Berscheid et al., 1973).

The Hite Report on Male Sexuality presents somewhat different findings. Shere Hite's question was: "Do you think your genitals are beautiful? Do you think your penis is a good size?" She concluded: "Most men in answering this question wished over and over again that their penis would be just a little longer" (Hite, 1981:390). Other researchers confirm that "Men often fantasize about having larger penises" (Pietropinto and Simenauer, 1977:314). Indeed, despite Freud, penis envy is a characteristic male phenomenon rather than a female one. Statistically, presumably 50 percent of men have below average-size penises and, thus, 50 percent are above average; but many of the latter may think they are below, while some may want to be more above average, in the top 10 percentile—hence, as we shall see, phallectomies.

More interesting are some of the comments men have made about their penises. Many men are extremely proud of their penises, says Hite, frequently because of their size, and some are quite obsessive about measurements. Some comments are just funny (1981:392-7):

- "I think my penis is well proportioned and a beauty to look at when compared to others. It has been circumcised, is smooth and flawless, and it has a large head which is well appreciated in sexual intercourse (contrary to the adage that size does not matter) . . ."
- "Yes, I think my penis is beautiful. I take good care of it. It is bathed every day, kept nice and clean, lotion used on it to keep its skin smooth, and powder to keep it dry. My penis has given me very much joy and pleasure, and has given the same to many girls and women. It has seldom failed me, so I'm proud of it."

• "I think my penis is beautiful and I'm proud of it. I think when I die I'm going to have it bronzed."

• "They're O.K., just another part of my body. I wouldn't hang a portrait of my genitals on my living-room wall."

• "The male genitals look absurd. They are. God could have found a better way."

Women are also interested in the penis. A survey in *Psychology Today* asked women how they feel about the penis. "Very carefully!" is the old joke. But the actual responses varied widely as Table 6.1 indicates:

Table 6.1: How Women Feel About the Penis

	Length	Width
Care a great deal	8 percent	13 percent
Care moderately	34 percent	38 percent
Care a little	31 percent	28 percent
Care not at all	27 percent	21 percent

Source: Pertschuk, Trisdorfer and Allison, 1994:72.

Opinions are divided, with about two-thirds of the sample caring a little to moderately about length and width, and another quarter caring not at all, while 8-10 percent care a great deal. Note that while men care more about length, women seem to care more about width. I like the 21-27 percent who do not care about length or width. I suppose the attitude is, as long as he's got one, we're fine!

In a later survey on "Sex and Size" women were asked: "Does penis size matter?" Yes: 77 percent; No: 23 percent (Blanchard and Levine, 1996:46). The comments from women are quite interesting:

"Men with big penises are all too prone to think they've got all it takes, and therefore don't show much variety /ingenuity /empathy. Ordinary or even small-sized men have provided me with more orgasms."

• "It's not what a man has that matters so much as how he uses it."

• "If women says the size of a man's penis doesn't matter they haven't been with a man with a big one! Fabulous!"

• "I had a boyfriend who was huge. I was in pain every time we had sex, and I got tons of infections. Extra-large is not always excellent."

Some women explained that a thicker penis was preferable to a longer one since it stimulated the clitoris more. Others said that the ideal size depended on the type of sexual activity, and that smaller sizes were more pleasurable in fellatio and anal sex. But most women agreed (over 71 percent) that "Men seem too concerned with the size and shape of their genitals" (Pertschuk, Trisdorfer and Allison, 1994:72).

These concerns about size and shape might be somewhat intimidating to men who do not know the competition or the sample size (literally!) of their partner's experiences. Apart from size and shape, however, the aesthetics of the penis are also intriguing. In the *Marie Claire* survey of 300 men and women, 67 percent of women and 83 percent of men found penises "not ugly," in answer to the question "Are Penises Ugly? Not exactly glorious praise, perhaps!

Not surprisingly, men found them more attractive than women; but the range of attitudes is amusing, including:

- "No. I adore everything about men's genitals." (F)
- "Silly, yes; ugly, no." (M)
- "I used to think so, but now I find them very sexy." (F)
- "Some are. I remember one guy I dated whose thing had veins all over it; that's pretty unsightly." (F)

Perhaps surprisingly, two-thirds of the men surveyed said that their penis was of average size, while only 8 percent said that it was small and 26 percent believed that it was larger than average. It always seems to be the women's magazines that ask the embarrassing, and fascinating, questions—not the social scientists. After having surveyed men about their size, the *Marie Claire* survey asked men: "Have you ever measured it?" Men are, it is well known, always measuring: GDP, fish, engine capacity and, it seems, the penis, too: Yes: 63 percent; No 37 percent. Best comment: "A couple of times, back in grade school, with the same ruler I used in algebra class. I remember it was little—but, then, so was I." Then they asked: "Do you ever check out other men's equipment? Yes: 57 percent; No: 43 percent. A fairly even split. One man said: "Sure. It's the same as women looking at other women's breasts: As a biological creature, you gotta check out the competition's plumage." Another argued: "No. If you get busted, it means you're gay" (Blanchard and Levine, 1996:46, 48). Again, penis envy seems to be more a male than a female syndrome—and more often based in the imagination than reality-based.

Some men are not satisfied with their penis. Perhaps it is a mushroom cap or a pencil, in the charming phrasing of an aesthetic surgeon; or perhaps not. At any rate, about 10,000 penile enlargements or phallectomies are performed annually in the United States, for a total cost of about $12 million. Length can be increased by cutting two ligaments that attach the penis to the pubic bone, although increases are usually noticeable only in the flaccid states. Girth can be increased by injections of fat (Farnham, 1996:82). Such operations are often not medically necessary. One professor of urology states: "They want to look larger in the locker room. It's a macho thing." He added that, after seeing 25 men with post-operative problems, "Not one of them had a penis that was not perfectly normal to start with. Their real problem was between their ears, not between their legs" (Podolsky, 1996:74). The other problem is the dire phrase "post-operative problems."

Michael Kimmel has a problem not just with one man's personal endowment, but it seems with all penises across the land. Kimmel is a pioneer of "Men's Studies" in the United States, a distinguished sociologist and the author of numerous books on and about men. But he is very hostile to the poor penis and to men. He writes: "Perhaps we should slap a warning label on penises across the land. WARNING: OPERATING THIS INSTRUMENT CAN BE DANGEROUS TO YOUR AND OTHERS' HEALTH" (2004:565; emphasis in original).

I know! We have to wonder. Does he know where he came from? Does he have a Post-It note on his own penis? And, as a self-defined pro-feminist and person committed to equal rights, do you think he would advise readers to slap a warning label on women's vaginas? Of course not. That would be unconscionable and blatant anti-female misogynistic sexism. Yet this, too, is blatant sexism and misandry.

Germaine Greer also has problems: "The male perversion of violence is an essential condition of the degradation of women. The penis is conceived [!] as a weapon, and its action upon women is understood to be somehow destructive and hurtful" (1971:317).

Really? Sausages and wieners are weapons? Who knew? She goes on: "It has become a gun, and in English slang women cry when they want their mate to ejaculate, 'Shoot me! Shoot me'" (1971:317-8). All of them? Wow! I imagine that English women know the difference between a gun and a penis, and between being murdered by her partner and her partner having an orgasm. The differences are not that subtle.

But, then again, Greer, like Kimmel, is not exactly keen on men: "Women have very little idea of how much men hate them" (1971:249). Greer has very little idea of how much men love women: They spend most of their lives working to support and protect their wives and children. That is love.

But, perhaps, Greer did not experience much of this, generalizes from her own bad experiences and extrapolates to the entire sex.

It is curious how attitudes to the penis have changed in recent years—well, specifically, from patriarchy to feminism and from pre-pill to post-pill. In many cultures, the penis was and sometimes still is worshipped as a fertility symbol. In ancient Egypt, the god Min was represented holding his erect penis and was represented at the coronation of Pharaohs to ensure their fertility. In ancient Greece, the gods Dionysius and his son Priapus (hence priapic) were depicted with huge penises. The phallus is still worshipped in parts of India as an attribute of the god Shiva, and in parts of Borneo and Japan as, again, a fertility symbol (Vanggard, 1972; Monick, 1991). Indeed, one of the fascinating contrasts between Hinduism and so many other faiths and Judeo-Christian or post-Christian cultures has been the totally different attitudes to sex, sexuality and especially the penis: deified versus demonized, shotgun versus semi-automatic (Augier), dangerous (Kimmel), and weapon (Greer). Fertility versus killing. Birth versus death. It does not get much more polarized than that.

Sigmund Freud

Freud was one of the towering (a suitably phallic adjective) intellects of the twentieth century. A measure of his significance is the degree to which so many of his ideas are now taken for granted. His insights into the importance and the dynamics of sexuality in our lives have been of immense value. These would include his insights into the unconscious, dreams, parapraxes (Freudian slips of the tongue or the hand, and accidents), sibling rivalries, and the psychic apparatus of id and ego; and also his taxonomy of the psyche: resistance, rationalization, sublimation, repression, defensiveness, displacement, projection, transference, psycho-somatic illness, wish-fulfillment, the Oedipus and Electra complexes, the pleasure and reality principles, and the life and death instincts. His identification and naming of so much of what we all do was a magnificent achievement. We build on his foundations, and adapt them as necessary.

Wrestling with the problems of how identities, especially sexual identities, are created and learned, and how they differ between males and females, Freud postulated various stages of psycho-sexual development. The first stages he suggested were the oral and anal stages, determined by the primacy of the various erotogenic zones associated, first, with breastfeeding and, later, with toilet-training. In boys, the third stage is the phallic phase, which Freud discussed in a manner guaranteed to shock and dismay his readers: "When a boy (from the age of two or three) has entered the phallic phase of libidinal development, is feeling pleasurable sensations in his sexual organ and has learnt to procure these at will by manual stimulation, he becomes his mother's lover" (1973a:46).

Of course the boy loves his mother. Indeed, Freud lyrically describes "a mother's importance, unique, without parallel, established unalterably for a whole lifetime as the first and strongest love-object and as the prototype of all later love-relations—for both sexes" (1973a:45). But Freud was being provocative in describing the two-year-old as a lover — two is a bit young to be anyone's lover, as the word lover conventionally has other connotations. At any rate, the phallic phase, beginning with masturbation, initiates what he called the Oedipus complex: the boy's love for his mother coinciding with rivalry with the father "and whom he would like to get rid of." To cut a long story short, in an unpleasantly castrating image, the mother intervenes. She forbids her son his masturbation and "she threatens to take away from him the thing he is defying her with. Usually, in order to make the threat more frightening and more credible, she delegates its execution to the boy's father, saying that she will tell him and that he will cut the penis off." So the poor boy develops a castration complex: "the severest trauma of his young life" (1973a:46-7).

This is an amazing echo of the creation myth in Hesiod's *Theogeny*, in which Gaia, "the mother of us all," persuaded her son, Cronos, to castrate his father and her abusive husband, Uranus, which he did (Hesiod, 1989). So castration became a dominant theme in the Western canon.

All this seems too wild and fanciful—too Freudian. But Freud certainly did emphasize the prime role of masturbation in male pleasure and its central importance in male identity. The psycho-sexual development of girls is different. There is no phallic phase, by definition, nor is there a castration complex; but there is penis envy: " A female child has, of course, no need to fear the loss of a penis; she must however react to the fact of not having received one. From the very first she envies boys its possession; her whole development may be said to take place under the colours of envy for the penis (1973a:50; cf. Vol. 1:360; Vol. 7:114).

Again, there is no data for this grand assertion. Intuitively, one must suspect that there is some truth in this: Children always seem to want whatever someone else has, if they haven't got one, or even if they have—especially after the terrible twos. "I want!" is as loud as "No!" But even if some do, there is no apparent justification for the assertion that "the whole development" of women is centered on penis envy!

Freud has been widely criticized, notably by his biographer Ernest Jones (1954), for being "phallo-centric," i.e., for overestimating the significance of the penis in libidinal development and for seriously misunderstanding female sexuality. Some feminists have also been very enthusiastic in their attacks on Freud, while usually, unfortunately but understandably, failing to acknowledge his contributions.

Margaret Mead, who described herself as a "neo-Freudian," reinterpreted Freud's idea of penis envy as sex-role envy and status protest; not penis envy but phallus envy. She also presents the charming comment of a little girl who saw a little boy urinating: "Wouldn't that be a convenient thing to take on a picnic!" (1949:273).

The penis is not only an organ of pleasure, and also of procreation, and even a divine phallic symbol, it is also—and chronologically first, lest we forget—an unromantic waste-disposal system. It is what some men refer to as their "waterworks." As waterworks, the procedure is simple: unzip, point, shoot (downwind, obviously, a lesson learned early), shake, zip. This is quick, efficient and can be done anywhere, almost; but it also illustrates an instrumental attitude to their genitals, to their external and very visible genitals—one which women may not share in quite the same way with respect to their own genitals.

The boy's instrumental attitude to the penis persists until puberty, when the penis develops a "mind of its own." At that time, the function of urination as the most useful aspect of the penis is replaced by the function of masturbation as its most pleasurable aspect. Again, attitudes are likely to be instrumental, rather than (or as well as) emotional.

Soon after adolescence, however, the penis becomes socially more complicated: The private, personal, solo pleasures of the penis may be displaced by the intimate interpersonal pleasures of sex, either homosexual or heterosexual, or both. Now other people are involved.

To complicate penile matters still further, however, the young men and the young women involved may have very different ideas about sexual relations, or, of course, they may not; but the consequences and costs of intercourse weigh very differently on the two genders.

Certainly "The Penis Dialogues" would be very different from "The Vagina Monologues." For a start, it would be a dialogue because the penis is always in a dialogue with something or someone: urination, masturbation, erection, sex; or, simply, comparative analysis, performance anxiety, "customer satisfaction," and castration anxiety by other men, women, society or self (Monick, 1991). And it is moving around all day, in a dialogue with time and space, women and men, pleasure and pain, urine and semen, cotton and flesh: pretty much everything, even embarrassment and orgasms.

"Anatomy is destiny," said Freud (Vol. 7:1977:259, 320)—a phrase for which he has been much reviled, even though it was certainly more true in 1912, when he coined the phrase, than it is now, over 100 years later, and after the pill. The destiny of both men and women is certainly a variable and a choice; it is also a matter of statistics. And the destiny of men, compared to that of women, was that they are more likely to climb up to the pinnacles of economic and political power (hence Margaret Mead's theory that penis envy is really status envy); but they are also more likely to fall down to the depths of drug abuse, alcoholism, homelessness, violence, death by homicide, suicide, or accident, and workplace fatalities; and to have higher mortality rates from the leading causes of death, resulting in shorter life spans. This constitutes a binomial distribution of power and powerlessness compared to more of a bell curve for women. Today, anatomy is more a matter of differential probabilities rather than destinies, at least in many countries, both physical and social, including educational and occupational choices and even mortality rates. Anatomy may not be destiny but it is not totally irrelevant either.

The penis, small though it is, has generated enormous controversy, massive complexes and polarized destinies—which brings us, first, to Freud's theory of phallic symbols and, then, to ancient and modern theories of the phallus, which Freud did not discuss.

Dreams are a mystery to most people: Are they serious or nonsense? Do they tell us of past lives or of future ones or of lives lived simultaneously? Can they predict? What do they mean? Freud published his massive *The Interpretation of Dreams* in 1900, in which he effectively exposed the unconscious and the symbolic nature of its communication with the conscious—an historic achievement. Freud argued that "Dreams are nothing other than a particular *form* of thinking, made possible by the conditions of the state of sleep" (Vol. 4:650). Dream-work (his phrase) consists of two things, the thoughts and the symbolic ways these thoughts are expressed, which are completely different from the usual waking thoughts. Hence the confusion, and hence the need to interpret dream symbols. There are, Freud insisted, many types of dreams. Not all are sexual or wish-fulfillment. Many relate to fears and anxieties; and the person *thinks* about them during sleep, which is the dream work. But many dreams are about sex and relationships; and, here, Freud's theories of phallic and, effectively, vaginal symbolism apply. Oddly he only used the phrase phallic symbolism, not vaginal, reflecting perhaps his limited theory of female sexuality, or perhaps the delicate sensibilities of his times. In one dream interpretation, Freud insisted that "every word was a symbol" (Vol. 4:497). Still, he did point out the difficulty of interpreting symbols, but also their commonality in some circumstances (Vol. 4:467-70). Freud's discussion set the parameters for the debate; and he is, as usual, quite definitive:

> All elongated objects, such as sticks, tree-trunks and umbrellas (the opening of these last being comparable to an erection) may stand for the male organ—as well as all long, sharp weapons, such as knives, daggers and pikes . . . Boxes, cases, chests, cupboards and ovens represent the uterus, and also hollow objects, ships, and vessels of all kinds.—Rooms in dreams are usually women. (Vol. 4:470-1)

There is, of course, much more—not only animals, especially snakes, but also location, e.g., right = right and left = wrong. Furthermore, houses, rooms, and shoes are also female. Doors and gates are symbolic of genital orifices and so are mouths. Apples and peaches are symbolic of breasts and, therefore, females, as are landscapes and jewel cases. And sexual intercourse itself may be symbolized by certain rhythmic activities like riding, dancing and climbing. Hills and rocks symbolize male organs; gardens, blossoms and flowers symbolize female organs (Vol. 1:187-92). Freud added that "In general, weapons and tools always stand for what is male, while materials and things that are worked upon stand for what is female (Vol. 1:202). Add fountains, grain silos, spires and domes, the Eiffel Tower, the Empire State Building, the CN Tower, doughnuts, horseshoes, deltas, prisons, theatres and cinemas and classrooms and purses . . . and the puritan can go wild.

St. Augustine believed that everything symbolized God. Freud believed that much (most?) dream work symbolized sex. Indeed, for many people, at some time in their lives, sex is God and God is sex. Certainly dreams were never the same again after Freud; but, then, neither is the real world (though dreams are real too), in the sense that the symbols loop back from sleep to waking, and we see sex symbols everywhere: everything straight or curved, protuberantal or orificial, rising or falling—pretty much everything.

D. H. Lawrence

Freud brought the penis into the light, but it was D. H. Lawrence who brought it to the front and center stage, and introduced the penis into the literary world and high culture. Lawrence was the son of a Nottingham coal-miner and knew the mines and slag-heaps, poverty, violence and death in the new Jerusalem better than any other British novelist before him. Not surprisingly, he despised the civilization built on coal but he did not look to politics, socialism, unions or religion for salvation; rather, he looked to the phallus, John Thomas, J. T.

Lawrence was a prolific writer and his mission, as he saw it, was to criticize the development of British industrial civilization and to affirm the wonder and beauty of sex and sensuality, passion and life, in face of mass psychic destruction. His most famous and, indeed. notorious book was *Lady Chatterley's Lover* (1928), which scandalized his contemporaries and was banned as obscene in the United Kingdom in 1959—which, of course, guaranteed its later bestseller status. This was the most explicit account of sex and sexuality up to that time in the English language, and was free with such taboo words as fuck, cunt and penis. Almost as scandalous was that the relations were between a married and titled English lady and her husband's gamekeeper. So Lawrence not only capsized the traditional sexual value system and the traditional hierarchy of mind over body, he also capsized the British class system. Too much!

Lawrence, himself, wrote about *Lady Chatterley's Lover*: "This is the real point of this book. I want men and women to be able to think sex, fully, completely, honestly, and cleanly." He expected trouble: "It's what the world would call very improper. But you know it's not really improper—I always labour at the same thing, to make the sex relation valid and precious, instead of shameful. And this novel is the furthest I've gone. To me it is as beautiful and tender and frail as the naked self is (1961::xiii, xv).

Indeed, his novel was originally entitled *Tenderness*, which might have been a less contentious title and more emphatic of the rights and needs of the individual. Lawrence, however, can speak for himself; and while he does discuss more than the penis, the penis is central—to male identity, to female satisfaction and, indeed, to civilization. This crystalline formulation captures both his despair and his hope: ". . . our civilization is going to fall. It's going down the bottomless pit, down the chasm. And believe me, the only bridge across the chasm will be the phallus! (1961:78)

For Lawrence, capitalism, the love of money and the life of the mind are all curses on England and humanity. Indeed they are all different facets of the same curse. He returns to this theme time after time in many different ways. He contrasts the ugliness of the colliery and the mining town with the beauty of the bluebells in the woods in the spring sunshine; the clever, crippled and impotent war veteran, knight and husband with the whole, sensitive and lusty gamekeeper; the life of the mind and the life of the body; books and sex.

The basic problem is that England "was producing a new race of mankind, over-conscious in the money and social and political side, on the spontaneous, intuitive side dead, but dead. Half-corpses, all of them" (1961:159). The colliers, thought Connie as she watched "in some ways patient and good men. In other ways, non-existent. Something that men *should* have was bred out of them . . . they were only half, only the grey half of a human being . . . Men not men, but animas of coal and iron and clay" (1961:166). Her husband, Sir Clifford, debated this with her: ". . . they are *not* men. They are animals you don't understand and never could . . . The masses were always the same, and will always be the same . . . The masses are unalterable. It is one of the most momentous facts of social science" (1961:189-90). He adds that "I believe there is a gulf, and an absolute one, between the ruling and the serving classes. The two functions are opposed" (1961:191). Here, of course, he echoes Marx's analysis in *The Communist Manifesto* (1848) on the class war between the bourgeoisie and the proletariat, epitomized by the General Strike of 1926, two years before Lawrence wrote this book.

Sir Clifford's belief can be contrasted with Mellors, Lady Chatterly's lover, when she challenges him: "I do believe in something. I believe in being warm-hearted. I believe especially in being warm-hearted in love, in fucking with a warm heart (1961:215).

Mellors also describes Sir Clifford in opposite terms as "a bit like a lady, and no balls." Questioned by Connie to explain, he offers this superb review of types of men, bodies and "real" masculinity: "You say a man's got no brain, when he's a fool; and no heart, when he's mean; and no stomach when he's a funker. And when he's got none of that spunky wild bit of a man in him, you say he's got no balls. When he's sort of tame (1961:204).

Here he anticipates Robert Bly's description of men today in his bestselling *Iron John* as "soft" (1990:2). Real men are a bit "wild" — balls do it to them. But he also echoes Plato's theory of the three types of men in the *Republic*—men of gold, silver and bronze, defined by the triple hierarchy of dominant body-parts: head, heart and belly; but Lawrence added a fourth part, the most essential, balls.

Men, from colliers to knights, are deformed in different ways: half dead, broken by mining, or just tame, consumed by the mind. Sir Clifford is a great believer in the mind; he has published articles, his picture is in the paper, he reads Racine and Proust and derives great enjoyment from them, and he studies mining technologies to increase his wealth. Of course, he cannot get about much since he is paralyzed from the waist down. The final quarrel between the couple hinges on this: What rules, mind or body?

The argument began after Connie criticized a new book on the universe, which Sir Clifford had been explaining. He replied with a patronizing comment: "But then I suppose a woman doesn't take supreme pleasure in the life of the mind." Connie exploded—and the division between them becomes totally clear:

> Supreme pleasure?' she said, looking up at him. Is that sort of idiocy the supreme pleasure of the life of the mind? No thank you! Give me the body. I believe the life of the body is a greater reality than the life of the mind: when the body is really wakened to life. But so many people, like your famous wind-machine, have only got minds tacked on to their physical corpses.
>
> He looked at her in wonder.
>
> The life of the body, he said, is just the life of the animals.
> And that's better than the life of professional corpses. But it's not true! The human body is only just coming to real life. With the Greeks it gave a lovely flicker, then Plato and Aristotle killed it, and Jesus finished it off. But now the body is coming really to life, it is really rising from the tomb. And it will be a lovely, lovely life in the lovely universe, the life of the human body. (1961:224-5)

Lawrence was not single-handedly responsible for the resurrection of the body in Western culture in the 1920s; the tango was also part of it, and so were jazz, Hollywood, the flappers and the "magic bullet" cure for syphilis; also, Sigmund Freud and the sexologist Havelock Ellis, whose seven-volume work *Studies in the Psychology of Sex* was published from 1898-1928, contemporaneous with Freud's work. Margaret Mead's *Coming of Age in Samoa* (1928) portrayed a Pacific paradise and implied that permissiveness is normal and natural, good for you—a polar opposite to the repression of sexuality in Freud's Europe. The suffragettes and the struggle for the vote and political emancipation may have contributed to women's sexual emancipation, and men's. Margaret Sanger also fought for birth control rights and sexual emancipation. Perhaps this resurrection of the body was also a response to the massive death toll of World War I: about 10 million. Not that one should overemphasize the degree to which attitudes and practice have changed. Attitudes to sex and the genitals are still ambivalent. Michelangelo's "David" still cannot usually be placed in storefront windows — still less a penis without David attached.

Lawrence, however, in his quest for a solution, was the first to present vivid verbal portraits of the penis, and also admiring portraits of the body, legs and hair, particularly. He did enjoy describing bodies and love-making; but here Connie relaxes after "a night of sensual passion."

> In the short summer night she learnt so much. She would have thought a woman would have died of shame. Instead of which the shame died. Shame, which is fear: the deep organic shame; the old, old physical fear which crouches in the bodily roots of us, and can only be chased away by the sensual fire, at last it was roused up and routed by the phallic hunt of the man, and she came to the very heart of the jungle of herself. She felt, now, she had come to the real bed-rock of her nature, and was essentially shameless. She was her sensual self, naked and unashamed. She felt a triumph, almost a vainglory. So! That was how it was! That was life! That was how oneself really was! There was nothing left to disguise or be ashamed of. She shared her ultimate nakedness with a man, another being. (1961:258)

The "phallic hunt of the man" had dissolved shame, exposed the bedrock of her nature: "She was her sensual self, naked and unashamed" as Eve and Adam were originally in the Garden of Eden. Such is the power of the penis with the right warm-hearted couple. Each needs the other to find their true selves, and to survive as real among the half-corpses of industrial England. Connie was grateful: "Ah, God, how rare a thing a man is! They are all dogs that trot and sniff and copulate. To have found a man who was not afraid and not ashamed" (1961:258-9). Mellors, too, was grateful: "Tha'rt real, tha art!" Evidently, Mallory did not think that many women were real. "Thank God I've got a woman! Thank God I've got a woman who is with me, and tender and aware of me" (1961:232, 290).

The book ends with the two lovers apart, trying to get their divorces, and Mellors writes the last line: "John Thomas says goodnight to Lady Jane, a little droopingly, but with a hopeful heart" (1961:314).

Lawrence's divinization of the penis, however, is most clearly expressed in *Aaron's Rod* (1922). The rod is, first of all, Aaron's flute, which he plays beautifully and, second, in the usual Freudian symbolism, his penis. The two converge in the end of the novel, as Aaron's flute playing awakens the long-lost singing ability and soul of the Marchesa, and, in so doing, also awakens Aaron's long lost libido:

> And now came his desire back. But strong, fierce as iron. Like the strength of an eagle with the lightning in its talons. Something to glory in, something overweening, the powerful male passion, arrogant, royal, Jove's thunderbolt. Aaron's black rod of power, blossoming again with red Florentine lilies and fierce thorns. He moved about in the splendour of his own male lightning, invested in the thunder of the male passion-power. He had got it back, the male godliness, the male godhead. (Ch. 18; 1972:300-1)

This is a magnificent paean in praise of the penis, purple prose and all. Yet this divinization of the penis has proved extremely controversial. Kate Millett, for instance, has argued that however liberating his views may have been for men, they were oppressive of women; she charged him with "The transformation of masculine ascendancy into a mystical religion, international, possibly institutionalized. This is sexual politics in its most overpowering form" (1970:238).

Millett's assumption is that this is a zero-sum game: that what is liberating for men must be oppressive for women. But I disagree. Indeed, feminists have usually argued the other way, and very persuasively, that what was liberating for women would also be liberating for men. And, in many respects, surely they were correct.

But Millett's attack on the penis is more than a concern about Lawrence's alleged sexism; it is also part of a more general attack on male sexuality and, therefore, on men in general. This is clear from her extended criticisms not only of Lawrence but also of Henry Miller, Norman Mailer and Jean Genet. Her well-known book *Sexual Politics* (1970) was one of the inspirational works of the second wave of the feminist movement, most notable for its toppling of male icons. Attacking Miller, for instance, she writes: "What Miller did articulate was the disgust, the contempt, the hostility, the violence and the sense of filth with which our culture, or more specifically its masculine sensibility surrounds sexuality" (1970:295-7). One does not need to be a great admirer of Miller to be able to spot Millett's vast generalization from one writer to allegations about an entire culture, and her binary sexist values.

If the penis was a biological piston for Miller, then for Mailer it is by and large a weapon, which conquers women; but, also, Millett asserts it is a conquest over the man's own fears for his masculinity—for to fail at any enterprise, especially sex, is to become female in Mailer's machismo (Millett, 1970:3-7). The penis is not an organ of procreation, nor an instrument of love, but a weapon of coercive sexuality, she says.

In Mailer's world, the penis conquers women; in Genet's world it conquers men. The son of a prostitute, illegitimate and abandoned, Jean Genet illuminates his homosexual world, arguing that "a male who fucks a male is double male." Discussing his pimp, he explains to himself: "It's perfectly natural. He's a prick and I'm a cunt" (In Millett, 1970:340, 343). This is reductionism carried to its logical absurdity: The self is surely more than an organ of the self. But, either way, for him the penis is an instrument of conquest.

Millett's concern is to show that the sexual politics of the penis in the writings of these men is expressive of male misogyny and also oppressive of women. But Genet was gay and he was not very interested in gender politics; and Lawrence's goal was the sexual liberation of both women and men, and his praise of the penis did not imply hostility to women; on the contrary, his joy in the one implied his joy with the other. Similarly, I doubt that Millett would have condemned the divinization of the vagina by Blackledge and Wolf as overpowering "sexual politics." In hindsight, what I now find interesting in Millett's work is precisely the reverse of what she found, namely, that *her* writings are expressive of female sexism and oppressive of men.

How different the women's movement might have been if Millett, Greer, Augier, Ensler, Kimmel and others, instead of demonizing men and the penis, had been more humanitarian and, perhaps, valorized men's and women's enjoyment of sexuality and each other in loving relationships; then we could all worship the vagina *and* the penis in loving passion and passionate love.

Sperm

Having a penis carries its own risks, not only of Bobbitt-type castration, circumcision and botched circumcisions, which may cause death (Proctor, 2002) or catastrophic sex change (Colapinto, 2000), but also (as for women) STIs and unwanted pregnancies and child support (Morgan, 1999). U.S. legislation on the rights and duties relative to conception are clear in law, less clear in justice. One section of Morgan's article deals with cases of fraudulent misrepresentation and is titled "Yes, I lied. Now pay your child support." Women can and sometimes do claim that they are on the pill, when they are not, or they may claim that they are infertile, when they are not. The men become fathers, which they did not want to be, and are now on the hook for child support for the next 18 or so years. Some might think that women have agency, and that deception, if proven, might have its share of responsibility—maybe total. Not so. Courts have argued variously that they do not wish to intervene in purely personal matters; that the moral offence is not a crime; that contraception is not 100 percent effective, so the man should have taken responsibility for his actions; and, basically, that your sperm is your responsibility, not that of the state. The needs and rights of the child, not the father, come first. "The courts have universally held that the father's allegations [even if proven by others] that the mother had deceived him were totally irrelevant to the issues of paternity and support." This must be a huge encouragement for more deceptions and money transfers down the road.

Next: "Yes, you were underage. Now pay your child support." Even in cases of statutory rape by the woman, the male is still liable for child support. As one court judgment concluded: "This minor child, the only true innocent party, is entitled to support from both her parents regardless of their ages"—and regardless that the male was legally incapable of consent.

Even in cases when guys donate their sperm to a friend, so that she can become pregnant, with prior agreement that he has no parental responsibilities—men should be aware that she may change her mind. Verbal or even written agreements have no legal validity unless they follow the provisions of the various state or federal jurisdictions, including the Uniform Status of Children of Assisted Conception Act or the Uniform Parentage Act.

Some cases are bizarre:

• In Louisiana, Mr. Frisard was visiting a sick relative in the hospital. A nurse's aide offered to perform oral sex on him, and he agreed. The aide requested that he use a condom, so he did. She took it and, unknown to him, inseminated herself, became pregnant, sued and won child support.

• In Alabama, S. F. got totally drunk at a party, passed out, a woman had sex with him, i.e., without his knowledge or consent, became pregnant, told a friend that it saved her a trip to a sperm bank, sued for support and won. The man had argued that this was rape. The court did not rule on the alleged rape.

• In Kansas, two couples went for a drive, but they only had one condom. The couple in the back seat went first, then passed the condom to the couple in the front. Someone emptied and inverted it, but the woman in front got pregnant. But the father was the guy in the back seat; he did not even have sex with her, but his sperm was responsible. Don't you just hate that? At the time of publication, the issue was before the court.

Morgan's recommendations after her survey of these cases are: "Shut up and put on a condom and dispose of it yourself." To which I would add, "Not just any condom, your own; do not pass it on; and don't pass out at a party in Alabama."

*

So there stands the penis: admired and loved by some, despised and hated by others; worshipped as a fertility symbol—the phallus—in many cultures past and present, like the vagina, as we have seen; a turning point in the psycho-sexual development of boys for Freud, and symbolically ever-present in our dreams; analyzed statistically by Kinsey and physiologically by Masters and Johnson; praised lyrically by D. H. Lawrence; largely ignored artistically, except in men's washrooms occasionally, and by Aubrey Beardsley and Greek, Roman, Indian and Japanese erotic artists or sculptors, including Michelangelo's David. Yet the penis is an engineering marvel of simultaneous life-creation and waste-disposal, as well as a usually willing donor of so much pleasure to both men and women. Not bad for such a relatively small organ.

Chapter 7
BREASTS

Breasts are everywhere, especially women's breasts. They are in magazines and movies, on television and blown up on billboards. They sell everything from Pirelli tires to bras and photo magazines. They attract men's eyes like magnets from yards away, so T-shirts are adorned with the slogans "Look Up!" or "Grow Your Own!"

Breasts are powerful: they are sex symbols, erogenous zones, organs of nutrition, sites of cancer, marketing tools for many products, and also loci of cosmetic surgery, self-esteem and capital value. Indeed the West is very much a breast-centric culture. The British tabloid *The Sun* features women proudly exhibiting their breasts every day on page 3. Given their significance to both women and men, this is perhaps not too surprising; but it is ironic that the self-esteem of many young women may arise, and rise, from their cup-size, especially if it is largely silicone. Sad, maybe? But then penis-size fulfils the same self-esteem raising function for many men. Size often matters.

Breasts are sanctuaries for babies and lovers—places where we can snuggle and be open, naked, vulnerable, and held. Leah Cohen says this well: "In this place we fall asleep. We cry. We listen to a voice rich in the chest of the speaker . . . In this place we rise and fall. We speak quietly. We are comforted" (1999:79).

Life and death, food, comfort, pleasure, beauty and power are all located in these mammary glands. Breasts are far more than mere biology.

Breasts are also highly political: police, lawyers and judges are all deeply concerned about breasts. Several recent cases illustrate the controversial nature of these glands, notably the confusion over food and sex, nutrition and eroticism, making milk and making love. Specific social issues include visibility, appearance, aesthetic attitudes, cosmetic surgery and breastfeeding—all amazingly controversial. This is not a medical sociology book, so breast cancer, its etiology, the utility of mammograms, and the pink ribbon campaign are not discussed here.

• When Justin Timberlake ripped open Janet Jackson's top during the 2004 Super Bowl halftime show, one breast escaped—and it was televised. Shock! The head of the U.S. Federal Communications Commission called it a "classless, crass and deplorable stunt." There would be an inquiry. Pundits talked about the effects on children and sexual assault and male violence. Highbrow American papers offered no photos. Lowbrow papers showed the recapture. But virtually all the British papers showed the exposure, from the tabloids to the *Times*. This does seem to indicate different attitudes both by class and by national culture. The fact that Jackson said the stunt had been agreed upon beforehand also indicates the range of attitudes to the breast within American culture. Crass or fun?

• In Rio de Janeiro police cracked down on topless sunbathers at a popular beach, arresting one woman who refused to comply and clubbing down her 60-year-old boyfriend. This incident was captured on television and widely shown. Brazilians were furious and complained of hypocrisy; they noted that such sunbathing has been practiced since the seventies and is popular at Carnival also. Topless protesters carried placards stating "Down with sexism, long live hedonism," and "Just like a woman, breasts deserve respect." In the face of massive popular opposition, the policy was reversed, and the mayor declared that summer to be "Topless Summer" (Hall, 2000).

• In Canada, there was a famous case in which Gwen Jacobs was arrested for strolling topless on a hot summer day in a small Ontario town in 1991. She was fined $75 and appealed. Her conviction was overturned five years later (it takes a while), allowing women to go top-free except for commercial gain or sexual purposes. So, ironically, all women save sex workers and erotic dancers can go top-free. Seems like occupational discrimination.

• In the second decade of the New Millennium, breasts still remain contested territory. In 2013, Angelina Jolie, whom some believe to be the most beautiful and sexiest woman in the world, had a preventative double mastectomy followed by cosmetic surgery; and she told the world about it in the *New York Times*. She learned that she had a genetic mutation in the BRCA1 gene, which put her at a very high risk of contracting breast cancer and ovarian cancer. Her mother had the same genetic mutation and had just died of ovarian cancer, at the age of 56. She explained: "Once I knew all this was my reality, I decided to be proactive and minimize the risk as much as I could." She added: "On a personal note, I do not feel any less of a woman. I feel empowered that I made a strong choice that in no way diminishes my femininity" (Kluger and Park, 2013:30). The disassociation of breasts from femininity is a major redefinition of beauty, and the empowering of other women who may face similar cost-benefit analyses is itself a huge gift.

A second theme is the research on breastfeeding and social mobility. Using survey data on over 30,000 individuals from British studies in 1958 and 1970, researchers discovered that breastfed individuals were more likely to be upwardly mobile (by 24 percent) and less likely to be downwardly mobile (by about 20 percent) than those who were not breast-fed—and that was holding constant such variables as parental education, alcohol consumption by the mother, and other factors. The rise or fall was determined by comparison with the social class of the father. When interviewed, the lead author insisted that other factors may well be more important than breastfeeding, but that the benefits are not negligible in terms of brain development and reduced stress levels; whether the beneficial "mechanisms" (an odd choice of word!), however, are the nutrients, the bonding, or both is not clear; probably both, she thought (Anderssen, 2013).

A recent longitudinal study in Brazil, of over 3,000 adults who had been followed from birth in 1982, found that those who had been breastfed for more than a year had IQs four points higher than those who had been breastfed for less than a month, they had stayed in school for a year longer and also had incomes 15 percent higher. Family income was not a factor. Winston Churchill said: "There is no finer investment than putting milk into babies." Mother's milk, especially (*Economist* 21, March 2015:70)

A third theme is the emergence of topless protests by the members of Femen, a "sextremist" feminist organization founded in Ukraine in 2008, which has staged hundreds of demonstrations around the world. (*Economist* 25, May 2013). Breasts that once were hidden are now exposed, and which once were sex symbols are now (also) political symbols. The meanings are multiple and in perpetual flux.

Breasts have interested many people over the millennia for different reasons, and they still do: women and their babies first, no doubt, and their lovers, but also priests, photographers and pornographers, prostitutes, oncologists and surgeons, artists and sculptors, police, lawyers and judges, psychologists, pediatricians, historians, feminists, anthropologists, sociologists, and those in the bra industry, the fashion industry, the advertising industry, and the film industry.

One of the (many) reasons that men are so fascinated by or, some would say, obsessed with breasts is, of course, that they do not have breasts as complex or, on average, as large as those of women. Breasts are not only classic examples of sexual dimorphism,* but they are also unique to humans among the other primates. Monkeys and the great apes do breastfeed and they have nipples, but they are relatively flatchested. Why, then, did women develop breasts: mammary glands? Evidently, not solely for milk storage. Desmond Morris notes that the other primates walk on all fours and demonstrate sexual signals of coming into estrus on their rear ends—by swelling, coloration or odor. Humans, he suggests, developed breasts as a "primeval sexual signal," "a pair of mimic buttocks on her chest"—rounded, protuberantal, soft, i.e., as visual sexual stimuli, and, perhaps, also nasal and tactile. The twin hemispheres and cleavages echo each other, and their evolutionary purpose is to sexually incite and excite men—which, when visible and not hidden away they seem to do, for better and for worse (Morris, 2004:146; 1985:161-72). Hence, the cosmetic surgeries and the push-up bras.

Love and Hate

Some women love their breasts, some hate them; some want them bigger, some smaller, and some enjoy them just as they are. Some are ashamed of them and their perceived imperfections, some are shy, and some flaunt them; some have cosmetic surgery while others reject the idea. Breastfeeding and mastectomies and lovers—all can radically transform previous attitudes to breasts. Some attribute their fortunes, their misfortunes, or both to their breasts.

Attitudes to this terrain are complex and surprisingly under-researched. There are far more books on breast cancer than on "breast power" and related attitudes and meanings. On a personal level, Daphna Ayalah and Isaac Weinstock (1979) interviewed over 200 women about their breasts and photographed them in all their rich individualities. Comparative and historical reviews are presented by Wilson (1974), Blum (1995) and Yalom (1997). And Meema Spadola more recently produced a documentary film, "Breasts," in which she interviewed 22 women, then interviewed still more and published a book of the same name, in which women tell their stories.

The slang terms for breast tell some of the story, with or without respect, adoration and amazement: bazongas, bazooms, melons, tomatoes, headlights, knockers, hooters, boobies, tits, udders, jugs, love pillows, marshmallow mountains, sweater meat . . . readers may add their own personal favorites. Desmond Morris adds his own long list, including the variations over the centuries (2004:142).

The stories, however, are more illuminating, since stories about breasts are often, but not always, stories about identity. One woman notes that "How women are has a great deal to do with how their *breasts* are—our breasts are so involved with who we are." Another said: "I recently told a friend that I thought smaller breasts would look very elegant. He said to me that he didn't think I'd be who I am if I had small breasts, and when I thought about it I agreed" (Ayala and Weinstock, 1979:22-3).

Nora Ephron went public with her obsession: "I am obsessed by breasts. I cannot help it . . . Well, what can I tell you? If I had had them, I would have been a completely different person. I honestly believe that" (2006:51).

Dolly Parton, frank as ever, had to cancel a tour on the advice of her doctor. She commented: "Hey, you try wagging these puppies around a while and see if you don't have back problems" (*Time* 25, February 2008:11).

How do breasts have such a defining role on identity, one wonders? And what sort of "completely different person" would someone be in a parallel universe? Women offer different ideas and experiences on this.

There is power. One woman, a self-confessed tease says, "Ah, power. I have power with these things." A woman related how, on one hot and humid night in California, when her male friends were all wandering around in their shorts, she took off her shirt, too: "I still remember the look of shock on their faces. I felt incredibly empowered" (Spadola, 1998:44, 61).

There are different types of power. A mother of three comments: "They make me feel powerful because these breasts grew three gorgeous children—solely on the milk that they produced. That's power" (Spadola,1998:61).

And there is pleasure, first usually self-induced and then induced by others, often in the context of baseball metaphor. Breasts are "second base." "We were kissing," Carol recalls about her eighth-grade boyfriend, "and then for the first time ever, he put his hand underneath my shirt and into my bra. Oh God, that was like fireworks going off. I don't think it's ever felt as good as the initial touch" (Spadola, 1998:45-6). Too bad.

Then again, there may be pleasure in the power. Birgitte obviously enjoys male attention:

> Men love big breasts. They'll do crazy things for big breasts. Recently I wore this beautiful red evening gown with a lot of cleavage to the most exclusive nightclub in New York City. I had men running back and forth to the bar, getting me drinks, wanting to fly me to Paris, wanting to put me in a limousine for the night, and bringing me flowers." (Spadola, 1998: 122)

So it goes. Others feel a bit more vulnerable either physically—and have reduction surgery—or emotionally. Feelings about breasts are as varied as the breasts themselves; and the stories are endless, and not always positive. "Breasts can be like a prison," said one woman—quite the opposite of power. Another says wearily: "With my large breasts I've never had trouble getting jobs. The trouble begins once I have the job. Always . . . Always!" And another woman reported: "My breasts have caused me to have an angry, hard attitude toward men. I had something they wanted, the shitheads, but I learned that men weren't really sensitive to me!" (Ayala and Weinstock, 1979:16, 22-3)

Breasts are almost all things to all people: adorable or disgusting, too big, too small, power, pleasure, milk, job offers, prisons, door openers, trouble, sex, private but also public, controversial and, for some, identity. One woman recalled:

> Recently I read about an ancient Minoan culture that worshipped the Mother Goddess and where women were the high priestesses. They lived on the island of Crete around 3,000 B.C. Carved in one of their temples was a statement that proclaimed, "I have breasts, therefore I am!" It struck me, so I thought about it for a while and, you know, I think there's something to it. (1979:24)

The contrast to Descartes' "I think, therefore I am" is remarkable. The polarization of breasts to head—suckling to thinking—captures precisely the Cartesian and Platonist dualism of body and mind, which has plagued us for so long. A philosophy built upon the breast would have been radically different (and surely far more humane) than Cartesian mechanism.

So women's breasts may be many things: a prison, an economic asset (the waitress), a health hazard (Dolly), a sex symbol (for better and for worse), a source of nutrition, a legal issue, even a political one or a moral one—not a simple biological fact. Female breasts are imbued with a range of meanings and values.

Breasts are most naturally a female sign. One Native American, a great-grandmother, describes what her breasts mean to her: "My breasts have meant a great deal in teaching me to be 'Woman.' Their sensitivity tells me I am 'Woman' because women are sensitive beings. . . . As old as I am my breasts are still a constant reminder that I am 'Woman'" (1979:273).

Aesthetics

Americans spent about $12.9 billion on 15.6 million cosmetic surgeries in 2014, up 11 percent since 2000, according to the latest statistics from the American Society of Plastic Surgeons. This would be an underestimate, since not all surgeons are board certified. Ninety-two percent of the procedures were on women, and the vast majority of the procedures were "minimally invasive" (Botox and the like). Breast augmentation was the most common surgery, with (numbers are rounded) 286,000 procedures on augmentation, 24,000 on implant removals, 93,000 on lifts, 41,000 on reduction and 26,000 on men for reduction. Prices vary across the country and also depend upon the implant, silicone or saline, and the "specials" being offered (www.plasticsurgery.org, accessed October 11, 2015); so probably about $1.5 billion on breasts all told. These are clearly valuable commodities and a huge investment, usually in breast hugeness.

Breasts come in all shapes and sizes and colors and textures. Most women are satisfied with theirs, but according to various surveys, breast-dissatisfaction, like body-dissatisfaction, is rising among women. A 1972 survey found that 26 percent of women were dissatisfied with their breasts, increasing to 34 percent in a 1997 survey. Furthermore, in 1972, 25 percent of women (and only 15 percent of men) expressed their dissatisfaction with their "overall appearance," but this more than doubled for both women and men by 1997 to 56 percent and 43 percent, respectively (Garner, 1997:42).

This is not a representative sample of the United States, but it may be fairly representative of the middle-class; either way, if about one-third of middle-class American women are dissatisfied with their breasts, this could indicate a problem. The problem, however, is not in the breasts, suggests Judith Rodin; the real problem is women's preoccupation with the body. "Body preoccupation has become a societal mania. We've become a nation of appearance junkies" (1992:57). The attention given to the amply and artificially endowed Pamela Lee Anderson, and to so many other women, certainly does not help. Indeed, the ideal breast size is now artificial! This is totally bizarre! And it raises the matter of aesthetic surgery.

The expenditures cited above indicate, once again, the close identification between the body and the self. To some, investment in breasts is seen as investment in the self , and also as investments in women's relations with others. To dismiss all these women as "appearance junkies" is surely a bit disrespectful. Perhaps they have a clear understanding of the personal and social values of appearance in the real world as it is, as opposed to the world that others think it should be.

The women speak for themselves. Here, Dorothy complains about her "puny little breasts":

> The thing is, Doctor, not my husband, mother, or best friend, or anybody really has any sympathy for me. My husband says, 'So what? I married you, didn't I?' Yet every time he sees a girl with big breasts, he's all eyes, and when we go swimming, I might as well not be there because he's so busy ogling . . . My mother thinks I'm crazy to tamper with nature. She says that as long as I'm healthy, I should be thankful and let well enough alone. I can't get her to see

that having puny little breasts like mine just isn't well enough. It's awful! (Stallings, 1980:39)

It's "awful" not only because her husband ignores her and her mother doesn't understand, but also because it made her unhappy and apparently she took out her feelings on others in antisocial and aggressive behavior. Breast augmentation began the reversal of this process, beginning with a more positive body image.

There may also be pecuniary benefits. Simply, market value increases with bra size. As one bartender/university student explained after her breast enlargement: "They look totally natural; they don't feel like coconuts. I feel feminine and sexy, I can't explain it, it's amazing." Furthermore, customers' tips have increased by 15 per cent. As she said: "When I leave at the end of the night, I come home with $200 in my pocket because someone was looking at my breasts. It pays for school" (*Maclean's,* August 7, 1996:40).

The connections between women's breasts, men's eyes and cash are almost magical! Geography, psychology and economics are all connected here.

Breast reduction can be equally liberating. Prior to surgery, Marion explained: "I'm tired of being so top-heavy that I feel like a freak. I'm tired of buying the larger bra cup available and still it's too small. And I'm tired of going around stooped over from the weight pulling down on my shoulders and having a backache most of the time. After surgery, however, things were different: "I could wear a 36C bra and I couldn't wait to go into a store and buy sweaters I had never dared to wear and a bathing suit to show off my new figure. Best of all, there's no back pain nagging at me anymore and I'm learning to stand straight and square my shoulders like a young woman who's proud of her body and doesn't care who knows it! (Stallings, 1980:45, 47)

Radical mastectomy can have the most devastating impact on a woman's sense of self and body image. Deborah, 27, a happy wife and mother, went to the hospital for what she hoped would be a routine biopsy, and woke up with no right breast. "I lay in bed blind with pain that was as much mental as physical. I felt such revulsion toward my own body that I was sure my husband would pity me, but not be able to bear looking at me or touching me. Would we ever be able to make love again? How could our marriage survive? Could I function as a wife and mother when I only felt like half a woman?" (Stallings, 1980:56).

It was like a nightmare. Her relations with her husband deteriorated "and I guess it was mostly my fault because I couldn't feel desirable as a woman;" and her relations with others also deteriorated, as "I had been a rather cheerful and outgoing person, but I became more and more withdrawn" (Stallings, 1980:57). It is a familiar story for other women who have had mastectomies. As another woman said: "When you look at yourself and see that your chest is flatter than your husband's, every nerve in your body protests, 'Why me?'" (Stallings, 1980:59-60).

Reconstruction surgery can have dramatic benefits, as two women attest:

• I can't really express how it feels to have breasts again, any more than I can describe how it was not to have any. I'm thrilled, and so is my husband. He's simply amazed and I can't get over how well they look. Life has a whole new meaning to me now.

• I would say to any woman who has to have one or both breasts removed to find out where the nearest doctor is who can do the operation and have him DO IT! It is wonderful to have your husband look at you and see an expression in his eyes that hasn't been there for a very long time. At last I can say I AM A WOMAN (Stallings, 1980:63, 61).

Certainly, some women's identification with their breasts is intense, e.g., the woman who lost one breast and said "I only felt like half a woman;" and the woman who reported, after reconstructive surgery: "At last I can say I AM A WOMAN." Here the breasts equate exactly with the female self. The mammary gland is the identity. Other women do not identify so closely with their breasts, and losses may not be so traumatic. "Big deal!" exclaimed one woman, "I'm alive!" Angelina Jolie's operation and attitude may, however, help others to identify differently—perhaps not so closely with the now disposable breasts.

Nonetheless, the range of possibilities is great. Breast sizes go in and out of fashion. In the 1920s, the flappers bound their breasts for the slim, willowy look. Jane Russell brought breasts back into the public eye in the movie "The Outlaw" (1943), and was followed by Jayne Mansfield, Sophia Loren, Raquel Welch and others. Twiggy took them back out of fashion again in the 1960s. Then, Dolly Parton and Pamela Lee Anderson flaunted them, and still do. Kate Moss, however, offers the alternative look. So there are options for women. The aesthetics are very much a matter of personal preference.

There is a certain irony (as well as expense and risk) in all this cosmetic surgery, mostly for women—not just breasts but also butts and bellies and eyes and noses and, nowadays, even vaginas. For decades, feminists complained about the objectification of women by men—how men regarded women as objects, perhaps even as "pieces of meat" (to be consumed); and not just in beauty competitions, but all the time. It was the protest at the 1968 beauty competition in Atlantic City that significantly helped launch the modern women's movement.

Now here are so many women engaging in self-objectification, trying to maximize their beauty, desirability and attractiveness—perhaps for their own personal satisfaction and self-gratification, no doubt, and perhaps also to attract men's eyes, fire up their lust, increase their tips and maximize their market value (or, in the jargon, their "social capital"). And investment in beautification brings excellent returns: attractive men are paid 5 percent more than the less attractive, and attractive women 4 percent more. Over the course of a lifetime, that amounts to about $250,000, on average, for the above-average looking man. Not as much as an undergraduate degree over leaving high-school (which is 40 percent), but still, not bad (Rice 2010:52, 50). Put some of those extra earnings from your degree into your face or your body, and you're all set.

Some people object to all this (mostly male) objectification, and some to the (mostly female) self-objectification; and each responds to each. Others obviously do not object, and consider that subjects are free to make the most of their assets and asses—or bust.

Nipples

Nipples do not have quite the same social visibility as breasts do, in advertising, movies and dress. Breast display and cleavage are the focus of lenses, as nipples remain demurely hidden, usually, at least in public. The American reaction to Janet Jackson's decorated (concealed) nipple appearing in public demonstrates that point. The incident has even been labeled "nipplegate."

Yet nipples are interesting as erogenous zones, sources of milk, sites for piercing these days, private areas not usually available to the public gaze, and also as fashion accessories: Now you see them, now you don't.

Nipples are usually less visible than breasts, since cleavage and décolletage are intended to expose the latter, rather than the former. Their scarcity value is, therefore, high and inspirational. Robert Herrick, a seventeenth-century English poet, was certainly inspired by the nipples of Julia's breasts:

Have ye beheld (with much delight)
A red-Rose peeping through a white?
Or else a Cherrie (double grac't)
Within a Lillie? Center plac't?
Or ever mark't the pretty beam,

A Strawberry shewes halfe drown'd in Creame?
Or seen rich Rubies blushing through
A pure smooth Pearle, and Orient too?
So like to this, nay all the rest,
Is each neate Niplet of her breast.

Three centuries later, "each neate Niplet" may be pierced. Nipple piercing is one of those "extreme" body practices that appalls many people in the "vanilla world." One woman, Sheree Rose from Los Angeles, explained that "the sensation of actually being pierced is a rush;" asked "How do the piercings feel now?" she replied, "Now, it's great! They're constantly erect, and because they're erect you notice them all the time." She added that "There are some women who say they can experience orgasms just from having their nipple piercings played with, and I can believe that" (Vale and Juno, 1991:109-10).

A man who had his nipples pierced spoke in similar terms: "My nipples were a dead zone before they got pierced. Then they became a whole new discovery. It was nice—like being female as well. . . . So I discovered nipples, which was good—two more erogenous zones added (Vale and Juno, 1991:176).

One of the mysteries of nipples is why men have them. They would seem to serve no evolutionary purpose, and to be the only organ of the human body that has no use or function. Could male nipples be a mistake of nature? Of course not. They indicate that males and females have a common embryonic source. At about three months, after the nipples have developed, the Y chromosome will signal a testosterone wash and the embryo switches from female to male. Women come first.

Breast Feeding

In the beginning was the breast," affirms Marilyn Yalom (1997:9) in her superb *A History of the Breast.* (Marvin Harris said it was the foot and St. John said it was the word, but I say it was sex; we are, however, talking about different beginnings.) Yet breast-feeding remains contested territory in some parts of the world.

- In London, some of the 120 women elected to the House of Commons in 1997 were having babies, and searching for somewhere to nurse their babies. There is no creche, there are no highchairs, and the Speaker of the House, a woman, had taken a tough line forbidding nursing anywhere but in a toilet and the Lady Members' Room. "The attitudes are antediluvian," fumed one MP. A committee was struck to recommend a new policy! (*Economist*, 22 April 2002). There is something very Monty Pythony about the "Mother of Parliaments," which legislates for 60 million people in the U.K., and which debates war, nuclear power and Europe, stumbling over babies and breastfeedings! Powerful things, breasts, to paralyze a parliament.

• In Chicago, a six-year-old boy was removed from his mother's care because she was still breastfeeding him. The mother accused the social workers of "cultural bias." An anthropologist testified in the case, based mostly on studies of nonhuman primates, that the "natural" age for weaning is between two-and- a-half and seven; and that weaning should be "child-led." A nanny, who had called the authorities, testified that the boy was being made to suckle against his will. The judge stated that "Instead of helping him mature emotionally, [his mother] continued to put her own needs first" (Pearson, 2000; Owens, 2000).

• In Toronto, there have been so many complaints from mothers about harassment while breastfeeding that the Ontario Human Rights Office and other organizations have sponsored an ad campaign to promote greater acceptance of breastfeeding in public. Posters feature babies in police mugshots with the caption: "Breastfeeding in public is not a crime" (Lindgren, 2000).

• More recently, near Montreal, a mother breastfeeding her son was asked to leave the store. But she blogged her expulsion and about 100 breast-feeding mothers turned up at the store to protest. A lactation consultant noted that 88 percent of Montreal mothers start breastfeeding but only 4 percent are still nursing six months later, due, she thought, primarily to lack of public support (Cornacchia, 2011).

• A particularly pathetic case in Nova Scotia illustrates the problem, though attitudes may have changed by now. A mother was nursing her six-week-old son and was asked to leave when a man entered the store. She did, but as she left she noticed the woman feeding her dog. She commented: "It was pretty bad that she could feed her dog, but I couldn't feed my child" (Globe and Mail 26 June 1998).

Certainly the breast is the beginning of physical life for the baby, or a breast-substitute, the bottle; but Freud pointed out that the breast is also the beginning of erotic life for the baby. He suggests that "A child's first erotic object is the mother's breast that nourishes it; love has its origin in attachment to the satisfied need for nourishment" (1973a:45). Love begins with the breast—what a beautiful idea of Freud's, though he does seem to emphasize the comfort food aspect of the breast rather than the erotic.

The breast provides nourishment but it also provides pleasure—hence the later identification of food and sex, in various ways (e.g., comfort food), and also the persistent, almost subconscious, fascination with the breast for both men and women, albeit in different ways. Freud explains: " The baby's obstinate persistence in sucking gives evidence at an early stage of a need for satisfaction which, though it originates from and is instigated by the taking of nourishment, nevertheless strives to obtain pleasure independently of nourishment and for that reason may and should be termed *sexual*" (1973a:11; emphasis in original).

Sexual? This picture of the little angel as a cuddly "sex maniac" at the breast may be a shock, but the sweet neonate does derive immense pleasure as well as nutrition from suckling. In this sense, Freud is surely correct that the mouth is the "first organ to emerge as an erotogenic zone" (1973a:10).

Breastfeeding may be the beginning not only of infants' survival lives but also of their pleasure lives, though that contention is still highly controversial in Western cultures, if not necessarily in other cultures, as we shall see. It is often the case that whatever is life-giving and pleasurable in our culture is also automatically, reliably and puritanically defined as wrong elsewhere.

The body is not strange but our attitudes to it certainly are. It is an essential source of food for infants, but it is forbidden to feed infants in so many restaurants, public places and corporations. Many people are disgusted at the sight. Others think it inappropriate. Every year some special case of a nursing mother being asked to leave a public place makes headlines. It is strange that anyone can eat in restaurants except babies! Some people find it difficult to recognize the twin—but confusing—roles of breasts as both sources of nutrition and sex symbols and erogenous zones.

It is strange that something so normal, natural and pleasurable as masturbation should have been banned by so many religious and medical authorities, and that something so normal, natural and apparently pleasurable as breastfeeding, wholeheartedly endorsed by the medical authorities, should have been, and often still is, so widely ignored or deprecated by so many mothers as well as corporate and political authorities. Emily Martin has castigated American norms: "This lack of institutional support in the United States makes it very difficult for women to be whole people—productive and reproductive at the same time . . . [Indeed] the current structure of work-places in the United States does not easily allow any woman to live with her bodily functions, whether she be menstruating or pregnant" (1989:100-1).

"Or breastfeeding," I would add. I would also add that our norms do not make it easy for *babies* to be whole people; they are so often restricted to eating in bathrooms, including the toilet stall—not the most congenial environment for a delicious and nutritious snack; or they are switched prematurely to the bottle.

The World Health Organization (WHO) and UNICEF have recommended for decades that "Breastfeeding is the normal way of providing young infants with the nutrients they need for healthy growth and development," and that "Colostrum . . . is recommended as the perfect food for the newborn." Also, breastfeeding is recommended exclusively for the first six months of life, and for up to two years or beyond. While this is not intended as a medical text, the WHO summarizes the advantages of breast milk over other formulae:

• it is uniquely suited to the baby's nutritional needs, being species specific.

• it is easy to digest and contains nutrients and antibodies that build the immune system, protect against allergies and help prevent infections.

• it builds emotional bonds.

• it is a readily available supply on demand, cheap, clean (sterile), fresh, and, at the correct temperature, error and contaminant free.

The WHO asserts that:

• Under-nutrition is associated with 45 percent of child deaths.

• About 36 percent of infants zero to six months are exclusively breastfed.

• About 800,000 children's lives could be saved among children under five, if all children 0-23 months were optimally breastfed (www.who.int/topics; accessed 11 October 2015).

Recent research suggests that breastfeeding not only improves health and saves lives but also it seems to have beneficial results on children's intelligence, as measured by I.Q. tests. Furthermore, it is thought to be beneficial for the mother, resulting in lower rates of breast and uterine cancer, and it halves the risk of contracting Type 2 diabetes, which is due, apparently, to a superior ability to lose weight. Despite these purported benefits, only 14 percent of mothers in the U.S. breastfeed for as long as the recommended duration of at least six months (*Time*, 13 September 2010:20).

Breastfeeding is particularly advisable in Third World countries, where water is sometimes scarce or contaminated, energy supplies may be limited or erratic and equipment cannot easily be sterilized. These countries are precisely where many of the infant formula corporations have targeted their advertising, hyping their products as symbols of modernity, despite the often catastrophic effects on infants' health. One of the very successful marketing techniques of the infant formula industry was to distribute gift packs free in hospitals. By the time the supply ran out, the baby often could not, or would not, suckle and the mother could not lactate, so both became increasingly dependent on the inferior and expensive product of the industry. This situation resulted in a boycott of Nestle in 1977 in the U.S. Since then, far more attention has been given to the value of breastfeeding and to the slogan that "The breast is best."

Despite the well-publicized benefits of breastfeeding—nutritional, emotional, economic and even intellectual—breastfeeding is still not the norm in many parts of the world, either for the initiation or for the duration. Reasons for not breastfeeding are many and varied, but many mothers say that they have inadequate or insufficient milk, or that it's inconvenient, or that they have sore nipples, and so on. Another reason for the relatively low rate of breastfeeding after the first few weeks is the paramount need for so many mothers to return to work—and the correlative, almost complete failure of the business world to establish facilities for nursing mothers. Our priorities, familial and corporate, are all wrong in these respects, and, as a result, our children and our futures suffer. Family values are deeply subordinate to wealth values.

By contrast, in other cultures breastfeeding is not only done in public, like any other eating, but breasts themselves may be bare, without any complaints about the "objectification of the female body." Indeed, breasts may be shared by children, who may be passed from one to another as convenient. I remember one acquaintance of mine who was breastfeeding complaining that "I feel like a cow!" But other people rejoice. One new mother wrote:

> [I] took plain joy in my baby's fatness (eight and three-quarter pounds at birth, and consistently weighing in at the ninetieth percentile), knowing that every ounce of him came straight from my body. *I* could feed a person. It was a melody, a hymn, an ode to direct action . . . As a child I'd sort of gathered that cows alchemically turned grass into milk; now I was in that league, and what pure delight to see my milk metamorphose within his body into round wristlets, echoing chins, cheeks like ripe cheeses, a stomach like the moon. My milk made his tiny nails grow long; it

> made the drool that dripped from his curly lips; it made his eyelashes which didn't appear for a few weeks … What woman engaged in such a project could not love her body? (Cohen, 1999:84; emphasis in original)

Certainly women's bodies are miraculous, converting food into milk, with the milk converting back into food for their babies, growing them. And the feeding is itself a bonding experience: "It is cuddly and restful, satisfying and poignant, a form of primitive physical love, and a mutual, functional act of complete connectedness . . . I would gaze down at my son suckling at my breast, and I have never drunk in such beauty" (Cohen, 1999:86).

The anthropologist Margaret Mead has offered an enchanting description of breastfeeding among the Arapesh of New Guinea, from her research in the 1930s:

> This is an experience that the mother enjoys as much as the child. From the time the little child is old enough to play with her breasts, the mother takes an active part in the suckling process. She holds her breast in her hand and gently vibrates the nipple inside the child's lips….She blows in the child's ear, or tickles its ears, or playfully slaps its genitals, or tickles its toes. The child in turn plays little tattoos on its mother's body and its own, plays with one breast while suckling the other, teases the breast with its hands, plays with its own genitals, laughs and coos and makes a long, easy game of the suckling. Thus the whole matter of nourishment is made into an occasion of high affectivity and becomes a means by which the child develops and maintains a sensitivity to caresses in every part of its body. It is no question of a completely clothed infant being given a cool hard bottle and firmly persuaded to drink its milk and get to sleep at once so that the mother's aching arms can stop holding the bottle. Instead, nursing is, for mother and child, one long delightful and highly charged game, in which the easy warm affectivity of a lifetime is set up. (Mead, 1956:40-1)

Yet, even in our relatively nontactile culture, the psychic importance of breastfeeding should not be underestimated. In the feeding, pleasuring and caring for the child, says Freud, "lies the root of a mother's importance, unique, without parallel, established unalterably for a whole lifetime as the first and strongest love-object and as the prototype of all later love-relations—for both sexes" (1973a:11). Amazing to think that our first love and our prototype of all later loves is formed at the breast, founded on milk, and is probably totally forgotten.

The last word goes to the British pupil who, when asked, "What are the advantages of mother's milk over other forms of milk?" replied: "It's cleaner, it's cheaper, and the cat can't get it!" (*Globe and Mail,* 12 December 1996).

*

So, in the end, what are breasts? And what do they mean? Yalom answers this well: "Babies see food. Men see sex. Doctors see disease. Businessmen [and women?] see dollar signs. Religious authorities transform breasts into spiritual symbols, whereas politicians appropriate them for nationalistic ends. Psychoanalysts place them at the center of the unconscious" (1997:275).

Many women also see power, even identity, self-esteem, femininity, cash and attractiveness in their breasts, making them central to their social lives, as well as at the beginning of our personal lives, and deeply influencing, according to Freud, our love lives. Our own lives have likely depended on them, as will the lives of future generations. They are the fountains of life.

Chapter 8
Buttocks

Buttocks and butts, buns and the bum, the behind, the bottom, the posterior, the backside, the seat, the rump or, cutely, *la derrière* or, crassly, the arse or ass—these slang terms for the buttocks testify to their immense social significance and, perhaps, to some embarrassment about them. Indeed, attitudes are polarized between the friendly "bum" and the cute "butt" or the athletic "buns of steel" to the insulting arse—which becomes more insulting with the additives "hole" or "licker," and still more insulting with the precursors "bloody" or "stupid" or worse.

The buttocks are not only linguistically polarized, but also behaviorally. On the one cheek, the double symmetrical convex curves of the bottom may be alluring and the object of interested glances and affectionate pats; on the other cheek, mooning is insulting, unwanted pats may be grounds for sexual harassment lawsuits, and the buttocks are a favorite site for the infliction of pain, e.g., via spanking and pinching.

Again, buttocks are curious because they are public but also private: Although their size may vary from the petite and almost invisible to the gigantic and totally awesome, they are usually concealed, at least in public, but sometimes flaunted in bikini bottoms or thongs on beaches. Admirers may look but not touch. This is still private property, even if publicly displayed. Indeed, buttocks, as protuberantal, like breasts, are potentially visible and may either be displayed and flaunted or concealed by dress—depending on local culture and personal taste. It is curious that top/front protuberances mirror the bottom/behind protuberances not only physically but also socially.

So buttocks are paradoxical: They may be visually admired but also used as insults; caressed by lovers but harassed by strangers; flaunted or hidden; public and private.

Admirers may look and even take photographs—as California photographer Christie Jenkins, evidently a connoisseur, did, in her published collection *Buns* (1980). She shot men's buns in various states of dress and undress, described them evocatively in such terms as "a good piece of art" or "English muffins," and gave the names of the athletes, celebrities or dancers involved. As an experienced "buns-watcher," she advises women: "Take a look at your guy's buns. If you see mostly keys and wallets, invest quickly in pocketless pants." This is buns as sexy and fun, not as high art, nor even as political objectification.

Despite some aesthetic joy in buns, buttocks have a precarious position in the geographic hierarchy of our anatomy. They are bottoms in societies that value tops, as evidenced in expressions such as the top dog, number one, the head of state (or the table or the bed), the apex of achievement, and the brains of the organization. We may spend our lives trying to climb up the ladder of success to reach the top, the pinnacle, the summit. At all costs, we try to avoid hitting rock bottom—being a loser or being a "bum" or a beggar; "bumming" money from hard-working taxpayers. They may be designated by one of the insulting epithets mentioned earlier. Symbolically, bottoms are polar opposites of the dominant head: the source of reason, truth and light, and the pride of humanity. Incidentally, toes and feet are similarly polar opposites. Bottoms and feet, therefore, compete for the *lowest* status parts of the social body. One organ expels dirt and the other is mired in it.

By the same geography, buttocks are behinds, in societies that valorize the front—indeed, the forefront—leading the way bravely, not just left behind, last again, dragging arse, so to speak. Not everyone wants to lead the way or to be the head of anything, but no one wants to be left behind or at the bottom of the social hierarchy, still less a "bum." Buttocks, therefore, as bottoms and behinds, would seem to be doubly stigmatized.

Desmond Morris calls the buttocks the "joke zone" of the body, because it is the butt (sorry!) of so many "dirty" jokes (1985:197)—which it is, but it is far more than that. For many, it is also an erogenous zone (buttock display on beaches and strip clubs), an insult zone (mooning, slang), and, certainly, a legal zone, since exposure of the buttocks in a public area could be regarded as indecent and the grounds for arrest.

Buttocks are clearly powerful social forces, capable of arousing a wide range of emotions, from adoration to disgust to anger to laughter, depending on the circumstances.

Despite the jokes and polarities, bottoms and behinds are much beloved, fondly caressed, proudly swung and carefully watched. Indeed, they are probably the most pinched, petted and patted parts of the human anatomy, by men to women, certainly, whether appreciated or not; women to men; and also men to men — as we see when watching football and other athletic games on television. The shoulder pat or back slap is given more as congratulations, but the bum pat is more intimate, because closer to the taboo, private zones of the body.

Buttocks are particularly appreciated by Southerners, at least according to Rosario Ferré, who writes:

> I've always had a positive feeling about my butt. It's a part of my body I like, and I am very conscious of it when I walk down the streets of Old San Juan. The rear end is an instant lodestone, a magnet for male eyes in Puerto Rico. If I'm depressed because I've had an argument with my husband, I slip on my tightest tubo skirt, climb on my spiked heels and swing down Calle Fortaleza to La Bombonera. There I sit at the counter, my behind sticking out on the red leather like a bull's-eye, and order a sweet, squashed, buttered mallorca and a *café con leché* loudly, enjoying the amorous looks of neighboring males … I don't know why, but I can't feel happy unless I know someone wants to squash my butt like a sweet, buttered mallorca. (2000:193)

She protests the feminist discourse that "today disapproves of the exposed female backside, the sexual object par excellence." This is objectification of the female; but she loves it and says that in Puerto Rico the female ass, the mythical Tembandumba's, in particular, is "an affirmation of Puerto Rican national pride, of its energy and joy" (2000:194). Surely, the ass, to many no doubt, beats the bald eagle, the lion, the beaver and, surely, thistles, leeks and shamrocks as national symbols.

Ferré is certainly an enthusiast, as are most Puerto Rican women who "are proud of their gourd-like buttocks, which they like to shake at every opportunity." Indeed, she insists: "The pivot of the soul is always the butt, where everything is expressed and evil spirits are expelled." The bigger the better. Evolution has its own logic. Also, "Women with small bottoms are chumbas—figs with sunken cheeks" (2000:195). And it does not get much worse than that—no soul, you see.

Ferré describes how cultural norms vary. She enjoyed one man who yelled at her (in Spanish, in the original): "Blessed be the butt that birthed you and the tits that nursed you." This is almost biblical in its essence. But when she visited Teheran, she says: "I never heard a compliment or heard a disrespectful whistle, and also felt frustratingly invisible" (2000:193). Butts appreciated make women visible and feel good . . . in Puerto Rico and elsewhere but not in Teheran. And such compliments and "wolf whistles" would not be politically correct in New York, Tokyo or London.

Reluctantly we will have to leave Ferré to enjoy her *mallorca*, the "amorous looks" and enthusiastic yells so appreciative of her assets, and return to quieter art appreciation classes.

The historian Edward Lucie-Smith (2000) presented a "cheeky" (his pun!) artistic history of the bottom, painted famously by the ancient Greeks, especially Praxiteles, who sculpted Aphrodite's famous behind. Bottoms disappeared for a while, artistically speaking, during the Dark Ages, but caught the eye of Michelangelo ("David") and Leonardo da Vinci, particularly during the Renaissance. Later, Rubens, Renoir, Watteau and Boucher became intoxicated with bottoms, particularly female ones. But the first was the Venus of Willendorf (about 20,000 B.C.), amply endowed fore and aft in complementary measure, and testament (whatever its purpose) to an appreciation of the feminine figure.

Similarly, Christine Blass (2001) presents a cheerful selection of backsides from 5,000 B.C. to the present, in sculpture, paintings and, more recently, erotic photographs. The beauty of the bum, male and female, is amply exposed.

Today, bottoms are everywhere—in films, advertising and tight jeans, which is a form of self-advertising that has become far more provocative (or self-objectifying) since the addition of tattoos on the lower back; and they are a staple of the joke postcards so popular in the U.K., but also in tourist regions everywhere, especially as seen in the highly photogenic lineup of multi-shaded bums in the sun. Again, *derrières* are a staple of films and even plays and respectable live shows these days, not to mention the exotic dancers—the new name for strippers—in nightclubs everywhere. On some beaches, thongs divide the hemispheres for all to admire, and on nude beaches, the undressed world can watch the thongless spheres in orbit.

Yet, it is not 100 years since Victorian ladies visiting the seaside often only paddled, lifting up their dresses; and if swimming, they would be virtually fully dressed as depicted in the film "Mrs. Brown" (1997).

Indeed, bums have wandered out of the clothes in which they were once so invisible. The elegant curvature, soft texture, voluptuous movements and personal intimacy of the ideal butt is now, thanks to tight jeans, much more visible. The smooth rounded orb of the bum mirrors the similar orbs of the breasts and the smooth rounded heads of infants. Humans seem to be drawn to these shapes and to feel for them, literally and metaphorically, in a way that we do not feel for, nor caress, harsh angular objects — except, perhaps, diamonds (but there the appeal is financial rather than sensual).

Such an attraction is well-deserved, for buttocks are, like the relative size of the brain, the opposable thumb and binocular vision, one of the distinguishing features of *Homo sapiens*. The large gluteus muscles enable humans to stand erect on two legs and walk—and to eventually have circled the globe. The other 192 living species of primates walk on four legs. Indeed, *Homo sapiens* is the only primate that has the protuberantal hemispherical buttocks of the gluteal muscles. The evolution of the buttocks has been critical in human evolution and, in turn, in the evolution of the breast (Morris, 1985). In the beginning was the butt.

Both the buttocks and the breasts act as sexual signals, signals that may be emphasized in some cultures by more fat, and, therefore, more protrusion, more undulation, and also by such extraneous fashion attributes as cinched waists, high heels, "spray-on" spandex tights or jeans, and low-cut jeans. Such sexual advertising may be maximized or minimized but can and does contribute to sexual selection in the evolution of the human species, as Charles Darwin suggested (1981/1871).

Despite being bottoms in a world of tops, and behinds in a world of forward-looking leaders, buttocks do have the singular luck, for both men and women, of being sex symbols. There may be, therefore, some sort of moral equivalence in the differential evaluation of body parts.

It is curious and unfortunate that so much has been written on the brain and reason as the distinguishing feature of humanity from Plato to Descartes, and so little about the buttocks that enabled both of them to get up in the morning to walk and to sit on, in order to write. Had they reversed their priorities, how different Western philosophy would be.

The orb itself is vertically bisected into left and right hemispheres, east and west. This bisection into two cheeks mirrors the cheeks of the face, as the sphere itself mirrors the head and, to carry the looking-glass theme a bit further, as the anus mirrors and connects with the mouth. Thus, top and bottom are mirror images of, and connected with, each other: spheres, hemispheres and orifices.

A similar mirroring is evident both physically and linguistically in the lips of the vagina and the lips of the face. It's not clear if mimicry serves evolutionary purposes, but it seems likely that it is neither purely coincidental nor simply a matter of packaged engineering. That the body should be symmetrical from side to side, left and right, seems readily understandable; but that it should be so symmetrical from top to bottom and front and back does seem surprising.

The butt, however, is also interesting as the site of the private and publically taboo process of defecation, and the noxious odors that may attend such a process, as well as a number of unpleasant medical disorders, like haemorrhoids, Crohn's, constipation, diarrhoea and operations like colostomies. All these situations provide us with an immense range of so-called "dirty jokes" (as Morris said) — joking being, as Freud pointed out, one of our most effective defense mechanisms; in these examples, defenses against embarrassment, shame and disgust associated with the poor, unfortunate butt.

Such contradictory and bipolar evaluations of any geographical part of the body are unusual, as is also the intensity of the emotional reactions. No such contradictions and no such intensities are evoked by most other body parts, e.g., the ears, arms or legs.

So public and private, admiration and disgust, fine art, humor and taboo, evolution and sexual selection, all meet in the buttocks. So does pain. And so does politics.

Nature

Nature has been good to the rear end, especially in the avian kingdom. We might think of the peacock, the lyre bird, the pheasant, the ostrich, the turkey, the bantam cock, the bird of paradise, so highly prized in New Guinea; the tail feathers of the eagle, so highly prized by the Plains Indians. The rarer the bird, the more highly valued its feathers. Nature also does well by the head, the breast, the throat, and the wings too, but it is the parson's nose we are examining now.

Nature has also been good to the rear ends of the non-avian kingdom: the cotton tail of the rabbit, the white-tipped brush of the fox, the tails of horses and all the different species of dogs and of monkeys. All these tails have different functions and meanings, whether for courtship display, as with so many birds, or as warning signals, as with rabbits, hares and white-tail deer, whose tails flash like lightning as they vanish; as a tool for fly-flicking with horses; as emotional display, with the ferocious tail-wagging, or occasionally the tail-between-the-legs ("I'm sorry about that!") of dogs; and, of course, the tails of monkeys (but not the apes) as a transport system. Tails are useful and important.

While humans have lost their tails and their tail-feathers, we still have the remnants of this system in the coccyx: the last bone in the spinal column. Nonetheless, we surely cannot underestimate the roles of our tail-ends in courtship display, and even well past courtship. Indeed, the books and articles that advertise the development of "buns of steel" are not read to maximize the pleasures of sitting down but to maximize posterior sex appeal.

In his delightful book on the bottom, *The Rear View*, Jean-Luc Hennig comments on "the impure thoughts which rose from women's buttocks into men's brains" (1996:45). Indeed, rumor has it, and Christie Jenkins (1980) confirms, that similar impure thoughts may rise from men's buns to women's brains, and also to other men's brains, so evocative are these wonderful instruments of nature. All this may explain why buttock augmentations are the fastest growing types of aesthetic surgery in the U.S.: up 86 percent from 2013 to 2014, according to the American Society for Aesthetic Plastic Surgery.

So buns speak directly to the brain or, perhaps, lower down and just around the corner. Buns, perky and cute or heavy, sad and drooping, wiggling or wobbling, striated with muscle or wattles and cellulite or smooth as a baby's — they all speak a fascinating and well-understood language, impelling, compelling or repelling, as the case may be. They speak to the eye, the heart and the loins: and the brain just follows along, late as usual.

Pain

The bum is the preferred location for the infliction of corporal punishment in many families and schools, though such punishment is now illegal in most schools in North America and in much of Europe. Indeed, the criminalization of spanking is currently a matter of some debate. Some argue that violence is out of place in both the family and the school. Others believe that a good spanking has its uses, especially for young boys.

The back is the preferred site for floggings, usually in public, in Islamic countries. Not coincidentally, they tend to have very low crime rates. In Singapore, however, the bare buttocks are considered the ideal target for caning—so much quicker and cheaper than prison and, also, it appears, far more effective.

Corporal punishment is a vexed topic, whether administered by parents, teachers or the state. People have different opinions on whether violence is a legitimate method of social control in the family, the school or the nation. However, the Council of Europe recently reprimanded France for failing to outlaw the spanking of children. French law recognizes this as a parental right, and nearly 70 percent of parents admit to having smacked their children (*Economist*, 7 March 2015:20). This is something of a tidal change: "national surveys in the U.S. in 1975 and 1985 found that more than 90 percent of parents spanked their 3-year-olds." A 2007 study reported that less than 9 percent of parents said that they spanked their children; but, strangely, 40 percent said that they were spanked as children (lower than one might expect) and did the same to their children (so much for the 9 percent). One expert thought that spanking was less prevalent, and that fewer people were admitting to it, both of which were good, since spanking is an ineffective disciplinary measure and the denial factor suggests a measure of guilt and a shift in cultural norms (*Newsweek*, 5 February 2007:16).

Anatole France has suggested that spanking is the best way of "inculcating virtues through the bottom" (Hennig, 1996:73). By that criterion, I should be very virtuous, particularly since the Jesuits by whom I was educated considered the hands as well as the bottoms to be effective virtue-inculcation organs. Personally, I doubt that spanking inculcates virtues, though it may certainly modify behavior. The prospect of manual or posterior pain does have an immediate impact on the brain. The three parts of the anatomy are obviously physiologically connected somehow.

But some people seem to enjoy such punishment. In his *Confessions*, Jean-Jacques Rousseau confessed how much he had enjoyed being spanked by his nurse. He explained that, although it was strange, ". . . this chastisement made me feel still more devoted to her who had inflicted it . . . for I had found in the pain, even in the disgrace, a mixture of sensuality which had left me less afraid than desirous of experiencing it again from the same hand." The second time he was spanked by his nurse, however, she seems to have noticed that the eight-year-old boy was enjoying it, so she stopped, abandoned the practice, and ejected him and his cousin from her bedroom, where they had used to sleep (1982:10-11).

Rousseau shows signs of an early masochism, and an early enjoyment of spanking which has sometimes been called the "English disease." Yet, in *Emile*, his classic work on education, he advises parents and teachers: "never punish him, for he does not know what it is to do wrong" (1984:56). On the contrary, recognizing the well-known brute fact that little children are always hungry, Rousseau's maxim is: "the best way to lead children is by the mouth" (1984:117). The carrot or, better still, the candy, rather than the stick or the flat of the hand, is what Rousseau recommended. But he did not practice what he preached; and despite writing the finest text on education since Plato, he committed his own five children to a foundling home.

The debates about the morality and the utility of spanking and physical punishment continue today; and despite all the research, the conclusions are not crystal clear. In one study, researchers analyzed U.S. National Survey data of 1996 and 1990, from over 800 mothers of children aged six to nine years. They compared levels of anti-social behavior (defined as including cheating, lying and bullying) of the spanked and unspanked children, and found what they called a boomerang effect: the higher the level of spanking at the beginning, the higher the level of anti-social behavior at the end of the study period (*Globe and Mail*, 15 August 1997). This would seem to indicate that spanking is counter-productive. Critics pointed out, however, that dysfunctional families spank more and create dysfunctional children; they suggested that the study is really only measuring the degree of dysfunction, not the effectiveness or otherwise of spanking.

Later research in the U.S. reported that 19 states continue to permit spanking in schools. One leading researcher states firmly: "The more kids are spanked, the more problematic their behavior is" (Park, 2012:17). A recent report from the Brookings Institution, a think-tank, reviewing nearly 30 studies from many countries concludes that children who are spanked frequently are more likely to become delinquent: take drugs, be depressed and become more aggressive and have slower cognitive development. The Economist summarized this brutally: "Spanking makes your children stupid." But 81 percent of American parents believe that spanking is sometimes necessary, especially born-again Christians, Southerners, blacks and Republicans. The children's views were ignored. 20 rich countries have banned spanking altogether, even by parents. The new theory of spanking is that it produces the very reality that it is trying to prevent: violence, in the so-called boomerang effect. The old theory asserted the utility of spanking and argues that since parents and teachers have given up their physical authority over children and students, the children and students have now picked up guns and turned them on both parents, teachers and other students. The abolition of corporal punishment (spanking) by one has led to the implementation of corporal punishment (gunfire) by the other, as in all the school shootings in the U.S. (15 Nov 2014:34). Take your pick. The evidence is tricky.

Dr. Shamsie, who founded the Institute for the Study of Anti-Social Behavior in Youth in Toronto, has some wise words on this matter: "How are you going to teach the child not to be aggressive when you hit him?" [or her?]. "By nurturing you can undo what nature has done. If you've got a difficult child you should almost bend over backwards to make sure you are not hitting the child." And: "I'm a child psychiatrist but I work with adults. Every time I fail it's because I was unable to modify the behavior of the parents" (Fine, 1999). There are so many other more effective methods to discipline children, but does he not sound exactly like the dog whisperer? (I like the understanding that children are not all born the same, some are born difficult!) (Synnott, 1983).

At bottom, as we have seen, buttocks are immensely controversial in some ways and also immensely powerful forces in the electrically charged anatomy of the body. As erotic zones, they may be wiggled or wobbled, displayed or danced to the best, most seductive, advantage. They are sculpted, painted and photographed by admirers, and tattooed and exercised by those who wish to be admired. And they are appreciated, watched, caressed, even pinched on occasion—sometimes evoking a smile, sometimes a lawsuit or a slap. They have also played an underappreciated but vital role in human evolution, which is ironic, since this same process has enabled humans to drive or be driven rather than to walk; and, partly as a result, some have now become so obese that they can no longer walk. Evolution comes full circle.

The downside of the buttocks is that they are bottoms in a world of tops, behinds in a world of leaders, and sterns in a world of bows. Buttocks are sat on, fallen on, caned and kicked—and all that hurts. They are the erotic camouflage for the anus, the site of the particularly taboo process of defecation, only popularized but also anesthetized and neutralized by "dirty jokes." Bums, literally and metaphorically, are bipolar: They are the outcasts of society but also ogled and lovingly caressed zones.

In the end, the number of buttock augmentations (11,505) in the U.S. performed in 2014 by board-certified surgeons is tiny compared to the 286,000 breast augmentation procedures (www.cosmeticsurgery.org). But Jennifer Lopez has set a high standard. Some believe that buttocks augmentation will become the breast augmentation of the 21st century, and that gluteal aesthetics will replace mammary aesthetics as the new competitive zone. Maybe, in the end, the last will be first.

The Anus

The anus is neither a frequent topic in polite conversation nor a subject area in sociology. It is probably the most despised and disliked zone of the body: a constant reminder that, despite our brilliance, charm and beauty, we are just animals. *Homo sapiens* shits. That said, both Lewin (1999) and Laporte (2000) have written learned works on feces, discussing hygiene, the rise of civilization, changing manners, sewage disposal and what Norbert Elias (1982) has called "the rising threshold of shame."

The anus (or "arsehole," to give one crass, slang synonym here) is quite literally as well as metaphorically at the bottom, the lowest rung, of the hierarchy of body parts. Indeed "asshole" is surely the most commonly used term of abuse; and the most effective insulting gestures achieve their power by reference to that organ, both the one or two-fingered "Up Yours" gestures and, also, the most dramatic of all, "mooning;" this is still more dramatic if the cheeks are spread, for maximum visibility and power.

Yet this maligned organ is, after all, an important component of the human body. As the old joke insists, if the arsehole does not work, the entire body shuts down. Not only is the poor thing not appreciated for the beauty of its biological functions but, to add insult to injury, it is surrounded by the warmly appreciated and often caressed bottom. Oh! The unfairness of it all!

And what is this anus? It is only the opposite end orifice to the mouth. And the mouth is lovingly kissed. And the mouth is made up with lipstick. And the mouth is checked carefully in mirrors every day as we shave or put on makeup or practice our smiles or grimaces or just check for crumbs. Not so the anus. We don't kiss it, decorate it or even look at it. We probably wouldn't recognize our own if we saw a picture of it.

Indeed, a kiss on the anus was Satan's kiss in the Middle Ages and warranted death. A kiss on the wrong end was immoral, a sin, and during the witchcraft trials could only be punished and redeemed by death, usually by fire.

The mouth is the input end of the digestive tract, which runs past the heart, liver, and lungs into the stomach, with the large and small intestines of the alimentary canal (some 24 to 36 feet long) to the output end at the anus. What goes in must come out, transformed by the digestive process.

Again, the intensity of this moral polarization of the two ends of the digestive tract—mouth and anus—is odd, mirroring the polarization of the beloved bottom and anus. The phrase "Kiss my arse!" is all the difference in the world from its opposite "Kiss me, you fool!"

Furthermore, the poor despised anus is only a perineum away from the valued and prized generative sex organs. Vagina or penis keeps the anus company, like old friends, sheltering under the same umbrella of underwear.

Odd that such geographic proximity is again allied with such extreme moral polarity: the organs of pleasure, creativity and god-like birth adjoining the organs of pain (often enough), waste-disposal and, historically, devil worship. Pleasure-pain, birth-waste, god-devil: the body is highly polarized.

Henry Ford was once asked what he thought about the engineering of the human body. "The ignition is too close to the exhaust," he replied. Nonetheless, it works—and usually lasts longer than any Ford creation.

Despite these multiple polarities of anus to mouth, anus to beloved bottom, and anus to genitals—output to input and exhaust to ignition—the anus has in common with the genitals and the buttocks that they are all the butt (an unavoidable pun) of so much of our humor.

Yet, what is most strange about our human geography is that we are hollow. A long organic cylinder weaves through us from top to bottom. At any given time, delicious food and drinks may be ingested at one end and miraculously converted into energy and heat, or solid and liquid waste, and excreted at the other end of the cylinder. The entire process of filling and emptying this cylinder demonstrates our hollowness.

In *The Waste Land*, T. S. Eliot argues that "We are the hollow men," but he meant this metaphorically. We are without moral fiber, without goals, without ethics, without a solid stainless steel core. He was a bit of a pessimist. But he was also correct in a literal sense. We really are hollow. Things pass straight through us like a hose pipe, the long tube of the alimentary tract. And despite our heft and weight and our "too too solid flesh," as Hamlet soliloquized, our hollowness is real. Filling it up is the prime requirement for survival and growth.

Humans may be hollow but we are also porous: two-way sieves with six different types of holes for women—mouth, nose, ears, vagina, urethra and anus—and five, of course, for men (though a friend says that the sexes are actually equal in this regard, since men also have a hole in the head). These holes are organs of reception for everything from sound waves to penises to food and drink to aromas to oxygen—a wide enough variety of biological possibilities, and most of them essential for the survival of the human individual or the species. These orifices might also receive virtually any and every object that human ingenuity can devise. Poking things into holes is something that humans do; it is practically a defining feature of the species.

These holes are also organs of emission, disposal and output: solid and liquid waste, sound, including speech, semen, blood, wax and vomit, gas, mucus and carbon dioxide, and, most notably and largely, babies. Again, as wide a mix of valuable and occasionally totally taboo items as may be imagined.

Such complexities of input and output are almost incredible. Who would imagine that our human orifices do so much to keep us alive and perform so many diverse functions in the process, and through such a large number of holes.

We would do well to respect our six or so orifices for all they are worth. We might first see them in their holistic unity as survival systems, rather than deconstructing them, so to speak, into their separate orifices. We might also admire the engineering and the aesthetics of appearances. Noses, ears, vaginas, penises, urethras, anuses and mouths have entirely different social functions, physical appearance, and aesthetic significance. We need them all and can appreciate them all, rather than rank them. True, we have no aesthetic criteria for some of these holes (noses, mouths and eyes, yes; ears and anus, not so much) but the principal is important. Also, it is interesting to relate the beauty of biological function to the beauty of social reality.

Humans are fascinated by holes. Children dig holes in the sand. Adults explore caves. We peer into holes in trees, look through holes in walls, and, perhaps, explore the holes in each other's bodies. It is part of our curiosity, which is the genesis of our knowledge and our civilizations.

Yet, holes are strange. By definition, they are an absence of something, a nothingness surrounded by something. So in digging a hole we are creating a nothing out of something. As such, we are the reverse of gods who create something out of nothing.

Jean-Paul Sartre: Anus and Nothingness

Although many have written about heads, faces and eyes—the privileged regions in the geography of the body—very few have written about the nether regions and about the anus. One of the few was Jean-Paul Sartre, writing his war diaries while he was stationed as a meteorologist in the French army, 20 kilometres behind the front lines during the "phony war" of 1939-40. His discussion is original, not to say quite bizarre, but it does make a change, for instance, from his abstractions on consciousness, will and time; and it is certainly time that we became conscious of this neglected component of the human anatomy. He begins in poetic vein: ". . . certainly the arsehole is the most alive of holes, a lyrical hole, which puckers like a brow, which tightens in the way a wounded beast contracts, which finally gapes — conquered and ready to yield up its secrets. It is the softest and most hidden of holes, what you will–I have nothing against the Freudians composing hymns to the anus" (1984:149).

The Freudians did not compose any such hymns; the nearest we have is Sartre's own composition. He then continues in what would almost seem to be self-parody, but isn't: he took himself very seriously; there are no jokes in his war diaries. " The world is a kingdom of holes," he writes. "I see, in fact, that the hole is bound up with refusal, with negation, with Nothingness. The hole is first and foremost what *is not* (1984:149-50; emphasis in original).

You can see where he is going: negation opposed to the affirmation, Nothingness and Being; and his entire philosophy founded on the arsehole!—the "most alive" of holes.

Sartre summarized his philosophy in various ways: "I *am* what I *will*" and "I will what I am" (1984:41) — which is reflective of Nietzsche and anticipates his later formulation. But still more interesting is this implied notion that "I have an arsehole, nothingness, therefore I am, I am Being" or "I have what is not, therefore I am." It seems that few have connected his war diaries to his existentialism, which is founded on the arsehole. (Freud stressed the mouth, but ingress is followed by egress. Freud was better, since ingress contributes to love, life, energy and growth, whereas egress is waste.)

Anyway, he develops all this, saying, "Thus the hole's nothingness is a nothingness of man; it's at once death and freedom, negation of the social" (1984:150). The arsehole is "freedom?" Rousseau and Patrick Henry might have objected. The French Revolution was fought for this? The U.S. Constitution sacralizes this right? Sartre does get carried away occasionally; nonetheless, it is interesting to follow him in the development of his ideas: "But the hole's nothingness is colored: it's a *black* nothingness, which causes another nature to intervene here, another cardinal category—Night. The nature of the hole is nocturnal . . . And precisely because it is nocturnal, it conceals. Daytime holes are slashes of night. In the depths of the night there is *something*. The hole is sacred because it conceals" (1984:150).

You could not parody this! So Sartre's imagination travels from lyrical description of arseholes to the "kingdom of holes" to negation and Nothingness, death and freedom, night and the sacred and, finally, to sex, which is where this panegyric has been leading us.

> Two bodies that fit together are made for each other. Fitting together magically entails fusion . . . [And it is] the categorical nature of the whole that will constitute the basic layer of signification for the various species of sexual hole: vagina, anus, mouth, etc. . . . The hole — nocturnal female organ of nature, skylight to Nothingness, symbol of chaste and violated refusals, mouth of shadow which engulfs and assimilates—reflects back to man the human image of his own possibilities. . . . (1984:151-2)

No, you really couldn't! Sartre developed this fanciful theme in *Being and Nothingness* a few years later; but his emphasis shifts to establishing "plenitude": filling up the holes in our lives to achieve wholeness. Why he starts with the anus rather than the mouth, since that is the first hole that the infant tries to fill, is not clear. And Freud has insisted that the oral phase of psycho-sexual development precedes the anal phase. Perhaps Sartre was fixated on the latter, hence his ignoring the former.

As a founder of existentialism, he is noteworthy for capsizing Cartesian mechanism, in which Descartes insisted on his "*cogito, ergo sum*"—I think therefore I am (adding that "this 'I', that is to say, the *mind* by which I am what I am, is entirely distinct from the body"). (1968:53-4; emphasis added). Not so, argued Sartre, insisting that the *body* is the self and the self is the body: "I *live* my body . . . The body is what I immediately am . . . I am my body to the extent that I *am*" (1969:428-30; cf. 460, 470). What do you think? Are you your mind or your body? (No, you can't just say both but, rather, assume here that you have to explain which and how and why and so what.) It is interesting to note in this context that Sartre contradicts his earlier, equally dogmatic assertion that "I *am* what I *will*."

This prioritizing of body, though more complicated than the above quotes would suggest, echoes Nietzsche: "Behind your thoughts and feelings, my brother, stands a mighty commander, an unknown sage—he is called Self. He lives in your body, he is your body . . . There is more reason in your body than in your best wisdom" (1985:62).

So, here the body is reason and wisdom, i.e., mind, as well as Self. This is intriguing and holistic rather than bipolar; but back to Sartre and the body. Only a reading of his war diaries and a close reading of *Being and Nothingness* would suggest that his abstract idea of the body boils down to his theory of the hole, and, in particular, the anus. The entire pyramid of his philosophy is built on the humble anus, the hole and Nothingness. You can't get much more existential than that.

In *Being and Nothingness* Sartre emphasized that the child "learns that his anus is a *hole*" and that "the *hole* is the symbol of a mode of being which existential psychoanalysis must elucidate" (1969:780-1; emphasis in original). In sketching out his attempt to do so, he argues—from the anus, remember—as follows: "Here at its origin we grasp one of the most fundamental tendencies of human reality—the tendency to fill . . . A good part of our life is passed in plugging up holes, in filling empty spaces, in realizing and symbolically establishing a plenitude" (1969:781).

Plenitude is one metaphor for one of our "fundamental tendencies;" others might be unity or direction or growth. But plenitude is fine and helpful. Certainly, in the most literal sense, eating is a filling-up of the self: "Are you full? Or do you want some more?" But, then, Sartre gets carried away. He argues that "When he [the child] puts his fingers in his mouth . . . he seeks again the density, the uniform and spherical plenitude of Parmenidean being" (1969:781-2). He does? I doubt it. He just seeks oral gratification with a nipple replacement. Sometimes a suck is just a suck.

Sartre's theory of holes shifts from the anus to the mouth to the vagina. Despite his womanizing, in this passage at least he is clearly misogynistic. "The obscenity of the feminine sex is that of everything which 'gapes open' . . . Beyond any doubt her sex is a mouth and a voracious mouth which devours the penis—a fact which can easily lead to the idea of castration. The amorous act is the castration of the man; but this is above all because sex is a hole" (1969:782).

It is strange that Sartre, so cerebral, yet so fixated on holes, forgot that it is through that very hole he found such an "obscenity" he was conceived; and that through that same hole he was born. It is also curious that Sartre should conflate the anus, the mouth and the vagina, and even more curious that he would base his theory of plenitude on the anus rather than the mouth, for the anus empties the body whereas the mouth fills it up: plenitude.

And to describe that "amorous act" as castration is equally strange, particularly since, according to his theory of plenitude—which he had just advanced and equally quickly forgotten—the woman's being "filled up," to put it crudely, should have contributed to the "spherical plenitude of Parmenidean being"—a component of the human need to establish plenitude, like eating.

Nonetheless, Sartre did draw our attention to holes, as Freud had done before him. In our human orifices, therefore, are the secrets of our lives, growth and development. Humanity evolves out of, and revolves around, our holes. His misogyny seems to have passed unnoticed.

Sigmund Freud: Gifts, Gold and Anal Eroticism

It was Freud who brought the anus and faeces out of the water closet. Travelers have noted that defecation customs are culturally relative, and historians have demonstrated that they have changed over time; but Freud was the first to discuss such taboo topics as anal eroticism, toilet training and anal characters, as well as the changing evaluation of feces with toilet training. In an essay on love, Freud (1912) points out the geographic proximity of the excretory and procreative organs: "The excremental is all too intimately and inseparably bound up with the sexual; the position of the genitals—*inter urinas et faeces*—remains the decisive and unchangeable factor" (Vol. 7:259). (His use of the word "too" suggests a residual repression in Freud's own psyche, perhaps a feeling that so "oceanic" and pleasurable a sensation as sex should not be associated with "dirt.")

Freud scandalized his contemporaries by saying that "A child's first erotic subject is the mother's breast that nourishes it; love has its origin in attachment to the satisfied need for nourishment" (1973a:45). The breast provides nourishment but also pleasure and, Freud insists, "for that reason may and should be termed *sexual*" (1973a:11; emphasis in original). "Sucking at the mother's breast is the starting-point of the whole of sexual life, the unmatched prototype of every later sexual satisfaction" (Vol.1:356). This pleasure is followed, often, by thumb sucking—the beginnings of auto-eroticism—and later by masturbation. Both the mouth and the genitals are discovered quite early to be "erotogenic zones."

To describe the "little angels" as "sexual" and to discover their "erotogenic zones" was bad enough; but Freud went further in discussing the pleasures of defecation, anal eroticism, the first repression of instinctual urges and the emergence of anal character-types. The personal world, and indeed civilization, is founded in toilet training, in his view.

Freud says that children's attitudes to their own excreta are quite different from adults' attitudes: "Infants have feelings of pleasure in the process of evacuating urine and faeces and . . . they soon contrive to arrange these actions in such a way as to give them the greatest pleasure." Furthermore, the infant "feels no disgust at his faeces, values them as a portion of his own body with which he will not readily part, and makes use of them as his first 'gift,' to distinguish people whom he values highly" (Vol. 1:357). Indeed, "by producing them [these gifts] he can express his entire compliance with his environment and, by withholding them, his disobedience." They are "a token of affection," or disaffection (Vol. 7:103-4, 299). This is the infant's first decision-making process and may be the foundation of future character development, in Freud's view.

The toilet training, however, is precisely a training—and a repression of instinctual urges. In this process, infants, for the first time, "encounter the external world as an inhibiting power, hostile to their desire for pleasure, and have a glimpse of later conflicts both external and internal. An infant must not produce his excreta at whatever moment he chooses, but when other people decide that he shall . . . This is where he is first obliged to exchange pleasure for social respectability" (Vol. 1:357).

This is the beginning of the self-repression upon which civilization is built; and it is built on the reconstruction of feces from "gift" to "dirt": nasty, horrid, bad. So children learn to use the toilet, the importance of cleanliness and also disgust. Infants learn their bodies first through their oral and anal zones, and as they learn their bodies, so they learn pleasure and also about relationships; and so, through this process, their characters are formed.

Freud was particularly intrigued by the idea of feces as gifts, and, therefore, as the symbolic equivalent of gold and money. Indeed he suggests the improbable: "Faeces—money—gift—baby—penis are treated there [in the unconscious and in language] as though they meant the same thing, and they are represented too by the same symbols" (Vol. 2:134). While we cannot track all the connections between these seemingly unconnected objects, we can point to some: feces are offered as gifts by infants, though money is a preferred gift as they grow up; money is itself sometimes referred to as "filthy" as in "filthy rich;" babies are often referred to as "gifts of love" and are born "*inter urinas et faeces*;" and the penis produces both urine (waste) and semen (the gift of life).

Freud drew several examples from mythology that connect the unlikely combination of gold and feces: "The gold which the devil gives his paramours turns into excrement after his departure, and the devil is certainly nothing else than the personification of the repressed unconscious instinctual life." He adds that "even according to the ancient Babylonian doctrine, gold is the faeces of hell." Hence, there is the ironic equation of "the most precious substance known to men and the most worthless, which they reject as waste matter" (Vol. 7:214).

He also suggested that, for girls, the penis envy he postulated (in a now discredited theory) gives way to a desire for a man as the possessor of a penis and, then, to a wish for a baby. Furthermore: "Faeces, penis and baby are all three solid bodies; they all three, by forcible entry or expulsion, stimulate a membranous passage, i.e., the rectum and the vagina . . ." (Vol. 7:299-302).

Freud concludes his discussion with an analysis of character development based on fixation at the anal stage of development. Such people, suggests Freud, "are especially *orderly, parsimonious* and *obstinate*" (Vol.7:209; emphasis in original). Indeed, the description of someone as anal-retentive captures Freud's point precisely. He suggests that as infants they were defiant, refusing to empty their bowels as required. They were "anal erotics," but he thought that this stage was usually outgrown except "with certain homosexuals" (Vol. 7: 210-15).

His ideas were considered scandalous by many for various reasons: He wrote about parts, processes and products of the body that his readers did not usually discuss; he argued that children took pleasure in either defecation or constipation; and, perhaps, mostly because he suggested that such a devalued and taboo part of the body as the anus should have such an important role in personality formation. This was a total capsize of the usual hierarchy of body geography: not the will or the mind or parental love but the excretory process determines the self; not the top but the bottom.

Indeed, his ideas and interests are still rather shocking to many people. Yet, surely, the widespread use of the description of people as anal retentive or, simply, as anal, does suggest that, shocking or not, people find his ideas useful; though not, perhaps, his theory of toilet training.

Today, the interest in anal eroticism is probably more in anal sex as a safe but, perhaps, painful method of birth control, as a site of pornography, and as controversial in debates (previously discussed) about whether it counts as sex or not, and how much that depends on who is doing it.

Chapter 9

Skin

Skin is almost magical. It keeps the world out and the self in. It is the boundary between self and non-self. It is so thin that it is virtually transparent, yet so strong that it keeps our 110 or 220 pounds together. It is also elastic, growing and stretching from birth to a larger and heavier maturity. It lets the water of perspiration out, but does not let the waters of oceans and rains in. And whatever the outside temperature may be, it helps to keep the body temperature relatively constant, changing a few degrees up or down during illness. The skin also metabolizes vitamin D, stores fat (sometimes too well), is self-healing, and teaches us so much through both pain and pleasure and trial and error. And skin even changes color in sunlight with tans, in prison with pallor or under emotional stress of rage, fear or embarrassment. It renews itself, a bit like a snake: The body sloughs off about a million dead skin cells every *hour*. In humans it transmutes into hair and nails, and in animals skin can become hide and horn and hoof. Furthermore, the skin prints of fingers, palms, toes and soles are all absolutely unique. And it is our most engaging erogenous zone. It is a fascinating phenomenon.

Socially, however, skin is even more extraordinary. It is the principal medium through which and in which we express who we are and symbolize ourselves. Indeed, we talk in skin language as we do in body language and face language. Our skin talks, whether we like it or not, and it may betray us.

Our lives are inscribed on our skins; everyone can read them. Our scars, scabs, wounds, scratches, bruises, stretch marks, callouses, spots, wrinkles, laughter lines, pallor, tans, broken veins, wattles and dewlaps . . . everything leaves its marks on our skins. Our skins tell our age and sex, our ethnic or racial group, perhaps our patterns of smoking, eating and drinking, exposure to inside or outside, our childbearing status in stretch-marks, and our hard or scarring contact with the physical worlds of fire, sharp objects, contact sports and violence. Our skins, like our faces, can indicate with remarkable precision both who we are and how we have lived our lives.

Skin is also a prime site for emotional display, particularly for whites. With a light base color, whites may go even paler with shock or fear, blanching; or they may become crimson in embarrassment, exertion, sunburn, anger or with excessive alcohol consumption. And everyone's skin may sweat in the heat or with high energy output, or get goose-bumps in the cold. We watch skins closely— unavoidably, of course, since we also watch faces and eyes—for clues to emotions, feelings and states of mind.

The health states of the self are often indicated by the skin. Skin disorders erupt on the boundaries and borders of the body physical just as military conflicts erupt on the borders of the body politic. These include the mini-syllabic acne, boils, hives, warts, rashes, cold sores, tumors, and the worse-sounding eczema, psoriasis, neurotic excoriation (compulsive scratching), and shingles. Some say that many illnesses have a psychic component. True enough, I think, but also too much like blaming the victims. It surely does not apply to Ebola, malaria, polio, mad cow disease and more. Still, emotional stress, or how we deal with it, can be physically stressful. Many disorders may be caused by a wide range of factors: bacteria, viruses, physical or chemical irritants, cancer, allergies, nutritional deficiencies, and heredity may also play a role; but they may also be symptoms of underlying emotional disorders. The skin is often the link between physical and emotional health, and the medium of emotional expression.

North Americans spend billions on cosmetics, cosmetic surgeries, and beautification thingies of all sorts: moisturizers, lipsticks, razors, perfumes, deodorants, nail-painting, tanning, gyms, memberships, exercise, steroids, equipment—all to look more beautiful (perhaps for themselves), to maximize their health (perhaps to attract others), or both. Others spend on tattooing, branding, piercing, cicatrisation, implants, amputation, tongue-splitting—whatever. The point seems to be either to increase one's individuality or to seriously increase one's erotic capital, with maybe a nose job, liposuction or hair implants.

The point here is that the skin and the body react to, and interact with, our emotional lives and our sex lives. As one friend remarked: "When my husband was unfaithful, I got sick." Freud discussed this body-mind unity in talking about what he called "conversion" (though the term implies difference rather than unity), and "the language of the body," and "the flight into illness." The skin and the body are talking to us, both in pathologies and in body language (Vol. 8: 75-9; 114). Mental health and physical health, mind and body, are one. They are not quite as distinct as Plato and Descartes thought.

Finally, the skin is the primary and most potent instrument of self-transformation and self-reinvention. We can and do transform ourselves in our skins, temporarily or permanently: a paint-job, nose-ring, tattoo, type of hair cut or color, cosmetic surgery—all of these and more can flick our identities like a switch from one to another to another, though clothing, bearing, language, etc. must also be consistent with the presentation of these new selves.

As an indicator of emotions and of health, a medium of communication, a sensory organ, an erogenous zone, a political symbol and the prime site of identity and identity change, as well as of beauty or ugliness, the skin is powerful, magical and precious (Lafrance, 2009; Synnott, 1993)

Indeed, the social value and importance of the skin matches its physiological roles in a different domain. No wonder we pay it so much attention and give it so much care: We wash it daily, fragrance it, decorate it, check it for blemishes—the dreaded acne or cold sores, cuts and bruises and unwanted hair—visit dermatologists (in a crisis) and touch each other's skins in all sorts of different ways, depending on the relationships.

An oblique indication of the extraordinary social and physiological importance of the skin is that it provides some of our richest metaphors for personality and mood. These cutaneous metaphors are often textural. We may describe people as prickly or smooth or rough around the edges; as a soft touch or as hard and tough; or, unpleasantly, as oily, greasy, slimy or slippery. They might get under our skin, particularly in ticklish or hairy situations. Yet others are painfully shy. The tactile metaphors may also be thermal: We describe others as hot or cold, real cool, warm or, worse, frigid; or still worse, tepid. These thermal metaphors, in particular, relate closely to sexuality from cold to hot.

The skin is an erogenous zone. Freud was the first to insist on this. In his *Three Essays on Sexuality* (1905) he wrote that "Everyone knows what a source of pleasure on the one hand and what an influx of fresh excitation on the other is afforded by tactile sensations of the skin of the sexual object" (Vol. 7:69). Though some parts are, of course, more erogenous than others.

While this is well known today, his esteemed predecessor in sexology, Richard von Krafft-Ebing, said nothing about the skin and touching explicitly in *Psychopathia Sexualis* (1946/1886), despite long discussions on sadism and masochism. In his *Psychology of Sex*, however, Havelock Ellis agreed with Freud on the sexual roles of touch and skin: "The skin is the foundation on which all forms of sensory perception have grown up;" and "touch is really the primary and primitive erotic sense" (1934:41, 42). He cites the remark of a contemporary that "the sexual act is primarily a skin reflex" (1934:44). Ellis and Freud admired each other's work greatly, and were the first to discuss the sexual significance of the skin.

Hugging, stroking, caressing, kissing, cuddling, massage—all are, or may be, explicitly sexual. Yet we are not all equally tactile. This is both a personal and a cultural property. The tactile and the nontactile in personality and culture may have a difficult sexual time of it. What is unusual for the former may be instinctive for the latter. This constitutes a sensory and sexual mismatch.

The Personal Touch

Politicians are expected to be good communicators, and touch is one medium of communication. The journalist James Rosen recently accompanied secretary of State John Kerry on a whirlwind 11-day tour of 10 different countries. He reported:

> Kerry's a toucher. The physical contact he initiated during our first 15 minutes on the plane together, as he strode the cabin and chatted with his new press corps, easily exceeded the sum total of my physical contact with cabinet officers in the previous 15 years. He would scrunch your shoulder while talking to someone else, like a kindly uncle...Near the end of our trip, when I arrived for our final one-on-one interview, Kerry shook my hand, then drew me in for a bear hug, like a fraternity brother. (*Time*, 2013:191)

But not everyone is a toucher. A *Time* magazine journalist reported vividly on the sensory mismatch in tactilities between Bob Dole and his running mate Jack Kemp in the 1996 presidential election campaign:

> Jack Kemp is a space invader. Anyone in his vicinity is likely to be hugged, grabbed, patted or poked. He can't see a shoulder without draping an arm around it. Bob Dole is an untouchable. He seems to have an invisible force field around him that repels physical intimacy. What happens when an irresistible toucher meets an immovable untouchable? Reserve begins to melt. After Dole's convention speech and the duo's first rally in San Diego on Friday morning, Kemp grabbed Dole's good (left) arm and lifted it high. Both times Dole kept his arm up for fewer than 10 seconds before wriggling free. But by afternoon, under a bright sky in downtown Denver, as Dole and Kemp came onstage, Dole reached for his running mate's passing arm and raised it into the air, then held it there some more. This time Kemp let go first. (*Time*, 26 August 1996)

That's just running mates. Think bed mates. Some people are more tactile than others, and such an incompatibility could bring sexual problems and intimacy issues, at least until reserves melt.

Such differences may begin at birth. Some babies are cuddlers, others do not like to be restricted. In one study, half the babies were cuddlers, a quarter were resisters and a quarter were in-between. Why this is so is not known. Some theorize that, perhaps, it was a difficult birth while others suggest it is congenital (Hardison, 1980:24-5, 170-2). Yet it should be possible to test these hypotheses. We could ask the mothers if they had relatively easy or difficult births (though there could be issues of subjectivity here) and correlate that with the "Cuddle Quotient" of their children.

Certainly the range in personalities is wide. One extreme example is Esther Walker, who explains that she hates the New Year season: "I hate the physical contact, you see. It's not that I have personal space issues, or am particularly picky about who gets close, but that I suffer from haphephobia, a fear of being touched" (2011:36).

She first realized this when she was 13, and hated all the hand-holding and hugging at school: "I felt like I was made of ice." At university: "I had less of a problem with boys I liked but there always came a point in the relationship when I would snap, 'Get off me' or visibly recoil when I saw them coming in for a hug. My husband has succeeded where others failed, though. He simply ignores the occasional flinching and flatly demands affection" (2011:36).

So, some people are haphephobics, some are haphephiliacs, and others are into pain. (See "Paraphilias" below.)

Touch and Gender

There is, or may be, a huge "tactility gap" between individuals with respect to their personal borders and boundaries and their comfort levels. Tactility and sexuality are not simply individual matters, however; they are also gendered and cultural, which can contribute to misunderstandings and sexual disconnects. What makes individuals more or less comfortable with tactility is not known. Some think it might be genetic, others that it might be rooted in a difficult birth, family upbringing and, certainly, culture. But whatever the explanation(s), the gender difference, such as it is, is surely also rooted in socialization.

It all begins in childhood, as mothers and fathers raise their sons and daughters in subtly different ways—not all the time in every way, obviously, but enough to be worth a mention. Fathers tend to roughhouse with their sons, tossing them in the air, throwing them over their shoulders, twirling them around; mothers, not so much—more cuddling, tickling and kissing. Plus, fathers treat their daughters more gently. Similarly, mothers treat their daughters more gently, too, but also with more caution. I don't think that this is controversial, but in case it is, two anecdotes:

- I was walking past the kindergarten where two of my grandsons went to school. A boy suddenly rode his tricycle straight into the curbstone—why, I don't know—fell off, and looked up at me. He was fine, so I looked down at him and said: "No blood. You're O.K." and kept going. He was fine, though, perhaps, a bit surprised by his nonexistent driving skills. But behind me I heard a scream rising to high C: "Johnny! Are you O.K.?" The voice begged for tears. (Different socialization styles, obviously, stoicism vs. emotional expressiveness; or, as I like to think, reality vs. craziness).
- Coming out of our local library, I watched a five-year-old girl strolling along the granite curb (maybe two inches high) between the lawn and the driveway. She was fine. But her mother, in a knee-jerk reaction, called: "Be careful, dear!" Be careful of what? Of falling? A tsunami? This was inculcating fear into the poor kid, I thought; she was fine, doing well.

Both parents apparently tend to identify more with their same-sex offspring—no surprises there, really—and see themselves in them; and both are likely to repeat the same types of familial socialization that they were exposed to, modified, of course, by the fact that their partners may have been exposed to different patterns.

In fact, socialization begins long before the infants are aware of the processes. They are snuggled into pink or blue blankets (or yellow, in some hospitals, for fear of kidnapping). Relatives and friends arrive to ooh and aah and comment in "gender-appropriate" phrases: "Oh he's a strong looking one, isn't he? He's going to be useful on the rugby (insert sport here) pitch, just like his dad." "Oh, isn't she beautiful, just like her mum." They all say that the babies are cute, which is the commonality; but after that, it is binaries—strength and beauty; and while the babies are not aware of it yet, their big brothers and sisters can hear the expectations and values clearly.

Then, at primary school, the boys and girls settle into apartheid groups, with the boys generally more physical and competitive, playing football, soccer, hockey, or other contact sports, such as wrestling or boxing; and the girls are quieter, playing more cooperatively in skip-rope or hop-scotch or chatting. One lot are honing their physical and teamwork skills while the other lot are developing their language and emotive skills. The deviants from the norm in each group can have a difficult time, perhaps as loners, or perhaps as bullied, until they can find a domain in which they can shine. But G. I. Joe and Barbie Doll, Superman and Frozen epitomize the gender gap.

At puberty, the sexual attractions begin to attract, but still the lifestyles diverge: more violent and dangerous contact sports for men, and cheerleading as a common ideal for women, along with tennis, aerobics and swimming. At the same time, almost all sports are now open for both sexes at the Olympics, including individual competitions and team co-operative sports. Indeed women's sports and athletics are far more popular, and much better funded, than they were 50 years ago.

So much has changed in gender socialization, suggesting that we might have overestimated the importance of nature in the nature/nurture debates, and certainly underestimated the importance of nurture. Still, for all the tactile variation within each sex and the behavioral changes over time, men and women do tend to be socialized into opposite tactile—and emotional—directions: high risk vs. prudent, stoïc vs. expressive. Boys are trained to use their bodies as tools, as weapons, to conquer their opponents physically and to endure the pain. Girls are often on the sidelines watching, as their friends show off their skateboarding skills, and tend to avoid such dangerous situations.

The American anthropologist Ashley Montagu, who wrote a fine book on touch, suggests that American women are much more comfortable with touch than American men (1986:185). This is probably true, given the differential socializations. He did not discuss how these discrepant comfort levels might affect sexual relations. Signals get mixed, messages are misunderstood, life goes on and relationships are renegotiated—or not.

In her well-known report on female sexuality, Shere Hite asked women: "Do you enjoy touching?" Many women were very enthusiastic: "Touching is the most important part of sex." And some preferred the touching to the sex: "Sex itself is not terribly important to me, but physical contact in the form of touching, hugs, embraces, caresses, etc. is most important. I am more interested in having that kind of physical contact than I am in having sex." Another woman explained more briefly: "I will take a really good hug over an orgasm any day." I doubt that many men would agree with that statement. Indeed, some women complained about male tactility or, rather, the lack of same, quite bluntly: "Men never want to touch and kiss without fucking." Another remarked that "Men most generally have but one end in mind when they touch you" (1987:556-62).

Evidently, there is a wide range in personal tactility from the haphephobic to the haphephiliac, but also, more generally, a disjunction between male and female tactilities, sensualities and sexualities. The gap is probably far less than it was in the past. Today both sexes may engage in any sport, from rugby to boxing, hang-gliding to ice-climbing; and both sexes compete in the same events at the Olympics. Men can be champion chefs and women have climbed Everest, sailed round the world single-handed, been elected presidents and prime ministers of many countries, and become CEOs of some of the Fortune 500 companies. We have come a long way from Tennyson's poem, "The Princess":

Man for the field and woman for the hearth:
Man for the sword and for the needle she:
Man with the head and woman with the heart:
Man to command and woman to obey:
All else confusion.

The old polarization is clear: field/hearth, outside/inside, world/home, sword/needle, head/heart, reason/emotion, command/obey, man/woman. The new rules and roles are not so clear.

For all the constant change, mobility and fluidity in post-modernity, along with role-reversal and gender-equality, the millennia-old traditions still linger on, perhaps rooted in biology. Men are far more likely to ignore their tactile "needs" and to see their body as a tool, as in manual labor, or even a weapon as in contact sports, and to hurl themselves through space at risk of bodily/tactile injury for fun or sport or occupational duty, e.g., police, fire-fighting, the military, and to risk their lives for others in war. Women, on the other hand, are far more likely to see their bodies as assets, treasures, plants—to be grown, cared for and nurtured—as they themselves looked after their dolls when they were children, and their mothers looked after them. (Their fathers did so, too, by working, but this is not so often regarded as loving, though it is. Today more mothers are working outside the home, so the old equation has changed.)

These gender binaries are minefields, such as the pink and blue, the Venus (goddess of love) and Mars (the god of war) binaries proposed by John Gray (1994), and the binaries of Tennyson. Gender is not so clean and clear in post-modernity, and neither is tactility—if it ever was. These tactile/non-tactile, cuddler/resister dichotomies are probably rather overstated in adult-hood. Most of us are surely in-between along the usual continuum, avoiding the haphephobia of Esther and the haphephilia of some of the respondents in the Hite survey.

For starters, touch is unavoidable, even if you want to avoid it. Take, for instance, as Desmond Morris phrases it, your "average modern lovers." He traces the development of their intimacy through increasing access to the body parts: public to semi-public to private parts; from seeing to touching to "doing." He suggests a 12-step process, or progress. This starts, often, with eye to body, eye to eye, voice to voice, hand to hand, arm to shoulder, arm to waist, mouth to mouth, hand to head, hand to body, mouth to breast, hand to genitals, and genitals to genitals. Obviously, these 12 steps can be leapt, as in rape, or by sex workers and their clients, or by the hot and horny. Or they can be stopped cold at step three: "Nope. Not interested." Or there could be more steps,, such as lips to hand, mouth to genitals, which Morris also discusses. And, as he notes, other cultures have other patterns of arousal, seduction and intimacy. Still, it is a fascinating journey around and into each other's bodies (1979:62-82). Indeed, the idea of eyes, ears, voices, arms, hands, mouth, breasts, tongues and genitals exploring the various geographic zones, like tourists, in increasing intimacy, is rather beguiling.

The sexologist Pamela Stephenson-Connolly is less worried about the alleged gender-gap in tactility than Hite or Montagu, and more concerned about the learning of both. She says that "the early pleasure of being held and caressed helps us to respond positively to sensual and sexual human contact later in life" (2011:19). So we learn to love ourselves and to take pleasure in our bodies. In later life, sexual pleasure is likely to take on different sensualities. "Many adults have forgotten the delights of non-coital sexuality because they have become accustomed to 'going straight for the money.' But women in particular tend to love slow romantic connection, sensuous embraces and seductive words" (2011:405). By "adults" above, I think she means mostly men, who should become less "goal-oriented" and more pleasure-oriented, and think more about quality, not quantity. She quotes Barbara Cartland: "Among men, sex sometimes results in intimacy, among women, intimacy sometimes results in sex" (2011:405). But both often agree that "Sex isn't as important as a relationship" (2011:361).

Touch and Culture

Just as individuals and genders vary widely in their tactility, so too do cultures. Paul Theroux commented on this in Spain:

> . . . What I saw (and it made me hopeful for the rest of my trip) was simple affection. In other travels I had not seen much affection between men and women, that is, open displays of physical intimacy—kissing, hand-holding, snogging, canoodling, a sudden hug; not lust but affection, friendship, reassurance, paddling palms

> and pinching fingers. I had hardly seen it in China. It was rare on the islands of Oceania. It did not exist in India.
>
> I saw it in Spain: old married couples holding hands, young people kissing, married ones embracing . . . It was deeply affecting, spontaneous and candid. I thought: I like this. (1976:73)

Theroux is an observant writer and presents us with a rank order of cultural tactility from high (Spain) to low (China and Oceania) to non-existent (India). But such observations are limited in scope and subjective to one observer; I like them, but they are not enough. Having recently returned from India (in 2013), I have to disagree with Theroux. I saw much affection: men holding hands with men, women with women, boys walking with their arms slung around their friends' shoulders, and much affection between parents and children. True, public displays of affection between members of the opposite sex were unusual, and the guidebooks warn tourists about observing those customs. Theroux missed that tactility is demonstrated in opposite ways in the U. S. and India.

The English

"Continental people have sex life: the English have hot-water bottles." So declared George Mikes, a Hungarian immigrant to Britain and an acute observer of the English. He later apologized for being completely out-of-date, citing an English women who wrote: "You are really behind the times . . . We are using electric blankets nowadays" (1966:84). Is the stereotype based in reality? A bit, according to Druckerman's *Lust in Translation*, as we have seen; but not entirely.

Kate Fox, an anthropologist, has thoroughly researched English culture in her own amused and amusing (often absolutely hilarious) style. She says that "the notion that the English do not have much sex, or have a laughably low sex-drive, is widely accepted as fact—even, indeed especially, among the English themselves" (2005:324). She dismissed this as a myth, stating that "the English have the highest rates of teenage sexual activity in the industrialized world, with 86 percent of unmarried girls sexually active by the age of nineteen"—beating the U.S. with only 75 percent (2005:324-5). Whether that is great or not is another matter, but it does demolish the myth that they prefer hot-water bottles or electric blankets. Still, she finds that the English really "are sexually inhibited" and have difficulty discussing sex except through humor. "In other parts of the world, sex may be regarded as a sin, an art form, a healthy leisure activity, a commodity, a political issue and/or a problem requiring years of therapy and umpteen self-help 'relationship' books. In England, it is a joke" (2005:326).

She returns to this theme again, with some comparative analysis: "Some cultures celebrate sex and the erotic; others (religious ones, mainly) neutralize sex by censorship; others (the US, parts of Scandinavia) neutralize it with po-faced, earnest political correctness. The English do it with humor" (2005:352).

But they do it! (And they do most things with humor, not just sex). The English also do it with alcohol: "The role of alcohol in the passing on of English DNA should not be underestimated" (2005:328); perhaps, as she suggests, because of the central role of pubs in social life.

We might wonder how sexuality relates to tactility, might we not? Very closely, probably, but I do not have scientific data on either. Travelers' tales do not suffice. But they raise excellent questions: Are we more tactile because we are more sexual or more sexual because we are more tactile? Or both? The latter seems probable, with reciprocal interaction in a virtuous circle. The answers, predictably, are complicated.

Ashley Montagu, whom we have already mentioned, talks to this issue: "Two of the great negative achievements of Christianity have been to make a sin of tactual pleasures, and by its repression to make of sex an obsession" (1986:312). Yet, he insists: "Sex . . . has been called the highest form of touch. In the profoundest sense touch is the true language of sex" (1986:204). He notes the wide variations in tactility by culture, class and gender, which we can only "touch" on. First, culture: he advises that "There are clearly contact peoples and non-contact peoples" (1986:357). This is a bit too binary: Probably there is a continuum, with most people somewhere in the middle. For Theroux, the extremes were Spain and India. Montagu, however, affirms the "absolute untouchability" of upper- and middle-class Englishmen. (He had studied at the London School of Economics, so he was somewhat familiar with some of them.) And he attributed this to a whole range of possible or probable factors, admittedly differing between families. These included negative attitudes to breastfeeding, functional orientations to bathing babies (not taken as an opportunity for fun and play), the transfer of parenting to nannies, the solitary sleeping arrangements for children (who may be "sent" to bed rather than "put" to bed with stories and kisses), the boarding-school system. He concluded: "Too often [all this] produced a rather emotionally arid human being who was quite incapable of warm human relationships. Such individuals made poor husbands, disastrous fathers, and efficient governors of the British Empire, since they were seldom capable of understanding genuine human needs" (1986:354).

We might surmise that Montagu was not an Anglophile. Still, if it is any consolation to any Brits who might read this, Montagu adds: "Even more far gone in nontactility, if such a thing can be imagined, than the English, are the Germans" (1986:356). And if it is any consolation to any Germans who might be reading this, the first edition of his book came out in 1971, and much has changed in the last 40-plus years. Montagu's theorizing that this "nontactility" creates "poor husbands, disastrous fathers . . . seldom capable of understanding genuine human needs" is intriguing. So, he implies, highly tactile cultures have lower levels of violence, due to the interpersonal empathy learned by tactile contact; and members of these cultures are more comfortable with their bodies and their sexuality—unlike, he says, many repressed, puritanical Americans who are obsessed with sex. And, we might infer, are more violent.

The data, however, contradict such simplistic theorizing. Central and South America are supposedly relatively tactile cultures, but the homicide rate in Honduras is now about 90.4 per 100,000, the highest in the world; in Venezuela it is 53.7 and in Belize it is 44.7, which is twice as high as Mexico at 21.5; but the homicide rate is less than one in Japan, New Zealand and—wait for it—Germany. Almost half a million people are killed by homicide every year, with the global average about 6.2 per 100,000 population (UNODC, 2014).

So the data indicate exactly the opposite of Montagu's assertion. It just may be that Montagu's prejudices got the better of him, and that he needed a more critical or broader perspective. Montagu's point that this trinity of variables (tactility, sex and aggression) are all causally related is too simple; they are mediated by other intervening variables: historical backgrounds, access to gun-ownership, drug wars, racism, gangs, poverty, inequality, police and judicial corruption and more.

And had he been more reflective, he might have wondered about the United States, where the once-standard work on raising children, *The Care and Feeding of Children* by Dr. L. E. Holt was first published in 1894 and last reprinted in 1943. He instructed parents: "Babies under six months should never be played with; and the less of it at any time the better" (Holt 1929:201). Holt objected to rocking babies, not having figured out that this must have been the norm for them in their mothers' wombs, as they moved about (1929:91). And he particularly objected to kissing babies: "Tuberculosis, diphtheria [and syphilis, he added later] and many other grave diseases may be communicated in this way . . . Infants should be kissed, if at all, upon the cheek or forehead, but the less even of this the better (1929: 93).

Holt was not unique in his time. John Watson, the founder of Behaviorism, wrote in his influential *Psychological Care of Infant and Child* (1928; reprinted as late as 1972): "There is a sensible way of treating children. Treat them as though they were young adults. Dress them, bathe them with care and circumspection. Let your behavior always be objective and kindly firm. Never hug and kiss them, never let them sit on your lap. If you must, kiss them once on the forehead when they say goodnight. Shake hands with them in the morning" (Watson, 1972: 81-2).

Strangely unaware of the advice of his compatriots, Holt and Watson, and of the possible consequences of their advice, Montagu was aware that tactile deprivation is the primary cause of "failure to thrive" in infants, and even of their deaths (Montagu, 1986; Synnott, 1993; Classen, 2005).

The French

And now for something completely different: the French. The French benefit from the positive stereotype that they are a very sexy people—in stark contrast to their neighbors—the English, the Germans and the Swiss—but also to the Americans. The stereotype is based on some realities, not least Brigitte Bardot, and also their leadership in the perfume industry and the fashion industry (Coco Chanel, Dior, Pierre Cardin); their sensual gastronomy; their womanizing politicians and the public tolerance of same for so long; and the beauty and style of French women. The award-winning American journalist Elaine Sciolino has written a magnificent book on the French entitled *La Seduction*—for seduction, she argues, sexual and otherwise, is the key to understanding the French and French culture.

Some stories and statistics to illustrate the sexy bits: one Saturday morning in downtown Paris, an acting teacher had two of her students demonstrate kissing to the watching crowd—the French kiss: "See, hold her head. That's very good! The back of her neck!" Then, the American kiss: "more technically welcoming to the camera. They are going to simply move their jaws. It's called 'mouth-eating'." Sciolino thought that, back in the States, "you would be more likely to find a demonstration of a device to cut potatoes in ten ways" (2012:50).

For both lingerie and perfume, statistics tell much of the story about the French and sexuality: For lingerie, one survey found that 91 percent of French women and 83 percent of French men consider lingerie important in life. I doubt if anyone has asked Americans; they certainly haven't asked me. And French women aged 15-plus spend nearly 20 percent of their clothing budget on lingerie, more than the women elsewhere in Europe (2012:140). So, yes, they consider it important. For perfume, the French apparently spend more than $40 per person on fragrances annually—more than anywhere else in the world; and that's about $2.5 billion. She tells the story of one friend who asked her what perfume she used. She responded by asking why she wanted to know. Her friend answered: "I want to get to know you better" (2012:166). That's (non-sexual) seduction too.

Yet, there is some mythology here. The Durex sex survey, already mentioned, reported that the French have sex, on average, 120 times a year, which puts them at #11 on the sex league table, far behind the Greeks at 164 and Brazilians at 145, and far ahead of Americans at 85. For the record, this survey is contradicted by other research, which reports that not only do the French have sex less frequently than the Americans, but also that they have fewer sexual partners; on the other hand, French women over 50 are more sexually active than same-age American women (2012:52-3).

In some respects, France and the United States are opposite in terms of sexuality. The French could not understand the fuss about the Clinton-Lewinsky scandal; one deputy (male) explained: "Americans are the puritan descendants of the Mayflower . . . In truth, what is scandalous across the Atlantic is one of the favourite traditions in France." Another deputy (female) seemed to applaud Clinton: "He loves women, this man." Adultery is a major reason for divorce in both France and the United States, but they seem to see it differently. "For Americans, infidelity is betrayal. For the French, what Americans call infidelity is often the glue that keeps the order of things: parents stay together; the children are spared emotional trauma; property stays in the family; financial security is maintained . . ." (2012:215, 58).

Another comparison: "In America, the goal is to conquer as efficiently as possible and, if you're lucky, to live happily ever after. In France, the excitement comes less from gratification than desire." It's the difference between sex and pleasure. It's not about notches (2012:42).

Yet, times change very rapidly, and particularly in the empire of sex. The womanizing of successive French presidents—Giscard d'Estaing, Mitterand, Chirac, Sarkozy—rather rudely listed by *Time* (27 January 2014), which omitted Kennedy, Johnson and Clinton, was abruptly challenged by the Dominique Strauss-Kahn affair, and the accusations against him of rape in New York and engaging prostitutes in France, which cost him his bid for the French presidency. Then the integrity and credibility of President Hollande was impaired after his alleged affair with an actress. In France, the private is no longer private. The culture is changing.

So: different cultures, different sex norms. The differences are illustrated by the covers of these two aforementioned books. Fox's anthropology of the English features a rather dispirited couple seated under an umbrella, presumably in the rain, in empty football stands, with the woman reading a newspaper; Sciolino's shows a woman's shapely legs in high heels climbing the stairs. But both are better than the cover of Susan Bordo's book, *The Male Body,* which has a nude, presumably male, body, segmented into four parts, minus most of the arms, legs, half his head and all of his penis. Castration, again! Not too hard to deconstruct that American portrait.

Kissing

We kiss each other all the time, in greetings and farewells, to say goodnight; to heal, as in kissing it better; to celebrate: the winners kiss the golden or silver trophy; to show respect, as we kiss the bishop's ring or the lady's outstretched hand; even to betray, as in the Judas kiss and the Mafia kiss—the kiss of death; and we kiss and make up. And, mostly, we kiss to express our love and affection.

Lovers love to kiss. The union of lips equates with the union of souls and lives. Hence, Shelley's lovely line: "Soul meets soul on lover's lips;" and Sara Teasdale's poem "The Look," about the kiss that never was, and the various types of kiss too:

> Strephon kissed me in the spring
> Robin in the fall
> But Colin only looked at me
> And never kissed at all.
> Strephon's love was lost in jest
> Robin's lost in play
> But the kiss in Colin's eyes
> Haunts me night and day.

Ah, well! *C'est la vie*! A verse from Stevie Smith's poem "Conviction" is quite blissful:

> I like to laugh and be happy
> With a beautiful kiss,
> I tell you, in all the world
> There is no bliss like this.

The origins of kissing are thought to lie in breastfeeding; this is why we like it; it is associated with our earliest pleasures, sucking at the breast, with the oral gratification and the overall physical gratification, the full tummy, which ensues. Adrianne Blue, who has written the definitive work on kissing, suggests (following Freud): "We love to kiss because kissing was present in our first great affair" (1996:51), i.e., with our mothers. (Others note that kissing is not, or was not, a universal custom; and it may have developed from mouth feeding, by which mothers chew the food first.)

There is a certain symmetry here, in that as soon as we are born we enjoy kissing and sucking the breast; and then, in maturity, we enjoy the kissing again, feel passionate, perhaps, and what with one thing and another, another baby is born who also enjoys the kissing. So kissing the lips escalates the first great love of kissing the nipples. The kiss is the nurturer of life both in infancy and in maturity, albeit in varied styles.

It is also sheer delight, as in Doisneau's famous photograph of two lovers kissing and Rodin's equally famous sculpture. As so many women told Shere Hite: "Kissing is very important to me. I can sometimes almost orgasm from kissing. Tons of kissing is what I relish. Gentle and passionate kissing especially on my neck—ahhh . . ." (Hite, 1987:569).

Despite our love of kissing and its importance in so many sectors of our lives, kissing is not a cultural universal. Greetings and intimacy are expressed differently elsewhere. The Maoris of New Zealand traditionally greeted each other with the "hongi," or nose press, as did the Inuit of Canada. South and West and North meet, however, in the positioning of the faces together, whether with nose or lips. The Japanese greet each other with graceful bows, and with no physical contact. Even shaking hands is not the norm.

Not that Western customs are identical. They are not. The English kiss on one cheek. The Quebecers kiss on both cheeks. Negotiating which one, or which one first, can be quite confusing and nose-dislocating. The French and Lebanese often kiss three times. Men may kiss each other in France and Russia and in Arabic and Persian cultures, but not usually in the U.K. or North America. As the anthropologists have told us, kissing norms vary, and some cultures are much more tactile than others.

There are, of course, many types of kisses, conveying different roles and causing different states of mind and, indeed, body. There is the peck, the smack and the smooch, the air kiss (or lipstick-avoidance kiss), the vacuum kiss, the lip-o-suction kiss, the upside-down kiss, the exchange kiss (of candy or wine), the electric kiss, the French kiss, the Aussie kiss (the same as the French kiss, but down under), and so on (Blue, 1996:34-6).

The Kama Sutra has a chapter on kissing and mentions 21 types. These include the straight, bent and turned kisses, the "moderate, contracted, pressed, and soft, according to the different parts of the body that are kissed," and so on down the list. But in its listing of positions and types, it is more anal than erotic: it is an accountancy of kissing.

The journalist Lynn Snowden has observed several kissing styles in Hollywood movies: There is the Harrison Ford style: "watch his co-star's face get twisted out of shape from the sheer force. This is also why they are panting afterward. It's not from desire; it's oxygen deprivation." One of her friends fainted when her kisser prevented her from breathing with his mouth and cheek. Then there is the Lizard-King style of Tom Cruise in "Top Gun," with the tongue prematurely sliding out. The Road-runner-eats-birdseed is epitomized by Woody Allen in "Hannah and Her Sisters," as he pecks away at Dianne Wiest with smacking sounds. Daniel Day-Lewis wins an award for his "Best Use of Hands," caressing his co-stars's hair. For good measure, she tells her readers the difference between a good kisser and a bad one: "A bad kisser, regardless of whether he likes to secrete a gallon of drool or waggle his head like a dog menacing a bone, seems to be simultaneously thinking: 'When can we get to step two? And three and four?' . . . He sees kissing as the necessary first step in a carnal quest. The good kisser, however, sees the kiss as the destination itself" (1995:41-2). Or seems to.

There are now books on how to kiss. It is a learned art, it seems, either from books or the hard but happier way. One slim volume, mostly for teenagers, has sweet chapters on Flirting, Developing Courage, and How to Become a Successful Kisser—and the stories and lists of Dos and Don'ts are cute (Terry and Mike,1984). Another is mostly a list of the different types of erotic kisses. Perhaps the longest kiss is 417 hours, as stated in the *Guinness Book of Records*. Didn't they sleep? Eat? The author doesn't say (Cane, 1995).

And then there is the first kiss, which some people can remember even decades later (Cane, 1995:26, 28):

• My heart exploded. I was one happy rubber-chested gal the next day. A New Year's party. I was fourteen or fifteen. His name was Gary, a boy my age, a schoolmate. My first experience drinking hard liquor (or any kind of liquor). I let him touch my breasts under my shirt. We kissed for hours on a couch in a den of a friend's house. Then he drove me to a place where we watched planes take off from the airport, soaring, blasting close overhead. More kissing. More thrill to the bone marrow. I still remember his breath, and occasionally the scent comes back to me.

• I was fourteen years old, and I kissed a girl I had a crush on named Karen. It felt great, though she was eight inches taller than I was. I felt like I was floating on a cloud. I was a little embarrassed because she kissed me in front of my whole soccer team.

• My first kiss was incredible. I was fourteen and we were playing truth-or-dare at a party, and someone dared me to French-kiss a girl that I (and every other guy in my school) wanted very badly. She was an extremely attractive girl with a fantastic mouth. I had no emotional connection with her, but the kiss was fantastic, and she also seemed to be pleased. That thrill will follow me for the rest of my days.

The imagery is so vivid, so poetic, so intense: "My heart exploded," "thrill to the bone marrow," "floating on a cloud," "That thrill will follow me for the rest of my days." These kisses were not just kisses: they were ecstasy, turning points in life, powerful unions with another person, and still remembered . . . not all quite so happily. One friend remembers that the first boy who kissed her remarked that "it was like kissing a brick wall." At best, they touch on the perfect union between two human beings. Reading these accounts—and there are many more in Shere Hite, Adrienne Blue and William Cane, as well as in your own memory—is almost enough to restore one's faith in human nature!

Mary Karr, now an English professor, described her first kisses in a kissing game with three boys and her girlfriend. Her description runs over three pages and is far more sensual than the *Kama Sutra*. The first is Bobbie "who holds my elbows as if we are about to spin toplike through the dark. His lips are chapped dry and sweet . . . [then] Davie Hawks is on me. His lips are blubbery and wet . . . [then] John Cleary draws me to him, and there's such a surge inside me I can't locate where it's bubbled up from" So the game continues and "my whole body is purring" (2000:74-6).

There is also the forbidden kiss: the taboo kiss of incest. An acclaimed American novelist, Kathryn Harrison, described meeting her father for the first time as an adult. He had left his wife and her before her first birthday, only seen her three times as a child, and then returned into their lives when Harrison was a beautiful, blonde, 20-year-old university student. She drove him to the airport, and he kisses her goodbye, his hand behind her head: "My father pushes his tongue deep into my mouth: wet, insistent, exploring, then withdrawn." She added: "I am frightened by the kiss. I know it is wrong, and its wrongness is what lets me know, too, that it is a secret."

This kiss is not only wrong and a secret, Harrison shows that it is much more: "In years to come, I'll think of the kiss as a kind of transforming sting, like that of a scorpion: a narcotic that spreads from my mouth to my brain. The kiss is the point at which I begin, slowly, inexorably, to fall asleep, to surrender volition, to become paralyzed. It's the drug my father administers in order that he might consume me. That I might desire to be consumed" (1997:69-71).

Her affair with her father lasted five years, and her memoir about it is entitled *The Kiss* (1997). It took the death of her grandfather and then the death of her mother before it was over. And as it was a kiss that put her to sleep, so it was another kiss that awakened her—kissing her dead grandfather goodbye: "The kiss I place on his unyielding cheek begins to wake me, just as my father's in the airport put me to sleep" (1997:190).

Her memoir is a cool analysis of the vortex of emotions and the tangled knots of the relationships between her and her divorced parents, theirs with each other, the grandmother, and the new wife. A curious dance of lovers. But in an interview in *Mirabella*, Harrison sliced through the Gordian knot: "I wanted my father . . . And I got him" (March-April 1997:41). So the villain and victim changed places. Perhaps it was *her* kiss that was the sting of the scorpion.

Susanna Kaysen, she with the painful vagina, is lyrical about kissing:

> "The moment before you kiss someone is the best moment of all, and I want to extend it. Once you've kissed, once you've tasted each other, entered each other's bodies, the entire business has been concluded in some way. This is why a kiss equals an infidelity. A fuck is just a full-body kiss. The kiss is what breaches the separation between two people. Nothing is the same after a kiss" (2001:144).

And it was not the same after the most famous kiss in history, when Judas Iscariot kissed Jesus Christ in the Garden of Gethsemane almost 2000 years ago.

You may (or may not) have wondered about this. What is it like to kiss Matt Damon? Michael Douglas, playing Liberace, kisses him in "Behind the Candelabra," and was asked by an interviewer for *Maclean's* magazine: "Everybody wants to know what it was like to kiss Matt Damon." His enigmatic answer: "You know, it doesn't matter, does it, if it's a man or a woman. It's a kiss. We had to show affection, in some places, love, passion in other places. A kiss is just a kiss. I mean, we'd have our fun" (Johnson, 2013:14-5).

The urge and desire to physically connect with other people—by hand-holding, head-caressing, kissing or nose-rubbing (or even without touching, by bowing or smiling, glancing or staring)—is, surely, hard-wired and with evolutionary functions. It is after the kiss that one might decide to try to take it to "the next level," as they say. Kissing is more than touching. And many animals kiss. Chimpanzees kiss for mutual assurance, in greeting and in joy. Bonobos, who are the primates closest to humans, engage in what we call French kissing, but what we should probably call bonobo kissing—as one zookeeper discovered to his surprise (Blue, 1996:69-72). And our dogs insist on licking our faces, especially our lips, preferably immediately after they have been cleaning rather personal parts of their anatomy. Wolves, who are described by their researchers as very affectionate and nurturing animals, engage in mutual face-licking—what we would call kissing—in tender moments; and there are numerous photographs to prove it (Brandenburg, 1993). Sometimes these actions are submission behaviors, which maintain pack hierarchies, but often they are affection behaviors, which maintain pack unity and pair bonding. As Darwin (1872) noted so long ago, and as we so often forget, we cannot look at animal behaviors and emotions without seeing the similarities to human behaviors and emotions.

The big difference is that human beings have to be very careful who they kiss, when, where, how and why. Kissing is now highly political: grounds for sexual harassment charges and potential career breakers. But sometimes it all gets ridiculous, as in the case of Johnathan Prevette, six years old, of Lexington, North Carolina. He kissed a classmate, because he liked her and because, he said, she had asked him to. A teacher saw him. He was expelled for the day. The press picked up the story and Prevette became an international star, a cause célèbre, and a symbol, to quote Camille Paglia, of "archfeminist ideology gone amuck" (*Time*, 7 October 1996).

"A kiss is just a kiss," goes part of the lyric of the featured song in "Casablanca"—except when it isn't. xx Love.

*

Skin is the first site of "fresh excitation" (Freud) and "the primary and primitive erotic sense" (Ellis). But personal boundaries, borders and sensitivities are immensely variable between individuals, between the two sexes and, especially, between cultures; and they change all the time as values change. "Mad Men" is only 50 years—but light years—from "Sex and the City." Hugging, caressing, kissing, stroking, massages, and all forms of touch are all, or may be, intensely erotic and also intensely controversial.

Section 3—The Goings On

Introduction

The goings on are hard to keep track of. Here we will just explore a few issues related to sex and sexualities. First, there are the debates about nakedness and nudity in Chapter 10. What is the difference? And how do they reflect and create attitudes about the body, from shame to pride?

These matters are developed further in Chapter 11, on the vexed issue of pornography and erotica, and depictions not just of naked or nude bodies but of people having sex. What is the distinction between pornography and erotica? Is it purely subjective? How does pornography impact society? And sexuality? Some are for porn, some are against it, and some simply want better porn. The arguments are continuing. Still, the range in erotica cross-culturally is fascinating, e.g., *shunga* among the Japanese, the cult of the lotus among the Chinese, and the temple carvings in ancient Hindu India. And beauty is highly erotic—though in the eye and culture of the beholder.

Then, there is the amazing history of masturbation in chapter 12, from wrong to right, from sin to disease to neurosis to fun to a right; and it is even, according to a pamphlet published by the British National Health Service, a duty to one's sexual health (which was later withdrawn).

Paraphilias are discussed in chapter 13, describing the wide range of sexualities, first reviewed by Krafft-Ebing as pathologies. Some are harmless, some anxiety-provoking, and some are lethal. The principal focus here is on BDSM (an overlapping abbreviation of bondage, discipline, dominance, submission, sadism and masochism), with Count Masoch and the Marquis de Sade; also, there is the story of former Colonel Russell Williams in Canada, whose paraphilias escalated rapidly, from the relatively harmless to homicide. Now the international best-selling *Fifty Shades of Grey* trilogy has brought them forward into pop culture.

Finally, we explore the different theories of love, and some of the research on love, as well as the role of sexual attraction in human evolution, according to Charles Darwin and, more recently, Jared Diamond. Love seems so simple, yet it is so complicated and so fascinating, there are so many types and so many theories, and it is, perhaps, the greatest power in our universe.

Chapter 10
The Naked and the Nude

Isn't it odd that artists do not paint "naked" people? They paint "nudes." This is so much more refined, high class, intellectual, asexual, less gross. No nasty, smelly, naked bodies here. Ugh! Simply elegant and beautiful women with curvy lines gazing at you gazing at them, and pondering mutually salacious thoughts; until, that is, the twentieth century, with Picasso's bizarre canvases, Lucian Freud's famous, very large naked lady, and the rise of gay male portraiture. The distinction between the naked and the nude has been complexified, however, as these comments indicate: "The English language, with its elaborate generosity, distinguishes between the naked and the nude. To be naked is to be deprived of our clothes, and the condition implies some of the embarrassment most of us feel in that condition. The word 'nude,' on the other hand, carries, in educated circles, no uncomfortable overtone" (Clark, 1956:3).

So, Sir Kenneth Clark, the distinguished art historian, opens his classic volume on *The Nude*. He suggests there is "a short answer to the question, 'What is the nude?' It is an art form invented by the Greeks in the fifth century, just as opera is an art form invented in seventeenth century Italy" (1959:4). But all this is open to discussion, and invites it. (So when the police arrest you for wandering around downtown with no clothes on, you can enquire: "Why me, officer?" "Because you are naked in public, and that is against the law." "But officer, I'm not naked. I'm nude. And this is an ancient Greek art form. Sir Kenneth Clark said so." "Oh. Did he? Well that's OK then. Off you go. Keep warm." But I digress.)

Yet surely, the prior question should be: "What is the difference between the naked and the nude?" The two words mean exactly the same: they are synonyms. My *Concise Oxford Dictionary* defines naked as nude and nude as naked. The etymologies are different, it is true: The former is from the Old English, Old High German and Old Norse, while the latter is from the Latin. But even though the words have identical meanings, the emotional connotations are subtly different. The classic illustration of this is the title of Clark's own book, *The Nude*. A gentleman in his "educated circles" would not call it "Naked People!" But why not? Artists just do not paint naked people. They paint nudes. This is an example of words as camouflage for naked truths. Again, why? And my second issue is that nudes are not just art forms invented in fifth century Greece. Nudes are people, too. So, then, why the different emotional connotations? Quick answer: circumstances and attitudes.

Circumstances: We are naked (not nude) when we are born, and the first thing they do is swaddle us; and, after that, we are hardly ever without clothes, especially in public. We are naked by ourselves in the shower, but with others looking at us in the locker room at the gym, things can get a bit more complicated. We might be a bit more self-conscious, for example, suck in the gut, and, if you are a man, discreetly "fluff" the old penis to try to impress the competition. Not having had the opportunity to research women's behavior patterns in the locker rooms, I cannot speak for them; but my colleague, Andrew Nicholls, says that men can be divided into the strutters and the hiders: The former stroll around happily, showing off their equipment, with their towels slung casually over their shoulders, and their "second face," so to speak, in your face. The hiders may not even take a shower after their workout, especially if the showers do not have private stalls or cubicles; but, if they do, they will hide their equipment with their towels, modestly. Younger men are more accustomed to privacy than the older ones, who, perhaps, grew up with compulsory showers after compulsory games. The privatization of showering by the building of separate cubicles with curtains has raised what sociologist Norbert Elias (1982) has called "the shame threshold." The naked body must be hidden in public; it is way too pubic for public consumption. The pubic and the public seem to be antithetical.

The hiders and the strutters might be seen as somewhere along a continuum between the naked and the nude. The naked include the baby, who is totally unselfconscious, but also the mad. Years ago I was walking past what was then called the Lunatic Asylum in Port of Spain, Trinidad. The asylum adjoined the road, and a wire fence surrounded the inmates. Most of them had taken their clothes off and were sitting on the tarmac in the sun, utterly unselfconscious, too. The nude, on the other hand—whether in the picture on the wall for which she has posed or in the bedroom—is very much self-aware, and proud of it. The portraits show women (usually) and their pride in their beauty, their awareness of their sexuality and their confidence in their sex appeal. It is all there in so many of the portraits and photographs.

In contrast, in Japan, in rural areas, men and women may bathe together, naked, in the public baths. Nakedness, therefore, does not have quite the same erotic appeal as it does in the Occident. This explains why, in *shunga,* the active participants in sex are usually clothed. Shame thresholds are different or nonexistent (Baruma, 1984).

John Berger has also addressed this state of undress:

> To be naked is to be oneself. To be nude is to be seen naked by others and yet not recognized for oneself. A naked body has to be seen as an object in order to become a nude. Nakedness reveals itself. Nudity is placed on display. To be naked is to be without disguise. To be on display is to have the surface of one's own skin, the hairs of one's own body, turned into a disguise which, in that situation, can never be discarded. The nude is condemned to never being naked. Nudity is a form of dress. (1979:54)

Well, I don't know. Naked or nude, we can still be recognized for ourselves. Nor is one's nude friend "condemned" to anything; he or she will certainly be naked later on, or somewhere else. And, surely, it is unduly oxymoronic to say that "Nudity is a form of dress." It is a presentation of the self to the other, and a form of undress. And, anyway, the nude person is not so much "placed on display" as he or she deliberately places himself or herself on display—in a bedroom or a strip club or an artist's studio—perhaps to incite desire or to raise cash and hopes. True, the portrait may be placed on display, but the nude is first of all the person, not the portrait.

The renowned art historian Edward Lucie-Smith has also joined the debate. The distinction between the naked and the nude, in his view, resides here: "naked (that is, conspicuously without clothing), rather than as nude (without clothing, but somehow translated into an ideal sphere)" (1998:112), e.g. as a work of art. In other words, you are naked but my portrait of you (or your self-portrait) makes you a nude—except that some portraits and self-portraits (Schiele, Freud) are horribly unidealized. No halos there.

Ruth Barcan (2004:14) has written an authoritative volume, *Nudity*, in which she developed a typology comparing various characteristics of nakedness and clothing:

Nakedness	**Clothing**
Natural	cultural
Unchanging	changing
Invisible	visible
Truth	lies
Pure	corrupt
Human nature	human society
Pre-non-anti-social	social

Such evaluations are also contextual, as she admits, and may be more of a continuum; naked, for example, can be quite social. But this typology does relate to two common aphorisms: the human as the "clothed ape" and founder of civilization, and the idea that "the clothes make the man." Not quite; other factors are relevant, but change the clothes and you start to change the man and the woman. The "Pygmalion effect."

There are complications here, for the nude in art and the naked individual cannot be conflated. The nude in art has historically (except for Michelangelo) been mostly female, and, therefore, subject to the old feminist criticism of the ubiquitous "male gaze" objectifying women; and there is the related criticism of the male artists prettifying and beautifying women, rather than painting them realistically. Rembrandt's "Three Graces" would be one exception

The real naked body is often less than the perfect ideal; subject to male and female gazes, whether in lust or disgust; and highly regulated by law and custom, especially in naturist camps.

Still, there are plenty of occasions for nudity. Some display themselves for fun, as with the people who gather in different cities to be photographed all nude by Spencer Tunick; streak through games or shows; play nude rugby in Australia; do nude bungee-jumping—all illustrated in full color, and full frontal, in Carr-Gomm's *A Brief History of Nakdness* (2010).

Some consider nudity to be healthier than being clothed—physically, psychologically, or both. Exhibitionists might go nude in porn videos, for fun or cash. Others think it is necessary for their art and feel empowered. The actress Elizabeth Olsen was naked in a couple of films, and explained: "I truly believe in the films I've chosen to be nude [in]. It helps tell a more grotesque story. There's nothing gratuitous about it. I find it empowering" (*Times of India*, 1 December 2013).

Some go naked to protest, e.g., Lady Godiva, the most famous in mythology; bit naked men and women have protested a wide range of causes over the years (Carr-Gomm, 2010). In 2012, university and college students in Quebec went on strike to protest a provincial government proposal to raise student fees. The protest took many forms: blocking highways and a bridge, occupying classrooms, preventing students entering universities or classrooms, marching, banging pots. Predictably, there was some vandalism and violence. But one summer evening, the tactics were to disrobe and stroll through the streets naked or topless, sometimes with the symbols of the protest—red Velcro squares—placed strategically on their bodies. Asked why they were doing this, one student replied that transparency was essential in dealing with the premier and the Ministry of Education. The students said that they had nothing to hide; also, they hoped that the police would be gentler with them if they were arrested (Lalonde, 2012). And I missed the whole thing!

Our attitudes to bodies, naked, nude or clothed, depend heavily on our circumstances, goals and values, as well as on our cultural and religious backgrounds. It is ironic that so many authorities prohibit both public nudity and the veil in public.

Genesis

"Genesis"—the first book of the *Torah* (also commonly referred to as the "Old Testament" or "Five Books of Moses")—speaks to the beginnings of widespread Judeo-Christian negativism about the body and sex, from which post-Christian cultures are recovering and rebounding off of—in the other direction of sex-obsession. The legacy is still strong, however, and worth a glance.

In the beginning, God forbade Adam to eat of the fruit of the tree of the knowledge of good and evil, "for in the day that thou eatest thereof thou shalt surely die." Then God created Eve. "And they were both naked, the man and his wife, and they were not ashamed" (Gen 2: 17; 25). Enter the serpent:

> And the serpent said unto the woman, Ye shall not surely die: for God doth know that in the day ye eat thereof, then your eyes shall be opened, and ye shall be as gods, knowing good and evil. And when the woman saw that the tree was good for food, and that it was pleasant to the eyes, and a tree to be desired to make one wise, she took of the fruit thereof, and did eat, and gave also unto her husband with her; and he did eat. And the eyes of both

> of them were opened, and they knew that they were naked; and they sewed fig leaves together, and made themselves aprons. (Gen 3: 4-7).

Nakedness is obviously an issue here. Innocent, they were naked and unashamed. Guilty, they were ashamed of nakedness: It is evidence of and a symbol of their sin. And why aprons not masks? The answer would seem to be to camouflage their genitals. The knowledge of evil, in this general interpretation, is the knowledge of sex, leading to a hiding of the body and the clothing of the body. "The Lord arrived in the Garden and called Adam. And he said, I heard thy voice in the garden, and I was afraid, because I was naked; and I hid myself. And he said, Who told thee that thou wast naked? Hast thou eaten of the tree whereof I commanded thee that thou shouldest not eat?" (Gen 3:10-1).

So, the blame game began. Adam blamed the woman, the woman blamed the serpent, the Lord blamed and cursed everyone—and expelled Adam and Eve from the Garden of Eden (which did not end so well when Cain killed Abel). This association of nakedness with innocence and clothing and sex with sin and shame was not an auspicious start to gender relations. This was the beginning of the battle of the sexes and the negative evaluation of sex.

This biblical account of the "Fall," which many people hold to be mythological, is interesting for several reasons: It accounts for evil with a serpent—the devil—extraneous to the self; and it purports to explain the relations between men and women, God and creation, good and evil, and the origins of dress. Before the Fall, as mentioned, the original couple were naked, innocent and not ashamed; after this original sin, they were ashamed and got dressed and have been ashamed ever since. Clothes cover the sinful body. That must have been the message for centuries – until nudism. Clothes cover the body, but not the whole body, only the genitals in early Christian art—symbolic of sin. The message of Genesis was clear.

The basic equation in the Judeo-Christian tradition is that innocence = naked and vice versa; conversely, guilt and shame = clothed, and vice versa. Barcan states that clothing symbolizes the alienation of humanity from God and from the self (2004:50). But she lives in Australia and not Montreal or New York in the winter, so she might be overstating her point.

The fig leaf theory of clothes as modesty is sweet but not entirely persuasive. One may be immodest in clothes as well as out of them. Indeed, Bernard Rudofsky reverses the argument, suggesting that "modesty, rather than being the cause for wearing clothes, is its result;" and he complains that the absurd and unhealthy situation has now arisen in which "in our society the naked body is believed to be incomplete – a body minus clothes" (1974: 27).

He cites a fashion theorist who is more forceful: "In modern civilization there has grown up an immodesty which was lacking in more ancient cultures. We are ashamed of our bodies. Whether the practice of concealing the body is the cause of our uncleanliness of mind, or whether our obscenity is rather the cause of concealment, is a debated question (1974:78).

The traditional theory states that moral shame caused clothing, while the new theory states that clothes cause bodily shame and modesty. The two theories may be complementary rather than contradictory; some people are not or have not been ashamed of their bodies – some proudly flaunt them. And in many cultures nakedness is the norm not the exception (see below).

Meanwhile, *Cosmopolitan* (April, 2010) suggests on its cover: "50 Things to Do Butt Naked" – which is obviously more naked than just plain, ordinary naked. And Paris, Britney and Lindsay have been known to go panty-free—clothing most of their body *except* their genitals, which is quite the reverse of Adam and Eve in traditional art. For some, it is clear that the *pudenda* are now not only *amanda* but also *demonstranda.*

Michelangelo and Art

The Dark Ages, from the fall of the Roman Empire to the dawn of the Italian Renaissance, have been described as a thousand years without a bath. This was something of an exaggeration, but a thousand years without a nude would probably be more accurate.

To Greek and Roman sensibilities, the nude and the depiction of sex were not alien. Neither body nor sex was considered shameful, and both decorated household utensils as well as walls. The rise and spread of Christianity coincided with the fall of Rome. St. Augustine insisted that it did not cause this fall (in *City of God*), but it probably did cause both the fall of nudes from their pedestals and a rethinking of bodies and sex. All secular reality should be subordinate to spiritual reality, as in Christ's commandment: "Seek ye first the Kingdom of God."

Yet nudes returned, as nudes will. The turning point in this re-evaluation of body, beauty and sex was the Italian Renaissance in general and Michelangelo in particular. Commissioned by the pope to paint the ceiling of the Sistine Chapel (1508-12), he created this magnificent work, absolutely glorious; and, not to trivialize it, one of the major differences between then and the past as well as then and now is the flagrant display of male nudes and penises.

The centerpiece is the Creation, with God (portrayed in the likeness of an elderly, white male) creating Adam, who is lying down, naked, with his penis flopped over his right thigh. Surrounding this primal scene are 19 more naked young men. There were originally 20 but one was destroyed. Penises are everywhere; no shame attached (Copplestone 2002:281, 285-7).

He had earlier been commissioned to paint a portrait of the Holy Family, which he did in vivid colors (1503-4). He also threw in a few full-frontal nude young men as background, for reasons best known to himself. The painting was rejected, which is not really surprising. Copplestone, author of a definitive work on Michelangelo, comments that "His interest, almost a pre-occupation, with the nude male figure in his paintings has led, with other matters, to the suggestion of homosexuality . . ."—but he added that the question had not been settled (2002:252-5). Other matters included that he never married and that he wrote love letters to a young, male friend. But as Copplestone says, nothing is settled: he may have been a latent and the love may have been platonic. Having read some of the poems, I go with platonic and surely at least latent.

Later (1537-40), Michelangelo painted "The Last Judgement" on the wall behind the altar of the chapel, which contained more nudes of both sexes, but they were not so central. Meanwhile, many of his sculptures had expressed his interest in male nudity, notably David, Bacchus and even a naked Christ on the cross, as well as a series on slaves, all male and nude (2002: 174-7, 198-9, 196, 236-43). To be fair, he did also paint naked women, notably Eve in "The Last Judgement" and two amazing sculptures of nude women, Dawn and Night, at the tombs of two Medici brothers in Florence. Still, he was not an equal opportunity artist.

Michelangelo was not the first in the Renaissance to paint nudes, and, as Nead and Berger have noted, female nudes were the norm. They were usually painted in biblical or classical themes, e.g., Masaccio's "The Expulsion from the Garden" (c. 1425), with the penis on display and the vagina gracefully hidden, and da Panicale's "The Fall from Grace" (c. 1427), with nothing hidden. Van Eyck also painted a nude Adam and Eve on his Ghent altarpiece (1425-32), again with the genitals hidden; and Botticelli painted "The Birth of Venus" (1485), with her long blonde hair curling modestly.

After Michelangelo, it seems that the artistic culture changed. More nudes appeared. Raphael's "Madonna" features a full-frontal Baby Jesus. Bosch (c. 1510) painted "The Garden of Earthly Delights," featuring numerous nudes. The spectacular "Allegory of Love" by Bronzini (c. 1543) features the very nude Venus and Cupid, who is caressing her breast.

At the same time, Cellini (1543) crafted a magnificent, gold salt- cellar for King Francis I, embellished rather unnecessarily for the distribution of salt with two golden nudes, one male and one female, reclining gracefully on the golden lips, and gazing at each other while she fondles her breast. It is not something one would find, even in plastic, in your local Walmart.

So nudity became increasingly acceptable, at least as an art form. The most notable works were all about women, with Adam appearing with Eve occasionally, e.g., Durer's "Adam and Eve" (1507), Georgione's "Reclining Venus" (c. 1518), Cranach's "Adam and Eve" (1528), Titian's "Venus of Urbino" (1538), and Tintoretto's "Leda and the Swan" (c. 1552-8). Indeed, most of the greatest artists of the Renaissance painted naked people, often in churches, sacralized and institutionalized.

Leonardo da Vinci, the other towering genius of the Renaissance (and of all time) was a contemporary of Michelangelo, and less "preoccupied" with young male nudes. His portraits of women are far more attractive than Michelangelo's, with sweet gentle smiles, e.g., on "The Virgin of the Rocks" and "Virgin and Child with St. Anne" and the famous, enigmatic smile on probably the most famous picture in the world, the "Mona Lisa." He also drew "The Vitruvian Man" (1492), a picture of a full-frontal nude male framed within a square and a circle, to illustrate proportionality: The penis is the halfway point from head to toe, and the (four) arms and legs outstretched fill the frame of the square and the circle. He also, perhaps, symbolized the archetype of being human, as Comar (2013) has suggested. In this, he followed the ancient Greek sculptures of men as warriors, virile and naked, while the women were clothed.

Hazarding a guess, if both Michelangelo and da Vinci were gay (da Vinci was arrested for sodomy in his youth), as many assume, then, in the opinion of this author, they take Kameny's slogan of "Gay is good" to a new level: "Gay is great!"

Later artists continued the theme of nudity, particularly female nudity. To list some of the more well-known: Rubens and "The Three Graces"

(1636-8), Velasquez and "The Rokeby Venus" (c. 1648-51), Rembrandt and "Bathsheba" (1654), Boucher and "Louise O'Murphy" (1752), Goya and "Maya Nuda" (c. 1797), David and "Madame Recamier" (1800), and Ingres and "Odalisque" (1814) and "The Turkish Bath" (1863); and so it has continued with too many to mention. This will simply indicate the widespread acceptability of the genre.

Nudes began to turn around, so to speak, at the end of the nineteenth century. Several developments were initiated at that time. Whereas earlier, the female nudes were often classical goddesses or biblical heroines, later attention shifted to the female herself, and beauty—at first, quite often Eve in the idyllic garden of Eden, with all the animals at peace and the beautiful flowers. The French artists from Gauguin to Bonnard especially developed this (the English kept their would-be nudes clothed), and then Picasso, after that. The first shift was, perhaps, when artists at the French Academy were allowed to paint female nudes, in 1863: This was progress of a sort. Gauguin's portraits of Polynesian women as Eve, naked and unashamed, were influential in shifting attitudes about women, bodies and, no doubt, sexuality. Then, Klimt's portrait of a very beautiful nude woman "Nuda Veritas" (note the equation – this is not a Grecian urn) outraged the Parisian audience, when exhibited in 1898. Chagall, Cezanne, Rodin and Bonnard followed suit. And so began the romanticization and pedestalization of the female as beauty, truth, goodness, mother/love and, implicitly, sexy. She replaced or complemented the iconic status of the male from Aristotle through Paul to Da Vinci's Vitruvian Man. (Most of these and many other nudes can be found in Clark, 1956; Blass, 2001; Gill, 1989; Nead, 1994; Lucie-Smith, 1998, 2000; Stuckenbrock and Topper, 2011; Musee Bonnard, 2013). The capsize in values became evident across the Atlantic when Mother's Day was declared a national holiday in the U.S. in 1914, followed by the declaration of Father's Day as a national holiday in . . . wait for it . . . 1972. This does indicate a profound shift in values

Male nudes were painted, but not so much during the Renaissance, with the one conspicuous exception noted earlier. Comar shows that the themes of male nudity shifted over time, with some overlaps. The initial Greco-Roman theme was the warrior. The Renaissance introduced the cosmic ideal, as with "Vitruvian Man" and the English philosopher Robert Fludd; and, also, the anatomical male of skeletons and musculature by Durer, Da Vinci and Vesalius from the fifteenth to the early seventeenth centuries; the portraits of men as heroic (Atlas, Hercules, kings) complemented the emphasis on dress and feminine beauty through many centuries. In the twentieth century, men might be portrayed as emaciated, deformed or wounded (Egon Schiele), but curiously, not as a result of war; the posing of men generated the realistic male as nude, resulting in Lucian Freud's self-portrait, which is not in the least seductive or romantic. At the same time, males were presented in nature (Cezanne, Munch) and in photography, which desexualized the nakedness or camouflaged it. From Michelangelo to Hockney, men have been presented as desirable. These shifts, from warrior to skeletal to muscular to deformed to natural to desirable, exemplify the ways that nudes may be presented and evaluated, though the themes often overlapped chronologically (Lucie-Smith, 1998; Comar, 2013). Values are hidden in the portraits and the nudes.

Men emerged into their limelight with the relatively recent emergence of female artists and gay artists, as earlier with the Greeks and Romans. The development is interesting, from the worship of the male body as the epitome of humanity, in the ancient world, to the delight in the female body as beautiful and, maybe, presumably, sexy, and the virtual ignoring of the male body.

Today, different artists paint whatever they like or admire, according to their various predilections. Male nudes have been portrayed in a remarkable funerary statue in Greece from the sixth century BCE – it was not clothes that made the man, but the body; how different from most portraiture. Such a statue would not be permitted in a cemetery today. The rules are clear. And a statue of a satyr with a full erection would not be permitted anywhere, except in Greece, 540-530 BCE (Comar, 2013).

Nudism and the Nuer

Nudism emerged as a practice and a philosophy first in Germany, towards the end of the nineteenth century, arising out of some concern with the health of the German people. Proponents argued that the exposure of the whole naked body to sunlight, fresh air and exercise would be beneficial to health and happiness. They were particularly critical of the education system for privileging the mind over the body and of the Christian churches for body-negativism and sex-negativism. The movement spread to France, with a more congenial climate in the south. It was later sponsored by the National Socialist government, which added eugenics and racial purity into the mix. After the war, the movement expanded without the racial ideology, was transformed with a name change to naturism, and is now global, with national and international organizations and magazines. In Germany and

France, nudity is sometimes permitted on public beaches, and also in public parks in Germany (Ross, 2005). Not so much in the U.S. or the U.K.

In some respects, these developments were congruent with the thinking in other parts of the world. This included the founding of the YMCA in 1844; the rise of Muscular Christianity, founded by Charles Kingsley in England in the 1850s; the emergence of rugby (1823) and the beginnings of organized competitive sports in schools and universities; the publication of *Tom Brown's Schooldays* (Hughes, 1857); the revival of the Olympics (1896); and, later, the founding of the Boy Scouts (1908) by Baden-Powell (Putney, 2003; Haley, 1978). The Anglo-American efforts to revive manliness in the face of what was perceived to be the feminization of religion did not, however, include nudity. This is only recently becoming more acceptable.

Nudists, or "naturists," in the new terminology (which thus avoids the emotive word) are interesting for their practice of a behavior quite opposite that of the majority. Martin Weinberg has defined the ideology of the nudist camps as follows: Nudism and sexuality are unrelated; there is nothing shameful about exposing the human body; the abandonment of clothing can lead to a feeling of freedom and natural pleasure; and nude activities, especially full bodily exposure to the sun, leads to a feeling of physical, mental and spiritual well-being (1965:314).

The nudist camp is not a Garden of Eden. The organizers take stringent precautions against intruders, including demanding proof of identification, the removal of clothes upon access, prohibiting access of unaccompanied young males (no mention of females), and generally trying to enforce the rules. The rules include no staring, no cameras, no alcohol, no sex jokes or 'dirty jokes' (sex as dirty is part of the puritan problem), no touching, no nude dancing, and modesty of posture will be maintained (1965: 315-8).

While Americans are usually more diffident about public nudity than many Europeans, particularly the Germans, nudism is becoming increasingly popular, and organized. The American Association for Nude Recreation (AANR) states that nude tourism generates more than $440 million a year. There are now more than 250 nude or clothing-optional resorts in the United States, and business is booming with "cottontails" (white-bummed novices) (*Economist*, 5 July 2014:27).

Few such issues of rules or embarrassment are raised among the Nuer. The English anthropologist E. E. Evans-Pritchard was requested by the government of the Anglo-Egyptian Sudan to study the Nuer and report back, which he did in his 1940 book *The Nuer*. He reported on their cattle—they were a pastoral people—and their political, economic and lineage systems; and he illustrated his work with photographs of the Nuer people, villages and cattle. It was and is a classic ethnology, peppered with humor; and in an almost throwaway remark, he states: "No high barriers of culture divide men from beasts in their common home, but the stark nakedness of Nuer amid their cattle and the intimacy of their contact with them present a classic picture of savagery" (1967:40). We may disregard the apparent negative value-judgment here, for he greatly admired their skills and knowledge, and was even fond of the Nuer, though occasionally exasperated (e.g., 1967: 12-15). But the point that has interested others most was the nakedness. The lack of shame and embarrassment is apparent in the full-frontal photographs of men and women, including the leopard-skin chief, who did wear something, a skin around his shoulders. The genitals were not covered.

E-P, as he was known, did not devote much attention to this nakedness. It just was. Nakedness was not an uncommon practice in warm regions, including the South Pacific, Australia and parts of South America. One question raised, of course, is the definition of nakedness. Most of the Nuer in the photographs wore a waistband, or a necklace, or bracelets on the arms, wrists or ankles. This self-decoration might be defined as dress. Furthermore, rules and taboos governed "dress": Some women might wear fragments when married, or might not; girls wore grass dresses for ceremonial occasions; and young boys wore six parallel scars incised on their foreheads, as initiation into manhood.

Were the Nuer naked or clothed? By their standards, perhaps they might have been dressed in the height of fashion. By ours, the position is debated. By whose criteria does one judge? And should one? The point here is that no shame or shyness or embarrassment attached to nakedness. This indicates a fascinating cultural difference from "Western" (redefined in this context as "Northern") norms. The Nuer do not need nudist camps.

More recent discussion has explored the issue of Nuer nakedness, with which E-P was not particularly concerned. In the enigmatically titled article, "The Clothes of the Naked Nuer," H. Fischer (1978) has explained that the Nuer men and women do wear clothes, occasionally; and the women do when married, if they wish, or when cold or at dances; and the men do, before taboo individuals—usually in-laws. Then again, dress relates to eating together and defecation. The rules are complicated.

More recent work indicates that this custom of nakedness has not changed. Leni Riefenstahl (1976, 1984) photographed the people of Eastern and North-Eastern Africa in all their glorious nakedness. No shame attached to nakedness and, apparently, no eroticism either.

Clothing

Why do we wear clothes, if we do, when we do not have to, such as in hot climates (some don't), apartments, and offices? Numerous researchers have pondered the meanings, functions and origins of clothing and its corollary, fashion. James Laver, an early theorist of dress, suggested three principal functions: utility, seduction and hierarchy. Utility refers to protection from the elements and from particular threats, e.g., armor, diving suits, football uniforms. Apart from that, he added, "We dress either to attract the other sex or to demonstrate our position in society" (1953: ix-x, 33); or, we might add, to attract the same sex.

That is a start, but others have added more items to this "language of clothes." They include: self-expression, which is very evident on the street; magic, including decorations against the evil eye; ritual, such as vestments, coronation robes, wedding dresses, and graduation robes; threat-display, such as is worn, for example, by riot police; disguise, including masks and hoodies; anti-seduction and anti-status garb, to play down both; and clothing to demonstrate group identity, e.g., as among teams, scouts, regiments, Rastafarians, and Orthodox Jews. That is 10, but my students have added modesty and to conform to cultural norms, for a total of 12.

The seduction-beauty function has proved immensely controversial. Isaiah inveighed against immodesty, status display and narcissism:

> The Lord said: Because the daughters of Zion are haughty and walk with outstretched necks, glancing wantonly with their eyes, mincing along as they go; tinkling with their feet; the Lord will smite with a scab, the heads of the daughters of Zion, and the Lord will bare their secret parts…instead of perfume there will be rottenness; and instead of a girdle, a rope; and instead of well-set hair, baldness; and instead of a rich robe, a girding sackcloth; instead of beauty, shame. (Is 3: 16-7, 24)

Christ's dictum on dress was more moderate: "Consider the lilies of the field, how they grow; they toil not, neither do they spin: And yet I say unto you that even Solomon in all his glory was not arrayed like one of these" (Mat 6:28).

Here extravagant clothing is seen as a problem, and even, according to Isaiah, as a sin. Elsewhere, nudity or semi-nudity is seen as the problem and, according to the police, a crime. In the late 1960s, the Tanzanian Government passed legislation to require the Masai to wear trousers, in order to civilize them: So, in this case, civilization = trousers (Mazrui, 1971). Some did, some did not. The equation of civilization with clothing is almost as curious as nature with nudity.

Similarly, the efforts of some Muslim religious authorities to require women to wear the veil, the hijab, burkha or niqab are as controversial as the efforts of some government authorities to make the niqab, in particular, illegal in public or in government jobs. Some hide the face and the body. Others flaunt them. And so many people from Isaiah to the present will try to interfere, particularly with women's dress or undress. The politics of the clothing of the body never cease to amaze.

But dress is not just about flaunting or modesty, it is also about status display: gender, rank, occupation, faith, etc. "The apparel oft' proclaims the man" (or woman), exclaimed Polonius. Indeed, to paraphrase Voltaire, if clothes did not exist, it would be necessary to invent them. The occupations of bus drivers, nurses, the police, the military, besuited businessmen, even students, are written in their uniforms; and the rings on the cuffs and epaulettes and stars and medal ribbons, silver and gold braid, indicate rank and service. Religion may be evidenced by turban or cross or Zoroastrian eagle or kippa or niqab. Wealth is evidenced by the quality of dress as well as the accessories of diamonds and gold and, of course, the Timex or Rolex. Colors, too, speak the language: the saffron robes of Buddhist monks, the black and white of Catholic clergy, the black of widows from Mediterranean lands, the ubiquitous blue business suit, the blue jeans of informality, the pink of some girls, and the colors of the flags waved by enthusiastic nationals. Almost everything we wear screams our identity.

Laver summarized the three main principles of costume: "It is possible that the Seduction Principle (dressing to attract the opposite) may outlive the Hierarchical Principle (dressing to indicate one's position in society) and the Utility Principle (dressing for warmth and comfort)" (1953:273). These principles are not necessarily mutually exclusive, but they do make the point that dress is as much about the mind as the body; and despite "Genesis," seduction is far from shame—it might even be shameless.

Certainly if everyone went naked in this anonymous society, confusion would result very rapidly. As Kemper remarked drily: "A lawyer or a judge would be indistinguishable from the prisoner at the bar; there's often little enough difference as it is" (1977: 12). In this sense, clothes and their accoutrements hold society together, as well as splitting it apart.

A cartoon in the *New Yorker* (1968) illustrates this point. An elderly gentleman is standing by a swimming pool in his swimsuit being addressed by a bikini-clad, young woman: "A general! Goodness gracious, you don't *look* like a general."

In other cultures less given to wearing clothes, status may be written in the body directly, whether by body painting, scarification, piercing, tooth or finger removal, and tattooing, circumcision or clitoridectomy. The people in every culture modify their bodies or self-decorate, often for the sake of beauty or bravery (Brain, 1979; Ebin, 1979; Kirk, 1981; Fisher, 1984; Riefenstahl, 1986.) As these authors and others have demonstrated, the creative human ingenuity in presenting both individuality and community is most impressive, if sometimes surprising.

*

The nude and the naked are semantically identical. The interesting thing is that even undressed we are always sending messages about ourselves. In this we are sort of dressed. Our lives are inscribed in our bodies: how we wear our hair and our faces, our weight and shape, our bloodshot eyes or nicotine stained fingers or squashed toes and bunions, our smile, our animation, how we carry ourselves, our tattoos, tans, piercings, stretch marks, scars…and circumcisions or clitoridectomies.

Even without clothes on, our bodies symbolize and demonstrate who we are. The fancy clothes or expensively and fashionably slashed jeans or dress uniforms or Oscar dresses just make the messages of nudity and nakedness more complicated, and camouflage the self underneath.

Chapter 11
Pornography and Erotica

What is pornographic? And what is erotic? Can we distinguish between them? Or is the distinction purely subjective, culturally relative and contingent upon historical circumstances? Are there any formal standards or criteria to distinguish them? Are they mutually exclusive? Or do we have a continuum, whereby the pornographic is or may be erotic, and the erotic is or may be pornographic? Then again, is pornography bad for you as an individual and for all of us as a society, e.g., as a phenomenon that objectifies everyone, especially women, or that is addictive or promotes violence or deviance? Perhaps it depends on the individual, the type of porn consumed, and the quantity. But how much is too much? How would you tell? (By the consequences, one might reasonably surmise.) And is erotica good for you as an individual and for all of us as a society, e.g., for sustaining sexual health and sex-positive attitudes, perhaps, and maximizing mutual sexual pleasure? And what role does the state play in these delicate, ultra-sensitive realms? What roles should it play? Opinions vary, as always.

These are sticky questions, ticklish and controversial. But before tackling the range of opinions, we will consider some of the data. About 25 percent of porn viewers are women, according to PornHub, which is the biggest commercial porn website. Researchers calculate that of the million most visited websites, 4 percent are dedicated to porn—which equals 40,000—though others also include some porn. The greatest consumers of porn are in the United States, with 38 percent of PornHub traffic, and Britain is next, at about 13 percent, with no other country above 10 percent. Total visits numbered over 18 billion in 2014, with nearly 80 billion video viewings. Pornography accounts for more than 10 percent of all Internet searches. Is that good or bad? The moral panic generated by the porn industry is still pervasive, as it was with the girlie magazines in the 1950s and rental videos in the 1980s, but concern has shifted from the objectification of women and the promotion of violence to the effects on the viewers—particularly teenagers, and in promoting addiction and false expectations of sexualities—though many researchers seem less alarmed than others. The future seems to be in the education of teenagers about porn (though the prospect of research grants is low) and also in VirtualRealityPorn (VRP), with VR linked to sex toys (*Economist*, 26 September 2015: 18, 58-62).

Natasha Vargas-Cooper points out that the Chicago Sex Survey of 1992, mentioned earlier (Michael et al., 1994), reported that 20 percent of women aged 25-29 stated that they had had anal sex. A later study in 2010 found that this number in the same age group had more than doubled to 46 percent, and, furthermore, that now 20 percent of the 18-19 age cohort had had anal sex. She comments on what she calls "brute male desire" and added:

> Never was this made plainer to me than during a one-night stand . . . We quickly progressed to his bed, and things did not go well. He couldn't stay aroused. Over the course of the tryst, I trotted out every parlor trick and sexual persona I knew . . . in a moment of exasperation, he asked if we could have anal sex. I asked why . . . He answered, almost without thought, "Because that's the only thing that will make you uncomfortable." This was, perhaps, the greatest moment of sexual honesty I've ever experienced—and without hesitation I complied. (Vargas-Cooper, 2011:100)

To this I can only say "Wow!" and that I consider it "too much information," though I have to wonder how it went. Probably not too well, since it remained a one-night stand. For me, however, the image refuses to go away.

Life is full of ironies and contradictions. Sex is healthy, it is said, but videos about it are porn—unless offered for sale by accredited professionals with PhDs, in which case they are educational. We can probably all agree that people will disagree, but how much they disagree is amazing. Millions watched the Miss World Beauty Pageant held in Nigeria in 2002—but hundreds were killed protesting the Pageant. Clearly some find beautiful and erotic what others consider deeply offensive. Opinions vary. Beliefs are different. But we cannot just subside into solipsism and relativism; we will examine the borders and boundaries and values, and the varying assessments of costs and benefits.

Pornography is widely believed to be the principal cause of the so-called "epidemic" of sex addiction in the U.S. About 40 million Americans log onto a multitude or porn websites every day (figures are hard to determine, but the studies on the prevalence of porn sites vary from many thousands to several million). Not that all the visitors to the sites are addicts but, as we saw earlier, the Society for the Advancement of Sexual Health estimates that 3-5 percent of the U.S. population, or about nine million people, may be sex addicts (Lee, 2011). Some cite environmental factors (abandonment), or biological ones (dopamine deficiency), or pornography availability, though a combination seems probable. Few cite Wall Street, yet it is corporate capitalism that finances and profits from pornography. The pornographers wear suits and silk ties and look respectable. A special report by the *New York Times* exposed that pornography in the U.S. was a $10 billion industry in 2000 (how much more today?). GM sells more "graphic sex films" every year than Larry Flynt, the notorious founder of the "Hustler" empire. EchoStar Communications, whose financial backers include Mr. Murdoch, makes more money on porn than *Playboy*. AT &T has its own porn channel and sells sex videos to hotels. The hotels, including the Marriott and Hilton chains, do very well on this—more than their bars and meals, apparently. And, no doubt, all these well-educated corporate executives justify their marketing by their need to supply demand and to reward their shareholders (Egan, 2010).

Two fundamental questions arise about pornography: "How does pornography differ from erotica?" and "Is pornography harmful?" Etymology is a start. "Pornography" is from the Greek *porne* (prostitute) and *graphos* (to write), so "pornography" equates to "writing about prostitutes," i.e., sex; though why the Greeks restricted sex to prostitutes is not clear, except, perhaps, that prostitutes, as "sex workers"—in our more modern idiom—were presumably more experienced and professional and, therefore, better in bed; and, perhaps, they enjoyed both the sex and the money more! That is plausible. "Erotic" is also from the Greek: Eros was the god of (sexual) love and was later transformed by the Romans into Cupid, who is associated with desire and love and well-known for his sharp and painful arrows (and his bad aim). So etymologically, the distinction between pornography and erotica is fairly, but not totally, clear: it is that between sex and love, the financial and the emotional, the free spirits (formerly permissive, and before that promiscuous) and the committed exclusivists; but these seemingly clear distinctions are crossed and blurred by the common factor of sex. And in real life, much of Internet porn is posted by enthusiastic amateur exhibitionists for fun rather than for profit.

Gloria Steinem suggested that the difference is that pornography demeans women and erotica does not: It is egalitarian; "there is equal power and mutuality." This is a fair enough starting point, though I would add that it may demean men as well as women, and also that BDSM is all about men and women who *want* to be demeaned and humiliated and hurt and, as we shall see, they may not be "sick." Still, her point that "there is so little erotica . . . and so much pornography" seems to me to be valid. Her argument that pornography legitimizes "real antiwoman warfare" seems hyperbolic, and was unsubstantiated by any data (1983:8). It was a provocative essay, which raised the flag about the dangers of pornography and the benefits of erotica, clearly distinguished.

Historically, pornography is a relatively recent invention, under 400 years old. The Greeks and Romans reveled in the depiction of naked bodies and sexual intercourse, decorating their houses and pottery with all sorts of erections and positions. But this was erotica, since sex was not shameful and the genitals were not *pudenda*. Similarly, the artists of the Italian Renaissance painted all sorts of naked or semi-naked people, usually in classical or religious contexts, to facilitate worship or to instill virtue by reminding viewers of the fires of hell. Yet Michelangelo's naked "David," in a shop window or a faculty club, would likely evoke protests today (Nathan, 2007:15-8).

The point about pornography is that it is taboo. Debbie Nathan, an award-winning, New York-based journalist has offered a three-part description of pornography: it must depict sexual situations emphasizing the genitals; it is intended to arouse; and "Third, and most important, pornography should seem 'dirty' or taboo: fantasy anyway" (2007:16, 36).

Yet the idea that sex is "dirty" is problematic. It may have its origin in Plato's dualism, privileging mind over body, and more recently in Christian dualism, privileging spirit over body—a dualism later reinforced by Descartes. Or, perhaps, the origins of shame lie more in the male supremacism of Aristotle and the traditions of misogyny and patriarchy that persist in some quarters, including the Internet, today. Or it could be both, with mind/body dualism reinforcing male/female dualism and expressed in literature—in the beautiful but evil Pandora and the sinful Eve, the two founding women; all, perhaps, created by male misogyny and/or patriarchy (Synnott, 1993; Gilmore, 2001).

The question of origins is, perhaps, academic, but Nathan tracks the rise of modern pornography. It is almost funny how every invention was subverted to sex. The invention of the printing press by Johannes Gutenberg in 1450 led first to the publication of the Bible, and within 100 years to the publication of *I Modi* (1524), 16 engravings of different sexual positions: sex as physical pleasure. This eventually provoked the pope to ban the work as obscene and to publish the *Index* (*Librorum Prohibitorum*), a list of prohibited books, in 1559. The book was immediately pirated and expanded, of course. The *Index* listed books determined to be dangerous to faith or morals and was finally abolished in 1963 by the Second Vatican Council. Perhaps this *Index* was the beginning of pornography: the first definition of portrayals of sex as obscene.

This was followed by Rabelais' *Gargantua and Pantagruel* (1530-40), which was banned as dangerous to both faith and morality by the Italians and the French. The English were a bit slower. *Fanny Hill*, purporting to be the memoirs of a prostitute, did not appear until 1749, though bawdy tales had been around since the "Pardoner's" story in Chaucer's *The Canterbury Tales*, in about 1387 (Ginzburg, 1958). This was sex as humor.

The invention of the printing press was followed centuries later by the invention of the camera (1827), and photographs of the naked and of sex were sold as postcards; then came films, with those featuring sex often called "blue movies;" then *Playboy* (1953) arrived on the scene, followed by mainstream movies featuring such stars as Brigitte Bardot in "And God Created Woman" (1958); then came by porn movies, followed by the invention of the VCR in 1975, and the World Wide Web (1994), and . . . one thing after another: web cams, chat rooms, video streaming, electronics and dildonics, plastics and dolls, cell phones and sexting . . . Every new invention has enabled sex to flourish, including, of course, the automobile—think Ford: personal mobility and autonomy, and also back seats (Nathan, 2007:15-27). There is no looking back, except, perhaps, with nostalgia and a smile or a frown.

Is that progress or regress? Opinions vary, but surely it depends on the individual, how much is watched, the type of porn, the expense, and the effects on partners and family. But what about the effects on gender relations and on society? That too is debated.

Pornography and Pornification

Pornography is big business. In 2015, the global industry was estimated to be worth about $97 billion, according to sociologist Kassia Wosick, assistant professor at Mexico State University, with the U.S. industry estimated at about $13 billion (up from $10 billion in 2000), rivaling the market worth of all the major Hollywood studios combined. According to several estimates (Nathan, 2007:41; Dines, 2010:47), this figure derived from about 4.2 million websites, up from 60,000 in 2000 and 1.6 million in 2004. But the industry has contracted sharply with the rise of free porn, perhaps 75 percent according to one estimate (*Economist*, 26 Sept 2015: 61).

This changed sexual climate is indicated with particular clarity in a *Time* magazine analysis of the Oscar-winning films from 1970 to 2012, and the nine nominees for 2013. The authors apply six criteria: theme, character, sex, violence, storytelling and setting. Sex includes five themes: female nudity, male nudity, masturbation, prostitution and sex standing up. Two of the nominees include all five sexual scenes (five films had none of the above, and two had two scenes) for a total of nine; yet in the previous 42 years, the maximum number of boxes checked was three, and all were in only one film, "American Beauty" (Wilson and Jones, 2014). So in 2013, Hollywood shifted American popular culture "sexwards," for better or for worse, and presumably for the almighty dollar. The "hypersexual society" identified by Boudrillard way back in 1983, and exposed by Kammeyer (2008), is being further hypersexualized even as we watch the Oscars (which I am actually doing, as I write).

The rise of pornography has generated considerable concern over the years. The first attempt at censorship, by the pope in 1559, was followed by others, three in particular. First, the battles waged by Anthony Comstock in the U.S. to prevent the sales of pretty much anything to do with what he described as "obscenity," "smut," and "filth", whether books, songs, or pamphlets. Comstock was successful in having Congress pass the so-called Comstock Act, which prohibited the circulation of anything by the U.S. mail deemed ""obscene, lewd, or lascivious." This later included the birth control information distributed by Margaret Sanger. Comstock died in 1915, and interest in his efforts gradually declined (Kammeyer, 2008: 44-7). The second was the trials of publishers of various books in the U.S. and the U.K. in the 1960s that were considered obscene, including *Lady Chatterley's Lover* and *Ulysses*. The victory of the publishers in both countries led to a vast increase in sexually explicit material in film, theater, books and magazines. The sexual revolution was accelerating, The third was the effort by Catherine MacKinnon and Andrea Dworkin in 1983 to ban pornography as exploitive of women, first in Minneapolis and then in Indianapolis. Both efforts failed. Then, in 1992, MacKinnon presented a brief to the Supreme Court in Canada in a pornography case, which influenced new legislation banning obscene materials. Ironically, two of the banned books confiscated by Canadian Customs were by Dworkin (Kammeyer, 2008; Paul, 2005: 63-6).

Despite attempts at censorship, several government Commissions found no cause for concern. The U.S. Commission on Obscenity and Pornography (1970) rejected the idea that pornography leads to violence against women, as did a British Home Office report (1979) and a Canadian Department of Justice report (1984). But that was a long while back. It is difficult to research this topic. Surveys, interviews and clinical testing are all methodologically flawed. But cross-cultural research suggests that even though the consumption of porn—including XXX porn—has increased dramatically for most demographic groups, violence against women (and men) has declined in both the U.S. and Canada. Furthermore, the same seems to apply to both Denmark and Japan—heavy producers and, perhaps, consumers with low rates of rape (Nathan, 2007: 42-50). Some researchers think that the data indicate an inverse relation between porn consumption and violence against women, and that the worst effects may be on both high consumers of porn and the quality of marital relations (*Economist,* 26 September 2015:58).

Still, pornography has changed – one hesitates to say evolved – from the soft core, by today's standards, of *Playboy* (1953) to *Penthouse* (1969) to *Hustler* (1974), and, in general, the 1970s and 1980s. Explicit sexuality (though not technically porn) is now mainstream on TV with, for example, the groundbreaking HBO series "Sex and the City," about the sex lives of four New York women, which premiered in 1998, and "Girls Gone Wild," which was sanitized as pop culture and youth culture rather than as porn culture. The trend was further popularized and glamorized by Jenna Jameson, in her popular *How to Make Love like a Porn Star* (2004), who declared that she sometimes made $50,000 a week. Then Belle de Jour (2007) told tales of her time as a call girl in London, which made the bestseller lists in the U.K. All this was routinized by Howard Stern on Sirius radio, and reached its apex, or nadir, in "gonzo porn" (see below for discussion).

Despite government reports, there are several areas of concern: a moral argument against pornography from religious authorities already noted, and a political argument from some feminists. In the past, some have had a vexed relationship with men, masculinity, heterosexual sex and pornography. This is not surprising, really, if you define men as oppressive of women, sexist, misogynistic, violent, morally inferior, and objectifying women in patriarchal societies!

Robin Morgan famously stated: "Pornography is the theory, rape is the practice." Not true, of course. Perhaps she had not realized that some women watch porn, or noticed that some even participate and star in porn, and (today at least) some produce and direct it; and that even though so many men and women consume porn, most do not rape anyone. Still, it was great misandry, conflating anti-porn activism with anti-male politics.

In *Pornified* (2005), Pamela Paul interviewed over 100 men and women (80 percent male) about their use of and views on pornography and its impact on their lives in general and sex lives in particular. She complemented this by commissioning a random poll of Americans by the Harris polling agency. She cautions that we do not have to be polarized on this, a "Larry Flynt or Andrea Dworkin"—but we do have to be better informed. Porn is everywhere today in popular culture—and respectable in memoirs, on HBO and other TV networks, in public appearances in malls and universities by porn stars, in lyrics, and, of course, on the web. Society, she suggests, is "pornified" (2005:2-11).

Proponents of porn argue that it is just fantasy, harmless, not cheating—indeed, that it even prevents cheating; it is human nature (well, male nature anyway), sexually satisfying, and fun, easy, educational and safe. It adds "salt and pepper" to our sex lives; it is "almost an aphrodisiac" say two of Paul's respondents (2005: 9, 141-3).

Yet significant numbers in her Harris Poll believe that pornography harms relationships: 47 percent of women and 33 percent of men. Only 22 percent of Americans think that it improves the sex lives of those who watch porn, though the gender breakdown is not given (probably more men than women). Still, that leaves an astonishing 38 percent who must have been in the "Don't know" or "Refused to answer" categories (2005:141-3). It is also not clear whether these responses are experientially or ideologically based. Has it benefitted or harmed *your personal* sex life and relationships? We cannot tell with certainty, but the statistical data above (about 40 percent on average vs. 22 percent) suggests more harm than good, with a large percentage who do not know or are undecided.

The interviews tell more compelling and personal stories. While men often enjoyed their porn, even regardless of how their partners felt, most women seem to have been upset. Some were jealous; some felt that they could not compete with the porn stars, and their body image and self-esteem fell; they felt insecure, that the men were cheating on them, and that their partners preferred porn to them. They also felt that they were spending time and money, secretly, damaging their families. And their sexual performance was increasingly unsatisfactory (2005: 155-71). Paul did not bother to cross-tabulate time or type of porn watched with decreased satisfaction, but some of the men admitted that they preferred the porn to the real women in their lives. The fantasy replaces the reality.

The various experts and therapists tend to agree with the women that heavy (five hours or more per week) and solitary users of hard core porn become desensitized, sexually callous, selfish and, therefore, lousy lovers (2005: 151-5). The effects of watching porn seem to depend on so many variables: the time and money spent, the type of porn, whether both parties watch together, who chooses, and the degree of (usually male) obsession. It may be "salt and pepper" on special occasions or totally destructive of relationships. In one poll, one-in-four divorced respondents said that porn had contributed to the split. Divorce lawyers at a 2003 conference of the American Academy of Matrimonial Lawyers reported a sharp rise in the number of cases related to porn use; it figured in 58 percent of the cases, compared to almost none eight years earlier, according to the president of the association (2005:166-7). Not such fun. Not so harmless.

Gail Dines, professor of sociology and women's studies, has studied pornography for two decades. Her book, *Pornland: How Porn has Hijacked Our Sexuality* (2010), lists some of the Fortune 500 corporations involved in the profitable production and distribution of pornography and its horizontal integration, i.e., the ripple effects with industries other than the film and video industries, notably the banking, advertising, fashion, cosmetic surgery, computer, hotel, and communications industries. The corporatization of pornography permeates the economy; and, as this sector of the economy expands (see above), then, Dines notes, "so too will the pornification of our society" (2010:58).

Gonzo porn is the prime target of Dines' powerful, well researched and documented attack. She defines pornography as "any product that is produced for the primary purpose of facilitating arousal and masturbation" (2010:171). Fair enough, though the same might apply to erotica; and there does not seem to be anything intrinsically evil about all that (see below), though the teachings of the Vatican disagree (but, of course, many Catholics disagree with the Vatican). But gonzo is different. Indeed, Dines is furious in her condemnation of gonzo, for a number of reasons. It is physically destructive, including simultaneous triple orifice penetration, double anal, double vaginal, gagging (by penis), ass-to-mouth without washing, bukkake. It is medically risky with the dangers of STDs, including HIV, the tearing of the anus, vagina and throat and Chlamydia of the eye (2010: xiii-iv, xxviii). It is violent physically, verbally and emotionally. In sum, it is degrading to women and dehumanizing; more about assault than sex; and more about hate than love. Not all porn, Dines makes clear, is like the increasingly marketed and cheap gonzo porn.

Furthermore, it is not only sexist but also racist in its particular treatment, both physically and economically, of black women (2010:121-40). Again, the pornographers are increasingly upping the ante, as their viewers become bored, accustomed to the same old/same old; so they are turning to child pornography, real or simulated (2010:141-62). It is a sick old world out there, and gonzo porn is not about female empowerment, as some pornographers would say, but making money off cruelty and catering to misogynists.

Dines is an activist in this domain. It must be a vocation. She has published widely and lectures at universities and colleges across the United States. She is appalled at what she sees on the various websites (I confess, I did not go there), what she reads of the horrifying comments men make, which she cites, and by the impact of such porn on the female and male students with whom she talks.

Many men and women watch porn. Listening to men, Dines notes several themes: first, porn is addictive for some men; second, it is incremental, like alcohol, requiring increasing stimuli for the same effect; third, it "leaks" over from fantasy into reality, quietly, almost unnoticed into their sex lives and love lives, with detrimental effects; and fourth, it has huge costs in terms of money and time spent on porn sites. She comments that "Whenever I hear these stories, I feel both sad for the men and outraged at the porn industry for hijacking the men's sexuality to the point that they feel so out of control" (2010:93).

The impact on the female students has been equally disastrous. Impelled into a hook-up culture in which men expect that the porn culture will be replicated, and faced on the websites with many beautiful, professional, toned, surgically enhanced and acrobatic women who will do anything for the almighty dollar, many women find their relationships fraught. Plus, to quote Dines: "Harriet Nelson and June Cleaver have morphed into Britney, Rihanna, Beyonce, Paris, Lindsay, and so on" (2010:102). Now we can add Miley (the former, teen star of the TV show "Hannah Montana," on the Disney Channel). She notes that "what porn does is create what some feminists call a 'rape culture' by normalizing, legitimizing, and condoning violence against women" (2010:96). To comment, in this context, the notion of a "rape culture" at a time when rape is criminalized and rates of both rape and violence against women are falling, perhaps due to the rise of porn, as some researchers have suggested, is part of the moral panic and climate of fear of men and misandry that some feminists seem to think make for equal rights. The violence is declining yet the fear seems to be rising, in short, perhaps as much thanks to violent TV as to concerned feminists.

Erotica

The British Museum has published a little book entitled *Erotica*, with pictures of some of the artifacts in its collections. The author advises that while erotica are usually understood today in Anglo-American culture as sexually stimulating, in other cultures and times sexual imagery may have had other meanings: as expressions of spirituality in Hinduism and Buddhism; as tenderness; as good luck charms; as fertility symbols; and also, in England and France, as political satire or humor. The common theme is sex, and interest in sex, both ancient and modern, which is here, there and everywhere.

A Babylonian plaque from c. 1,800 BC and a wall painting from Egypt (c. 1,200 BC) depict men penetrating women from behind (very much like contemporary "toilet art"). A figurine from the Judean desert (c. 11,000 BC) features a woman sitting on a man's lap and facing him. And there is more from China, Japan, England, Rome and elsewhere. The author comments on a Hindu temple carving, saying that it expresses "a delight in human sexuality which was permanently lost to western culture once Greco-Roman paganism had been superseded by the Christian Byzantine Empire" (Johns, 2012: 30). Maybe some of that delight is beginning to reappear with amateur exhibitionist porn, rather than gonzo, which seems strictly business and joyless.

We have briefly explored some aspects of English, French and American sexualities and erotica, but traditional Hindu, Japanese and Chinese erotics shine other lights on erotica.

Khajuraho: Hindu Eroticism

Indian erotica constitutes a class of its own. India is the birthplace of the fourth century *Kama Sutra,* and Europe had nothing to compare with that. Then, Tantric yoga emerged in the eighth century. Then, came the amazing, magnificent erotic stone carvings that adorn the Khajuraho temples in North-Central India, within a cluster of 25 temples, which were sculpted between the early tenth and late eleventh centuries by the Chandella rulers of the area. Apparently, there were over 85 similar temples, but many were destroyed by time of the Moghul invaders who ruled from the still extant Red Fort in Delhi from 1206-1555 (Panda, undated: 9). Only 25 now remain on that site, though there are others scattered elsewhere across the subcontinent.

The 20,000 or so carvings at Khajuraho depict everyday scenes of normal life: a teacher with his class of students; a woman removing a thorn from her foot; another woman applying khol to her eyes, dancing, flute-playing; many animals, including elephants, dogs, pigs, bulls, boars, scorpions, and monkeys; hunting scenes; battle scenes; and gods and goddesses in their many incarnations and manifestations, including the elephant god, Ganesh, the monkey god, and the snake god. About 7 percent of the sculptures depict sexual behavior of many sorts – surprising to occidentals not only for their display, but also because the display is on temples.

These include a nine-person orgy, masturbation, fellatio, "69," many couples in various positions, homosexuality (though widely disapproved of in India today), threesomes of both combinations, bestiality, and semen collection. (The semen, mixed with wine, was served to men as a Viagra-type aphrodisiac, so my guide explained with a grin.) What all this work means, or meant, to the sculptors has been a matter of some debate. Chandwani, who has written an authoritative text on the subject, offers some of the prevailing theories: that the erotic scenes are "a glorification of the marriage of Shiva and Shakti"; that the whole complex is a picture of all aspects of life for teaching purposes; or that they depict the *Kama Sutra.* All this is contextualized within the history of fertility cults, dating back to depictions of sexual acts in about 2,000 BCE; the belief in creation by sexual union in the *Rig Veda*, dating back to about 1,000 BCE; and the worship of Shiva as *lingam* and Shakti as *yoni.* Sexuality was intrinsic to India and Hinduism for centuries, within a spiritual and divine context, and was institutionalized more deeply with the rise of Tantrism from the eighth century (2006:56-8; Panda, undated: 48).

Chandwani concludes that "whatever the meaning of eroticism, the artists have taken the meaning with them, but have left behind worlds of wonder for posterity to marvel and to ponder upon" (2006:72). True. And I pondered upon the totally opposite construction of sexuality in Christianity, with masturbation, threesomes, orgies and bestiality all condemned. I also wondered about the marvels of these sex scenes, so scandalous to so many eyes. Gandhi was appalled by them and gave his blessing to vandals who wanted to clean the temples of these "indecent and embarrassing" aspects of Indian culture. Only a letter from Tagore prevented further destruction (Panda, undated: 9). They are contextualized in such a wide variety of options within the day-to-day normal life; but, as carved on temples, they sacralize the secular and valorize sex as "symbolizing the spiritual ecstasy of the Soul merging with the Divine." This was *Moksha* (salvation), the ultimate and fourth goal of Hinduism (Chandwani, 2006: 36, 56). Panda (undated: 48) speaks in similar vein: "Instead of considering these erotic sculptures as vulgar or obscene, they should be taken as ecstasy, the beauty and the truth." Thus, sexual union transcends and integrates the sacred and the secular, the divine and the earthy, love and sex, the gods and the humans.

Shunga: Eroticism in Japan

Shunga, the Japanese term for the art of depicting sex, flourished in Japan for centuries during the Edo Period of the Tokugawa Shogunate (1600-1868), though it was prohibited after the Meiji Restoration in 1868. Some of this artwork was on exhibition at the British Museum in 2013-14, which I was able to see and admire. As at the temples in India, I was amazed at the beauty, the tenderness and the explicitness of these works of art.

Shunga means "spring pictures" or "spring light," but the art was also known by such charming terms as "laughter pictures" and "pillow pictures." They displayed a wide variety of sex and sexualities: homosexual, heterosexual, egosexual, orgies, involving ghosts, some violence, with maids watching (amused) or a cat watching (not amused). The background is often romantic, with a full moon, cherry blossom or Mount Fuji visible through open windows. The participants are usually fully dressed, in brilliant silks, and have engorged genitals. Some are simply explicit portraits of different penises and vaginas – a bit of a surprise as one wanders through the austere portals of the British Museum.

One authority describes shunga as "one of the glories of world erotic art," to which I would add not just erotic art but all art. Another adds that the "veneration of both male and female sex organs . . . to increase fertility or ward off evil, had since ancient times been a central strand of . . . Japanese folk religion." (Clark et al, 2013:14-19). Still another is more prosaic, arguing that shunga was designed to facilitate masturbation (Screech, 2009). These ideas may be complementary, as so often is the case. There is some agreement that the egalitarian sexual relations displayed were not historically accurate; gender relations were very unequal but sexual relations may have been more equal. Shinto was more open, relaxed and permissive than Confucianism or Buddhism; and the early creation myths of Japan featured conjugal sex between deities, giving human sexuality a very different aura than Genesis or Hesiod, Eve and Pandora (Clark et al, 2013: 23-4).

Meanwhile, in Europe the pope had banned the production and publication of erotica, whether artistic or literary – a ban that became less effective over the decades; but still there was nothing like shunga in all its explicit detail and luxurious plurisexuality, with the exception of Rowlandson's bawdy satires and some drawings by Turner.

Monta suggests that shunga was widely enjoyed by both sexes and all classes. It was not considered "smut" or "dirty" or "obscene" but, rather, normal, natural, interesting and even laughable. Monta cites numerous examples, including this verse from one shunga: "Looking at *shunga* / The lord's ladies, like the 'rocks offshore' / Are wet below, out of sight." Customarily, sets of shunga—12 pictures in each set—were presented to brides at their weddings. Monta quotes an American businessman visiting Japan in 1859 who was horrified by these "vile pictures"—and, later, by the interest shown in them by the wife of an acquaintance. His host showed him "three or four very obscene pictures. His wife stood close by and it was apparent from the demeanor of both of them that there was not a shadow of suspicion in their minds of the immodesty of the act or of the pictures themselves." He considered shunga as "evidence of the depraved taste of this people," rather than as evidence of the repressive sex-negative attitudes of his own people. He, himself, was born by similar "immodesty." We are only now beginning to appreciate that the ancient Indian and less ancient Japanese attitudes to sexualities might have been superior – more humane and realistic – than our contemporary attitudes. But shunga was more than just about sex, since sex was partly sacred; so shunga were used as talismans: protection in battle, to prevent fires in storage facilities, etc. A Confucian scholar was asked to write a poem on a shunga picture. He wrote: "The truths of the universe are indeed dark and deep/All the mysteries of life are born through this dark gate" (in Clark et al, 2013: 37, 41, 44).

Although almost all of the major artists of this time painted shunga, despite the prohibitions of the Meiji emperors, the interest began to wane after 1900. The paintings began to be seen as vulgar, perhaps reflecting Western norms about sexuality, which, misunderstanding shunga, may have equated them with pornography or, perhaps, reflected the changing political times. The attack on Japan by Commodore Perry and his "black ships" in 1854 signaled the military weakness of Japan, the beginnings of the end of feudalism and Samurai rule, and the rise of a new Japan. The successive Meiji emperors initiated a campaign of modernization, industrialization, expansionism and militarism, very successfully, with victories in the first Sino-Japanese War (1894-95), the Russo-Japanese War (1904-05) and World War I (1914-18). This militarism persisted with the rise of fascism and the invasion of Manchuria in 1931, and the second Sino-Japanese War in 1937, which merged into World War II.

It may be that shunga eroticism declined with the rise of militarism (sexual and military aesthetics do seem to be opposed), or with the rise of photography, but eroticism may also have been displaced onto other traditional aesthetics, such as calligraphy, the tea ceremony, flower arranging, or geisha culture. In any event, the rapid economic growth rate of Japan from 1945 to today—when Japan is second in the world in GDP—has coincided with an equally rapid decline in the population growth rate, which is among the lowest in the world. This inverse relationship between economic growth rates and population growth rates is now a political concern, not least for its social and economic implications in the future. Noting the difference between contemporary Japanese attitudes and the past, Monta concludes: "It is time for the taboo to be lifted from *shunga* so that it can be critically studied and exhibited" (2013:47).

The Lotus: Chinese Eroticism

The lotus was the custom of binding the feet of women in China. It lasted for around a thousand years, beginning sometime between the end of the T'ang dynasty and the Sung dynasty (960-1279), and gradually dying out after the Chinese revolution in 1911. Howard Levy (1966) interviewed a number of elderly women who still bound their feet in Taiwan in the 1960s, and he found that, after all those years, the pain of unbinding equaled the earlier pain of binding.

The binding involved tying a bandage around each foot. The bandage, usually about two to three inches wide and about six feet long, was placed on the instep and over the toes to force them underneath the sole of the foot. The big toe, however, was left unbound. Then the bandage was wrapped around the foot in a figure-eight loop, to force the heel and the toes together, which resulted in the small foot, known as the lotus.

The pain was intense but the beauty and erotic attraction of the lotus was highly valued both by men and women. Yet bones were broken, and the odor of putrefaction was pervasive. The lotus, explained one woman "was more important than the face, for it represented wealth, beauty and nobility. Big feet indicated that the girl was humble, ugly and poor." The equations were simple: lotus=beauty=wealth; big feet=ugliness=poverty.

One woman explained: "At first I suffered very much, and often spent sleepless nights because of the pain. But I did it to be beautiful." No pain, no gain.

The lotus was evaluated carefully. The golden lotus was three to four inches long; the silver lotus was five inches long; and the iron lotus was even longer. One might not be able to resist some comparisons with the evaluations of the length of the penis, or with Plato's discussion of the three types of men with the three types of lotus. The lotus did incapacitate the women who practiced it; not everyone did, especially in the rural areas. It was a function of wealth. Thus, wealth bought beauty. In the Euro-American cultures, the converse is probably more true: Beauty, especially female beauty, buys wealth.

The lotus was at the heart of traditional Chinese aesthetics and erotics. In the misnamed "West," people generally pay little attention to feet, physiologically and aesthetically, though women pay much more attention than men, with pedicures and polish and shoes. The shoes, however, are often misshapen (prettily triangular, distorting the shape of the feet) and high-heeled, causing both bunions and twisted ankles. Indeed, as the podiatrists constantly reiterate, if we paid as much attention to our feet as we do to our faces and hands, we would have far fewer foot problems in middle and old age. Consider the remark "My feet are killing me!"

Most people have a limited descriptive vocabulary for the shape or qualities of their feet. One Chinese authority described 58 types of lotus, rather poetically. There was lotus petal, new moon, harmonious bow, bamboo, water chestnut, the Buddha's head, and more. The three qualities of a foot were plumpness, softness and fineness, with nine gradations of excellence corresponding to the nine orders official ranks of the empire, from Divine Quality (A1) to False Article (C3), which had such a large heel that she looked like a climbing monkey. Wondrous Quality (A2) was weak and slender, like a willow branch leaning for support and bending in the breeze, while another was long and thin like the neck of a goose or a duck in flight. Evidently Chinese aesthetics were highly developed.

For the aesthete, even the smell of unwashed feet was perfume, described as "fragrant bed aroma." The lotus, like the breast in the United States and elsewhere, was a powerful sex symbol. One enthusiast wrote that the relation of sex to lotus was like that of mouth to taste. Lovers of the lotus penetrated the profoundest mysteries, mysteries which can be recaptured not in words but only through experience. It was the psychological and not the visual impact which really mattered. Oh, Lotus, Lotus!

Manuals instructed how to hold the lotus. Ladies told their lovers where to press the lotus. And men bathed, fondled, kissed, smelled and rubbed the lotus. Their special joy was to take the whole lotus in their mouths. One man said: "When I loved a woman, I went all the way and wished I could swallow her up. But only the tiny feet could be placed in the mouth." Another man explained: "The smaller the feet, the more intense the sex urge." Whether he was referring to the urge of the man, the woman, or both was not clear.

The origins of this custom are obscure. One theory is that it arose from admiration of the dancers at the Imperial Court, with their lightly bound feet (not unlike the feet of today's ballet dancers), and then the custom trickled down from the court to the rest of the empire. Another theory was that it derived from an empress who had a club foot, and persuaded her husband to order the girls at court to bind their feet in emulation—so it became a model of beauty. There were also mythological accounts and practical explanations: "Why must the foot be bound? To prevent the barbarous from running around!" This would be the ancient equivalent of a chastity belt and a form of social control.

The Mongols, led by Ghengis Khan and his grandson, Kublai Khan, conquered China in the early thirteenth century, and big feet were now the symbol of the enemy. But by the Ming dynasty (1368-1644), the lotus received official sanction. Then the Manchu conquerors (1644-1911) outlawed the custom, though to little effect, as some of the Manchu women practiced the lotus. By the end of the nineteenth century, however, opposition had developed. Reformers condemned the custom as barbaric and stupid. The weakness of women endangered their health and safety, was thought by some to be transmitted to their children, and also affected China militarily. By then, China had lost the Opium War of 1839-42 (despite having invented gunpowder) and been forced to cede Hong Kong to Britain and open five ports for trade. Then, in 1900 Britain and other nations violently suppressed the Boxer Uprising. Meanwhile, around the same time, anti-foreign resentment was increasing, leading to the formation of the reformist and nationalist Kuomintang Party in 1891, led by Sun Yat-sen. The lotus now began to symbolize the old world, anti-modernity and Chinese weakness, not beauty and sexiness. A new slogan was coined: "Everything new is beautiful, everything old is ugly." Hence, a complete reversal of the old aesthetics and a new union of politics and aesthetics.

Opposition to foot-binding steadily increased. An empress banned it in 1902. A poet lamented: One pair of bound feet/But two cisterns of tears.

After the 1911 revolution, Sun Yat-sen prohibited the custom. Similarly, in Taiwan the Japanese banned foot-binding in 1915, 20 years after their conquest of Taiwan. A tradition that had lasted around a thousand years was abolished in about 20 years, due in part to severe sanctions. The lotus, originally a symbol of beauty and sexiness, and then, under the Mongol and Manchu conquests, a symbol of China itself, became a symbol of national weakness and obsolescence.

A couple of points might clarify the lotus, which seems so bizarre to many people. First, while the lotus was still popular, elite Western women were binding their waists in steel or whalebone corsets, and damaging, by compression, not only the lungs and kidneys but also the upper and lower intestines and the womb. Some women even had their lower or floating ribs surgically removed to minimize their waists. Men could girdle the waist with their strong manly hands. Similarly, as mentioned earlier, women's shoes in both shape and heels often deform women's feet. Common to both China and the Anglo-American aesthetics are the value of smallness and being "petite." The values of sexual dimorphism are not so far removed after all.

On the other hand, while liposuction is a favored surgery for size reduction, breast augmentation, of course, usually increases size. This dimorphism is in contrast to the "breastlessness" of men and, in a breast-obsessed culture, maximizes sex appeal. "Petite" below but ample above.

And the pain! Why did so many women endure so much pain for so long? The answer was simple, as one woman said: "for beauty" and, therefore, marriage. Plus, they had no choice if and when their mothers decided on this project (it was not universal), when they were around three to seven years old. As is evident, the endurance of pain for the sake of beauty is not only a Chinese norm.

Men and women may subject themselves to similar pain in ritual cicatrization of faces and bodies, especially in parts of Africa, and by tattooing, particularly in Japan. The Maori men might endure the *moko:* the incision of symmetrical patterns of scars on the face, with charcoal rubbed on for the terrifying aspect of the fierce warrior. Anyone brave enough to endure that rite of passage was not afraid of anything. The same logic applied to the male circumcision rites among some African and Aboriginal Australian peoples.

Then there is the matter of female incapacitation, either by choice or not. The lotus certainly incapacitated women, which was one of the arguments against the lotus from the reformers and modernizers. But other cultures had or have a similar process. The classic example is the use of brass rings around the necks of the Karen (or Padaung) people of Myanmar (Burma). Their weight compresses the collar bones down so the muscles atrophy and, if the rings are removed, the muscles cannot sustain the head. It was argued that the rings protected women working in the fields from tiger attacks, so they were protection. But, of course, with many rings around their necks, the women could not work in the fields anyway, since they could not bend over. So the rings became, like the lotus, both a status symbol and an attribute of beauty. Only the wealthy could be beautiful, as with the lotus. (Keshishian, 1979; Brain, 1979). The situation has changed somewhat since the 1970s, due to war and poverty. The women can no longer afford the brass so the practice has declined. Refugees, however, have found a home in parts of Thailand where the government has set up refugee camps, and the "giraffe people" are a revenue-producing tourist attraction and asset. Now girl children are preferred to boys (Mydans, 2001).

Two other examples of female incapacitation are worth mentioning. In the Admiralty Islands of the South Sea, women might have their two front incisors knocked out, usually by a specialist using a rock, giving them the toothless smile of, say, an unlucky NFL linebacker. This must have been very painful as well as hindered their eating – but all in the name of beauty. Similarly, in New Guinea women might have fingers removed as evidence of their pain and grief in the loss of loved ones. Some shed tears, others shed fingers. There were limits, however: The thumbs and first fingers were retained, since without them the women could not pound the grain. (Brain, 1979; Ebin, !979).

A third example is clitoridectomy, now widely, but not universally, outlawed. A fourth example is male circumcision, which, like clitoridectomy, is often part of a religious ritual, and therefore difficult to comment on. Is it the word of God or superstition or valid medical practice supported by contemporary medical experts? Condemnation of either practice is sometimes condemned as cultural racism, and is thus difficult to negotiate. In this context, it is interesting to note that, in New York, the city's board of health voted unanimously to require parental assent for Jewish ritual circumcisions that require the practice of *metzita bepeh:* direct oral-genital suction of the blood of the circumcision. The city health commissioner explained that 11 babies circumcised in this way between 2000 and 2011 contracted herpes, and two died. Some Ultra-Orthodox rabbis believe that this ritual is God's commandment, and state that they will refuse to follow the new directive and would even sacrifice their lives to obey this commandment. Two hundred Haredi rabbis signed a statement accusing the health department of lying (Ettinger, 2012).

*

Erotica have been around for millennia and everywhere, as the British Museum collection indicates. What we now call pornography has only developed in the last 400 or so years, but has expanded globally since the inventions of printing, the camera, film, the Internet, video, and corporate investment. The benefits may be high for some, the costs high for others; it all depends. And for society? This is debated: sexual amusement and/or liberation? Sin? Raunch culture (Levy, 2005)? Pornified (Paul, 2005)? Hypersexualization (Baudrillard, 1983; Kammeyer, 2008)? Now, into Pornland (Dines, 2010), and the entire scene nicely reviewed and summarized by Campbell (2012).

The range of erotica from, possibly, the Venus of Willendorf through Egyptian, Judaic, Greco-Roman, Hindu, Japanese, Chinese and European erotica indicate both the power of sex and the power of love and attraction. Erotica are defined as benevolent, loving and egalitarian, with pornography defined as the opposite: injurious, exploitative and harmful, especially to the female participants, and also potentially dangerous in its real and simulated violence, not only to participants but also to consumers.

There are concerns about the personal and social impacts of pornography, but it is far too profitable a corporate enterprise to expect it to disappear, though the cost-benefit ratio may be adjustable. Perhaps consumers will become more aware of the potential hazards, as with the use of tobacco or alcohol; or, perhaps, not. Perhaps producers will develop more erotic porn, with love, equality, respect and tenderness permeating the sexual relations, and more concern for female sexual satisfaction, as Caitlin desires. The rise of gonzo, however, suggests that producers will go in the other direction. Presumably they will follow the money, at whatever the social cost. And maybe consumers will follow the media, for better and for worse.

Depictions of sexual activity may be pornographic and obscene (though definitions vary) or loving and tender, and everything and anything between. It does seem that not much was considered obscene by the Greeks and Romans or by those who carved the temples at Khajuraho. The shunga of Japan do not portray such a wide range of sexual action as the temples, but a fair range, nonetheless, including violence. But the eroticism in both cultures is imbued with spirituality, which gives it a different tone and meaning than, say, Augustine's prayer and the Index. The lotus, in contrast, was loved for its eroticism in the imagination——no sculptures or paintings were required.

The classic definitions of criminal sex stress that the participants must give consent, must not be minors (though the age of maturity is defined differently in different places) and must not be violent (but some consenting adults are sadists, and there seem to be enough masochists around to keep them happy – see Chapter 13). So, defining the difference between pornography and erotica is difficult if not impossible – well, actually, easy enough to define but not easy enough to get agreement. Even XXX gonzo porn has its viewers who enjoy it and find it erotic. Concerns about the leakage of fantasy into reality seem to be warranted, to the detriment of both men and women. Censorship of the Internet is not impossible; governments do it all the time, but there does not appear to be any demand for that. Consumers will have to self-censor, as they do (or do not) with drugs, alcohol and tobacco.

Chapter 12
Masturbation

Oscar Wilde famously remarked that masturbation was so much better than sex with other people, because it is "cleaner, more efficient, and you meet a better class of people." Woody Allen later echoed this: "Don't knock masturbation. It's sex with someone you love." Despite these views, which are by no means universal, masturbation has had a crazy history for two main reasons: first, because attitudes have changed so rapidly in the last 100 years, especially in the last 30 years; and second, because although masturbation is widely practiced, attitudes are still highly conflicted.

The benefits of going solo over having sex with someone else are now loudly trumpeted by the sexperts. It is praised as the most important source of sexual gratification for many people, especially adolescents and the old; the second most important source for most men and women after coitus; and the form of sexual activity that most reliably causes orgasms and multiple orgasms for women. It is convenient, safe, free and causes no worries about STIs or pregnancies, which is a great relief (Kinsey, 1953: 132). From this list, one may ask, "Why would anyone have sex any other way?"

Many people masturbate, sometimes with greater or lesser frequency, depending on their sex drive, age, values and the availability of other partners; but it is not often discussed. The Chicago University study, which included only participants from the U.S. between the ages of 18 and 59, reported that over 60 percent of the men and over 40 percent of the women had masturbated in the past year (Michael,1994:158). That leaves about 50 percent of the participants who did not. It is still taboo in some circles; for others it is their primary sexual outlet.

Many other mammals masturbate, according to the Kinsey Report (1953:135): horses, rats, ferrets, baboons, cows, porcupines (very carefully, I imagine), elephants, rabbits, chimpanzees and man's second best friend, the dog (though how they all do it is not explained).

Masturbation has a long, checkered and interesting history. It was once regarded as a grave sin, and still is by some. Then, in the eighteenth and nineteenth centuries, established medical opinion began to redefine it as a disease—a disease sometimes remedied by circumcision for boys and clitoridectomies for girls. In the early twentieth century, Freud argued that it was not a sin or a disease but a neurosis. Then, in the 1950s, Kinsey entered the fray, redefining masturbation, yet again, as a normal sexual activity; and he was followed by other sexologists. In the 1960s, masturbation joined popular culture with a bestseller *Portnoy's Complaint* (1969), which played masturbation for shock value and as taboo-breaking.

The two Hite reports in the 1970s and 1980s exposed women's and men's ideas and practices of masturbation, which was by then renamed "going solo," in graphic detail, and indicated that the activity was much loved, though many women and men felt guilty about it. She reported: "Most women said they enjoyed masturbation physically (after all it did lead to orgasm), but usually not psychologically. . . . Psychologically they felt lonely, guilty, unwanted, selfish, silly and generally bad . . . As one woman said, 'to me, masturbation seems lonely, childish and self-absorbed; everything I'd rather *not* have as part of any sex experience. I do it sometimes, but I wouldn't brag about it in public'" (1987:62; cf 1981:486-7).

Well, no, one would not generally brag about it in public, but the disjunction between the physical pleasure and the psychological discomfort is very curious. Hite insisted that masturbation was not only a common practice but even a right: "Men have a right to love themselves and give themselves pleasure" (1981: 289). Women, too, presumably, for Hite's views had firmed up between her two reports. But the rapid shift from sin through disease to neurosis to right is amazing. Soon it would be a duty.

Recently, David Lodge's novel *Therapy* plays masturbation for laughs. The scene is a man writing his memoir:

> After I wrote that last bit, I undressed and lay on the bed with a towel handy and tried to jerk myself off. It's a long time since I did this, getting on for thirty-five years in fact, and I was out of practice. I couldn't find any Vaseline in the bathroom cabinet, and it so happened that I'd just run out of olive oil in the kitchen, so I lubricated my cock with Paul Newman's Own Salad Dressing, which was a mistake. First of all it was freezing cold from the fridge and had a shrivelling effect at first, secondly the vinegar and lemon juice in it stung like hell, and thirdly I began to smell like Gabrielli's *pollo alla cacciatore* . . . (1995:93)

Salad dressing may be one aid to orgasm, but there are others. Here are a few ludicrous examples: The place is Hong Kong. The date is August 2008. Forty-one- year-old Le King, strolling in a local park, noticed that the benches had holes in them – for drainage, presumably, but, perhaps, for other purposes, which Mr. King attempted. He got in, but could not get out. Police eventually arrived, found him face-down on the bench, carted him and his beloved park bench to hospital where, four hours later, they were separated. Moral: Don't have sex with a park bench. Another man was totally wrecked by his vacuum cleaner hosepipe. The doctor advised him to wrap a cardboard toilet paper roll around the pipe in the future. Another had tried his luck with an old-fashioned urinal, and cycled six miles to the hospital with it hanging on to his penis like grim death. The doctor smashed it with a hammer, the urinal that is, not the penis (Northcutt, 2010:79-86)

Sin

The negative definition of masturbation as sin and vice goes back to the story of Onan, or an interpretation of it:

> And Er, Judah's first-born, was wicked in the sight of the Lord; and the Lord slew him. And Judah said unto Onan, go in unto thy brother's wife, and marry her, and raise up seed to thy brother. And Onan knew that the seed should not be his; and it came to pass, when he went in unto his brother's wife, that he spilled it on the ground, lest that he should give seed to his brother. And the thing which he did displeased the Lord: wherefore he slew him. (Genesis 38: 7-10)

Masturbate and die! No wonder some people felt a bit worried. The scholars debate whether the Lord's displeasure was with Onan's disobedience to the law of levirate marriage or with masturbation or *coitus interruptus*. But the teaching of the Catholic Church has been firm: Masturbation is a sin and a vice because it perverts the purpose of sex, namely procreation.

Vatican authorities are very serious about it. In 1930, Pope Pius XI issued an encyclical "*Casti Connubii*" (On Christian Marriage) forbidding any artificial regulation of fertility, most notably contraception and masturbation: "Any use whatsoever of matrimony exercised in such a way that the [sex] act is deliberately frustrated in its natural power to generate life is an offense against the law of God and of nature, and those who indulge in such are branded with the guilt of a grave sin," i.e., as I was taught, a mortal sin. This teaching was reinforced by another encyclical from Pope Paul VI in 1968: "*Humane Vitae*" (On Human Life). But that was eight years after the Food and Drug Administration (FDA) approved the pill; and by 1974, 83 percent of American Catholics approved of contraception, despite papal pronouncements (Petersen, 1999:146, 275).

It always amazes me how many people profess to know the mind and will of God, and how profoundly they disagree about what it is. Yet they are often absolutely certain, and willing to kill or die for these beliefs.

In 1983, the pope affirmed the traditional view, when he condemned masturbation as "regressive," which reaffirmed his 1976 condemnation of masturbation as a "grave moral disorder" (*Newsweek*, 26 January 1976). The Holy Office has forbidden masturbation even to obtain a semen specimen for the detection and cure of gonorrhea. The *New Catholic Encyclopedia* states: "It has been the constant and clear teaching of the Church from principles found in Holy Scripture that masturbation is a serious sin that will keep one from heaven (e.g., I Corinthians 6:10; Catholic University, 1967: Vol. 9:438-40). In short, you will go to hell! (My reading of this verse does not support this conclusion.)

A senior Catholic theologian, responding to a question as to whether it was sinful to masturbate, explained that it was like owning a Ferrari and driving only in first gear. "Driving only in first gear, not only do you prevent the Ferrari expressing its full power, but gradually you wear it out and thereby ruin a masterpiece of technology" (*National Post*, 10 July 1999). This surely gives new meaning to "auto-eroticism."

How many Catholics subscribe to these condemnations is not known, but the threats of being slain and sent to hell are intimidating; and I humbly submit that the punishments seem a bit disproportionate to the alleged offence, especially since procreation is not always an option.

The Jewish tradition is gentler: Ejaculation only requires a bath and ritual purification (Leviticus 15: 16-7); this seems to contradict the Catholic interpretation of Onan, since it does not appear to be *that* offensive to the Lord.

The Welsh tradition is well documented and provides some arithmetic of vice. A Welsh penitential known as The Synod of North Britain (about 520 CE) provides for one year's penance for an adult masturbator. A later penitential (about 570 CE) is interesting as providing a scale of sinfulness: two years penance for masturbation (so it doubled in 50 years, for some reason), two-and-a-half for bestialities, three for adultery and for coitus *in femoribus* and four for coitus *in ano*. In the arithmetic of penance, anal intercourse seems to have been twice as bad as masturbation. A sixth century Irish penitentiary attributed to St. Columba required one year's penance from a married man but one-and-a-half from a single man. Female masturbation was not mentioned (Bullough, 1976:357-9).

St. Thomas Aquinas (1225-74), the great Dominican philosopher and theologian, dominated Christian thought until the end of the Middle Ages, and his influence is still paramount in the Catholic Church. In his *Summa Theologiae* (1981:2.2, Question 154, Arts 11, 12), Aquinas defined "unnatural vice" [homosexuality] as doubly sinful, for not only is it "in conflict with right reason" but also it is "in conflict with the natural pattern of sexuality for the benefit of the species." It is, therefore, "the worst of all kinds of lust" and "the gravest of sins" – worse, in his view, than sacrilege, rape, adultery or incest. In order of gravity, the worst of the sins against nature is bestiality ("which does not observe the due species"), then sodomy ("which does not observe the due sex"), then "the lechery which does not observe the due mode of intercourse" and, finally, masturbation or the solitary sin, "where the intercourse of one with another is omitted" (1981:245-9).

Masturbation may have been widely condemned in the Christian domain, but evidently it was still practiced sufficiently frequently to merit such detailed discussion over the centuries.

Disease

The dawn of the age of reason saw medical science reinforcing the teachings of religious faith. Thomas Laqueur has written a massive 501 page tome on the subject, and declared that "in or around 1712" masturbation was invented as a new and pernicious disease. This was due to the publication of the immensely popular *Onania*, or *The Heinous Sin of Self-Pollution, and All its Frightful Consequences, in Both Sexes Consider'd.* The author's main point was not its sinfulness, which was well known, but that masturbation caused diseases. The "Frightful Consequences" included stunted growth and many a phymosis and paraphymosis, of which he wrote: "I shall not explain these terms any further, let it suffice that they are very painful and troublesome." Examples are stranguries, priaprisms and gonorrheas, loss of erection, premature ejaculation and infertility. Women masturbators have most of the same troubles that afflict men, but also imbecility, discharges, hysteric fits, barrenness and a "total ineptitude to the act of generation itself." Those children that survive are weak and sickly and a "misery to themselves, a dishonour to the human race, and a scandal to their parents" (Laqueur, 2004: 23ff; MacDonald, 1967:423-5). Masturbation was not only a sin, therefore, but also a disease and a nuisance to everyone.

Various pamphleteers developed these themes, but the classic work on the subject in the eighteenth century was *L'Onanisme* by S.A.D. Tissot. It was first published in Latin in 1759, then translated into French, English, Italian and German, and was last published as recently as 1905. Tissot also listed the effects of masturbation: It causes weakening of the digestive system, a loss of appetite or an excessive appetite, vomiting and indigestion; and it can cause a breakdown of the respiratory system and inhibit the nervous system, hysteria, jaundice, stomach cramps, prolapse and ulceration of the womb. More specifically, he stated that masturbation caused impotence, gonorrhea, priapism, tumors in the bladder, constipation, hemorrhoids, pimples, blisters, headaches, rheumatic pains, a general weakness resulting in coughs, fevers and consumption, feeble-mindedness and even insanity. Women were affected in similar ways to men, but were also susceptible to stomach cramps, prolapse and ulceration of the womb, clitoral rashes, tremors of the uterus, etc. While Tissot believed that masturbation had more pernicious effects on women than men, he also believed that the effects were worse for young people, and for women who engaged in mutual fondling. This list of "Frightful Consequences" differs only in degree from that presented by the author of *Onania*; but Tissot's contribution was to attempt to explain, through medical science, how masturbation caused these consequences. He argued, first, that the body is drained and weakened by the loss of seminal fluid: one drop of semen, he said, is equivalent to 40 drops of blood; and second, the orgasm, which is a convulsive spasm of nervous energy, can damage the brain. This loss of fluid and brain damage, in turn, affect the other systems of the body, with catastrophic effects (Laqueur, 2004; MacDonald, 1967:427-8; Bullough, 1976:496-8).

Tissot, in turn, deeply influenced Rousseau, who condemned masturbation in his classic text on education, *Emile*, though he enjoyed it in his *Confessions*, published posthumously. And Rousseau was enormously influential (Laqueur, 2004).

By the end of the eighteenth century, masturbation was defined as morally wrong and physically harmful, and was condemned by church and medical science alike. There was a certain logic to these attitudes, for if masturbation were sinful, then how could it be good for you? Sin must be bad for the sinner, surely. It's tricky if sins are good for you. There also seemed to be a certain justice: for the sins of the fathers (and mothers) were not only visited upon the children, as the Bible said, but also upon the father and mothers themselves. Tissot, and the author of *Onania* had added a material sanction to a spiritual sanction against masturbation; so masturbation not only deserved hell after death but it also caused a hell on earth.

Although these ideas about masturbation grew increasingly popular in the eighteenth century, they were not entirely unchallenged. In France the philosophers did not take Tissot too seriously. Diderot wrote that "religious institutions have attached the labels 'vice' and 'virtue' to actions that are completely independent of morality." Like Rousseau, he believed in the "natural man," but "then an artificial man was built up inside him. Since then a civil war had been raging continuously within his breast," and the natural man always had the "moral man's foot on his neck" (Bullough, 1976:494). Very Pauline, but with reversed valences.

In Germany, Kant was furiously against masturbation, which is "contrary to morality in the highest degree," worse than suicide, which is against the law of self-preservation, because it is against the law of the preservation of the species. As such it is (Laqueur glosses the texts) an act of "moral madness" for Kant. (2004: 59-60).

In the United States, Benjamin Rush (1745-1813), one of the signers of the Declaration of Independence and a well-known abolitionist and reformer, was also the author of the first American textbook on psychiatry. He argued that sexual excess, including masturbation, caused insanity and a long list of other problems: seminal weakness, impotence, dysuria, tabes dorsalis, pulmonary consumption, dyspepsia, dimness of sight, vertigo, epilepsy, hypochondriasis, loss of memory, manalgie, fatuity and death (Bullough, 1976:542-3).

Following on, in 1874, Dr. Sylvester Graham, most famous for his crackers, explained with eloquence why masturbation is so pernicious: "In the first place, it is wholly unnatural; and, in every respect, does violence to nature . . . it is generally commenced very early in life. [It inhibits growth and development and the victims] fall prematurely into the grave . . . it is a secret and a solitary vice, [and] it impairs the intellectual and moral faculties, and debases the mind, in the greatest degree" (1974:40-45; [1874]). He goes on to explain that it affects the stomach, the nervous system, the heart and arteries, the genital organs, the lungs, the liver and kidneys and even the skin. The body wastes away, tissue deteriorates, "bones become dry and brittle," the chest and spine are distorted, teeth fall out and lips lose their color. The sense of touch becomes "obtuse," the sense of taste is "blunted," the sense of smell is "impaired," and the sense of sight is affected worse, as blindness often results. Even the masturbator's brain is affected, as "his mind seems confused, clouded and crippled. Death is often the result" (1974:58). He was quite carried away:

> Sometimes this general mental decay continues with the continued abuses, till the wretched transgressor sinks into a miserable fatuity, and finally becomes a confirmed and degraded idiot, whose deeply sunken and vacant, glossy eye, and livid, shriveled countenance, and ulcerous, toothless gums, and foetid breath, and feeble, broken voice, and emaciated and dwarfish and crooked body, and almost hairless head – covered, perhaps, with suppurating blisters and running sores – denote a premature old age! a blighted body – and a ruined soul! – and he drags out the remnant of his loathsome existence, in exclusive devotion to his horridly abominable sensuality. (1974:58)

Dr. J. H. Kellogg, better known for his breakfast cereals, was also enthusiastic in his condemnation of this "awful sin against nature and against God" (1888:339): "The sin of self-pollution is one of the vilest, basest, and the most degrading that a human being can commit. It is worse than beastly. Those who commit it place themselves far below the meanest brute that breathes. The most loathsome reptile, rolling in the slush and slime of its stagnant pool, would not demean itself thus . . . a boy who is thus guilty, ought to be ashamed to look into the eyes of an honest dog."

Perhaps Dr. Kellogg had not noticed that even honest dogs apparently masturbate. (I have not noticed it either). In any event, his particular contribution was to include some tragic case histories. One young man, for example, was driven to theft and thence to prison; another committed suicide and "with his own hand finished the work of destruction which he had himself begun." And a third was castrated by his father (1888:359-63).

Krafft-Ebing (1840-1902), the founder of modern sexual pathology and author of the immensely influential *Psychopathia Sexualis* (1886: twelfth edition, 1946) argued that masturbation caused homosexuality, injured not only the mind but also the body, including "neuroses of the sexual apparatus;" and he added for good measure that "every masturbator is more or less a coward" (1946:286-7). So this was the official medical consensus from 1700 to 1902, though as always there were exceptions (MacDonald, 1967:428-9).

So great was popular concern over masturbation that various devices were marketed to prevent it, notably "thigh-spreaders"—two leather straps connected by an iron bar, which prevented the poor child from masturbating by rubbing the thighs together. Cardboard rolls and aluminum mitts were also recommended: Tthey prevented both masturbation and thumb-sucking (Beekman, 1977:121-2).

Nonetheless, by the end of the nineteenth century, the conventional wisdom of the medical, psychiatric and religious professions was that masturbation caused (or exacerbated) a wide range of physical and mental illnesses, moral problems and crimes, but, notably, insanity, homicide, suicide, blindness, impotence, venereal disease, sterility, homosexuality and even death.

Neurosis

The turn of the century witnessed the gradual demise of what Hare (1962) has termed "the insanity hypothesis," but was gradually transmuted into what we may describe as "the neurosis hypothesis." The turning point was Freud. Freud paid considerable attention to masturbation; he avoided the use of such emotive terms as "unnatural," "immoral," "vile," "repulsive," and so on, and attempted to adopt a scientific method in his interviews and case studies. He regarded masturbation as "the executive agent of infantile sexuality," and distinguished between infantile masturbation, which he regarded as normal, and late infantile (about age four) and adolescent masturbation – both of which can be problematic (Vols. 2:161; 7:106; 9:197-8). In 1917, he insisted that "An unsuspectedly large proportion of obsessional actions may be traced back to masturbation, of which they are disguised repetitions and modifications" (Vol. 1:351; see Vol. 10:48, 56, 100). And in his well-known case study known as "Rat Man," Freud was sure he had proved that it was in masturbation that "the aetiology of subsequent neuroses must be sought" (Vol. 9:83).

In his last work, *An Outline of Psychoanalysis* (1938), Freud affirmed the differential significance of masturbation for boys and girls, particularly in the resolution of the Oedipus complex and the castration complex. The theory is a little fanciful, and may owe more to Freud's imagination than to his patients' histories. He begins with boys in the Oedipal phase, masturbating and having "fantasies of carrying out some sort of activity with it in relation to his mother." He continues:

> The boy's mother has understood quite well that his sexual excitation relates to herself. Sooner or later she reflects that it is not right for it to continue. She thinks she is doing the correct thing in forbidding him to handle his genital organ. . . . At last his mother adopts the severest measures; she threatens to take away from him the thing he is defying her with. Usually, in order to make the threat more frightening and more terrible, she delegates its execution to the boy's father, saying that she will tell him and that he will cut his penis off. (1973a:46)

Freud described this whole process as "the central experience of the years of childhood, the greatest problem of early life and the strongest sources of later inadequacy" (1973a:48). For masturbation crystallized in one process a (sexual) love for the mother, a jealous hatred of the father, and the repression of both emotions from a fear of castration. In Freud's mature view, therefore, masturbation is not just a more or less harmless habit; it is a profound expression of contradictory emotions that must be repressed but which must inevitably return at puberty with damaging consequences.

Masturbation could be equally traumatic for girls, Freud believed, but in a different way:

> If during the phallic phase she tries to get pleasure like a boy by the manual stimulation of her genitals, it often happens that she fails to obtain sufficient satisfaction and extends her judgement of inferiority from her stunted penis to her whole self. As a rule she soon gives up masturbating, since she has no wish to be reminded of the superiority of her brother or playmate, and turns away from sexuality altogether." (1973:50a; cf. 12)

Penis envy, therefore, facilitates the girls' transition from the clitoris to the vagina as a "leading erotogenic zone;" but this transition is one of "the chief determinants of the greater proneness of women to neurosis and especially to hysteria" (Vol. 7:142-4, cf. 2:160-1).

Freud's views on adolescent and adult masturbation are not entirely clear, but there are some indications that he thought that *attitudes* towards masturbation were more significant in the etiology of neurosis than the masturbation itself. This is apparent in the hypothetical story of the landlord's daughter and the caretaker's girl: both are likely to masturbate, but the former, who is better educated, will be without guilt feelings; the latter will think she has done something wrong, because of an education into false ideals, so she will repress her sexual impulses and, finally, "a neurosis breaks out in her which cheats her of marriage and her hopes in life," and she turns away from sexual intercourse with "unexplained disgust" (Vol. 1:398-9). All this catastrophe from not enjoying masturbation!

Freud had three sons and three daughters. One wonders how he coped with this "executive agent." For all his scholarship and concern, Freud refused to offer any practical advice to parents and educators (Vol. 2:161). Despite Freud's refusal to offer advice to parents, there were many others who did offer advice. For example, Wilhelm Reich (1897-1957), the controversial Austrian psychiatrist, advocated frequent sexual release to avoid neurosis, and was teaching masturbation techniques as part of his sex therapy in the 1920s. But his views found little favor and he was ultimately imprisoned for them.

In 1904, Dr. L. Emmett Holt stated, in the standard book on child-rearing in the United States, *The Care and Feeding of Children,* that "Masturbation is the most injurious of all the bad habits and should be broken up just as early as possible." In the 1924 edition of his work, he omitted that sentence, but added that masturbation is an *effect* rather than a *cause* of insanity (Beekman, 1977:124). ("Sorry! Just got things the wrong way round!" This would be a doubtful consolation for a worried parent: "No, of course it doesn't *cause* insanity, my dear! The poor child is insane already!")

Lord Baden-Powell, the defender of Mafeking and founder of the Boy Scouts, was equally against masturbation, but for different reasons. In *Rovering to Success* (1922), he stated that masturbation prevents semen from getting its full chance of making one the strong manly man he would otherwise be: "You are throwing away the seed that has been handed down to you as a trust instead of keeping it and ripening it for bringing a son to you later on."

Holt and Baden-Powell were the last speakers for the Victorian age—believers that masturbation caused psychological problems. A pediatrician, Erwin Wexberg, associated with the Adler Institute, argued the reverse: "Deficient courage and self-confidence are the very causes of (the children's) bad habit" (Beekman, 1977:124, 141). Cause and effect had changed places: Now psychological problems caused masturbation.

By the 1930s, however, expert opinion was changing again: masturbation had its *advantages.* The most thorough discussion of the topic was offered by the distinguished psychologist, Havelock Ellis, who concluded:

> Reviewing the general question of the supposed grave symptoms and signs of masturbation, and its pernicious results, we may teach the conclusion that in the case of moderate masturbation in healthy, wellborn individuals, no seriously pernicious results necessarily follow . . . It must always be remembered, however, that [the practice of masturbation is] in the absence of normal sexual relationships, frequently not without good results. (1934:128-9, 132)

However, Ellis warned against the dangers of masturbation "in excess." Unfortunately, what is normal and what is excessive was not defined, so the anxiety about possible negative physical or psychological consequences was hardly allayed (Ellis, 1934:129; cf. Kinsey, 1953:515).

The redefinitions continued in the 1940s and 1950s. One pediatrician described masturbation as simply a mannerism like ear-pulling, nail biting and baby talk (Tisdall, 1942:261). Another even advised: "Let your young baby discover and play with his genitals" (Beekman, 1977:185). The Child Study Association of America answered parents' questions:

> Is masturbation dangerous? No, not in the sense that generations of parents have worried about. It definitely does not lead to ailments or injuries of any kind and is, in fact, coming to be regarded as a normal part of sexual development. . . . What can happen, however, is that a child will develop unhealthy feelings of anxiety and guilt, especially if he has been scolded or punished for masturbating... The only real harm from masturbation is the worry and anxiety that go with it. (1954:16, 37)

And this introduced a new problem: Masturbation "does not lead to ailments and injuries," but scolding and punishing do! Two pediatricians from the Gesell Institute, which had developed from the Yale Clinic, suggested that "masturbation not only does not do harm, but that excessive efforts on the part of parents to stop or prevent it actually may in themselves be harmful" (Ilg and Ames, 1956:165). Masturbation is, therefore, still dangerous, not because of what a child does but because of what the parent does!

The third turning point in the thinking about masturbation came with the publication of the scholarly Kinsey Reports *Sexual Behavior in the Human Male* (1948) and *Sexual Behavior in the Human Female* (1953). (For "Human," read American.) The Kinsey team quickly demolished ideas that masturbation was "infantile," that there was danger in "excess" or that there were negative physical or psychological consequences. They reassured many Americans and others by reporting that almost all American men and two-thirds of all American women had masturbated to orgasm, and that many still did. The "hidden vice" was now out in the open, and was no longer even a vice—it was normal.

The team even gave the practice a certain halo by observing that high status men were more autoerotic than working-class men. Masturbation was in! Or almost. Furthermore, they not only said that masturbation was not bad for you, they even said that *not* masturbating was probably bad for people: "The individual may become nervous, irritable, incapable of concentrating on any sort of problem, and difficult to live with" (1953:166). They also observed that masturbation in women "may actually contribute to the female's capacity to respond in her coital relations in marriage;" and that the major problem with masturbation lay not in the act itself, but in how it was regarded: Worry and guilt caused problems, masturbation did not (1953:172, 168).

Now this was a *volte-face.* Previous authors gave lists of the problems that masturbation caused, and later authors gave lists of the problems that caused masturbation. Kinsey and his team listed, for the first time, the benefits and joys of masturbation, and the list of problems that resulted from *not* masturbating.

Dr. Spock reflected these emerging new ideas in his famous *Baby and Child Care* (1946). He distinguished between masturbation at different ages; in the infant it is "wholesome curiosity." "You can distract him with a toy if you want, but don't feel that you've *got* to. It's better not to give him the idea that he is bad or that his genitals are bad." He added that "At any age there are a few children who handle their genitals a great deal. . . . They are usually tense or worried children. They aren't nervous because they are masturbating; they are masturbating because they were nervous." Finally, Dr. Spock tried to overturn beliefs into which his generation had been educated: "Most of us heard in childhood the threat that masturbation would lead to insanity. This belief is untrue. It grew up because certain adolescents and young adults who are becoming seriously ill mentally masturbate a great deal. But they aren't becoming insane because they are masturbating. The excessive masturbation is just one symptom of the nervous breakdown" (Spock, 1958:372-5).

To the survey data and statistical tables of the Kinsey Reports, Masters and Johnson added detailed analyses of the physiology of sexual responses, based on clinical research in their laboratories and interviews with a sample of over 700 men and women. They concluded that, among men, orgasms reached by masturbation were more intense than coital orgasms, although, they added, "not necessarily as satisfying." This intensity was partly because it was easier to have multiple orgasms (1966:133, 314, 65). And they dismissed fears of excessive masturbation as one of many "phallic fallacies" or vaginal fallacies in our society (1966:200-3).

Fun, Healthy and a Right

By the 1970s, the research of the Kinsey team and Masters and Johnson and others was being translated into mass-market paperback bestsellers. Dr. Reuben was first, and advised that masturbation is "fun" and also helpful for female frigidity. "The only thing harmful about masturbation is the guilt that is drummed into children." He discussed genital, anal and urethral masturbation, plus dildos, vibrators and ben-wa balls, and concluded that masturbation was the primary sexual activity for most people, shortly after they came into the world. It may be their main source of sexual pleasure shortly before they leave this world. "In between, if they can arrange it, sexual intercourse is a lot more fun" (Reuben, 1970:188-213).

Fun, fun, fun—the Beach Boys' message from California to the1970s-—was also the message of "J" and "M," authors of *The Sensuous Woman* and *The Sensuous Man*, respectively. "J" assures everyone that masturbation is "good for you," "wholesome, normal and sound," "one of the most gratifying human experiences" and a great way to train for lovemaking. She offers plenty of ideas for techniques and urges everyone to "go for it"—10 to 25 orgasms in a single session (1971:38-52). "M" was just as excited about his good news: "Masturbation is terrific . . . one of our greatest tension-relievers. And it is completely harmless to self and society" (1971:45-52). Alex Comfort, in his widely read and fully illustrated *The Joy of Sex,* goes on to say that masturbation is good "exercise" (1972:165). And if the fun of masturbation sometimes sounds like a cross between a valium and a workout, it is certainly different from sin, disease and insanity.

It is remarkable how quickly and dramatically attitudes have changed: In the first half of the twentieth century masturbation was referred to as onanism (and we know what happened to him), self-pollution and self-abuse; in the second half of the century, it is described as self-love, auto-manipulation, auto-eroticism, and going "solo," as well as great fun and good exercise. As Laqueur notes: "the surest road to ruin has become for some a road to self-realization" (2004:23).

The second development in the 1970s was the impact of the women's movement. Perhaps the first book to treat masturbation "politically," rather than clinically (like the sexologists) or hedonistically (like Reuben, Comfort, "M" and "J"), was the well-known *Our Bodies, Ourselves* by the Boston Women's Collective, which was first published in 1971. The authors described the "confusion and shame we had been made to feel, and often still felt, about touching our bodies in a sexual way" (1979:12); but, they added: "If you have never masturbated, we invite you to try." They pointed out that it would improve self-understanding and the sex life; they offered advice in learning to masturbate and recommended books and exercises. Masturbation is now not just pleasurable but liberating—and political (Laqueur, 2004: 75-7; 400).

One of the outstanding works on masturbation for women was *Liberating Masturbation* by Betty Dodson (1974), which included 15 line drawings of vulvas and suggested a reorientation to masturbation, which she called "a meditation on self-love." She stated: "Masturbation is our primary sex life. It is our sexual base. Everything we do beyond that is simply how we choose to socialize our sex life." About the same time as Dodson's book, Nancy Friday's *My Secret Garden: Women's Sexual Fantasies* (1973) became a best-seller. Meanwhile sex shops were opening up and continuing to redefine sex (Laqueur, 2004: 77-9).

The third major contribution to the debate on masturbation in the 1970s came from clinical psychologists. The second Kinsey Report (1953) had noted that between 10 and 15 percent of women had never achieved orgasm. By 1970, therefore, Masters and Johnson had developed a therapeutic program for nonorgasmic women, and reported that 84 percent of the 193 women in their two-week program successfully achieved orgasm through masturbation.

Other sex therapists developed their own, even more successful, treatment programs. The new attitudes generated a new terminology: Masturbation was now "going solo" or "getting there alone" to "hit the jackpot" or "reach the big O."

Male sexuality was also considered, and another sexologist noted: "You can use it [masturbation] to learn more about your body and its requirements, and to acquire skills useful in sex with a partner. We have found masturbation exercises very helpful in developing ejaculatory control and in dealing with erection problems" (Zilberger, 1978:169).

Various exercises were suggested, but there is no mention of fun. In the 1980s, Letty Pogrebin, noting that 40 percent of young women had not achieved orgasm by the age of 18, said this is "like having healthy eyes and not opening them." She cited the new breed of medical experts who described adolescent girls who did not masturbate as "sexually deprived," and said they were less likely to be orgasmic as mature women, may be prone to vasocongestion, which can cause cystic changes in the breasts, ovaries and uterus and may cause damage to the sensory system and parts of the central nervous system (Pogrebin, 1981:248-51). More fear—but this is fear if you do NOT masturbate: yet another capsize.

The "big M" now seems to be the *cure* for almost all the diseases it was once thought to have caused; and the diseases themselves are now believed to be caused by *not* masturbating! The only thing that remains the same in this arena is the climate of vague threats, fear and terror.

In the 1990s, masturbation was virtually routinized. Madonna and Michael Jackson, for example, simulated masturbation onstage, with crotch-grabbing antics, and advertisements implied it. Singers sang about it. It was no longer hidden, but everywhere, and flaunted. Jack-off clubs have been formed in many cities. And masturbation is featured in popular culture: Films, TV, art, including Annie Sprinkle's performance art, and of course, the worldwide web (Laqueur, 2004:79-82; 407-20).

Tides ebb and flow. In 1994, despite the antics and the positive publicity, the U.S. Surgeon-General, Dr. Jocelyn Elders, was fired by President Clinton for asserting at a U.N. AIDS Conference that maybe masturbation could be taught in schools, which might help to reduce the spread of HIV/AIDS and STI infections, as well as reduce the rate of teenage pregnancies (Laqueur, 2004: 416).

But that was then, in the U.S.; meanwhile in the U.K., the National Health Service circulated a pamphlet to teachers, parents and youth workers asserting that "an orgasm a day keeps the doctor away." "Health promotion experts advocate five portions of fruit and veg a day and 30 minutes physical activity three times a week. What about sex or masturbation twice a week?" It added that students have a "right" to an enjoyable sex life, and that it is good for cardiovascular health. Plus it accused experts of concentrating too much on safe sex and love and not enough on pleasure (Martin, 2009). Radical!

The pamphlet was withdrawn after protests asserting that such advice would increase the number of teenage pregnancies, which number about

40,000 every year in the U.K., of which more than half end in abortion; that it would increase the number of STIs, and frequency of underage sex; and that if the National Health Service wanted to improve teenage health, it should focus on reducing smoking and alcohol use (Martin, 2009).

Meanwhile, the sexologist Pamela Stephenson-Connolly discussed the importance of masturbation at different stages of the life cycle from her survey data, interviews and clinical practice. My favorite: "Mum caught me masturbating once. I was lying on the bed with my dick in my hand. 'Oh God, Brian', she said. 'Are you coming to dinner?'" (2011:23).

Caitlin Moran is far more explicit and hilarious: In many pages, she describes her first effort, at age 13, and of trying, over the next few years, different positions and locations. Then she discovers porn. Bliss. "This new hobby is amazing. It doesn't cost anything. I don't have to leave the house, and it isn't making me fat. I wonder if everyone knows about it" (2011:26). They do now.

All these redefinitions of masturbation, from sin to disease to neurosis to normal to fun to duty to right, were also redefinitions from unhealthy problematic to healthy egosexual – just in time for the Internet porn explosion.

Times may be changing but, perhaps, not so much, and certainly not all for the good. In 2013, a high school student in California, Matthew Burdette, masturbated in a stall and was videotaped by another student, who then posted the video on the Internet. The video went viral and Matthew committed suicide (Scowen, 2014).

In sum, the social construction of masturbation is a fascinating exercise in the evolution of both medical science and ethics. In antiquity and the Middle Ages, it was widely regarded as a sin and sometimes as a crime. In the eighteenth and nineteenth centuries, it was redefined as a disease (and was still considered a sin) that *caused* insanity, so various mechanical devices to prevent this vice were marketed, and circumcisions and clitoridectomies were occasionally performed to remedy the disease. In the twentieth century, masturbation was redefined again, this time as a *cause* of neurosis (Freud), then as a *symptom* (effect) of insanity, then as a *symptom* of neurosis, then as a harmless mannerism. After the 1950s, it was redefined, yet again, as a principal source of sexual release, a pleasure, fun, morally right (although not everyone agreed), and essential for physical and emotional well-being and sexual satisfaction.

Masturbation is now defined as being the cure for almost everything it was once thought of as causing! "Self-abuse" and "self-pollution" have been redefined as "self-loving" and "self-pleasuring;" the vice is virtue, the wrong is a right, and the right is a duty to the sensuous self.

Yet, masturbation is still controversial in some quarters, and Matthew Burdette was one of the casualties of our sexual and gender attitudes. Still, the changing, expert medical testimony does make one worry about the validity of any of it, just as one might be concerned about the changing definitions of mental illness in the ongoing editions of the *Diagnostic and Statistical Manual* (DSM).

Chapter 13
Paraphilias

The Greek prefix *phil* means "having a strong affinity or love for," and is found in many terms, e.g., philosophy, philanthropy, philanderer and "paraphilias"—or unusual loves. Paraphilic disorders are indications of mental illness and may be criminal.

In *The Diagnostic and Statistical Manual of Mental Disorders* (DSM-5), which is published by the American Psychiatric Association (APA) and often referred to as the "Bible" of psychiatry, "paraphilia" is defined as "any intense or persistent sexual interest other than sexual interest in genital stimulation or preparatory fondling with phenotypically normal, psychologically mature, consenting human partners." It becomes a disorder when the paraphilia "is currently causing distress or impairment to the individual or . . . has entailed personal harm or risk of harm to others" (2013:685-6). A shorter definition is that they are "disorders characterized by a disturbance in the object of sexual gratification or in the expression of sexual gratification" (Andreason and Black, 2005:466).

The APA lists the most common paraphilias as follows:

Exhibitionism	exposure of genitals
Fetishism	use of non-living objects
Frotteurism	touching or rubbing against a non-consenting person.
Pedophilia	focus on prepubescent child
Sexual masochism	receiving humiliation or suffering
Sexual sadism	inflicting humiliation or suffering
Transvestic fetishism	cross-dressing
Voyeurism	observing the activity of others, especially secretively

There are many other paraphilias: "telephone scatalogia (obscene phone calls), necrophilia (corpses), zoophilia (animals), coprophilia (feces), klismaphilia (enemas), or urophilia (urine)" (APA, 2013:705). Some case studies and commentaries on some of these paraphilias are presented in "The DSM-IV Casebook" (Spitzer et al., 1994).

According to one textbook, about 80,000 Americans, mostly men, are arrested annually on sexually related charges (excluding rape), mostly for pedophilia or exhibitionism; and about 90,000 people are in prison for criminal paraphiliac activities (Andreason and Black, 2005:468).

The classic account of pedophilia in the literature is Nabokov's *Lolita*, and the classic account of zoophilia is Edward Albee's Pulitzer-winning play "The Goat," about a man who falls in love with a goat.

But there is more—sexuality is so amazing! Among them are apotemophilia, an attraction to the idea of being an amputee, and acrotomophilia, a sexual attraction to amputees. These two paraphilias first came to public attention in 2000, during the controversy surrounding a surgeon in Scotland who amputated the legs of two perfectly healthy individuals at their request. There is some question as to whether this desire is a paraphilia or a body dismorphia, which is a different disorder – and even whether it is a disorder at all. Carl Elliott notes that while there is little scholarly research on this topic, there are numerous Internet listserves and websites on both "wannabes" (apotemophiles), "devotees" (acrotomophiles) and "pretenders." The stories the wannabes tell, the language they use, and the feelings they express are strikingly similar to those who wish to change their sex, e.g.,: "I have always felt I should be an amputee;" "I felt, this is who I was;" "My left foot was not part of me;" And some have felt this desire since early childhood (Elliott, 2000).

Another paraphilia is autogynephilia, which is "the [male] propensity to be sexually aroused by the thought or image of oneself as a woman." This paraphilia is, therefore, not about objects or other people, but about oneself; and such men are described by one authority as "men trapped in men's bodies" (Elliott, 2000:80).

Havelock Ellis, an early sexologist and one of the first to advocate the decriminalization of homosexuality, has a few more paraphilias. He used the term "sexual deviation" to replace the earlier term "perversion," which, he pointed out, implied a moral judgment. But he insisted on the "vast range of kind and degree in the deviations of the sexual impulse," from the "innocent and amiable attractions" to "the random murderous outrages of a Jack the Ripper" (1934:151).

Ellis included presbyophila, the love of the old; iconolognia, or Pygmalionism, a sexual attraction to statues or presumably mannequins; ophresiolagnia or ozolognia, "sexual pleasure aroused by body odors;" algolognia, sexual pleasure aroused by the giving or receiving of pain (now redefined as sexual sadism and masochism); kleptolagnia, the pleasure aroused by theft; pyrolagnia, sexual pleasure aroused by fire; undinism, pleasure aroused by water, especially urination. The list goes on, and then there is "Mixoscopic zoophilia. Sexual pleasure in the spectacle of animals copulating" (1934:367-9).

One could make a poem out of all these lovely-sounding philias and isms, which describe an awful lot of deviations from the straight and narrow, e.g., fire, water, pain, theft, smells. Indeed, deviation seems to be the norm. Which it may well be. The "bible" of psychiatry is being revised—again. But the trouble with being a revised bible is that one wonders, What is the truth? It seems likely that many of these paraphilias, formerly deviations, formerly perversions, now disorders, will be modified in ongoing editions of the *DSM*. Thus, many former paraphiliacs will no longer be paraphiliacs: They will just be part of the normal, broad range of human sexuality (hopefully "innocent and amiable"). And it also seems likely that some new types of paraphiliacs will be added.

Psychiatry is not an exact science. On the one hand, it is disturbing that the experts can change their wisdom so drastically over time, and that, therefore, we do not know who or what we are; but on the other hand, it is reassuring to know that our understanding of ourselves has increased. We are getting to know ourselves better. That must be consoling to all of our "innocent and amiable" paraphiliacs.

Colonel R. Williams

But not all paraphilias, of course, are so "amiable and innocent." A recent horrific case is that of Colonel Russell Williams, 47, base commander at Canadian Forces Base Trenton, Canada's largest air force base. Williams was a rising star in the force. He had piloted Queen Elizabeth, Prince Philip and the Governor-General, and was a widely respected officer. In 2010, however, he was arrested, charged, and found guilty of two first-degree murders, two sexual assaults and 82 home invasions, in which he stole the underwear of young women, some as young as 12, then put them on, masturbated, and photographed himself masturbating in front of mirrors or on the beds. He kept complete records of his crimes on his computer, and collections of the undergarments were hidden in his house.

It all began with home invasions and thefts. Homeowners in rural Ontario did not always lock their doors, and many never realized that anything had been stolen. Then Williams escalated from fetishism and pedophilia to leaving clues, by breaking-in or disturbing items or, in one case, leaving a message on a computer. So he created fear. This led to press reports, which he copied and filed. These relatively minor crimes escalated further when he assaulted two women, tied them up and photographed them: sadism. Then it escalated again with two murders, which he recorded on film.

Williams was finally caught both by excellent police work and good luck. The police had found tire tracks in the snow at the site of his latest victim and set up road blocks. A police officer noticed that they matched the tires of Williams' Pathfinder, and he was called in for questioning. At the station his boots were printed and found to match the bootprints at the crime scene. And he confessed. But he could have taken his BMW to work that day and worn shoes, to lessen the chance of being considered a suspect.

He was sentenced to 25 years with no possibility of parole. No one seems to understand how this man could have lived such parallel lives. How could no one have spotted this psychopath before? He not only passed all the Canadian Air Force psychological tests, but he also impressed his experienced superior officers, who recommended him for promotions. Nonetheless, his seemingly relatively harmless fetish, an interest in women's underwear, which might have begun when he was younger, escalated incrementally to sadistic murder in the span of two-and-a-half years.

Sex may be sexy, but it can take us into dark places, not only into bedrooms with the lights out but into minds—also with the lights out. Williams was, perhaps, a psychopath, but psychopathology is not well understood. Many researchers think that psychopathy is a neuro-developmental disorder resulting from a combination of genetic and environmental (usually familial) factors, and causing brain deficits that impair emotional development. Brain scans indicate quantifiable differences in brain structure in criminals considered to be psychopaths (most are not)—even in five year old children. Some are researching genetic factors, which may be heritable in terms of predispositions; others are more concerned with early family trauma: abuse, neglect, violence. Yet, they say, many children are abused but few of them become psychopaths. Psychopathy is not listed in the *DSM-5*; but it does refer to an "anti-social personality disorder." Some argue that such a pathology is a mental illness, should be treated as such, and, therefore, exculpates the "criminal" – who himself or herself is a victim of illness. Others insist that while psychopaths may feel little or no empathy for others and have a low Emotional Quotient (EQ), which is a disputed concept, they know right from wrong and plan their crimes very carefully—as did Williams. Perhaps 1 percent of men are psychopaths, according to some researchers (no estimates are offered for women), but not all commit homicides; some, in fact, are rising stars in our community.

The judge summed it up: "Although not insane, it appears that Mr. Williams was and remains a very sick individual but a very dangerous man, nevertheless" (McIlroy and Anderssen, 2010; Appleby, 2010). Sane, but very sick, but not sick enough to be insane: These are tricky waters. From private fetishism to criminal theft to sexual assault to first degree homicide—it is all very worrying, and brain scans of children do not seem to be a viable option.

The Marquis de Sade

Sadism derives its name from the Marquis de Sade (1740-1814), referring to both the life he lived and (some of) his writings—for he practiced what he preached; and, as a result, he spent almost half his adult life in prison, about 30 years. He is most famous, or infamous, for two of his many books, both written in prison: *The 120 Days of Sodom* (1785) and *Justine* (1791).

De Sade has been interpreted in many different ways, almost as many ways as there are interpreters. In the last century there was, says a biographer, "the surrealist Sade, the Marxist Sade, the existentialist Sade, and, most surprisingly of all perhaps, the postmodern Sade." And there is the sexist, misogynistic and sadistic Sade. He has certainly aroused considerable interest and continues to do so. In October 2004, an Internet search for the Marquis de Sade produced 128,000 hits; In November 2010, a Google search produced 791,000 hits; and in January 2016, the same search produced 1,050,000 hits—a nearly tenfold increased in 12 years! In addition, at least nine films have been made about him (Phillips, 2005:118; 129-30).

I suspect that the principal interest in the man is not about his plays, political tracts and philosophical writings, most of which were not obscene, but, rather, about his obscene, sadistic work. That would gel with and be a sign of the times. Obscenity and sadism are in – or at least accelerating.

Camille Paglia (1991) writes brilliantly about him and contextualizes his work within a general theme of decadent sexualities, from Blake and Coleridge to Baudelaire, Swinburne, Oscar Wilde and Emily Dickinson, among many others I had never before thought of as decadent. She opposed the Apollonian (rational and positive about human nature, like Rousseau, Nature itself, notably Wordsworth, and ourselves, "If it's natural, it's good!") to the Dionysian (violent, sexy, passionate, with negative views of both human nature and Nature itself). We can enjoy the beautiful sunsets and birdsongs or be horrified by the destructive floods, earthquakes, tornadoes, typhoons, lightning strikes, forest fires, tsunamis – all natural – which destroy our Apollonian, ordered worlds. We can enjoy civilization and its benefits, civility, politeness, altruism, the rule of law, and be horrified by de Sade and Mr. Williams and Jack the Ripper and all the other murderers, plus the thieves, liars, cheats and rapists we read about, and even encounter, so often.

Paglia insists that de Sade destroyed Rousseau and the Apollonian ideal. Rousseau introduced *The Social Contract* (1762) with the famous words: "Man is born free, and everywhere he is in chains" (1963:3). The chains originate in poverty and the simultaneous creation of civil society, inequality, despotism and all manner of evils (1963:181). "The first man who, having enclosed a piece of ground, bethought himself of saying 'This is mine,' and found people simple enough to believe him, was the real founder of civil society" (1963:192). (And, one might add, evil society, in Rousseau's view). Rousseau not only believed that people are born free and equal but also good. So he began *Emile* (1762) in equally definitive terms: "God makes all things good: man meddles with them and they become evil" (1984:5; cf. 1963:222). The evils of crime, cruelty, violence, injustice, slavery and despotism are outlined. And he denied explicitly and casually the Catholic doctrine of original sin. There was no deep theological discussion with St. Augustine on the origin of evil—simply the calm assertion that "There is no original sin in the human heart" (1984:56). He also raised the topic of revolution against the despot: "As he was maintained by force alone, it is force alone that overthrows him" (1963:219). Not surprisingly, this "apostle of democracy" was not popular in some quarters, but he inspired both the American and the French Revolutions.

The U.S. Declaration of Independence affirmed: "We hold these truths to be self-evident, that all men are created equal . . ." And the French revolutionaries adopted the slogan of "Liberty, Equality, Fraternity." These were the high-minded statements of principle of the Enlightenment, capsizing the ancient tradition of the *inequality* of Man, from Plato onwards; but it was also blindingly hypocritical, given the persistence and significance not only of inequality but, especially, of slavery. Not much freedom or equality there. But over the centuries, these values have transformed society, albeit with some considerable violence. In France, the storming of the Bastille (1789) was followed by the execution of the king and queen (1793); then the "Terror," from March 1793 to July 1794, when over 2,500 men and women were guillotined; and then came the Napoleonic Wars, from the disastrous invasion of Russia to the Battle of Waterloo (1815). In the U.S., the War of Independence (1775-83) was followed by the Civil War (1861-65), with 600,000 dead.

The guillotine barely missed the Marquis de Sade, whose vision of humanity is the polar opposite of Rousseau's. He demonstrates the *inequality* of Man, the *evil* of Man—male and female, alike—and the primacy of the sex drive as related to power, and insists that neither sex is *better* than the other. (Both are horrible! Oh, well!)

In any event, whatever others have said about him, and for whatever reasons we might read his work (or not), he is pretty clear about himself. In a letter to his wife in 1781, he wrote: "I am a libertine, but I am neither *a criminal* nor *a murderer* . . . I am a libertine, but three families residing in your area have for five years lived off my charity, and I have saved them from the farthest depths of poverty . . . [and] I saved a child – at the risk of my life – who was on the verge of being crushed beneath the wheels of a runaway horse-drawn cart" (1966:xi; emphasis in original). A libertine, but generous and brave, in his view; but also a criminal, despite his denial, in the view of the state. It may be mentioned in this context that "libertine" is an interesting word choice, since it is expressive of liberty, particularly sexual liberty. The problem arises with respect to the sexual liberty of others – which he did not respect at all – and is why he spent so much of his life in prison — not at liberty, which is ironic, really.

Full disclosure: I could not read *The 120 Days of Sodom* – it was too disgusting. A biographer describes it as "above all, a mission, unique in literature, to describe, catalogue, and illustrate all possible manifestations of human sexuality" (Phillips, 2005:64) – to which I would add criminality, since it includes tortures, rapes and murder. Four wealthy libertines conspire to indulge all their sexual desires and pleasures at any expense—not only economic but also moral. So the book is a catalogue, not so much of sexuality as of perversions and paraphilias and, as we would say today, of abuses of human rights. More than that, as one of the four explains: "It is not the object of libertine intentions which fires us, but the idea of evil, and [. . .] consequently it is thanks only to evil and only in the name of evil one stiffens, not thanks to the object" (in Phillips, 2005:71).

The glorification of evil could get one into trouble in eighteenth century France, and it did. *The 120 Days* was followed by *Justine* (1791), with his dedication that clarifies his values and also camouflages them. De Sade was nothing if not smart. Bored with conventional novels that moralistically illustrated the triumph of virtue over vice, he intended "to present Vice triumphant and Virtue the victim of its sacrifices" (1966:xxv). Justine was the virtuous, beautiful, innocent young lass who always chose virtue over vice and was victimized for it: raped, sodomized, mauled by dogs, and found guilty by the courts (though innocent); but, still, she survived until struck dead by a bolt of lightning, just when we hoped a happy ending would be the reward for her virtue. Sudden death was her reward.

The Story of Juliette came out soon afterwards. It is the story of Justine's older sister, who was not a victim but a sadistic victimizer, in a reversal of the usual Sadean roles. De Sade's last years were spent in prison, until he was transferred to an asylum for the insane, convicted first of moderation during the revolution (narrowly escaping the guillotine), and then of corrupting morals. The corruption, or attempted corruption, was multi-layered. He was a precursor of Nietzsche in his "transvaluation of values," notably in his valorization of vice over virtue and evil over good – which, he said, reflected reality and Nature and the triumph of the strong over the weak (which might make him, like Nietzsche, a precursor of Social Darwinism, fascism and Hitler). His "transvaluation of values" also included his atheism, assertion of extreme individualism, denial of the rights of others, glorification of sex and, well, sadism.

In one sense, these stories are simply products of the feverish imagination of a highly-sexed man, deeply frustrated by his imprisonment; but they are also occasions for him to propound his philosophies, so contrary to the spirit of the Enlightenment.

He attacked the fundamentals, such as that vice is preferable to virtue, reflecting how the world works. "Man is naturally wicked," asserts Justine. This is a valid enough assertion given her experiences, but also a contradiction of Rousseau, the Enlightenment and egalitarianism (1966: xxxx). De Sade's point is that, given freedom, men and women in a Hobbesian "state of nature" will take their pleasures where and when they can. The strongest, wealthiest and most powerful will win, as both Justine and Juliette demonstrate in their opposite ways, as victim and victimizer.

In defiance of the American and French revolutionary ideologies, he insists that "Men were all born alone, envious, cruel and despotic, desiring to possess everything and surrender nothing, and perpetually struggling to maintain either their ambitions or their rights. . . . But society is composed of the weak and the strong." And, he says, the "state of Nature" is a "state of perpetual war" (1966:40-1). Here, he echoes Thomas Hobbes, writing at the time of the English Civil War, that without a strong state, "Leviathan," men "are in that condition which is called war; and such a war, as is of every man, against every man . . . and the life of man, solitary, poor, nasty, brutish and short" (1960:82). He was also a misogynist, as a rather philosophical bandit explains about "women existing solely to serve men's pleasures" (which poor Justine does); and an atheist: "No; there is no God, Nature is sufficient into herself." Then again: "I believe . . . that if there were a God there would be less evil on the earth." But: "If he exists, your God, how I loathe him" (1966:34, 43, 245, 261). And there is no heaven or hell or justice: "Forget about the justice of God, its rewards or punishments to come: all those platitudes only serve to make us die of hunger . . . The heartlessness of the rich justifies the crimes of the poor" (1966:28). And those debates persist.

In his view, "egoism is the first law of Nature" and "lustful pleasures" are, or should be, "our sole motive" in life, for they are far superior to "merely intellectual pleasures." Nor do they have anything to do with love: "Love and pleasure are very different things; the proof of this is that we love every day without pleasure, and that even more often we experience pleasure without love." This is a monk explaining his philosophy to Justine, and illustrating de Sade's anti-clericalism (and his egoism and misogyny). He continues: "It is quite essential that the man reach ecstasy only at the woman's expense, and that he take from her all that may increase his own enjoyment without the slightest regard for the consequences. Indeed, women . . . are but the instruments of pleasure, whose sole function is to provide targets" (1966:152-3).

He expands on this idea of the weaker and "contemptible sex." Woman is:

> An insignificant creature, always inferior to man, infinitely less beautiful than him, less ingenious, less wise, whose outward form is repulsive and the exact contrary of what pleases and delights a man, one who is unwell three quarters of her life, incapable of satisfying her husband whenever Nature compels her to bear children, and of a sour, peevish, and imperious disposition; a tyrant if she is given her way, a fawning slave if held in check; but always false, always wicked, always dangerous. (1966:194)

Whether these truly were his beliefs or he was just having a bad day is not entirely clear. Certainly he charmed many women into bed; equally, he abused many women and was sent to prison. But this view is certainly consistent throughout his novels.

Well, enough of this. All through these novels, de Sade is totally obsessed with, in no particular order, sodomy, copraphilia, rape, incest, cruelty, pain, infibulations, masturbation, gigantic penises, flagellation, torture, murder, exhibitionism, voyeurism – a catalogue of paraphilias, crimes and vice triumphant.

Leopold von Sacher-Masoch

Most people love vanilla ice cream and vanilla sex; but some prefer chocolate and some strawberry. The masochist finds pleasure in pain and the sadist loves to inflict it. For them, vanilla is plain, white and boring.

There are so many crazy sexualities and paraphilias out there now, from acrotophilia and coprophilia to necrophilia, pedophilia and zoophilia. Then add fetishism, exhibitionism, sadism, masochism, voyeurism and more. It is hard to keep track of them all. And, unfortunately for the enthusiast of paraphilias, one cannot practice all of them at once because some of them are contradictory: The exhibitionist does not want to be a voyeur nor the masochist a sadist, and vice versa.

Richard von Krafft-Ebing was the pioneer of sexual pathology with his monumental work *Psychopathia Sexualis,* first published in 1886. In my copy of his revised and enlarged 12th edition of 1946, he argued that "The gratification of the sexual instinct seems to be the primary motive in man as well as beast." (1946: v). But he wrote that this gratification is sometimes found in unusual ways, and described his case studies as well as included letters he received from all over the world, from men and women discussing their pathologies. He had some sympathy for his patients afflicted by such pathologies: ". . . large numbers of people find in [my book] instruction and relief in the frequently enigmatical manifestations of sexual life. . . . Compassion and sympathy are strongly elicited by the perusal of these letters . . . They reveal sufferings of the soul in comparison to which all the other afflictions dealt out by Fate appears as trifles" (1946: vii). Despite this sympathy, he was realistic that masochism was not always consensual and could, and occasionally did, result in murder—evil. He described Baron Sacher-Masoch as "a remarkable example of the powerful influence exercised by the *vita sexualis* - be it in the good or evil sense – over the formation and direction of a man's mind" (1946:133).

Venus in Furs is the semi-autobiographical novel by Baron Leopold von Sacher-Masoch, from whom Krafft-Ebing derived the word masochism, over the protests of the Baron's admirers. He described the Baron as "afflicted with an anomaly of his sexual feelings" (1946:132). Published in 1870, the short novel is both a psychological analysis of masochism and a critique of Christian values and practices, which echoed de Sade and anticipated Nietzsche.

The novel begins with a dream: The narrator is in the presence of Venus—the Goddess of Love—marble and wrapped in fur. Venus explains love: "It is woman's true nature to give herself wherever she loves, and to love whatever pleases her." He protests that this is cruel. She explains that "Woman is faithful as long as she loves, but you demand that she be faithful without love and give herself without enjoyment. Who is cruel then, woman or man? You northerners take love too seriously. You speak of duty where it is purely a question of pleasure" (1989:144-5).

The battle is joined now between men and women, Christianity and paganism, duty and pleasure. Venus continues: "It is man who desires, woman who is desired; this is woman's only advantage, but it is a decisive one. By making man so vulnerable to passion, nature has placed him at woman's mercy, and she who has not the sense to treat him like a humble subject, a slave, a plaything, and finally to betray him with a laugh – well, she is a woman of little wisdom" (1989:146).

The narrator, Severin (Masoch, we assume) tells his dream to his friend, who is familiar with the issue and cites Goethe's words: "Be the anvil or be the hammer . . . Woman's power lies in the passion she can arouse in man and which she will exploit to her own advantage . . . Man has only one choice: to be a slave or to be a tyrant" (1989:150).

And Severin tells his story of falling in love with the statue of a woman in a garden, and then meeting a real Venus, in furs. She explains herself and her views to him:

> I admire the serene sensuality of the Greeks—pleasure without pain, it is the ideal I strive to realize. I do not believe in the love produced by Christianity . . . I am a pagan.
>
> It was Christianity, whose cruel emblem, the cross, has always seemed to me somewhat horrific, that first brought an alien and hostile element into nature and its innocent instincts.

> The struggle of the spirit against the senses is the gospel of modern man. I do not wish to have any part of it. (1989:159)

This anticipates *Lady Chatterley's Lover* in its glorification of sensuality and pleasure. Both met the same condemnation, though only Count Masoch is memorialized in the *DSM- 5*. Venus continues: "I shall deny myself nothing, I shall love everyone who attracts me and give happiness to everyone I love. Is that such a dreadful thing? No . . . I am young, rich and beautiful, and I live for pleasure" (1989:161).

Poor Severin is desperately in love with Venus, whose name is Wanda. She is fond of him, but says that she can only "imagine belonging to one man for life, but he would have to be a real man who commands my respect and *enslaves* me" (1989:168; emphasis added). But if men fall in love with her, they become weak, fall on their knees and are, effectively, enslaved. Which is precisely what happens to Severin.

As the story develops, Severin begs Wanda to marry him. She refuses, saying maybe after a year. Severin replies, remarkably, that he would accept "no half-measures, no lukewarm compromises. I prefer to be at the mercy of a woman without virtue, fidelity or pity, for she is also my ideal, in her magnificent selfishness. If I cannot enjoy to the full love's perfect bliss, then let me empty to the dregs its cup of bitterness and woe, let me be ill-treated by the woman I love, and the more cruelly the better. For this is also a form of pleasure" (1989:171).

After more discussion, Wanda eventually agrees that he will become her slave. She finds her inner sadist to complement his masochism. He begs to be whipped. She whips him, at first with compassion, later with enthusiasm; and the relationship escalates, with humiliation and pain piled on top of each other in ingenious new ways. After a final whipping by Wanda's new lover, and after they have left together, he returned home to look after his father and his estate and found himself cured.

The narrator asked what the moral of the tale was, and gave the following answer: "That I was a fool! . . . If only I had whipped her instead!" And again:

> The moral is that woman, as Nature created her and as man up to now has found her attractive, is man's enemy; she can be his slave or his mistress but never his companion. This she can only be when she has the same rights as he and is his equal in education and work. For the time being there is only one alternative: to be

> the hammer or the anvil . . . Hence the moral of the tale: whoever allows himself to be whipped deserves to be whipped. (1989:271)

The novel is an interesting exploration of obsessive masochism and the development of sadism in Wanda, but also of the relation between pleasure and pain and control in relationships. The conclusion might be seen either as misogyny or egalitarianism, with an implied plea for equal rights. There have to be options other than hammers and anvils.

Count Masoch was a professor of history at Graz, distinguished and honored in his lifetime; and he practiced what he preached. He enjoyed being tied up, experiencing punishment and even acute physical pain, inflicted by a fur-clad woman with a whip. He sometimes dressed up as a servant, used disguises, advertised in the press and even prostituted the women in his life (1989:10). So *Venus in Furs* is partly autobiographical; and note that just because someone is a professor of history, it does not mean that he or she is the stereotype you expect!

Nowadays, however, with our postmodern relativism and refusal to judge, people often just shrug and say, "Whatever turns you on!" – with a few exceptions, especially pedophilia (for a child is not an adult) and rape (for there is no consent). Sexual behaviors in or out of the bedroom between consenting adults are just considered normal variations within heterosexual, homosexual or bisexual sexualities. "Crazy" and "evil" are not within the professional vocabulary—not officially, anyway. Perhaps the normal and the perverse exist along a continuum, or in a mosaic, rather than in separate boxes.

But some people, of course, simply object to vanilla, and want, for example, pain: "Sex without pain is like food without taste," said the Marquis de Sade (Bergner, 2009:69). And there are those who agree. Most people strive to avoid pain; but some love pain and desire pain. A male-to-female transsexual liked being whipped. The journalist Daniel Bergner watched her being whipped and saw the blood flowing, then he interviewed her. She explained: "The beating here pulls out my inner female; it goes so deep; I want to receive. It's like heroin. . . . Everything gets brighter . . . The law firm was good enough to keep me on after my sex change, but this is where I belong. It's two different worlds, this and the vanilla. This one is totally alive. That one is dead" (Bergner, 2009: 65). And this is the world where they roasted a man tied to a spit over a grill for hours, and where the dominatrix, a sadist—apparently unusual in a woman—carved a V in a man's back, and kicked another man, a slave, hard in the crotch. He didn't seem to mind. This is not for everyone; and the why and the how are mysteries to both the psychologists interviewed by Bergner and the individuals involved as well. Intensity seems to be the value affirmed. But to feel dead unless you are in physical pain is strange psychic territory.

Again, in a book on the English, the journalist Jeremy Paxman interviewed a gentleman: "By day, he runs a merchant bank. At night, he likes to be spanked until the blood runs." He has had a bottom transplant, which cost almost one thousand pounds. His obsession began with beatings by his father, who praised him afterwards for not crying, so pain and pleasure became confused. He counted a grand total of 17 people who had beaten him on his behind in the course of their duties, including "parents, nanny, teachers, prefects" (1998:207). He had been to psychiatrists without success, but the last one advised him that he might as well accept who he was. His wife is apparently not thrilled, but accepts this and just insists that the children do not see. So he visits clubs where he can be spanked by sadists or friends, and women visit him when they need a spanking. Apparently the business is thriving (1998: 207-10).

Recently, the *50 Shades of Grey* series of three novels about BDSM by E. L. James became international best sellers, during 2011-12. They are romance novels—but with a painful twist. They generated a shelf or two of copycat novels almost immediately, and then Sophie Morgan's already mentioned autobiographical memoir, *Diary of a Submissive* (2012) was published. It all seems quite fashionable suddenly.

*

Paraphilias are ambiguous territory, where the unusual may escalate into the criminal, the painful is pleasurable, and the abnormal may be redefined as normal. The sadistic murders by Mr. Williams, the new glorying in BDSM in the novels by James, and the sexography of Morgan all indicate the complexity of these matters. Add the popularity of the work of Belle de Jour and Jenna Jameson, in their respective domains of prostitution and pornography, and the field is wide open. There are many more paraphilias that may tempt the emerging novelist or paraphiliac.

Climax

Sex may be wonderful but, clearly, given the extraordinary and amazing range of behaviors, attitudes, meanings, sexes and sexualities, both personally and culturally, and the intensity of feelings about what is right and wrong, it is pretty weird. Or people are.

Indeed, the point of this work is to offer some of the lenses through which people now live and understand their sex lives, or did in the past, and to try to underscore this complex practice called sex, so intimately imbricated with changing and even conflicting values and policies worldwide. Genitals may be deified or vilified and sexualities are too many to count. The abnormal to one is normal to another and vice versa. Pleasure comes in many forms, but what pleases one may pain another, and, as we have seen, that which pains may also please.

Every week and every day brings more news about sex and the conflicts which imbue it. While writing this book:

- China: The government ended its one-child policy due to expected future labor shortages and a ratio of 130 to 140 men and boys to 100 women and girls, with about 30-40 million female deaths due to forced abortions, infanticide and sex selection.
- Mexico: A 14-year-old lesbian, protesting discrimination against her, received national attention and forced the school to apologize.
- India: A four-year-old girl was raped. In India this may bring the death penalty.
- Canada: A 22-day-old baby died due to a botched circumcision. It took two years to be reported in the media.
- Vatican: It eased its stance on divorce, permitting divorced Catholics to receive communion.
- U.S.: Texas withdrew funding for Planned Parenthood, making it more difficult for many women, especially poorer women, to have a legal abortion.

We have covered a lot of sexual ground here, including: AIDS; Shunga; the Lotus; desire; paraphilias; different attitudes and policies towards sex workers; the rise of lesbian, gay and transgender rights; the history of masturbation; the basic disagreements about what constitutes sex; Darwin on the role of beauty in human evolution; Freud on almost everything else regarding sex; double standards; jealousy; pornography;

Hindu eroticism; Chinese population policies; the erogenous zones; cosmetic surgery; lust . . . But there is so much more.

Meanwhile, the pleasure is still ours to enjoy.

Bibliography

Aldrich, Robert. 2012. *Gay Lives*. London: Thames and Hudson.

American Psychiatric Association. 2013. *Diagnostic and Statistical Manual of Mental Disorders 5*. Washington, D.C.: American Psychiatric Association.

American Society of Plastic Surgeons. 2014. *National Clearing House of Plastic Surgery Statistics*. www.asps.org.

Andahazi, Federico. 1998. *The Anatomist*. New York: Doubleday.

Anderssen, E. 2013. "Move your baby up the social "ladder." *Globe and Mail* 26 June.

Andreason, Nancy C. and Donald W. Black. 2005. *Introductory Textbook of Psychiatry*. 2nd Edition. Washington, D.C.: American Psychiatric Press.

Appleby, Timothy. 2010. "Williams begins serving life sentences." *Globe and Mail*. October 22: A7.

Aquinas, Thomas. 1981. *Summa Theologiae*. London: Blackfriars.

Aristotle. 1984. *The Complete Works*. Edited by Jonathan Barnes. N.J.: Princeton University Press.

Augier, Natalie. 1999. *Woman: An Intimate Geography*. New York: Houghton Mifflin.

Augustine, Saint. 1975. *Confessions*. Translated by R.S. Pine-Coffin. Penguin Books.

Augustine. 1958. *City of God*. Trans. G. G. Walsh. New York: Image Books.

Avery, Simon. 2000. "Wanted: One well-bred, smart, sporty Stanford egg. Price: $100,000." *National Post* 14 February.

Ayalah, Daphna and Isaac J. Weinstock. 1979. *Breasts*. New York: Summit Books.

Bacon, Francis. 1985 [1597]. *The Essays*. Penguin.

Barcan, Ruth. 2004. *Nudity. A Cultural Anatomy*. Oxford: Berg.

Baruma, Ian. 1984. *A Japanese Mirror*. London: Phoenix.

Baumgart, H. 1991. *Jealousy*. Chicago: University of Chicago Press.

Beech, H. 2013. "Why China needs more children." *Time* 1 Dec: 36-9.

Beekman, Daniel. 1977. *The Mechanical Baby*. New York: New American Library.

Benedict, Ruth. 1968. [1935]. *Patterns of Culture*. London: Routledge and Kegan Paul.

Berger, John. 1979. *Ways of Seeing*. London: BBC.

Bergner, Daniel. 2009a. *The Other Side of Desire*. New York: HarperCollins.

Bergner, Daniel. 2009b. "Women who want to want." *New York Times Magazine* 29 Nov: 42-7.

Berscheid, Ellen, Elaine Walster and George Bohrnstedt. 1973. The happy American body: A survey report. *Psychology Today*. November.

Bielski, Zosia. 2009. "Is the pill giving geeks an unfair chance?" *Globe and Mail* Sept. 10.

Bielski, Zosia. 2010. "The scent of a woman." *The_Globe and Mail* 2.1.10.

Bissinger, Buzz. 2015. "Call Me Caitlyn." *Vanity Fair*. July: 50-69, 105-6.

Blackburn, Simon. 2004. *Lust*. Oxford: Oxford University Press.

Blackledge, Catherine. 2003. *The Story of V. Opening Pandora's Box*. London: Weidenfeld and Nicolson.

Blanchard, Keith and Hallie Levine. 1996. "Sex and size." *Marie Claire*. August: 46-50.

Blass, Christine. 2001. *Bottoms*. London: Dumont/Monte.

Blue, Adrienne. 1996. *On Kissing: From the Metaphysical to the Erotic*. London: Victor Gollancz.

Blum, Linda M. 1995. *At the Breast*. Boston: Beacon Press.

Bly, Robert. 1990. *Iron John*. New York: Addison-Wesley.

Boellstorff, Tom. 2011. "But do not identify as gay: A proleptic genealogy of the MSM category." *Cultural Anthropologist* 26:2: 287-312.

Bogaert, Anthony. 2012. *Understanding Asexuality*. Lanham, ML: Rowan and Littlefield.

Bonaventure. 1978. *The Life of St. Francis*. New York: Paulist Press.

Bordo, Susan. 1999. *The Male Body*. New York: Farrar, Straus and Giroux.

Bornstein, Kate. 1995. *Gender Outlaw*. New York: Vintage.

Boston Women's Collective. 1979 [1971]. *Our Bodies, Ourselves*. New York: Simon and Schuster.

Brain, Robert. 1979. *The Decorated Body*. New York: Harper and Row.

Brandenburg, Jim. 1993. *Brother Wolf*. Toronto: Stoddart.

Bremer, Francis J. 2009. *Puritanism*. Oxford: Oxford University Press.

Brizendine, Louann. 2010. *The Male Brain*. New York: Broadway Books.

Brown, Chester. 2011. *Paying For It*. Drawn and Quarterly.

Bullough, Vern L. 1976. *Sexual Variance in Society and History*. New York: John Wiley.

Bullough, Vern L. 1979. *Homosexuality: A History*. New York: Signet.

Buss, David. 2000a. "Prescription for passion." *Psychology Today*. May/June: 54-61.

Buss, David. 2000b. *Jealousy: The Dangerous Passion.* New York: The Free Press.

Butler, Judith. 1990. *Gender Trouble.* London: Routledge.

Cahill, Thomas. 1996. *How the Irish Saved Civilization.* Anchor Books.

Campbell, Sara-Margaret. 2012. *Perspectives on Pornography and Erotica: Nudes, Prudes and Attitudes.* MA. Thesis. Department of Sociology and Anthropology, Concordia University, Montreal.

Cane, William. 1995. *The Art of Kissing.* New York: St. Martin's Press.

Canseco, José. 2005. *Juiced.* New York: Simon and Schuster.

Carr-Gomm, Philip. 2010. *A Brief History of Nakedness.* London: Reaktion.

Catholic University of America. 1967. *New Catholic Encyclopedia.* New York: McGraw-Hill.

Chandwani, Anupma. 2006. *Khajuraho.* New Delhi: Brijbasi Art Press.

Child Study Association of America. 1954. *Facts of Life for Children.* New York: Bobbs-Merrill.

Clark, Kenneth. 1956. *The_Nude.* London: John Murray

Clark, Timothy et al (eds). 2013. *Shunga. Sex and Pleasure in Japanese Art.* London: The British Museum.

Classen, Constance (ed.). 2005. *The Book of Touch.* Oxford: Berg.

Coelho, Paulo. 1998. *The Alchemist.* New York: HarperCollins.

Coelho, Paulo. 2005. *Eleven Minutes.* New York: Perennial.

Cohen, Leah Hager. 1999. "Breasts" in Sharon Sloan Fiffer and Steve Fiffer (eds) *Body*: 79-91.

Colapinto, J. 2000. *As Nature Made Him: The Boy Who was Raised as a Girl.* New York: HarperCollins.

Cole, Jeffrey 2006. "Reducing the damage: Dilemmas of anti-trafficking efforts among Nigerian prostitutes in Palermo." *Anthropologica.* Vol 48 No. 2: 217-228.

Comar, Philippe. 2013. *L'Homme Nu.* Paris: Gallimard.

Comfort, Alex. 1972. *The Joy of Sex.* New York: Simon and Schuster.

Cooper, Wendy. 1971. *Hair.* New York: Stein and Day.

Copplestone, Trewin. 2002. *Michelangelo.* Edison, N.J.: Regency House.

Cornacchia, Cheryl. 2011. "Nurse-in transforms shopping mall." *Gazette* 20 January.

Cotter, Adam. 2014. "Homicide in Canada." *Statistics Canada: Juristat.* Dec. Cat. No.:85-002-X

Darwin, Charles. 1955 [1872]. *The Expression of Emotions in Man and Animals.* New York: Philosophical Library.

Darwin, Charles. 1968 [1859]. *The Origin of Species*. Pelican Classics. New York: Penguin Books.

Darwin, Charles. 1981 [1871]. *The Descent of Man and Selection in Relation to Sex*. Princeton, N.J.: Princeton University Press.

Darwin, Francis. 1887. *The Life and Letters of Charles Darwin*. 2 Vols. London: John Murray.

de Beauvoir, Simone. 1953. *The Second Sex*. Trans. H. M. Parshley. New York: Knopf.

De Jour, Belle. 2007. *The Intimate Adventures of a London Call Girl*. London: Phoenix.

de Sade, The Marquis. 1966 [1791]. *Justine or The Misfortunes of Virtue*. Trans. Helen Weaver. New York: Putnam's.

de Waal, Frans. 2009. "Obviously, says the monkey" in the John Templeton Foundation (ed.) *Does Evolution Explain Human Nature?* www.templeton.org/evolution:4-7.

DeBruine, Lisa M. 2002. "Facial resemblance enhances trust." *Proceedings of the Royal Society*. London B. Vol. 269: 1307-1312.

DeBruine, Lisa M. 2004. "Facial resemblance increases the attractiveness of same-sex faces more than other-sex faces." *Proceedings of the Royal Society*. London. B: Vol. 271:2085-2090.

DeBruine, Lisa M. 2005. "Trustworthy but not lust-worthy: Context-specific effects of facial resemblance." *Proceedings of the Royal Society*. London B: 272: 919-922.

Deleuze, Gilles. 1989. *Masochism*. New York: Zone Books.

Descartes, René. 1968 [1637]. *Discourse on Method and the Meditations*. Trans. F.E. Sutcliffe. Penguin Books.

Diamond, Jared. 1997. *Why is Sex Fun? The Evolution of Human Sexuality*. New York: Basic Books.

Dines, Gail. 2010. *Pornland. How Porn has Hijacked Our Sexuality*. Boston: Beacon.

Dowd, Maureen. 2005. *Are Men Necessary? When Sexes Collide*. New York: Putnam's.

Driedger, Sharon. 1997. "What is a father?" *Maclean's* 9 June 62-3.

Druckerman, Pamela. 2007. *Lust in Translation. The Rules of Infidelity from Tokyo to Tennessee*. New York: The Penguin Press.

Dundes, Alan. 1980. "The number three in American culture." *Interpreting Folklore*. Bloomington: Indiana University Press: 134-59, 276-8.

Dunn, Winnie. 2008. *Living Sensationally. Understanding Your Senses.* London: Jessica Kingsley.

Dutcher, Jim with Richard Ballantine. 1996. *The Sawtooth Wolves.* New York: Rufus.

Ebin, Victoria. 1979. *The Body Decorated.* London: Thames and Hudson.

Egan, Timothy. 2010. "Erotica Inc." *New York Times* 23 October.

Elias, Norbert. 1982 [1939]. *The Civilizing Process Vol. 1. The History of Manners.* Trans. Edmund Jephcott. New York: Pantheon Books.

Elliott, Carl. 2000. "To be mad." *Atlantic Monthly.* December: 73-84.

Ellis, Havelock. 1934. *Psychology of Sex: A Manual for Students.* New York: Ray Long and Richard R. Smith.

Ellwood-Clayton, Bella. 2012. *Sex Drive: In Pursuit of Female Desire.* Sydney: Allen and Unwin.

Ensler, Eve. 1998. *The Vagina Monologues.* New York: Villard.

Ephron, Nora. 2006. *I Feel Bad about My Neck.* New York: Vintage.

Ettinger, Yair. 2012. "New York to require consent from parents for brit milah practice." *Haaretz* 14 Sept A4.

Evans-Pritchard, E. E. 1967 [1940]. *The Nuer.* Oxford: The Clarendon Press.

Evans-Pritchard, E. E. 1974. *Man and Woman among the Azande.* London: Faber and Faber.

Faderman, Lillian. 2015. *The Gay Revolution.* New York: Simon and Schuster.

Faludi, Susan. 2010. "American Electra." *Harper's Magazine* October: 29-42.

Farnham, Alan. 1996. "You're so vain." *Fortune.* September 66-82.

Farrell, Warren. 1993. *The Myth of Male Power.* New York: Berkley Books.

Fausto-Sterling, Anne. 1993. "The five sexes." *The Sciences.* MarchApril: 20-4.

Ferré, Rosario. 2000. "The blessings of the butt" in Sharon Sloan Fiffer and Steve Fiffer (eds), *Body.* New York: Perennial.

Fischer, H. Th. 1978. "The clothes of the naked Nuer" in Ted Polhemus (ed.) *Social Aspects of the Human Body.* Pantheon Books. : 180-93.

Fisher, Angela. 1984. *Africa Adorned.* New York: Harry N. Abrams.

Fisher, Helen E. 1992. *Anatomy of Love.* New York: Norton.

Fisher, Helen. 2010. *Why Him? Why Her?* New York: Henry Holt.

Flew, Antony. 1984. *A Dictionary of Philosophy.* London: Pan.

Forsyth, Adrian. 1993. *A Natural History of Sex.* Shelburne, VT: Chapters Publishing.

Foucault, Michel. 1979. *Discipline and Punish.* Trans. Alan Sheridan. New York: Vintage Books.

Foucault, Michel. 1980. *The History of Sexuality*. Trans. Robert Hurley. New York: Vintage Books.

Fox, Kate. 2005. *Watching the English. The Hidden Rules of English Behaviour*. London: Hodder.

Friedman, David M. 2001. *A Mind of Its Own. A Cultural History of the Penis*. New York: The Free Press.

Freud, Sigmund. 1973a. *An Outline of Psychoanalysis*. Trans. James Strachey. London: Hogarth Press.

Freud, Sigmund. 1973b. *New Introductory Lectures on Psychoanalysis*. Pelican Freud Library. Vol. 2. Penguin.

Freud, Sigmund. 1977 [1908]. *On Sexuality*. Pelican Freud Library. Vol. 7. Penguin.

Freud, Sigmund. 1977 [1901; 1909]. Case Histories 1: "Dora" and "Little Hans." Pelican Freud library. Vol. 8. Penguin Books.

Freud, Sigmund. 1977. "Civilization and its discontents" in *Civilization, Society and Religion*. Pelican Freud Library, Vol. 12. Penguin Books.

Freud, Sigmund. 1981. *On Psychopathology*. Pelican Freud Library. Vol. 10. Penguin Books.

Freud, Sigmund. 1982. *Introductory Lectures on Psychoanalysis*. Pelican Freud Library Vol. 1 Penguin.

Freud, Sigmund. 1983. *The Interpretation of Dreams*. Pelican Freud Library. Vol. 4. Penguin.

Friday, Nancy. 1987. *Jealousy*. New York: Bantam Books.

Garner, David. 1997. "The 1997 'Body Image Survey' results." *Psychology Today*. February: 30-44, 75-8, 84.

Giddens, Anthony. 1992. *The Transformation of Intimacy: Sexuality, Love and Eroticism in Modern Societies*. Oxford: Polity.

Gill, Michael. 1989. *Image of the Body: Aspects of the Nude*. New York: Doubleday.

Gilmore, David. 2001. *Misogyny: The Male Malady*. Philadelphia: University of Pennsylvania Press.

Ginzburg, Ralph. 1958. *An Unhurried View of Erotica*. New York: Helmsman Press.

Gladwell, Malcolm. 2009. *What the Dog Saw*. New York: Back Bay Books.

Glaser, Gabrielle. 2002. *The Nose*. New York: Atria.

Godwin, Joscelyn. 1979. *Robert Fludd*. London: Thames and Hudson.

Goldberg, Michelle. 2014. "What is a woman?" *The New Yorker* 4 August: 24-8.

Gollaher, D. L. 2000. *Circumcision*. New York: Basic Books.

Graham, Sylvester. 1974 [1834]. *A Lecture to Young Men.* New York: Arno Reprints.

Gray, Eliza. 2013. "Number three: Edith Windsor: The unlikely activist" *Time* 11 Dec: 102-115.

Gray, John. 1994. *Men are from Mars, Women are from Venus.* New York: HarperCollins.

Greer, Germaine. 1971. *The Female Eunuch*. London: Paladin.

Grey, Eliza. 2014. Rape. "The crisis in higher education." *Time* 26 May: 20-9.

Grigoriadis, Vanessa. 2010. "Waking up from the pill." *New York* 6 December: 44-49, 123.

Haley, Bruce. 1978. *The Healthy Body and Victorian Culture.* Cambridge, MA: Harvard University Press.

Hall, Kevin. 2000. "A 'topless summer'." *National Post* 21 January.

Handler, Chelsea. 2005. My Horizontal Life. *A Collection of One-night Stands.* New York: Bloomsbury.

Hanlon, Michael. 2011. "The outcast who gave us the modern world." *The Sunday Times*. 20 Nov.

Hardison, James. 1980. *Let's Touch: How and Why To Do It.* Englewood Cliffs, N.J.: Prentice-Hall.

Hare, E. H. 1962. "Masturbating insanity: The history of an idea." *Journal of Mental Science*. Vol. 108, No. 452:1-25.

Harris, Misty. 2013. "Sex survey: Half of Canadians either have, or would have, threesomes." *Postmedia News* 5 February.

Harrison, Kathryn. 1997. *The Kiss*. New York: Random House.

Havranek, Carrie. 1998. "The new sex surgeries". *Cosmopolitan*. Nov.: 146, 148, 150.

Hennig, Jean-Luc. 1996. *The Rear View: A Brief and Elegant History of Bottoms through the Ages*. Trans. M. Crosland and E. Powell. London: Souvenir Press.

Henriques, F. 1961. *Love in Action: The Sociology of Sex*. London: Macgibbon and Kee.

Henry, Ronald. 2006. "The innocent third party: Victims of paternity fraud." *Family Law Quarterly* 40:1: 51-81.

Herdt, Gilbert. 1981. *Guardians of the Flute: Idioms of Masculinity*. New York: McGraw-Hill.

Herdt, Gilbert. 1987. *The Sambia: Ritual and Gender in New Guinea*. Harcourt, Brace and Jovanovich.

Herdt, Gilbert and Stephen Leavitt. 1998. *Adolescence in Pacific Island Societies.* University of Pittsburgh Press.

Hertz, Robert. 1960 [1909]. *Death and the Right Hand.* Trans. Rodney Needham. London: Cohen and West.

Hesiod. 1989. *Theogony.* Trans. D. Wender. Penguin Classics.

Hite, Shere. 1987 [1976]. *The Hite Report on Female Sexuality.* New York: Dell.

Hite, Shere. 1981. *The Hite Report on Male Sexuality.* New York: Knopf.

Hobbes, Thomas. 1960 [1651]. *Leviathan.* Oxford: Blackwell.

Hofmann, Corinne. 2007. *The White Masai.* New York: Amistad.

Holland, Jack. 2006. *A Brief History of Misogyny.* London: Robinson.

Holt, L. Emmet. 1929 [1894] *The Care and Feeding of Children.* New York: Appleton.

Hulse, Carl. 2010. "Senate ends military ban on Gays serving openly." *New York Times* 19 December.

Hunt, M. 1959. *The Natural History of Love.* New York: Knopf.

Ilg, Frances and Louise Bates Ames. 1956. *Child Behavior.* New York: Dell.

"J". 1971. *The Sensuous Woman.* New York: Dell.

Jacques, Juliet. 2014. "On the dispute between radical feminism and trans people." *New Statesman* 6 August.

Jameson, Jenna. 2004. *How to Make Love like a Porn Star.* New York: HarperCollins.

Jenkins, Christie. 1980. *Buns: A Woman Looks at Men's.* New York: Perigee Books.

Jenness, Diamond. 1972 [1928]. *The People of the Twilight.* Chicago: University of Chicago Press.

Johns, Catherine. 2012. *The British Museum Little Book of Erotica.* London: The British Museum Press.

Johnson, Brian. 2013. "On playing Liberace." *Maclean's* 3 June:14-5.

Johnson, Diane. 2015. "Who is not guilty of this vice?" *New York Review of Books* 8 Jan.25-6.

Jones, Ernest. 1954. *Sigmund Freud: Life and Work.* Vol 2. London: Hogarth.

Jung, C. G. 1983. *The Essential Jung.* Ed. Anthony Storr. Princeton, N.J.: Princeton University Press.

Kama Sutra. 2012. Trans. Sir Richard Burton. London: Hamlyn.

Kammeyer, Kenneth. 2008. *A Hypersexual Society: Sexual Discourse, Erotica, and Pornography Today.* New York: Palgrave Macmillan.

Karr, Mary. 2000. *Cherry.* New York: Viking.

Kaysen, Susanna. 2001. *The Camera My Mother Gave Me.* New York: Knopf.

Kellogg, J. H. 1974 [1888]. *Plain Facts for Old and Young*. New York: Arno Press Reprints. 1974.

Kemper, Rachel. 1977. *Costume*. New York : Newsweek Books.

Kempis, Thomas À. 1980. *The Imitation of Christ*. Penguin.

Keshishian, J. 1979. "Anatomy of a Burmese beauty secret." *National Geographic*. Vol. 155. No. 6. June: 798-801.

Kesterton, Michael. 2013. "Social studies." *Globe and Mail* 7 June.

Kimmel, Michael and Michael Messner (eds). 2004. *Men's Lives* (6th Edition). New York: Pearson.

King, R. J. 2013. "The lady vanishes." *Psychology Today* blog

Kinsey. Alfred C. et al. 1948. *Sexual Behavior in the Human Male*. Philadelphia: W. B. Saunders..

Kinsey, Alfred C. et al. 1953. *Sexual Behavior in the Human Female*. Philadelphia: W. B. Saunders.

Kirk, Malcolm. 1981. *Man as Art*. New York: Viking Press.

Kluger, J. and A. Park, 2013. "The Angelina Effect. " *Time* 27 May : 28-33.

Koedt, Anne. 1970. "The Myth of the vaginal orgasm." www.cwluherstory.org.

Kottak, C. 2014. *Mirror for Humanity*. (9th edition). New York: McGraw-Hill.

Krafft-Ebing, Richard von. 1946 [1886]. *Psychopathia Sexualis*. New York: Pioneer Publications.

Laertius, Diogenes. 1972. *Lives of Eminent Philosophers*. 2 Vols. Trans. R. M. Hicks. Cambridge, MA: Harvard University Press.

Lafrance, Marc. 2009. "Skin and the Self: Cultural theory and Anglo-American psychoanalysis." *Body and Society* 15:3:3-24.

Lalonde, Michelle. 2012. "Cocktails, cacophony, protests and arrests." *Gazette* 8 June.

Laporte, Dominique. 2000 [1978]. *History of Shit*. Cambridge, MA: MIT Press.

Laqueur, Thomas. 1990. *Making Sex: Body and Gender from the Greeks to Freud*. Cambridge, MA: Harvard University Press.

Laqueur, Thomas. 2004. *Solitary Sex: A Cultural History of Masturbation*. London: Zone.

Lau, E. 1989. *Runaway: Diary of a Street Kid*. New York: HarperCollins.

Laver, James. 1969. *A Concise History of Costume*. London: Thames and Hudson.

Lawrence, D. H. 1961 [1928]. *Lady Chatterley's Lover*. Penguin.

Lawrence, D. H. 1972 [1922]. *Aaron's Rod*. Penguin.

Lee, Chris. 2011. "This man is addicted to sex." *Newsweek* 5 December: 48-55.

Levy, Ariel. 2005. *Female Chauvinist Pigs: Women and the Rise of Raunch Culture.* New York: The Free Press.

Levy, Howard S. 1966. *Chinese Footbinding.* New York: Walton Rawls

Lewin, Ralph. 1999. *Merde.* New York: Random House.

Lindgren, April. 2000. "Subway ads seek to end discrimination over breast-feeding." *National Post* 3 October.

Lodge, David. 1995. *Therapy.* London: Secker and Warburg.

Loyola, Ignatius. 1963 [1548]. *The Spiritual Exercises.* Trans. Thomas Corbishley, S. J. London: Burns and Oates.

Lucie-Smith, Edward. 1998. *Adam.* New York: Rizzolli.

Lucie-Smith, Edward. 2000. *Bottoms.* New York: Barnes and Noble.

Lydon, Susan. 1970. "The politics of orgasm" in Robin Morgan (ed.) *Sisterhood is Powerful.* New York: Vintage: 197-205.

Lyons, Andrew and Harriet Lyons. 2006. "The new anthropology of sexuality." *Anthropologica* Vol. 48 No. 2: 153-158.

"M". 1971. *The Sensuous Man.* New York: Dell.

MacDonald, Robert H. 1967. "The frightful consequences of onanism: Notes on the history of a delusion." *Journal of the History of Ideas.*

Malinowski, Bronislaw. 1961 [1922]. *Argonauts of the Western Pacific.* New York: Dutton.

Malinowski, Bronislaw. 1929. *The Sexual Life of Savages.* London: George Allen and Unwin.

Martin, Daniel. 2009. "Pupils told they have a 'right' to a good sex life." *Daily Mail* 12 July.

Martin, Emily. 1989. *The Woman in the Body.* Boston: Beacon Press.

Masters, William H. and Virginia E. Johnson. 1966. *Human Sexual Response.* Boston: Little, Brown.

Mazrui, Ali. 1971. "The robes of rebellion: Sex, dress and politics in Africa." In Ted Polhemus (ed), *Social Aspects of the Human Body.* Penguin.

McDonough, Katie. 2013. "Death by cunnilingus." *Salon.* 30 January.

McIlroy, Anne and Erin Anderssen. 2010. "How a psychopath is made." *Globe and Mail.* October 23: F1.

McLennan, Natalie. 2008. *The Price: My Rise and Fall as Natalia. New York's #1 Escort.* Beverly Hills, CA: Phoenix.

McMillan, Terry. 2001. *A Day Late and a Dollar Short.* New York: Viking

McNeil, Donald G. 2010. "Precursor to HIV was in monkeys for millenniums." *New York Times* 16 September.

Mead, Margaret. 1949. *Male and Female*. New York: Morrow.

Mead, Margaret. 1956 [1935]. *Sex and Temperament in Three Primitive Societies*. New American Library/Mentor Books.

Mead, Margaret. 1968 [1928]. *Coming of Age in Samoa*. New York: Dell.

Michael, Robert, John H. Gagnon, Edward O. Laumann and Gina Kolata. 1994. *Sex in America*. New York: Little Brown.

Mikes, George. 1966. *How to Be Inimitable*. Penguin.

Miles, Rosalind. 1991. *The Rites of Man*. London: Grafton.

Millet, Catherine. 2003. *The Sexual Life of Catherine M*. New York: Grove Press.

Millett, Kate. 1970. *Sexual Politics*. New York: Ballantine Books.

Moir, Anne and David Jessel. 1991. *Brainsex*. London: Mandarin.

Monick, Eugene. 1987. *Phallos: Sacred Image of the Masculine*. Toronto: Inner City Books.

Monick, Eugene. 1991. *Castration and Male Rage*. Toronto: Inner City Books.

Montagu, Ashley. 1986. *Touching: The Human Significance of the Skin* (3rd Edition). New York: Harper and Row.

Moran, Caitlin. 2011. *How to be a Woman*. London: Ebury.

Morgan, L. W. 1999. "It's ten o'clock. Do you know where your sperm are?" *Divorce Litigation*. Vol. 11 No. 1.

Morgan, Robin. 1970. *Sisterhood is Powerful*. New York: Vantage.

Morgan, Sophie. 2012. *Diary of a Submissive*. London: Gotham.

Morris, Desmond. 1979. *Intimate Behaviour*. St. Albans: Triad Panther.

Morris, Desmond. 1985. *Bodywatching: A Field Guide to the Human Species*. London: Cape.

Morris, Desmond. 2004. *The Naked Woman: A Study of the Female Body*. London: Jonathan Cape.

Morris, Desmond. 2008. *The Naked Man: A Study of the Male Body*. New York: St. Martin's Press.

Morris, Jan. 1974. *Conundrum*. New York: Harcourt, Brace Jovanovich.

Mottier, Veronique. 2010. *Sexuality*. New York: Sterling.

Musee Bonnard. 2013. *The Nude from Gauguin to Bonnard*. Paris: Musee Bonnard.

Mydans, Seth. 2001. "Nat Soi's long-necked women." *New York Times* May 20.

Nanda, Serena. 1999. *Neither Man nor Woman: The Hijras of India*. 2nd edition. London: Wadsworth.

Nardi, Peter (Ed.). 2000. *Gay Masculinities*. London: Sage.

Nathan, Debbie. 2007. *Pornography*. Toronto: Groundwood.

Nead, Lynda 1994. *The Female Nude*. London: Routledge.

Needham, Rodney (ed.). 1973. *Right and Left*. Chicago: University of Chicago Press.

Needham, Rodney. 1979. *Symbolic Classification*. Santa Monica, CA: Goodyear.

Nelson, J. B. 1978. *Embodiment*. Minneapolis: Augsburg.

Nietzsche, Friedrich. 1985 [1885]. *Thus Spoke Zarathustra*. NY: Penguin.

Noack, Nick. 2015. "Sweden adopts 'nen' as neutral pronoun." *Gazette* 2 April.

Nolen, S. 2014. "For Brazil's sex workers, a brothel boom turned to dust." *Globe and Mail* 17 July.

Northcutt, Wendy. 2010. *The Darwin Awards: Countdown to Extinction*. New York: Dutton.

Nussbaum, Martha. 1999. "The professor of parody." *New Republic*. 22 February. www.akad-se/Nussbaum.pdf.

Oakely, Ann. 1998. "Gender, methodology and people's ways of knowing." *Sociology* Vol.32 No 4. November: 707-32.

O'Connor, Siobhan. 2015. "Why doctors are rethinking breast cancer treatment." *Time* 12 Oct: 28-36.

Ovid. 1988. *Metamorphoses*. Trans. A.D. Melville. Oxford: Oxford University Press.

Padawer, Ruth. 2009. "Losing fatherhood." *New York Times Magazine* 22 Nov: 38-44, 58, 60, 62.

Paglia, Camille. 1991. *Sexual Personae: Art and Decadence from Nefertiti to Emily Dickinson*. New York: Vintage Books.

Panda, Rajaram (ed). nd. *Khajuraho Temples and Orchha*. New Delhi: Mittal.

Park, Alice. 2012. "Spanking in the schools." *Time* 15 October: 17.

Park, Alice. 2014. "The end of AIDS." *Time* 20 November.

Park, Katharine. 1997. "The rediscovery of the clitoris" in David Hillman and Carla Mazzio (eds.) *The Body in Parts: Fantasies of Corporeality in Early Modern Europe*. London: Routledge.

Pascoe, C. J. 2007. *Dude, You're a Fag*. Berkeley: University of California Press.

Paul, Pamela. 2005. *Pornified: How Pornography is Changing Our Lives, Our Relationships and Our Families*. New York: Times Books.

Paxman, Jeremy. 1998. *The English: A Portrait of a People.* London: Michael Joseph.

Pearson, P. 2000. "Why breast-feeding is such a touchy subject." *National Post* 13 December.

Pertschuk, M., A. Trisdorfer and P. Allison. 1994. "Men's Looks—the survey." *Psychology Today.* Vol. 27. No. 6. Nov./Dec.: 33-9, 70, 72.

Petersen, James R. 1999. *The Century of Sex.* New York: Grove Press.

Phillips, John. 2005. *The Marquis de Sade.* Oxford: Oxford University Press.

Pickert, Kate. 2013. "What choice?" *Time* 14 January 38-46.

Pietropinto A. and J. Simonauer. 1977. *Beyond the Male Myth.* New York: Optimum.

Pines, Ayala. 1998. *Romantic Jealousy.* London: Routledge.

Ping, Wang. 2000. *Aching for Beauty: Footbinding in China.* Minneapolis University of Minnesota Press.

Plato. 1984. *The Collected Dialogues.* Edited by Edith Hamilton and Huntington Cairns. Bollingen Series. Princeton, N.J.: Princeton University Press.

Podolsky, Doug. 1996. "The price of vanity." *U.S. News and World Report* 14 October: 72-8.

Pogrebin, L. C. 1981. *Growing Up Free: Raising Your Children in the Eighties.* New York: Bantam.

Polhemus, Ted and Housk Randall. 1994. *Rituals of Love.* London: Picador.

Proctor, J. 2002. "B.C. infant dies after circumcision." *National Post* 29 August.

Putney, Clifford 2003. *Muscular Christianity.* Cambridge, MA: Harvard University Press.

Rabelais. 1972 [c.1535]. *Gargantua and Pantagruel.* Trans. J. M. Cohen. Penguin Books.

Ramirez, Rafael L. 1999. *What it Means to be a Man: Reflections on Puerto Rican Masculinity.* Trans. Rosa E. Casper. New Brunswick, N.J.: Rutgers University Press.

Ranke-Heinemann, Uta. 1990. *Eunuchs for the Kingdom of Heaven: Women, Sexuality and the Catholic Church.* New York: Doubleday.

Rawe, Julie. 2007. "So, who's your daddy?" *Time* 20 Jan: 38.

Rice, Andrew. 2010. "Putting a price on words." *New York Times Magazine* 16 May: 46-52.

Riefenstahl, Leni. 1976. *Africa.* London: Collins/Harvill.

Riefenstahl, Leni. 1984. *The People of Kau.* London: Collins.

Roach, Mary. 2008. *Bonk: The Curious Coupling of Science and Sex*. New York: Norton.

Rodin, Judith. 1992. "Body mania." *Psychology Today*. January-February: 56-60.

Ross, Chad. 2005. *Naked Germany: Health Race and Nation*. Oxford: Berg.

Rousseau, Jean-Jacques. 1963 [1762]. *The Social Contract and Discourses*. Trans. G. D. H. Cole. London: Dent. Everyman's Library.

Rousseau, Jean-Jacques. 1982 [1781]. *Confessions*. Penguin.

Rousseau, Jean-Jacques. 1984 [1762]. *Emile*. London: Dent.

Rudofsky, B. 1974. *The Unfashionable Human Body*. New York: Anchor Books.

Ryan, Christopher and Cacilda Jethá. 2010. *Sex at Dawn: The Prehistoric Origins of Modern Sexuality*. New York: Harper.

Sacher-Masoch, Count Leopold von. 1989. "Venus in furs" in Gilles Deleuze, *Masochism*. New York: Zone.

Salazar, C. 2006. *Anthropology and Sexual Morality*. New York: Bergahn.

Sartre, Jean-Paul. 1969 [1943]. *Being and Nothingness*. Trans. H. Barnes. New York: Washington Square Press.

Sartre, Jean-Paul. 1984 [1934-40]. *The War Diaries of Jean-Paul Sartre*. Trans. Q. Hoare. New York: Pantheon Books.

Sciolino, Elaine. 2012. *La Seduction: How the French Play the Game of Life*. New York: St. Martin's Griffin.

Scowen, Peter. 2014. "Masturbation is a sin." *Globe and Mail* 19 July.

Screech, Timon. 2009. *Sex and the Floating World: Erotic Images in Japan 1700-1820*. London: Reaktion Books.

Sharlet, Jeff. 2010. "Straight man's burden." *Harper's Magazine*. September: 36-48.

Snowden, Lynn. 1995. "How to kiss a woman." *Esquire*. Fall: 41-2.

Southworth, Natalie. 1999. "No sex, please, we're tired: Poll." *Globe and Mail* 5 November.

Spadola, Meema. 1998. *Breasts*. Berkeley, CA: Wildcat Canyon.

Spitzer, Robert L., Miriam Gibbon, Andrew E. Skodol, Janet B. W. Williams, and Michael B. First. 1994. *The DSM-IV Casebook*. Washington, D.C.: The American Psychiatric Association.

Spock, Dr. Benjamin. 1958 [1946]. *Baby and Child Care*. 2nd edition. London: Bodley Head.

Stallings, James O. 1980. *A New You*. New York: New American Library-/Signet Books.

Steinem, Gloria. 1983. *Outrageous Acts and Everyday Rebellion.* New York: Plume.

Steinem, Gloria. 1992. *Revolution from Within.* Boston: Little, Brown.

Steinmetz, Katie 2014. "America's transition." *Time* 9 June: 38-46.

Stephenson-Connolly, Pamela. 2011. *Sex Life. How Our Sexual Experiences Define Who We Are.* London: Vermilion.

Sternberg, Robert J. and Karin Weis. 2006. *The New Psychology of Love.* New Haven: Yale University Press.

Stuckenbrock, C. and B. Topper 2011. *1000 Masterpieces of European Painting.* Potsdam: N. F. Ullman.

Synnott, Anthony. 1983. "Little angels, little devils: A sociology of children." *Canadian Review of Sociology and Anthropology* 20:1: 79-95.

Synnott, Anthony. 1988. "Physical, mystical, spiritual: The body in Christian thought." *Sante, Culture, Health,* Vol. 5: 3: 267-89.

Synnott, Anthony and David Howes. 1992. "From measurement to meaning: Anthropologies of the body." *Anthropos* 87: 147-66.

Synnott, Anthony. 1993. *The Body Social: Symbolism, Self and Society.* London: Routledge.

Synnott, Anthony. 2009. *Re-Thinking Men: Heroes, Villains and Victims.* London: Ashgate.

Talese, Gay. 1983. *Thy Neighbor's Wife.* New York: Doubleday.

Tannahill, Reay. 1982. *Sex in History.* New York: Stein and Day.

Taylor, G. 2000. *Castration.* New York: Routledge.

Terry and Mike. 1984. *How to Kiss with Confidence.* New York: Bantam.

Theroux, Paul. 1976. *The Pillars of Hercules.* London: Putnam.

Tisdall, Frederick F. 1942. *The Home Care of the Infant and Child.* New York: The New Home Library.

UN AIDS 2014. *(Annual) Report on the Global AIDS Epidemic.* www.-unaids.org.

UN Office on Drugs and Crime. 2014. *(Annual) Global Report on Trafficking in Persons.* www.unodc.org.

UN Office on Drugs and Crime. *Global Homicide in 2013.* www.unodc.org.

Ussher, Jayne. 1997. *Body Talk.* London: Routledge.

Vale, V. and Andrea Juno (eds.). 1991. *Modern Primitives.* San Francisco: Re/Search Publications.

Van Biema, David. 2014. "The contraception showdown." *Time* 7 July: 28-33.

Vanggard, Thorkil. 1972. *Phallos: A Symbol and its History in the Male World.* New York: International Universities Press.

Vargas-Cooper, Natasha. 2011. "Hard core." *The Atlantic*. January-February: 97-104.

Viorst, Judith. 1977. "Confessions of a jealous wife." In G. Clanton and L. Smith (eds) *Jealousy*. Englewood Cliffs, N.J.: Prentice-Hall: 17-24.

Virel, Andre. 1980. *Decorated Man*. New York: Harry Abrams.

Walker, Esther. 2011. "I don't like being touched." *Psychologies Magazine*. January: 36.

Wallace, Lee 2003. *Sexual Encounters: Pacific Texts, Modern Sexualities*. Ithaca, New York: Cornell University Press.

Watson, John B. 1972 [1928]. *Psychological Care of Infant and Child*. New York: Arno.

Watson, Lyall. 1999. *Jacobson's Organ*. London: Allen Lane.

Weber, Max. 1968 [1920]. *The Protestant Ethic and the Spirit of Capitalism*. London: Unwin University Books.

Wedekind, C. et al. 1995. "MHC-dependent mate preferences in humans." Proceedings of the Royal Society of London. Series B. *Biological Sciences*. Vol 250 No. 1359: 245-9.

Weil, Elizabeth. 2006. "What if it's (sort of) a boy and (sort of) a girl?" *New York Times Magazine* 24 September.

Weinberg, M. 1965. "Sexual modesty, social meanings and the nudist camp." *Social Problems* 12:3: 311-8.

Wente, Margaret. 2014a. "The pronoun wars." *Globe and Mail* 19 June.

Wente, Margaret. 2014b. "The march of transgender rights." *Globe and Mail* 2 August.

Wilson, Chris and Heather Jones. 2014. "And the winning formula is…" *Time* 3 March: 56-7.

Wilson, Robert Anton. 1974. *The Book of the Breast*. Chicago: Playboy Press.

Wolf, Naomi. 2012. *Vagina: A New Biography*. New York: HarperCollins.

Yalom, Marilyn. 1997. *A History of the Breast*. New York: Knopf.

Zilberger, Bernie. 1978. *Male Sexuality*. New York: Bantam Books.

INDEX

www.ingramcontent.com/pod-product-compliance
Lightning Source LLC
Chambersburg PA
CBHW021848020426
42334CB00013B/237
* 9 7 8 1 8 8 4 0 9 2 2 1 3 *